It's Much Later Than You Think!

"And he saith unto me, Seal not the sayings of the prophecy of this book: for the time is at hand."

(Revelation 22:10)

Many things are supposedly going on in prophecy - as we speak. Most notable for the Christians who are "watching and praying" is the fact that we are sitting squarely on the other side of 2019 and Jesus Christ has not returned. If the continued catch-as-catch-can phrase of, "SOON!" is still adequate for you, then this book is not for you. But, if you have been watching and praying, you know something is "off¿" to say the least. Everyone is making excuses and no one is minding the Christian China Shop. This book is and addresses much of the BULL. Yeshua is coming. It's much later than you think.

"Who then is a faithful and wise servant, whom his lord hath made ruler over his household, to give them meat in due season?"

(Matthew 24:45)

It's Much Later Than You Think!

Timothy B. Merriman

IT'S MUCH LATER THAN YOU THINK!

It's Much Later Than You Think!

IT'S MUCH LATER THAN YOU THINK!

Walk with me through Biblical history to future Prophetic times. Understand shocking revelations from Your Holy Bible that reveal what time we are really in and how much time we have left.

TIMOTHY B. MERRIMAN

It's Much Later Than You Think!

*Some scriptural references in this book are paraphrased – however, the location of the reference itself is also listed for verification, accuracy and study.

**If a claim is made concerning the biblical witness, but the passage itself is not listed, we have made every effort to list the passage location in the Holy Bible. We highly encourage the reader to take the time to view it personally - *as with any witness* - read it from your own Holy Bible.

***With this bracket [*words contained*] within a Bible reference have been added by the author for point or clarification: i.e., *"...he* [**Jesus**] *preached in their synagogues throughout all Galilee, and cast out devils"* (Mark 1:39). [**Jesus**] was added.

****Unless otherwise indicated, all Scripture quotations are taken from the *King James Version* of the Holy Bible.

*****Original color schematics description will not match grayscale color design (pp. 142-143 – if applicable in book design).

Hourglass cover photo: ID 1683996 © Milosluz/Dreamstime.com | European Union's Parliament in Strasbourg / Louise Weiss Building / Photo #1 (p. 103) - ID 107216670 © Leonid Andronov / Dreamstime.com * Arial view: The European Union's Parliament in Strasbourg / Louise Weiss Building | Photo #2 (p. 103) © Jacky Hénin / Flickr.com * The Tower of Babel | photo #3 (p. 104) - Artist: Pieter Bruegel the Elder - 1563 / Photo by: Eduardo Urdangaray | flickr.com * Back cover face image: Microsoft Office 2007 clip art - Jewish Rabbi.

This book was printed in the United States of America. All rights reserved under International Copyright Law. Published by: FLR Publishing Group * Richfield, NC 28137 – 0352

ISBN: 978-1-7331889-6-8 Print
ISBN: 978-1-7331889-4-4 eBook

First Printing, 2020

FORWARDED

*Let's begin with a few questions. <u>Who **forwarded** the words that Yeshua spoke</u>?*

<u>Who approved of their contents and how they were presented</u>? <u>Was it Herod</u>?

***No.** Herod saw no miracles from the so-called Messiah and therefore he was*

angrily offended and disappointed. After mocking <u>Yeshua</u>, he sent him back to

*Pilate. <u>Was it Pilate</u>? **No.** Just after Pilate had sat down on his judgment seat,*

his wife warned him by a sent letter that he should have nothing to do with this,

*Yeshua. <u>Was it the Jewish leadership</u>? **<u>I think not</u>!** It was because of them that*

Yeshua was delivered to Pilate in the first place. <u>Was it the Jewish people</u>

<u>themselves</u>? You know; the people Yeshua allegedly worked all his miracles

*amongst!! <u>You really think it was</u> - **them**? It is because of **<u>them</u>** that many of **<u>us</u>***

are cursed today! Do you recall what those arrogant geniuses had to say when

they were called upon to testify? "<u>Let him be crucified...His blood be on us</u>,

***<u>AND ON OUR CHILDREN!¿</u>**" Wow! Thanks mom and dad! Despite, it would*

appear some 1987 years later; <u>The Word of the Lord</u> is flourishing throughout

the entire world. <u>Then who forwarded Yeshua's words</u>? <u>In those crucial early</u>

<u>days, it was his personal disciples</u>. One could argue, that is one main reason

*why **<u>The Gospel</u>** survived. I have no disciples for noting. The words I will speak,*

the tone I might sometimes take and the matters I have chosen to address in this

book might inspire too much scorn and negative criticisms; and garner way too

much theological heat for anyone of notoriety or anyone at all to endorse and

forward. But if truth be told here, for too long we have allowed other people tell

us <u>what to watch</u>, <u>what to wear</u>, <u>what to say</u>, <u>how to think</u> and <u>what to feel</u>, _where to go_ and **_what we are to read!_** _I did not seek an original endorsement. I most likely would not have been able to garner one anyway; especially from the mainstreams of Christianity - as far as the politics of forwarding go. I am content to leave it to the readers - to think for themselves and to judge independently as to the contents of this book. If you are reading this forwarding section, I suppose you have purchased and will read this book. You would be considered a free-thinker in my book. You should feel distinguished! There are not many of your kind left in this world today. I applaud you. And, you should give yourself a pat on the back. I am going to presume that you have no agenda for your reading. You are merely reading this book for information or perhaps biblical curiosity. Yet, I truly believe you will find this book spiritually valuable. After you have read it, then you can consider yourself as my honorary invitee. I encourage you to become an official forwarder of this book; even if you only find its information entertaining at best. I encourage all of its readers to commit and get this information before the eyes of others to read, ideally purchased of course. It might give cause for another book! With those being case and fact, literally it is all in your hands. That is, if I do well with my communication skills and you find a content value in this book. I pray you are captivated with such excitement; and the possibility of it being a small part of Yeshua's truth being revealed in these_ last minutes _of prophecy,_ before his return.

Your Special Page
(*For Forwarding*)

I asked the publishers to provide for you this *very special page* for your own personal forwarding comments; should you in your enthusiasm decide to get copies of this book for all of your friends.

Timothy B. Merriman

FORWARDED BY:

Print your name above
Your comments about this book below:

_____
Signature

...Enjoy the read

DEDICATION

This book is dedicated to my "SIX" (That's Right – SIX) loving daughters, Gwen, Lois, Philadelphia, Julia, Jennifer and Grace; but especially to my Lois and to my Jennifer. To Lois who was born with a rare chromosome deficiency and lived only nine years; because Lois showed me how to fight and be courageous and happy – no matter what life throws at you. Had she survived, Lois would have been twenty and nine years of age as of the year 2019. To my Jennifer because she showed me how to be content and thankful with even the simplest of things that life offered to her. I never saw her upset over anything. In fall 2014 Jennifer became a victim of murder through Domestic violence - when her brother-in-law gunned her down in cold blood. Jennifer was seventeen. I would be remiss if I did not mention my wife Andrea in my dedication. With the tragic loss of our daughter Jennifer, Andrea is determined not to let Jennifer's life become a forgotten statistic in the long tragic history of domestic violence; nor, if she has anything to do with it, any of those in similarly dangerous situations, be without their own voice and the opportunity for **H.E.L.P.** *(Hope, Empowerment, Life-skills and Prevention), her comprehensive support program offered through the advocacy of* **Feminine Life Rebuilders**; *the non-profit organization Andrea has founded. Andrea has shown me how to turn pain and anger into power and purpose. Believe me when I say that the ability to do so helps out a lot – especially when faith is the writing subject. I thank YHWH for all my girls; especially those two who I can no longer hold and tell them how much I love them. Lastly, my Eloah forbid me – if that in any way, I should fail to show Gwen, Philadelphia, Julia and Grace, the four daughters YHWH has left for me to treasure, how much they have meant to my continuous mental and spiritual wellness over all of these following years after our family's two tragedies. Saying, **"Thank you girls!"** is not enough. I pray that YHWH continue to richly bless you according to his own will and purpose. Because I am persuaded that nothing else could be more rewarding or could give you any more Joy and Holy Confidence, as we see the coming day of Messiah's return approaching.*

FOUNDATIONS AND MOTIVATIONS

This manuscript in its originality, is part of a larger unpublished work by Timothy B. Merriman entitled, "__DISCOVERY AND PERSPECTIVE__." The chapter from which most of the information and research you will read about in this book, was taken from a subtitled chapter within that book called, "My Walk Through Time." When Mr. Merriman made of that chapter its own independent book, he also took the opportunity to fine tune it. He expanded beyond its primary subject - Time - and added ever deeper time supporting events! We pray after reading, "__IT'S MUCH LATER THAN YOU THINK!__" you write and encourage Mr. Merriman to finish his original body of study and research. We are hopeful along with Mr. Merriman that you will be challenged - as well as blessed, by all of the insights contained in this book. If you should find information in Mr. Merriman's book important, then you will be doubly blessed to know that parts of the proceeds from the sales of this book will support an extremely urgent cause – by helping amplify urgently needed voices; which might otherwise be silenced and facilitating many committed efforts that fight against domestic violence through the 501 (c) (3) champion of advocacy organization, __Feminine Life Rebuilders__ and the comprehensive self-help program it sponsors - that offers __H.E.L.P.__ (Hope, Empowerment, Life skills and Prevention methods) for victims of, and those at risk for domestic violence.

H.E.L.P. Feminine Life Rebuilders

The Feminine Life Rebuilders, or (FLR) is a registered 501 (c) (3) organization. Any and all of additional contributions you will be inspired to give are tax-deductible. Feminine Life Rebuilders is a means by which we can all aid in the effort; so many of the victims of domestic violence will always be remembered and the needed voices of domestic violence survivors will be heard and will never be silenced in fear and shame ever again. FLR extends, "H.E.L.P." to facilitate programs that offer Hope, Empowerment, Life skills and Prevention methods to women by design - *the young and older*. Nevertheless - There are inclusions clauses that are set in place with FLR; which are dedicated to offering help and support to those that might be male, and male victims in the LGBTQ-IA communities. FLR works with their home state (N.C.) community partners as well as advocates in other state areas to find programs, services and safe shelter for all of their domestic violence victims in need. You should, and we encourage you to do so – visit the FLR site at: www.feminineliferebuilders.org. See what they are all about. Then if you will, make a donation. It will go a long way towards services for survivors and those at risk. This may include classes, training workshops, and/or funds needed to get to safety.

Disclosure

All of the Internet addresses given in this book (websites, etc) and contact information such as telephone numbers and addresses are given primarily as resources. They are not intended to be or imply an endorsement by the author. The author does not vouch for their contents or the continued accuracy of their information; to include the availability of claimed resources - for the life of this book. As with any and all personal interactions, it is the sole responsibility of the individual to conduct their own due diligence.

A personal note from the author

Greetings friends,

From my experiences, I have found usually; we can always say things better than we actually do. This is especially true, if we get a second chance and opportunity around. In truth, I will rarely go about something the way another person might have done them, or say things the way another person might have said them, and vice-versa. Because of a simple and obvious truth; I am me, and they are them. But know this. I will do my best to take every opportunity and make every effort when explaining myself concerning any claims and assertions, to make them as clear and simple as I possibly can; minus any awareness to respect of person, and to not engage in the slinging of existential insults. I pray YHWH bless you with the information contained herein. If the information in this book is beneficial to you, then I also asks for your prayers for this, and other possible future endeavors in making known YHWH's truths, to go to the world. However and regardless, thank you so much for the part you have played in contributing to the fundamental commitment for the broader open exchange of spiritual ideas, dialogues, personal truths and revelations, through your purchase of this book. Last but not least, before everybody gets started and become too deeply immersed in my book; permit me to make this disclaimer. While any or all would-be doctrine, reproofs, corrections or instructions in righteousness stated herein, could be argued on the basis of one's' religious beliefs and denominational preferences; to your open mind, I trust the numbers in this book will tell the story of our times past and of our time left. Which I argue within the context of this book and also the Holy Bible, our time is exhausted. I am confident, the numbers do not lie. IT'S MUCH LATER THAN YOU THINK!

Timothy B. Merriman

Author Contact Information:
Timothy B. Merriman
PO Box 231
Richfield, NC 28137-0231

Email Address: dayandhourministry@gmail.com

Please feel free to contact me (*preferably by email*) with any comment. If a response is warranted, I will make a genuine effort to respond to as many as I can. Please be patient.

Contents

It's Much Later Than You Think!

CHAPTER 1

WHY YOU SHOULD READ THIS BOOK

"[*Because*] *we speak wisdom among them that are mature: yet not the wisdom of this world, nor of the princes of this world, that come to naught: but we speak the wisdom of Eloah in a mystery, even the hidden wisdom, which Eloah ordained before the world unto our glory; which none of the princes of this world knew: for had they known it, they would not have crucified the Adon of glory. But as it is written, Eye hath not seen, nor ear heard, neither have entered into the heart of man, the things which Eloah hath prepared for them that love him. But Eloah hath revealed them unto us by his Spirit: for the Spirit searcheth all things, yea, the deep things of Eloah. For what man knoweth the things of a man, save the spirit of man which is in him? Even so the things of Eloah knoweth no man, but the Spirit of Eloah. Now we have received, not the spirit of the world, but the Spirit which is of Eloah; that we might know the things that are freely given to us of Eloah. Which these things also we speak, not in the words which man's wisdom teacheth, but which the Holy Spirit teacheth; comparing spiritual things with spiritual. But the natural man receiveth not the things of the Spirit of Eloah: for they are foolishness unto him: neither can he know them,*

because they are spiritually discerned. But he that is spiritual judgeth all things, yet he himself is judged of no man. For who hath known the mind of YHWH, that he may instruct him? But we have the mind of the Messiah." (*1st Corinthians 2:6-16*)
(King James and Hebraic Roots - *Author Merger Version*)

Nevertheless, I do not have all knowledge or perfect understanding of the knowledge that I professed to have. If I may be so bold as to say it. No person I know, has such levels of spiritual discernment. I do not think that I should need to justify my stated judgment, concerning the state of literally all of our spiritual statuses. Nonetheless, just between you and me, reflect on and keep it in mind when reading this book, the following remarks regarding an obscure "*prophetic*" passage.

"Let their habitation be desolate; *and* let none dwell in their tents."
(Psalms 69:25)

"Really!?" and "What!?" On my own, I would have no idea how in any way that verse would fit into prophecy. I would have never guessed it in a million years. That verse referenced specifically the betrayer of Messiah Yeshua - Judas Iscariot. I am afraid, I must say; only by our Messiah Yeshua revealing it to Shim'on Kefa (*Simon Peter*), do I and I dare say, we have its understanding today. Shim'on Kefa is recorded as having said the following words in reference to Yeshua's betrayal and Judas Iscariot's suicide hanging.

"Men and brethren, this Scripture must needs have been fulfilled, which the Holy [Spirit] by the mouth of David spake before

concerning Judas, which was guide to them that took [Yeshua]. For he was numbered with us, and had obtained part of this ministry. Now this man purchased a field with the reward of iniquity; and falling headlong, he burst asunder in the midst, and all his bowels gushed out. And it was known unto all the dwellers at Jerusalem; insomuch as that field is called, in their proper tongue, Aceldama, that is to say, The field of blood. For it is written in the book of Psalms, "Let his habitation be desolate, and let no man dwell therein:" and His bishopric let another take.
(Acts 1:16-20)

Now, I ask you. Would you have known Psalms 69:25 prophesied of Judas Iscariot and the taking away of his office of Bishop from amongst the twelve original Apostles? If not you, nor I, then who? Who would or could have known? I dare say, "**NO ONE!**" but by the revealing of the Holy Spirit. This will be my claim concerning certain portions of this book. As you will discover. There are things I will say in this book. The only way I could know them, is by the revelation of the Holy Spirit or depending on how you receive them, the deception of the Devil. I will rely on your wisdom to determine which. I only brought out this point of debate to illustrate my point that it is only by the Holy Spirit, hidden knowledge of truth is revealed. With this revealed knowledge and understanding, it is also only by the Holy Spirit that supplemental discernment is able to be seen, taken in and accepted as part of YHWH's Truth. If the Holy Spirit does not enlighten the person, then the person in question, becomes like some of the individuals that Apostle Shaul (*Paul*)

3

stated the Prophet Isaiah prophesied of saying, "...*Hearing ye shall hear, and shall not understand; and seeing ye shall see, and not perceive*" (Acts 28:26). Over modern history there is no doubt, many have made the kinds of claims I will make in this book. Over time most of their claims turned out to be errors. Is my book more of the same "*deceiving and being deceived*" dogma in a long line of Christian books written to sell religious sensationalism; presumptuously promoting mistruths and prophetic assertions sure to fail? God forbid! I do not claim that salvation is at risk in everything I will say here. But, I feel safe to say that a much clearer view can be gained on the basic theme of this book, "*what time it really is and how much time we have left.*"

CHAPTER 2

GETTING THE MINDSET TO READ THIS BOOK

What time are we really in? How much time do we have left? <u>Using</u> <u>only our Holy Bibles</u>, can we know? And if we use our Holy Bibles only, can we even trust it to tell us the truth? Many so-called theologians do not think so. What say you? While topics addressed in this book continue to be debated; most of the would-be prophets who have dared to *predict* anything about a date for this and a date for that in Biblical prophecy, all eventually over time have been debunked and defamed. And, as far as most of Christendom is concerned, these religious pundits have been debased from their presupposed high place with God. And in general, any remnants of trust in their prophetic gifts from "*Jesus Christ*" is gone. However, as far as most of these "*preacher*" personalities are concerned, there is no real need for concern. And, the proverbial "*Panic Button*" is rarely punched. They recognize "*inquiry minds*" wanting to know God's mysteries, are always offering up "$acrifice$" to preachers claiming to know spiritual things that no one in fact actually believes they know. But, as the poet Alexander Pope wrote; which clearly most parishioners cling to, "*hope springs eternal.*" And, those rivers of hope (*false as they may flow out to be at times*) will keep flooding minds from pulpits in America and over the world. We all need hope! So even if preachers are shown to have provided false hopes in the past; they just lay low for "*a spell¿*" Then, they come back; when the time is right, with a "*heartfelt*" reason to key members who fall under that "*spell;*" explaining why their prophesied event of hope did not come to fruition. Those key members bring calm and confidence back to the rest of the church membership. Believe it or not that strategy works more times than one might think!

People, and especially **spiritual people**, need some semblance of hope. It is one of their main reasons they tend to, "*heaped to themselves teachers* (Unfortunately at times, false teachers) *having itching ears*" (2nd Timothy 4:3). In this book, I am going to '**try**' not to make "predictions." Notwithstanding, what I am going to talk about and the path in which we are about to travel, will contain quite a bit of *godly claims and prophetic declarations*; whatever those mean. The information, insights, or if you choose to call them so, revelations you will find herein that may imply I am predicting, should not be confused as such. I can only hope and trust that any "revelations" that might be confused as any sort of prediction or date setting, will make for logical and spiritual sense and will speak for themselves. Additionally, insights you may or may not receive from this book should not be confused with or considered substitutes for actually living your life according to the essential standards of YHWH's biblical righteousness, holiness and godliness. As Apostle Shaul is understood to have said, even if we do have all understanding and knowledge, and still do not in actuality live and show a love **from the heart**; in truth, we still remain spiritually lost cases in terms of salvation. (1st Corinthians 13:1-3)

This book will be a spiritual aid to anyone able to consider its words without predisposed dogmatic beliefs. Some of its words and its ideas are not without debate. But, they should help answer some of those enduring questions over enigmatic events in the prophetic last days the Holy Bible speaks of. This book holds considerable implication for people who hold to their faith and hope, Yeshua or "Jesus" will return for his Millennial Reign - *in the case of most common Jewish believers* - Messiah comes at year 6001. Year 6001 begins YHWH's Millennial Sabbath. As of 2020, *AD wise*; we are in the Jewish year of 5780. If correct, it would mean we have 221 more years remaining on the Jewish prophetic clock; before the common religious Jew would be expected to be expecting their Messiah to come. Sadly, many Jews have become cynical by claims of lost time; due to inaccuracies caused by faulty time-keeping methods in their past. Evidently, even though personally I do not understand why; for Jewish historians and Rabbis, these unintended and unfortunate events for some reason, cloud their historical perspective. Many professing Christians it seems are also in the dark, as far as time goes; especially when it comes to when <u>and if</u> - **believe it or not** - they expect, "*Jesus Christ*" to return.

I would encourage every reader. If you are a seeker of the biblical truth. Open up your mind to this book with as much "<u>Love for the Truth</u>" as you can muster up. Armed with your "<u>Love for the Truth</u>" and a sense of righteousness, consider its insights of revelation and perspective. If you do this, then I will be comfortable with all praises or any criticisms you might attribute to my humble effort to expand your spiritual thought. With your existing understanding and lingering questions, along with the information in this book, come to your own determination as to the truth of these words, or at least the possibility of their truth. The things of what you will read about in this book might, and they should alter your divine insights for growth, **permanently and to your good**. So while you read, consider what it would mean for your Christian interactions with others - if you incorporated any of this book's revelations for your future spiritual conversations, with believers and nonbelievers alike. Whether most want to admit it or not that is an important consideration. Because, very few of us like to worship alone.

If one is not afraid, this book may show hidden Bible *"truths¿"* for discerning in context, what year we are really in. All my life I was of the faith that no one could know the truth of time and certainly no one could know *"that day and hour"* the Messiah was to return/come. Just as I had said earlier. According to the Jews reckoning of time; they feel, we most likely have another 221 years left as of the Gregorian calendar year of 2020. Even though many Jewish historians acknowledge that any given year they might list is most likely off by hundreds of years. After YHWH revealed to me what he did - *I wondered* - how could they or anyone be that far off. We *"Christians,"* with Gentile thinking minds, did we lose track too? It is hard to say what knowing the real date would mean to any one person. **Personally** – I think whether one knows the true date or not, salvation is not at stake. So then, why might it be important to any person to know *"that day and hour?"* In my humble opinion, I think that person would have to confer with YHWH to gain that piece of insight. What the knowledge meant to me had less to do with my initial epiphanies, from the Holy Spirit's revelations of biblical times; and more to do with its peripheral discernments. That is, once it was revealed to me about their importance. I felt, even though the peripherals were attention-grabbing, they were irrelevant Bible data, in light of my focus on Bible time. I felt they were only connected by chance to the revelations of time given me by YHWH - as I assert. I was wrong. As I hope you will discern to see.

As YHWH's divine calling to know his hidden truths would have it. The inherent dangers that came along with YHWH revealing those so-called, "_peripheral discernments_" to me, in my present understanding; and then, my later insight down the learning trail, were the main reasons YHWH revealed to me, the order of prophetic time. Because of this; and I do not want to sound insulting; even though I believe that it will sound that way to some; I must at times in this book speak with extra care and subtle wisdom – if I can. Based on the content of my omissions, the Holy Spirit in judgment of this truth; has determined that the majority of the readers of this book are not able at this time, to bear all of the revealed insight and understanding YHWH gave to me. Consequently, I will take great care as not to speak openly of what was for me, this major spiritual learning curve and life-changing revelations. However, that being said; YHWH has inspired me to write what I am to write and no matter what his reasons are, YHWH is now making known, what I at least hope will be those "_bearable portions_" of which I understand to the great majority, are some of YHWH's formerly hidden understandings or divine insights through this book. By way of their release into your heart, YHWH will reveal in his own way; what he wants you to gain from them, in his own time. In reflection of YHWH revealing those *"bearable portions"* and possibly what their values consists of; I will quote a passage of what I by my experience feel catches the essence of what Messiah is now saying in spirit by His Holy Spirit, to various readers of this book.

> "I have yet many things to say unto you, but ye cannot bear them now. Howbeit when he, the Spirit of truth, is come, he will guide you into all truth: for he shall not speak of himself; but whatsoever he shall hear, *that* shall he speak: and he will show you things to come. He shall glorify me: for he shall receive of mine, and shall show *it* unto you. **All things** that the Father hath are mine: therefore said I, that he shall take of mine, and shall show *it* unto you." - ***Yeshua***
> (John 16:12-15)

Here is a question to reflect on. Would not, *"**All things**"* include at that point in Yeshua's ministry time on the earth the formerly Top-Secret knowledge of *"that day and hour?"* Keep the above passage in mind as you read the rest of this book. And, as far as the matter of me opening your eyes to some tremendous truth and revelation goes, I must leave it at Yeshua's words. As you read this book and consider the information herein for yourself – proving all the things the best that you can – in your spirit, it will be left up to you, to **come to your own conclusions**. Be careful though. The last time I followed those instructions and actually did what it was I was asked to do (***come up*** *with my own conclusions*); I

came up getting expelled from my doctorate program in the "*Christian*" seminary school at the university I was attending. Administrators waited until my dissertation presentation before they acted; to inflict the most amount of harm plausible. I know right? I thought the same thing. Wow! The things "*loving Christians*" do to each other, in their intolerance for diverse levels of understanding.

Anyway – that is enough talk regarding that hurtful experience. Let us get back to the real subject at hand, **what year it is and how I came to understand it**. What my memory is allowing me to say at this time is this. I think, somewhat, how it all got started; as far as YHWH revealing this book section to me, is this. I have always wondered how it was that time got lost or confused in the first place. I am very used to hearing one well-respected historian estimating that **the event** happening around this date. Then another historian believing that **the same event** happened another date, sometimes being significant years apart. Later, I would hear preachers speaking about events that were going to happen in the end time just before "*Jesus Christ*" returns. They mention incredible things; like great stars falling from heaven and poisoning many people, people seeking out death and being unable to find it, the great tribulation, the antichrist and how "*Jesus*" was going to come as this thief in the night, rapture the church away just <u>before that great tribulation</u>; or in <u>the middle</u>

of the tribulation or just after the tribulation (*take your pick*) and the list goes on. I myself would think, how is "*Jesus*" going to sneak up on the world with all those events happening right in front of our faces? Maybe that is a subject to be answered in another book. However, the truth is, unless you are a pre-tribulation rapturist, mostly all of these prophetic events, must come to pass - *according to most all Christian doctrine* - before "*Jesus Christ*" can return – I think.

Thinking back, I am not sure why it was so important for me to know what time it was. I am certainly not sure why YHWH decided to give me insights concerning what time we are in. I am definitely not worthy. Nevertheless, YHWH gave me insights on the matter and I am going to share my insights with you in this book. Take the insights for whatever you think they are worth. And also, before some of you guys get all defensive and stuff and start calling me some kind of false prophet (*As I am sure a few of you have already done*); before you fire-off quoting that passage of scripture found at Matthew 24:36; I will go ahead to cite it for you from the King James Version. "But of that day and hour knoweth no man, no, not the angels of heaven, but my Father only." So, before any of you do what I claim others have done. And that is, you put a rather smug smile on your face. I want to make an observation and ask a question. Then, I will address that bull in my China Shop. This bull appears at first sight to be a dogmatic biblical disaster to my claim of possibly knowing

something perceptibly, it is impossible for any of us to know. I will now

remind some readers and inform other readers; in a standard King James

Version of the Bible, all the words written in *italics* were inserted by

translators. The words were meant for and in many cases did serve for

clearer understandings. But, they are not in the original Hebrew or Greek

text. A literal translation of the text could read, "*But of that day and hour*

knoweth no, not the angels of heaven, but my Father only." The passage,

when reread, **could** only be referring to what was known in the realm of

Eloah's third heaven. There is at least one passage of scripture that gives

support to this premise. It is cited from 1ˢᵗ Peter 1:6-12.

> "…greatly rejoice…for a season, if need be…that the trial of your
> faith…though it be tried with fire, might be found unto praise
> and honor and glory at the appearing of [Yeshua the Messiah]
> whom having not seen, ye love; in whom, though now ye see
> not, yet believing, ye rejoice with joy unspeakable and full of
> glory: receiving the end of your faith, the salvation of souls. Of
> which salvation the prophets have inquired and searched
> diligently...prophesied of the grace unto you: searching what, or
> what manner of time the Spirit of [Messiah] which was in them
> did signify, when it testified beforehand the sufferings of
> [Messiah], and the glory that should follow. Unto whom it was
> revealed, that not unto themselves, but unto us they did minister
> the things, which are now reported unto you by them that have
> preached the gospel unto you with the Holy [Spirit] sent down
> from heaven; **which things the angels desire to look into.**"

Now consider the question. Do you believe "**The Truth**" contained inside the "**WHOLE**" "**Holy Bible**?" Of course most readers, if they responded to my rhetorical question, would say, "**YES!**" So then, from here on out, I will carry on. Just for the sakes of those who say they do believe the "**WHOLE**" "**Holy Bible**." Since you say you do believe the "**WHOLE**" "**Holy Bible**," let me too remind you of some other passages from the "**WHOLE**" "**Holy Bible**," that give some speck of credibility to my claim of knowing a thing or two about the day and hour we are in as of AD 2020. Understand this. Many millions, perhaps billions suspected, "*Jesus*" might return in year AD 2000 or there about. **WE ALL KNOW THAT DID NOT HAPPEN**! Many have made end time predictions that miserably, predictably and sometimes tragically failed. Readers might consider me just another blowhard; seeking Christianity's attention with the sensationalism of my book's title. Is it sacred suicide to throw my hat into the prophetic ring with all of the other would-be end time prophets? You should be real skeptical. Because, within these end times; the Bible also says something about, "*many false prophets*" (Matthew 24:11).

With so much high-octane selling of "*breakthroughs and blessings*" going about, I suppose it can just be expected that some might imagine that I would be financially ecstatic to simply ride out the gravy train of literary sensationalism. After all, if it is packaged right, that means a lot of books sold – right? I see so many doing that today. Absolutely, I am delighted people are buying this book. But, more for the information and not to the point that I might have gained in this process. The truth is this. Before I put all of this information in book form, I tried to **give** this **same** information **free** to several of the local, national and international church organizations; in order to get its insights distributed worldwide faster. I received one reply. In that reply were those gracious words that were so memorable, they are seared into my spirit - even until this day. **"You Are Insane!"** I was simply strategizing. I figured many of them had the proper resources and could afford to distribute what significant truths they could extract from my research and get it to their fellowship circle, free of charge. I guess "free" was overrated. And, there is definitely a tremendous amount of truth to the saying, "If nobody wants it, you can't give it away. But, in the right wrap and presented the right way - you can sell it! Because then, people think it is valuable" (T.B. Merriman, 2018). And, even though I am throwing out a little bit of lighthearted sarcastic humor, there is a lot of truth inside what I just said. Because of my statement's inherent truth (*Not so much in that what **I am** offering has no value, it indeed does and very much so*); nevertheless, the truth of my circumstances has made me in my spiritual reality, a robbing hood. Take off the blinders. If I am telling you the truth in this book, I am selling some of the divine revelations of YHWH. Pray Eloah has mercy on me and bless me instead of cursing me. It is true. In my current circumstance and to get the words of this book out, I need spiritual curiosity to move people to buy my end time book. The purchase of this book will help get this book's thought-provoking messages and insights out into the world's broader Christian/Messianic/Jewish public.

> "Have I committed an offense in abasing myself that ye might be exalted, because I have [*not*] preached to you the gospel of God freely? I robbed other churches [*by selling my books*], taking wages *of them* [*and you*], to do you [*and them*] service."
>
> (2nd Corinthians 11:7&8)

I do not know if the information contained in this book will help you like it has helped me. I can only pray that it will. It helped me to be at ease with many questions I have asked and wondered about in the past. In my heart I believe; if you can receive its messages, it will do the same thing for you. And finally, to the challenge concerning the passage that emphatically states, "<u>But of that day and hour knoweth no *man, no, not the angels of heaven, but my Father only*</u>." I have come to my spiritual conclusion **"<u>of the moment</u>"** that it was true when it was spoken, but not essentially true now. I will most likely make this argument again before the end of this book. But, permit me to make it first, here and now. There are many passages in the Holy Scripture that for me, make it clear that in the end time; somebody will know the day and the hour the Son of man (*Messiah Yeshua*) will come. It is evident to me that this will be the case, even if nobody believes the words written in this book. In order to prove my point, I need for you as the reader to try and take an honest and a sober look at the following passages from your Bible, specifically if you are using the King James Version. *"Surely the Lord God will do nothing, but he revealeth his secret unto his servants the prophets"* (Amos 3:7).

"And I heard the man clothed in linen, which *was* upon the waters of the river, when he held up his right hand and his left hand unto heaven, and sware by him that liveth for ever, that *it shall be* for a time, times, and a half; and when he shall have accomplished to scatter the power of the holy people, all these *things* shall be finished. And I heard, but I understood not: then said I, O my Lord, what *shall be* the end of these *things?* And he said, Go thy way, Daniel: for the words *are* closed up and sealed [*un*]till the time of the end. Many shall be purified, and made white, and tried; but the wicked shall do wickedly: and none of the wicked shall understand; but the wise shall understand."

(Daniel 12:7-10)

"…[Yeshua]…said, I thank thee O Father, Lord of heaven and earth, because thou hast hid these things from the wise and prudent, and hast revealed them to babes. Even so, Father; for so it seemed good in thy sight. All things are delivered unto me of my Father [*Of necessity this would include knowledge of the day and hour*]: and no man knoweth the Son, but the Father; neither knoweth any man the Father, save the Son, and *he* to whomsoever the Son will reveal him" (Matthew 11:25-27).

"I have yet many things to say unto you, but ye cannot bear them now. Howbeit when he, the Spirit of truth, is come, **he will guide you into all truth**: for he shall not speak of himself; but whatsoever he shall hear, *that* shall he speak: and **he will show you things to come**. He shall glorify me: for **he shall receive of mine, and shall show** *it* **unto you**. All things that the Father hath are mine: therefore said I, that **he** shall take of mine, and **shall show** *it* **unto you**" (John 16:12-15).

"Let us hold fast the profession of *our* faith without wavering; for he *is* faithful that promised; and let us consider one another to provoke unto love and to good works: not forsaking the assembling of ourselves together...but exhorting *one another:* and so much the more, <u>as ye see the day approaching</u>."

(Hebrews 10:23-25)

There are other passages that support the belief Yeshúa will reveal to certain ones, "*that day and hour*" he will come, as we approach these last prophetic minutes before his Millennial Reign is to begin. But, because in truth, many people have been lied to so many times for so long and they have been bewitched and made drunk with the wine of fornication; for them, it is very difficult to receive new knowledge and insights. This is especially true when it comes to a controversial point of information that it seems that no one else has or is speaking. <u>Your point is well-taken.</u> But think about this. Church organizations and prominent evangelists are continually telling Christian parishioners and everyone who will listen to them that "*Jesus Christ*" could come back at any moment and we should all, "*be ready.*" While I wholeheartedly agree with the second part about, "*being ready,*" I have rational and biblical concerns about their, "*any moment now*" proclamations. Not to be offensive, but I am thinking the groups pushing such a narrative, are most likely pre-tribulation rapturist in their faith. The "*any moment now*" doctrine is less likely to be adopted by mid-tribulation and post-tribulation rapturists. If we listened carefully to their general narratives of the very last days by a significant number of popular televangelists, pastors and preachers (*There are Messianic and "Jesus Christ" prerequisites attached to their return doctrines that must take place before their most eagerly awaited and anticipated event* [The coming, return or rapture] *can take place.*); they will very likely include, but are not necessarily limited to the following appearances, happenings and/or events.

1. World War III – (*I would have to presume that would be the Great Tribulation.*)

2. The Antichrist comes on the scene.

3. The Antichrist makes some sort of seven-year Messianic-like covenant with the Jews.

4. The Third "Israelite/Jewish" Temple of YHWH is constructed.

5. The covenant is broken after three and a half years of civil, social and religious civility.

6. Christians or of the people who were left behind and Jews who have since determined the Antichrist is not their Messiah are massacred without mercy for not worshipping him.
   a. (Pre-tribulation view) left behind Christians for preaching the Gospel of "*Jesus Christ.*"
   b. Jews for simply being Jews and also preaching, "*Jesus Christ*" as the Messiah.

7. In time, surviving Christians and converted Jews preach the Gospel of *Jesus* to the world.

8. In some doctrines, there is a belief 144,000 Jews will be converted to Christianity and go forth to preach their newly attained faith to their fellow Jewish brethren and the world.

…And so forth and so on.

According to biblical prophecy, in theory at least (Matthew's 24th Chapter); if I supposedly covered all things in general - *as far as pre-messianic prophecies being fulfilled are concerned* - the next prophetic event that we would be expecting is the return of "*Jesus Christ*" or the coming of, or returning of - Messiah for the Jews and the Messianic believers respectively (verse 14). Of course, if one is a pre-tribulation rapturist, all bets are off. Because then – nothing truly kicks off, until the Rapture! Then after that event, **All HELL** breaks loose! If you have read Revelation, whether you take it in literally, symbolically or a little bit of both; you should have already asked yourself this question, "How could all this happen right up under everyone's noses and literally or virtually no one is able to notice any of it - as it happens?" That was a part of my attitude and questioning when I went to YHWH with my many concerns. I figured if I could not see some of these things after they had occurred and/or recognized some of these events as they were occurring; then in sobriety, I am forced to label myself as one of the wicked that could not understand. Those who Daniel prophesied about for the last days (12:10).

Billions will be deceived by Satan (Revelation 12:9). Deception is that spiritual cup no one really wants to drink from. I tried to justify in my own mind, why it was tolerable for me not to see and recognize - but the words of Daniel kept getting louder and clearer, "...**_none of the wicked would understand._**" I could not get past that Bible truth. **If I did not understand, then Daniel was prophesying about me!** I was left with no other choices. I had to drink from that cup of deception. After I drank from the cup (*Admitting I did not understand endtime prophecy*) it would not pass from me. Eventually, I would go to YHWH and I asked him to help me - **if he would**. You see, I had to also consider that possibility, YHWH had rejected me and I was cursed into being deceived. Again, I understood as many of you also understand. The word of YHWH says, "...**_many are called,_**" (Matthew 22:14), not <u>all are called</u>. That scared me; especially with me being a "*preacher*" and all. If I was a preacher and I had no divine understanding of end time prophetic matters; what does it say about me and my "*relationship*" with "*Jesus Christ?*" Perhaps one of the biggest reasons YHWH showed me what he did was because I became very honest with myself. I recognized that I was in that group of the unwise or as Daniel put it, "***the wicked.***" In truth, I **was** twisted (*that is what wicked means*) concerning truth and prophecy. My undesirable, but undeniable reality was as sure as hell. And it was as sure as hell; I did not understand the realities of end time prophecies – as in when they had occurred, were they occurring or when they were to occur.

I always thought if I had YHWH's Holy Spirit, understanding a good deal of YHWH's spiritual matters, to include several of the significant subjects of end time prophecies, should have been par for the course. In my divine logic, I felt that if I was part of the wise as Daniel described the wise I should recognize a few things like... *I don't know...* maybe like when wormwood would fall. Or at the least, recognize wormwood when it fell. Many of you have read Revelation and many if not all of the Holy Bible's prophecies. Daniel confirmed that if we were wise, our wisdom **"would"** eclipse that of all the wicked, so as to understanding prophetic happenings. When they (*the wicked*) would not and could not. <u>Do not we understand more than the wicked</u>? If we do not, what does it say about us? In my disappointment, I could not come to grips with why it was that way in my case with me. I could not understand why the theologians did not know what time it was so that we could at least have a general idea when to expect certain prophetic events to occur; instead of the religious pundits' usual and totally taxing, "<u>It's going to happen soon</u>" or "<u>Any day now</u>" predictions. YHWH revealed to me, the reason half of the ten virgins (*let alone the wicked of this world*), did not understand the true reality of prophetic time, was because they did not **live by** his basic word. So, he refused to reveal to them the mysteries of **The Truth** inside of His Holy Hebrew Scriptures. After YHWH's somewhat obvious and anticlimactic judgment – I could then understand why preachers did not know what time it was. YHWH explained to me that it was for the same reason. I then understood from YHWH's response that the answer to my unasked questions was in the Holy Scripture. Granted, I am paraphrasing my interactions with YHWH concerning this matter - because I really could not tell and explain to you all of the ways YHWH took me through verbatim. I can only hope that the revised, but deficient explanations I give and prophetic time routes I take you through will suffice. And, trust me when I say, I can somewhat understand any and all skepticism. I am merely asking that you allow me to make my case to you completely, as I bear out the path of recorded biblical history and future prophetic time.

Two more things I would ask from you; as you read and will surely come to controversial and thought-provoking views and ideas. Open your mind and enjoy the walk. Oh yeah. What was my unasked question? It is inside of this book's subtitle. Even those in our non-believing parts of the world know. We have just so much time down here as man. The Holy Bible is a witness to as much in saying, "*Is there* not an appointed time to man upon earth? *Are not* his days also like the days of a hireling?" (Job 7:1). Sure; I was unsure. But - I felt I needed to know it for my calling's sake. Was I truly called by YHWH Elohim or not. If I was I should know significant somethings - right? So I asked the no-no question. **My Adon,**

"What time are we really in and how much time do we have left?"

"THAT'S RIGHT! I ASKED HIM!"

Call me a sanctimonious idiot for asking, if you like. But, it was nothing like that. I am not sure that I had ever been so open, honest and humbled all at the same time in my life. So then - *please* - no prejudgments. Let me first retrace for you in a somewhat condensed account - the time walk YHWH took me on. And trust me when I say this. I understand you may not be able to use everything in this book. But, I believe the more you are able to process and incorporate, the better off you will be in the long run and in the end.

CHAPTER 3

WHERE DO WE START?

I suppose there are some basics - which I am sure you already know about. Nevertheless, and not to insult anyone intentionally; but, I believe it is better and safer not to assume too much about each other when it comes to Bible literacy and understanding. We will say things as clearly as we can and certainly try to prove as much as we can. Indeed, we are commanded by the words of Apostle Shaul (*Paul*), "*Prove all things...*" from the Holy Bible (1st Thessalonians 5:21). I will add to that. "*Prove all things...*" with the Holy Bible - as much as possible. With that said, understand. In the United States of America, our established standard for counting the years consist of the old B.C. (*Before Christ*) and A.D. (*Anno Domini*: Latin for "*in the year of the Lord*") and the more recent, B.C.E. (*Before Common Era*) and C.E. (*Common Era*). They are popular among traditional Jews and in secular society. Historically, B.C.E. aligns with B.C. and C.E. aligns with A.D. They cover the same periods of years. I see it clearly as an effort to avoid the "***Did Messiah come***?" or "***Is Jesus Christ divine?***" questions. For atheists any symbol of recognition to the divine is taboo. Thus is their leaning to exclusively use B.C.E. and C.E. over the Christian practice of B.C. and A.D. The corresponding years of B.C. and B.C.E. are the same and A.D. and C.E. are the same, (hereafter: BC, BCE, AD, CE). If we asked officially what are BCE/CE's purposes; I am sure there would be some scholarly response; to which, I care not to hear. I have given my view. The corresponding years being the same; the union point, is also the same. It is allegedly the birth of, or at the least, close to the birth of the biblical Messiah or Christian Savior. The Savior in the case of Christianity (*Catholics and Protestants*) is *Jesus Christ*. When it comes to most secular and religious Jews counting the years of man's time in existence, Jews start from the estimated – *more correct, **guesstimated*** – year one until now, year 5780. There is no entry on their calendar for the birth of a Messiah despite **Daniel 9:25-26**. I suppose for most Jews, YHWH is Messiah and he will "*restore again the kingdom to Israel*" (Acts 1:6) at the traditional "**Head of the Jewish Year**" in year 6001. But for now, the Jewish year is 5780. It corresponds closely to the AD/CE 2019-20 (*America, Great Britain and other professing Christian* *nations*). I mean to go over this again later; hopefully with added details.

But for now, armed only with an absolute faith in the authority of **The Holy Bible** *above all*, a fundamental knowledge of general mathematical principles - *to include* - but may not be limited to, basic and non-complex counting methods and the conversion processes to use ancient to modern numerical concepts; we will account for as much of biblical history as we can find. And, of course the inspiration and revelation of the Holy Spirit is absolutely essential for us. Without it, we would not be able to stay on YHWH's biblical trails without getting lost. It is impossible for a blind person to lead any other person to some place he has never been. YHWH created numbers and time. People have merely been allowed to borrow Elohim's mathematical numbers and use their concepts as best they can. That is what I have tried to do in this book. In my heart for a long time I had hoped YHWH would allow me to explore the time that has elapsed as compared to the total years he has ordained for mankind's natural existence. That said, I suppose in order to do it, one of the primary things I would need to know, is how much time prophetically if not literally, has been formally and divinely ordained for us from the beginning.

For individuals whose residence is in the USA, whether we are as naturalized, assimilated and I dare say even most of the non-citizens, we are aware our nation is living in AD time. For the Jew or non-Christians, the modern CE (*Common Era*) is likely preferred. The specific date and year during parts of this chapter's writing is January, year AD 2019. The initials "A.D." stands for the Latin term, "**anno Domini.**" **Anno Domini** means, "***In the year of the, or our Lord***" and is used to count or number the years on both their Julian and Gregorian calendars. That term is part of its completed or original phrase, "**anno Domini nostri Jesu Christi;**" which is translated to, "***In the year of our Lord Jesus Christ***" (odb.org). As an aside and in case we use it, the initials, "B.C." stands for, "*Before Christ.*" When the term was created and the initials of "A.D." is used, it is in essence saying with its use, whichever year AD is affixed to, it has been those many years since the birth of Christendom's Lord and Savior "*Jesus Christ.*" However, there is a troubling concern we see with AD. That is, if the date is true or even close to correct, as far as when the Christian Savior "*Jesus Christ*" was born. I am not saying this to be dismissive over the generally accepted time window given to support the assumption and the supposed birth year of "*Jesus Christ.*" I am merely addressing the obvious theological elephant and bull in the Christians' China Shop. They both seem ready and willing to wreak havoc or make a mockery not only of Christendom's theology; but every other professing Messianic faith. Which quite literally or at the least is said to contain in sobriety, our sense of time in relation to keeping accurate count. And, the

Holy Scriptures commands us in <u>Titus - Chapter 2</u>; to be sober minded. With that said, what I am about to ask next; I do not ask it with the spirit of foolishness. I speak it in the thought-provoking effort to uncover some clarity of truth; as it relates to our time-keeping inefficiencies. Success depends on if there is clarity of truth to be had in Biblical chronology connecting the days in our past to the present and then the future. It is not sacrilege to notate valid biblical events that show an invalid time-keeping format in our accounting of the years kept by carnal men. So... here goes.

<u>What happened to that great divine promise of his</u> (*Alluding to "Jesus Christ's"*) <u>glorious return?</u> Of course, I am speaking as a scoffer! But do not be alarmed. Be assured. I am no scoffer! Nevertheless, a legitimate question has been raised up. In view of our apparent reality that we are in AD 2020; those who are not in denial, spiritually drunk or completely blinded; are clearly face to face, nose to nose and eye to eye with the contemptuous glare of the scornful and the problematic challenges of the non-believer. "*Where is the promise of his coming?*" You know who and what I am talking about. That great promise Christendom has preached at us, should occur somewhere close to year of AD 2000; and fundamental Judaism has traditionalized to us that it should happen after 6000 years. "*...for since [their] fathers have fallen asleep* (<u>died</u>) *all things continue as they were from the beginning of the creation*" (2nd Peter 3:4).

As honest sober Christians, **we are forced to admit**, unless the **Holy Bible** is **Error** - **God forbid**! There is something wrong with our modern system for counting the years intellectual man has existed. How do you see it? We have a serious impasse when we consider the implications of the question itself. It is no less problematic if we were to view it from the arrogance of the "fools" who ask it with all seriousness. And to the fools, when *Christians* and believers who are at a loss, continue to respond with, "*He is coming soon or any day now*;" their defense for an apparent lie is shameful at worse and denial at best. But what else are *Christians* and believers to say? If fools ask such a question, is recognition being given? I want to address apparent givens briefly before moving on. My list is not full; but coming from the fool, I view them as possibly non-conscious confessions.

1) The term, "*creation*" suggests that there is indeed a master designer or a universal creator.

2) If a promise was made by a creator, was a time given when that promise should be fulfilled?

3) How do you know the fathers are only sleeping in death and are not just plain dead and gone - perished?

4) However, if they are asleep, then there needs to be a time for an awakening of some sort or resurrection date.
   a) By whose authority is this awakening or resurrection supposed to take place?

b) Does this authority also give a time when this awakening or resurrection is to take place?

Nonetheless, in all fairness no matter what we may think of scoffers; their enquiry is a legitimate challenge presented; to the Jew first, then to other believers and to the *Christians*. The scoffer and the fools' question remain, "*Where is the promise of his coming?*" In other words – why has not **The Messiah** for the Jews, **Yeshua** for most all Messianics and "***Jesus Christ***" for *Christians* come? These all have promised they would from 5780 to 6019 years (*Traditional Jews and Messianics faith*). 4000 years of BC added to the 2020 years of AD, combines for Christendom's total 6020 (*Catholics and Protestants*). These two are agreeing closely with many groups in the Messianic believers' movements. In all fairness, according to the Bible, it is a question believers in YHWH only (Jews), Messianic believers (Some Jews and Gentiles) and believers in "*Jesus Christ*" should all have a legitimate answer for when confronted by the unbelievers (1st Peter 3:15&16). **In this book we accept their challenge**. We will step up to the plate and address their question. And, as far as our response, they can believe it or not. This book will not ignore the ridicule of non-believer and fools; or the shame in the slackness of foolish virgins who reply to the unbelievers' scoffing with their own disingenuous moral scoffing, and their oftentimes illogical and their less than inspiring effort to counter ignorant challenges, presented by the powers of faithlessness.

Anybody, who in all seriousness, would make such an incredulous statement concerning the Messiah; I am sure in their own mind is skating solidly on the top side of sanity. But the cerebral ice holding them from a frigid plunge to sanity's underbelly (*insanity*), as far as my views go, is dangerously thin. If people take, "*scientific*" license or even religious liberty to ask "**that**" question; they imply, whether direct or indirectly, whether purposefully or unintentional; there is a God out in the cosmos or somewhere. Furthermore, no matter what so-called **_science_** may say; they, in all their arrogant anxiety know and understand, "...*it is **HE** that hath made us, and not we ourselves*" (Psalms 100:3). With general social and spiritual traditions in place in societies, these people (*scientists, non-believers and fools*) waltz all around YHWH with their faulty reasoning; and still fail to acknowledge him. One should think, due to our obvious frailties and failings in this temporal life and the natural hopelessness of existence imminent end in death (*mortality*); why would there not come from our intuitive senses, no matter how incomprehensible; **_God_** as an intellectual force exist? I for one believe he is. I went to this **_God_** for help in my lack of wisdom on biblical history, ordained and prophetic time.

For your perspective, I propose this consideration to your judgment. If we were able to in earnest and with a sober spiritual mind, self-debate those few questions above, and consider their implications, then is the possibility present that a major breakthrough for insights is right in front of our faces for acceptance? True enough, we may or may not know the exact of when, pertaining to when the dead will rise or when Messiah will return. That statement is at least for the moment, a fair judgment of our current understanding. But we (*you and I*) should be able to agree and come to this one and sure conclusion in faith. "*The Lord is not slack concerning his promise as some men count slackness; but is long-suffering to us-ward, not willing that any should perish, but that all should come to repentance*" (2nd Peter 3:9). If *Jesus* did not return when many *guesstimated* him to in AD 2000; it is obvious they did not see **the signs he was not coming**, at least not as clear as they possibly ought to have. Nevertheless, do not be too alarmed. If you will recall from the Holy Bible, the five wise virgins had gone to sleep right beside the five foolish virgins. Why was that? It would appear, because the bridegroom (Yeshua) did not return, even when those "*wise virgins*" thought that he would (Matthew 25:5). Looking past that worldly concealing and still spiritually revealing (*at the same time*) parable about those ten virgins; understanding the time element (*day and hour*) of Messiah's return was as of then, even unknown to Messiah's disciples. Right up until just the few moments before Yeshua's ascension and return to the heavens, his disciples were still questioning him, "*Lord, wilt thou at this time restore* *again the kingdom to Israel?*" (Acts 1:6) At that telling moment, they were yet still unaware of the years and times. And, even Yeshua himself, **would not** explain or tell it to them (Verse 7). That and other revelations would conversely be revealed unto their hearts, at some later date (John 16:12&13), particularly, "*at the time of the end*" (Daniel 12:10), by the power of the Holy Spirit. This is a promise in the Holy Scripture that we have from YHWH.

However, there are two edges to most swords. If we believe the Holy Bible is translated from original truth, we must conclude that the year AD 2020 is off – *somehow*. If it was not off, the Messiah in apparent theological theory at least, should have returned over nineteen years ago. AD 2000 as the year of Messiah's returning, should have been held up as **biblical fact**. That is, had we believed to incorporate the **Hebrew/Jewish** time guide of the **Millennial Week** - with no shortening of the days? The week includes a Millennial Sabbath. It is called in *Christian* circles the, "Millennial Reign." In Jewish theology, the end of the sixth millennial (*6000 years*); and by the way – **not equal** to AD 2000 from my current perspective, also demands an event like a Millennial Reign. Still, in the Jews' reality, Messiah comes and *restores the kingdom to Israel* forever.

Nevertheless, Revelation 20:4 supports the judgment for a Messianic Millennial Sabbath. It seems in BC/AD count, it is a simple add. 4000 years BC added to 2020 years AD is 6020 years total time. Clearly for me, something is very wrong! This is why I asked YHWH to help me walk through the time of intellectual man. I wanted to know. <u>What was wrong</u>? I asked if YHWH would penetrate my thick brain housing group and teach my dull spiritual common senses a thing or two, anything in truth. I asked if I could know how many years have passed since the first intellectual man Adam walked the earth. Understand, it was due to my darken senses; this journey for me was not a small order. Because in the back of my mind, I was consistently thinking. What if I ended up being wrong - or even worse? What if I had listened to some sort of wicked familiar spirit? I do not know about anybody else, but for me that latter "What if…" would have been a real spiritual nightmare. But, in loving kindness the Holy Bible informs us of a precious divine privilege that we have. It is designed to help us understand **Truth**. It helps us to find and understand in certain cases, what were once sealed Holy Bible mysteries. This divine privilege is available to those who seek true righteousness, holiness and godliness. Its promise is preserved to assist those of us who have come to see these last few minutes in end time biblical prophecies.

> "If any of you lack wisdom, let him ask of God, that giveth to all *men* liberally, and upbraideth not; and it shall be given him. But let him ask in faith, nothing wavering: for he that wavereth is like a wave of the sea driven with the wind and tossed. For let not that man

think that he shall receive any thing of the Lord"
(James 1:5-7).

Most of us already know about that passage. So yes, I understand your concerns. To read my words starting my journey to the knowledge that I claim to have today; one has to ask the question. Was I not, a bit wavy? **Yes**! I was really afraid on both ends. I was **afraid** YHWH would not reveal to me. Then again, I was **more afraid** he would reveal to me. At that time in my ignorance; I was not sure which one was the worse, responsibility wise. I felt like jurors inside that military courtroom; being berated and stupefied by the words of Colonel Nathan R. Jessup. He was the character actor Jack Nicholson portrayed in the movie, A Few Good Men. **No**! It was not, **"Here's Johnny!!"** That was in The Shining and arguably, Nicholson's most memorable quote. What Nicholson said in A Few Good Men was, **"You can't handle the truth!!"** I may not know Jack. But, I am sure Jack may not know in reality that he was describing the greater portions of human societies worldwide. Regardless to how I pictured myself then; I humbled myself and I asked of YHWH. Even though - I was scared to death. For some reason YHWH answered me. And now I am here before you, with what I believe to be new insights you all can glean from. YHWH has sent me out to you with this book, because he knows it is much later than everybody thinks. It does appear to me, YHWH wants me to help people by his Spirit's revelation; answer part of their lifelong questions on certain truths and prophecies. I suppose it is YHWH's final push to hopefully help them to build up their faith for them to fight an even better fight - in their effort to attain his eternal life.

I am wise to the idea that some of this book's readers; who consider themselves as, "*more knowledgeable*" about the Holy Scriptures than the "average Joe reader;" may find what I have to say in here not easy to accept. They may reject some of its contents or perhaps the entire book. And I myself must agree with them in a truth. They are absolutely correct should they contend.

> "*Mr. Merriman is not the first one, nor will he most likely be the last one; and he is certainly not the only one out here in the Christian world clamoring and claiming to know something no one else knows. There is always someone out here saying they know God like nobody else does. And God has delivered to them, "selectively," some great secret truth that no one else seems to have, can discern or recognize for the purpose of being able to understand its revelation.*"

Right now I have just three words for those who would be my detractors.

<u>"Guilty as Charged.</u>"

<u>"THAT'S RIGHT! I SAID IT!"</u>

<u>"GUILTY AS CHARGED!"</u>

As disbelieving as that criticism may be, their comment is pretty much spot-on. Believe it or not, there are no shortages, when it comes to all of the religious experts and scholars the world over, who sometimes imagine themselves as having the Holy Spirit inspired inside track to special truths, understandings and revelations. This is so in the Jewish community. This is especially true within the Christian and Jewish-like Messianic faiths. Many preachers and church organization inside some of the Protestant denominations have thought and preached as part of their message for the better part of almost 150 years that the Christian Messiah "*Jesus Christ*" "**should have**" come back "***generally***" around year AD 2000. In the case of the traditional Jewish faith, the coming of their Messiah is expected in the year 6001. This same 6001 year period is also expected in the case of many of the Messianic sects and some parts of the Christian faith. (*That is, by the **Hebrew** year 6001*). To better help you hold on to your bearing, in relation to my intended directional purpose of keeping a synchronized count; in the present as of the Gregorian calendar year 2019-2020, the Jewish State year is listed at their overall years since Adam was created at 5780. This is a significant understanding to keep in mind and remember; once we get started on our walk through recorded biblical history and future prophetic times. Of course, if you prefer - you are more than welcome to look all this stuff up. Then you can verify and prove it for yourself. I would highly recommend such action. It is readily available knowledge. It is listed in virtually every corner of the internet;

where teachings on various *Christian* religions and Jewish traditions are plentiful. I also encourage such studious activities; to verify all truths.

Since YHWH renewed of the face on the earth; as witnessed in the creation events, recorded in the Holy Bible from Genesis the first chapter until Genesis 2:1-3; and from the beginning and history of the Hebrew's oral tradition; there has been some form of a millennial week – seven day – or 7000-year cycle taught. There is an additional great day (*also 1000 years*) possibly mentioned and taught is at the end; to give space for the great white throne judgment. The ancient fathers and the Hebrew fathers taught it to all of their sons. Their sons taught it to their sons. This was so their understandings and culture was not lost. Oral traditions of beliefs were handed down from Adam to his son, to Abram - the first Hebrew. Then kept alive in the shadow pictures of scripture and from generation to generation in Jewish culture from their founding fathers, their great leader in Moses, the prophets of Israel, then the Jewish high priest and rabbis. Later on, even Christian scholars got in on the act; saying that YHWH in making a seven-day work week cycle, socially established the perpetual shadow-picture for some greater fulfillment regarding man's temporal existence in the flesh. Many churches teach that the shadow picture of YHWH's millennial week is seared into all cultures as man's everlasting time, through that literal seven-day week. I might venture to add; it is hereby cauterized with the self-destructive nature of the human sub-consciousness; offering instead of the obvious eventual extinction of our species, an utopian hope and promise of everlasting life. Through the concept of a millennial week, belief in life endured the joint-effort of war and history; those two intent on destroying most all faith. The expectancy of life at the end of this age, continues to defy its foes. Life has breached every barrier erected to hide from YHWH's faithful, the truth behind the cycle's millennial fulfillment – meaning each solar day of the creation week cycle, represent in shadow picture – a 1000 year period. With the ending of the six millennial day, the prophesied Israelite/Jewish Messiah is expected to return for His 1000-year seventh day (Sabbath) reign. The "paraphrased" Biblical passage below is lengthy. But, understanding its message is critical to a clearer picture and narrative; revealing a partly hidden truth of YHWH. He does indeed have a 7000 years plan for man.

> "I write to you; to stir up your minds to remembrance and <u>be mindful of the words spoken before by the holy prophets and of us the apostles of the Adon and Savior</u>. First, there will come in the last-days scoffers, walking after their own lusts, and saying, "Where is the promise of His coming?" Since the fathers <u>fell asleep</u> [*died*] all things continue as from the beginning of the creation. <u>For they are willingly ignorant to the promise</u> and the <u>authority of YHWH</u>, that just as the old world against the flood was judged; so too will not only the earth, but the heavens and perdition of ungodly men will be judged by the same YHWH with fire. <u>Beloved, do not be ignorant of this word and its revelation to us, one day with YHWH is as a thousand years and</u>

a thousand years is as one day. Do not be deceived, YHWH is not slack about His promise, as some men count slackness; but is long-suffering toward us, not willing that any human souls should perish, but that all should have opportunity to repent. Nevertheless, YHWH's Day will come to many as the thief in the night; after which the heavens shall pass away with a great noise and all the elements shall melt with unimaginable heat, the earth also and the works that are herein shall be burned up. All things being dissolved, what manner ought we to be in holy conversation and godliness, living eagerly and fasting to the coming of the Last Great Day of YHWH, wherein the heavens being on fire shall dissolve and the elements shall melt with fervent heat? Nevertheless, as non-survivable as all this is, we according to His promise [*and we trust that YHWH cannot lie*] we look forward to existing in the new heavens and a new earth, where righteousness will dwell. If you believe this beloved, and you expect such things, do not be foolish and do not fall prey to worthless and rebellious words; that you may be found in truth and peace of mind in Him, with no spots, and blameless."

(2ⁿᵈ Peter 3:1-14 - *paraphrased*).

One take-a-way from the above passage of scripture is a fundamentally uniting viewpoint contained within the Jewish faiths, in the Messianic faith and in much of the Christian faith. And that is primarily this.

"Shim'on Kefa (*Simon Peter*) was speaking the very same thing that the Hebrew Rabbis have taught for thousands of years. In that God created the heavens and the earth in six days and on the seventh-day he rested; what that means is that man will have his time of rule and reign on the earth for six thousand years. The Messiah will reign in the seventh or the Sabbath Millennium - The Day or the Millennium of the LORD." (Rood, M., 2000)

From my perspective, the thousand year reign of Messiah is clearly pictured in Revelation 20:4.

"And I saw thrones, and they sat upon them, and judgment was given unto them: and *I saw* the souls of them that were beheaded for the witness of [*Yeshua*], and for the word of Eloah, and which had not worshipped the beast, neither his image, neither had received *his* mark upon their foreheads, or in their hands; and they lived and reigned with [*Messiah*] a thousand years."

At my stage of discernment, I am able to accept the basic premise of Mr. Rood's statement. That is, before man's suicidal resolve consumes him, YHWH is allowing him six prophetic days, 1000 years each; to live by the Serpent's argument; in trying to prove the Dragon's word is truth. After Adam fails to do so - **and he will** - the Messiah will return and show man how life is really done. That time length in most of our Judeo-Christian theology is called the Millennial Reign. As I stated earlier, it is clearly recorded in Revelation. However, in debate various believers and theologians take those 1000 years to be figuratively. Other believers and theologians just as prominent take the 1000 years to be literal in nature. I am of the literal 1000-year persuasion. Nevertheless, after considerable introspection of my own understandings, I would like to take some time to interject. Of course, as with everything I will say inside of this book; you are welcome to accept or reject them. I will take no offense. At this point, my major goal is to help my readers see a fuller divinely enlighten view of YHWH's great jig-saw picture of truth in the times. I believe this book will aid you to put it together and establish momentum to race. It is your choice to accept. But here is my perspective. As far as I understand, the Holy Scriptures does not directly and precisely reveal how long YHWH took to create all of the heavens – including this earth. What we are given privy to in the book of Genesis and *other illuminating passages* on the subject matter, are the actions of YHWH creating an atmosphere and **_renewing_** *the face of the earth* in preparation for his creation of *man*.

> He looked on the earth and it was trembling: he touched the hills and they were smoking. Then YHWH sent forth his spirit to renew the face of the earth and all things were created. Afterwards, YHWH rejoiced in his works. And the glory of YHWH [*handiworks*] shall endure for ever.
> (Psalms 104:30-32 - paraphrased).

The renewal was necessary because of the great devastation place upon the earth by Satan and his angels. When the Scripture witnesses, "*...the heavens and the earth were finished, and all the host of them*" (Genesis 2:1); it was truly only referencing the immediate open parts of heaven and this earth alone. I apologize that I will only speak in such rudimental terms here, but bear me out. As far as I can determine at this point, **The Scriptures** reveal **four dimensions of heaven**, thus the term, "*heavens*" as in more than one is recorded. Apostle Shaul gave insight to the third dimension - whether he was in vision or in person (*I do not know*). Nonetheless, Apostle Shaul was witness to what some supposed for many (*Including myself – for a long period in my learning*) was the most glorious part of the "*heavens*."

> "It is not expedient for me doubtless to glory. I will come to visions and revelations of the Lord. I knew a man in Christ above fourteen years ago, (whether in the body, I cannot tell; or whether out of the body, I cannot tell: God knoweth) such a one caught up to the third heaven. And I knew such a man, (whether in the body, or out the body, I cannot tell: God knoweth)...he was caught up into paradise, and heard unspeakable words, which it is not lawful for a man to utter" (2nd Corinthians 12:1-4).

If there is a third heaven; logically, it makes sense there is a first and second heaven. The Bible reveals as much. Reflect on some of what The Scriptures say. "*And God said, Let the waters bring forth abundantly the moving creature that hath life, and fowl that may fly above the earth in the open firmament of heaven*" (Genesis 1:20). It is consistent to concede this. That is, if there is an open portion to the firmament of heaven; then, there is a closed portion to the firmament. It is what I believe is thinking and using spiritual common sense. What say you? If you meditate on it, I would like to think that you will come to a similar perspective that I have come to. There is an open part to the firmament. It is where the wind blows, birds fly and modern aircrafts zoom (*1st heaven*). There is a closed part to the firmament, where untold numbers of suns (*stars*), other earths, moons and man's rocket space ships and satellites venture (*2nd heaven*). And, there is yet at the least, one more level, another dimension of the heavens. It is beyond the birds, human aircrafts, satellites and spaceships.

It is beyond the stars, other earths, moons and comets. It is accessed by invitation only (*3rd heaven*). You, being the super sharp reader you are. You recall twenty-three (23) lines prior, not to include that passage from *2nd Corinthians*; I made the bold claim that there were at the least, four dimensions of heavens. I did. Some might ask, "Where is this fourth?" Most of you already know this fourth dimension of heaven exists. You have most likely read about it many times, but did not discern it. Discern today; and believe. The fourth dimension of heaven is in **The Light**. You know the light I am talking about; **"THE LIGHT!"** It is beyond space and time. Best I can say to illuminate. Elohim is the only one; "*dwelling in the light which no man can approach unto; whom no man (Enoch, Elijah, Shaul or Yochanan) hath seen, nor can see*" (1st Timothy 6:16).

Continuing on, YHWH likely used a much longer span of our time, when HE constructed the entire creation. HE likely took billions of years. Time means nothing to the **ETERNAL ONE** in reference to how long he takes to accomplish a thing. In that sense, time is only important to finite beings like men and angels. But again, that is another story for perhaps another time and book. Besides all of this, if we review a general passage that references the creative agent of **Elohim**; which I believe so many presume concerning and misinterpret in regards to; if we were to really look closer with our spiritual common sense, we should be able to see the obvious. **We were mistaken**. Consider again. "*Thus the heavens and the earth were finished and all the host of them*" (Genesis 2:1). **So, reason**. How could "***all the heavens***" be completed or be, "***finished;***" when all, except for this earth itself and alone, "was made subject to vanity...but by reason of him[YHWH] who hath subjected *the same* in hope; because the [*creation*] itself also **shall be** [*not already is*] delivered from the bondage of corruption" (Romans 8:20-21); which thus denotes it as incomplete or **"unfinished!"** I will say this to everybody here and now. It will be the divine ordination of the Sons of YHWH's, to go out into his "unfinished creation," at His command and under His authority of, to renew the face of the creation. I believe it is safe to say, such a magnitude of this kind of creative authority given would include visiting to every star, every planet and every moon. That includes comets and perhaps beyond. Don't forget.

> "But as it is written, Eye hath not seen, nor ear heard, neither have entered into the heart of man, the things which God hath prepared for them that love him. But God hath revealed *them* unto us by his Spirit: for the Spirit searcheth all things, yea, the deep things of God" (1st Corinthians 2:9).

Oh yeah, one other, "*minor*" thing concerning Mr. Rood's comments on the Day of YHWH. The Rabbis thousands of years ago, received their insights - many of them did - through the Hebrew's oral traditions. So the teaching of YHWH's millennium, likely has existed before Noah and with - *believe it or not* - Adam himself. I do admit, that hypothesis could be thoroughly debated to the positive or the negative. But keep it in mind along the way – anyway. It could very well apply to your good.

Here is most likely, something else you might want to think about. We are still waiting on year 6001; in the view of Jews and a few outlier Christian sects. That would begin the Millennial Reign of their Messiah. Recall the Jewish community contends; it is no more than the year 5780. But with various Messianic groups espousing that it is the year 6019-6020, then why is there still such a significant and influential mass inside the mainstream of "Christianity," and amongst its major denominations; which continue to preach that the Messiah or "*Jesus Christ*" could be returning at any instant now? That is, if all of the Christian organizations that continue evangelizing this doctrine, thought with any seriousness to its accuracy of time or spoke with any integrity when they know full well the Gregorian and the Julian calendar year sets at AD 2020. If you and I thought with soberness of mind in truth and without the some-times false denominational influences; based on our understanding of the seven day millennial calendar and man's 6000-year limit, we would have concluded if the various *Christian and some Messianic Jewish* prognosticators, who indoctrinate with their "*any day now*" theology were accurate, "*Jesus Christ*" **would** have returned - *if we are going to be forthcoming* - about twenty years ago. At its literal foundations, what this counting action in our *Christian* societies has been doing for the past 2020 years - whether intentional or unintentional, whether directly or indirectly, *"Christians"* were attempting to keep their eye out in history (*if you will*) by stamping into the civil unconsciousness year after year some kind of predictive due date for the return of *"Jesus Christ."* At its core *Christians* have crafted a religious prophecy in the mind of the broader social order without calling it a real religious prophecy in numerical sequence. What "<u>Anno Domini</u> - nostri Jesu Christi" (*In the year of our Lord Jesus Christ*) was intended to achieve in Catholicism, by its keeping up with time and the counting out of years; was a broad banded social religious effort to mark the actual return date of their *"Lord and Savior Jesus Christ."* Many might not admit to this purpose for their design. But, I believe if we were all being honest here and came clean with each other, we would all have to conclude and say, "What other purpose could using the term, *"in the year of the Lord"* mean, or stand for, or serve as? Again, it had to be Catholicism's and then later on, Christianity's attempt at predicting their *"Lord and Savior "Jesus Christ's" return."* Of course, now-a-days, if anyone else was to try and make such a bold claim or prediction, most of the time they would be met almost at once with religious jeers, strong distain and disbelief. In light of our spiritually blinded world, it is natural to expect and basically understandable that to go along with that knee-jerk reaction would be few inquiries and little hesitation to call any such prognosticator the infamous name of *"false prophet"* or *"deceiver."*

That type of reaction at its core is what I could easily describe at its extreme as hypocrisy and at the least of it as being ironic. Think about it honestly. If that was the case and in most instances it is. This incredulous condemnation would be perpetrated by our same *Christian* community that has been doing the same thing for well over 2000 years. Absolutely, Christians have been trying to predict *"Jesus Christ's"* return with the BC/AD count. In that social truth, I would find any condemnations of others predicting that Messianic event, highly suspect and disingenuous. This is especially true if we do so even after being confronted with our own *"20-year old"* flawed prophetic prediction. At this point, I am not really trying to be picky and difficult. I am just trying to establish a point.

If we have biblical confidence in the 7000-year prophetic cycle and then make the simple count of 4000 BC and AD 2000; minus any unseen conditions, we would have to conclude the true year after the birth of, *"Jesus Christ;"* **not** to be ***contextually***, AD 2020. What other choice do we have at this point, outsides of foolish chants such as, *"Where is the promise of his coming?"* Then again, maybe there is another explanation. I have to think such a scenario is at the least, possible. On the other hand, if we are to believe the Jews in Israel and their "***guesstimated***" year of

5780; then we have another 221 years before we can expect the Messiah to truly return. With whatever insights many of us think we have today, concerning Messiah Yeshua's return swirling around inside our minds; unless someone gets rid of all the so-called "Palestinians" in and around Israel, or my Eloah forbid, the Jews themselves - *in some abrupt manner and quickly* - the way things are shaping up in Israel at the moment, it seems reasonable to me at least, that it might very well take another 221 years and then some to even consider the real possibility of erecting **The Third Temple** in Jerusalem; which many Jews and Christians alike have suppose is one of the prerequisites for the return of the Messiah or "*Jesus Christ.*" Think about the time element. That would be the lifespan of another United States of America up until year 1997! The way things are shaping up in our own nation today, what I suspect will be the case with our **constitutional** U.S.A. is, we will not last another 221 years, at least not as this **FREE Representative Republic**. And literally, I believe most reading this book are thinking, neither will this world - meaning this age.

If 221 years are left, none of us will be alive, if or when that temple events occur. With the way things are going in the **United States**, at least as of now; how many readers really think this **Representative Republic** will be still standing - that far into the future? What does that say for our heritage, destiny and the future generations of our children? I fear to peer down that very dark path. But, I would like for you to consider this one question. Do you think it is going to take the perpetrators of terrorism 221 years to sneak a "dirty bomb" in through our porous U.S. southern border for its detonation in one of our cities? **CAN YOU SAY WWIII?** Personally and from my view, I find it to be highly unlikely and do not believe there will be our **United States of America** 221 years from now. From my vantage - **6019, AD 2020 and 5780** - were all three, distasteful dates for me. I suppose that is why I asked YHWH; would he heal my blinded eyes, unstop my death ears and give me an understanding heart. Then in tender mercy guide my ignorance; allow me to try and walk with him through as much of man's overall Bible history as my mind could receive from him. **And, he did!** I received knowledge that satisfied my ignorance to know what time it really is to a great degree. Eloah walked me along what I viewed to be the biblical history and ordained prophetic events of the first man Adam onward. In this book, I will make that walk through YHWH's ordained and revealed time, yet again. Only this time I will not be alone. I will have great company! I will have You! I hope you are ready! I truly believe this walk will be intriguing, enlightening and even a bit of fun - for the open minded. So then, let us begin in earnest.

We will start with an argument or if one would rather, the hypothesis that there are a total of eight millennial days or 8000 years that show the length of YHWH's ordained time for man in his current existence. From my perspective, this is not a very difficult argument to make from the pages and viewpoint of the Holy Scripture. With such being assumed for the moment; in order to know *what time we are really in and how much time we have left* – we must account for them all, in our walk through Adam's time. The eight millennial days or 8000 years or millennial week is symbolized or depicted in shadow picture, awaiting its future fulfilling at the end; or what most *"believers"* have come to see and understand is Judgment Day, during two of YHWH's appointed holy times in the fall. Our *"**tabernacling**"* is celebrated by many Jews at the festival of Sukkot or Sukkoth and at Shemini Atzeret. Shemini Atzeret literally means, *"the assembly of the eighth* (day)" (jewfaq.org). For a Jew it is the last biblical holy day and annual Sabbath of the year. Many Jews recognize Shemini Atzeret is in fact and have come to call it, "**The Last Great Day**." I am not going to try and dig too deep or explain too much (*this is not a book of doctrine, but numbers*). But, the first feast that I mentioned is Sukkot. Sukkot is routinely called The Feast of Tabernacles and is viewed for the most part as a holy time for the Jews. Sukkot is celebrated on the 15th, in their seventh religious month that is called Tishri. According to the Holy Scriptures, Sukkot is a seven days feast gathering (Leviticus 23:34). Not without debate, there is an eight day that is directly associated with

Sukkot, but for prophetic reason and fulfillment, that day is not biblically

apart of Sukkot. Keep in mind, Sukkot is a seven day celebration and is

only connected as far as Adam's life preparations for the great judgment.

When you can, read the entire chapter of Leviticus twenty-three. But for

now, consider the following.

> "...the Lord spoke unto Moses, saying, Speak unto the children
> of Israel, saying, the fifteenth day of this seventh month *shall be*
> the feast of tabernacles *for* seven days unto the Lord. On the first
> day *shall be* a holy convocation: ye shall do no servile work
> *therein.* Seven days ye shall offer an offering made by fire unto
> the Lord; on the eighth day shall be a holy convocation unto you,
> and ye shall offer an offering made by fire unto the Lord: it *is* a
> solemn assembly; *and* ye shall do no servile work *therein.*"
>
> (Leviticus 23:33-36)

The eight days: Sukkot (*The Feast of Tabernacles* at seven [7] days)

and Shemini Atzeret (*The Last Great Day* as in one [1]) represented in

their originality and in their shadow picture the total 8000 years of man's

ordained time on this earth; from year one until its full conclusion at the

end of **The Great White Throne Judgment** for all of mankind (*which*

includes angel kind too). So here again, if we accept the shadow pictures

presented in YHWH's Holy Days of scripture, we would simply need to

locate for accounting, the totality of no less than 8000 years from Bible

history to our present. Then we would simply add on the future biblically

anticipated prophetic fulfillments of those latter millennia. The last two

millennia will be a snap; being they have yet to occur. Being still in the future, we can simply put those (*2000 years*) on the back burners for now. After doing so, we are back down to the well-known, recognized and for the most part, the once well-received and anticipated 6000 years. Again, the question is, can we find them in the Holy Bible. We have to; in order to be able to view in realism, any possible Messianic return. We have to; before we are to expect or when we expected, think and thought the Messiah or Yeshua or "*Jesus*" will, would or should have returned to the earth for the restoration of Israel in Messiah's coming (*Jewish*) or Yeshua in his return with and for his Messianics, to set up his 1000-year kingdom or again, with "*Jesus*" and almost every professing *Christian* "*going to heaven.*" Whew! Well now. I believe that task sounds simple enough for all of us to spiritually get our heads around and then perhaps, biblically untangle inside the following pages of this book and definitely prove from the pages of the Holy Bible. Wouldn't you say so?

CHAPTER 4

OUR WALK THROUGH TIME

How is it, one person thinks he knows something - *it appears* - based on our Christian media and evangelists talk, the rest of the world has no real clue regarding it? That is a fair question to ask. Certainly, suggesting a serious date for Messiah's return falls into that category. In answering that question, I find it hard to explain. Because, pretty much everything that the Holy Spirit reveals to any person; will involve a certain amount of faith. But faith, is not a blind concept; nor is faith of an illogical mind. To be honest, I may not know entirely how all things will be or are in the end, how all things will get done; but with every explanation, all things have to be reasonable. Biblically, they must fit and they must make good sense to me; for me at least, to be able to consider their existence in final truth. So, when the questions of how did I come to conclude the matters I have judged in this book are asked of me; I have little pause to reply with the following. What people will read in this book is what YHWH's Spirit has revealed to me. And, as much as I could receive of what was shown to me and the revelations thereof, it made perfectly good sense to me. The things that were revealed and explained meshed well with even my elementary and middle school public educations. Nevertheless, the Spirit mandated that I reevaluate some of my long held Bible viewpoints. Some of them included major concepts and doctrines.

Clearly, if we are to make an effort in the counting of time; everyone involved will have to know at the least, the simple and established forms of general mathematics. So, speaking candidly; it is an insult to them and their ancient times, for us not to understand. While arguments could be made that literacy in the average citizenry may have been thin; along with knowing how to read and write; certain individuals in those ancient times certainly knew how to add, subtract, multiply, divide and convert. They accomplished extraordinary mathematical feats – like the pyramids. Architectural structures we still cannot duplicate today. We are left here to wonder how did they do them. Since we all should be in agreement on this. They clearly possessed less *"technology"* than we have today.

After I understood and learned to respect their intellectual abilities; I humbled myself before the Spirit of YHWH. Perhaps for those reasons or *other*, YHWH started to reveal things to me. Far as truth revealed goes, I emphasize, "*other*." At this time, I cannot really tell you the reason why YHWH revealed some of his hidden mysteries in the Bible to me. That is not important to most people anyway. What I see is important to people, is for YHWH to reveal to them also. So, I encourage praying; for YHWH to reveal to you these mysteries and even more. If YHWH allows you to believe the contents herein; then ask why he has done so, if you choose. I am advising this approach; because that is what I did. It was effective for my thinking and understanding. I am content with my spiritual situation. And, I cannot ask for anything more than that. I know, for the most parts; what is happening to me, why it is happening to me, why it will continue to happen to me and why things will escalate. You see, I understand this is the spiritual nature and strategy of antichrist. <u>The truth must be viewed by all of the interested masses as twisted personal opinions</u>. That way, all disagreeable revelation of truth can be immediately discounted and easily dismissed. That is antichrists' objective obtained - deception maintained.

I know what I know, because YHWH had mercy on me. He took the basic public education portions of my total educational experiences and revealed all the truth written in this book. It is not because I figured them out in any way. <u>If you have a basic public education, you can understand the revelations contained herein</u>. You just need to believe what YHWH's

Spirit reveals to your spirit. Again, we will be armed primarily with our absolute faith in the full authority of the Holy Scriptures, a fundamental knowledge of general mathematical principles - to include but might not be limited to, fundamental and supplemental counting procedures and the conversion process of ancient and modern numerical add ups - to account for as much of the Bible's chronological time as we can. Less we forget, the inspirations and revelations of the Holy Spirit is absolutely essential. Without him, we would not be able to walk accurately along the biblical trail of years. It would be impossible for me, *a blind man*, to lead you or anyone, to a place I had never been before. YHWH created numbers and time. Even with our borrowing of his fundamental mathematical systems and our pathetic attempts to mimic Elohim's absolute brilliance; when it comes to space and **time** – YHWH's mathematical concepts can only be scratched at the surface by humans. That is what I feel has been done in this book in order to know time. We have perhaps, scratched the surface.

Truth be told, in my search for divine truth, for a long time I had hoped YHWH would let me delve into the times that have elapsed as compared to the total years he has ordained for man's human existence. He did; and I have no words to express how humbled I am. I must let my living sacrifice (*my sense of godly worth*) endure whatever price YHWH wants me to pay by publishing out this book; as it suffers through the probable ridicule of, "scholarly criticisms" and worse. It is with a certain amount of anxiety that I have put myself out here into the arena of spiritual opinion, and abasing detractions. I am confident though, that it will all be worth it in the end. But, in any case, based on my Eloah's "*revelations,*" I will not have to put up with this "*persecution*" for long. Unlike the secular world and many others in this world, who are full of religions; I believe I understand now (*as looking through a glass, darkly – very darkly in my case*); it is much later than I first thought!

Perspective: We begin with the 6000-year premise. We have text below from the Bible showing Eloah ordained a limited time for Adam to train/qualify himself to take over the eternal reins to reign over YHWH's physical universe, "*to dress it and to keep it*" (Genesis 2:15). Eden was a mere microcosm for YHWH's entire creation. Consider the following.

> "What is man, that thou shouldest magnify him? and that thou shouldest set thine heart upon him? and that thou shouldest visit him every morning, and <u>try him every moment</u>?" (Job 7:17-18)

> "<u>What is man, that he should be clean? and he which is born of a woman, that he should be righteous?</u> Behold, he putteth no trust [*sovereign authority*] in his saints [*angels*]; yea, the heavens are not clean in his sight. How much more abominable and filthy is man, which drinketh iniquity like water? <u>I will show thee, hear me; and that which I have seen I will declare; which wise men [*prophets*] have told from their fathers, and have not hid it: unto whom alone the earth was given, and no stranger</u> [*other life forms*] <u>passed</u> [*is preeminent*] <u>among them</u>" (Job 15:14-19).

"When I consider thy heavens the work of thy fingers, the moon and the stars which thou hast ordained; what is man, that thou art mindful of him? and the son of man, that thou visitest him? For thou hast made him a little lower than the angels and hast crowned him with glory and honor. Thou madest him - to have dominion over the works of thy hands - thou hast put all things under his feet" (Psalms 8:3-6).

"For unto the angels hath he not put in subjection the world to come, whereof we speak. But one [*David*] in a certain place testified, saying, What is man, that thou art mindful of him? or the son of man, that thou visitest him? Thou madest him a little lower than the angels; thou crownedst him with glory and honor, and didst set him over the works of thy hands: thou hast put all things in subjection under his feet. For in that he put all in subjection under him, he left nothing that is not put under him. But now we see **"not yet"** all things put under him."

(Hebrews 2:5-8)

If we are starting out with a false premise concerning the concept of the millennial week; we must then trust in the Holy Spirit to make bear the error in our steps and to account and verify the truth, if possible. This is a must, if we are to trace and count the history and prophetic time of man. During our walk, we will need the narration not only for Adam's day one to the present, but the entire first six millennial days. We will also need to add into the mix, the Sabbath Millennial; or as most call it, the Millennial Reign of the Judeo-Christian/Messianic Messiah. And let us not discount the Last Great Day for the Judgment, another 1000 years. When we add all these together at their face values, the sum would equal 8000 years. In organizing all of our time, we can easily account for the

Millennial Sabbath and the Great Judgment Day. They have not occurred yet. So it is easy as well as sensible - *these two being future prophetic dates* - to simply place them at the end of our millennial calendar; before we begin our verification of the bible's history to present and beyond. In giving readers the flavor of things to come, take a look at our beginning millennial week; with days numbered as we have already stated. In my liberty, I circled the yet future Millennial Reign and Judgment Day as the Bible recognizes. (Revelation 20:4 & Zephaniah 1:14) Our Challenge, is to whether we can find the first 6000 years - in the same Holy Bible.

							Millennial	Judgment
1st Millennial Day	2nd Millennial Day	3rd Millennial Day	4th Millennial Day	5th Millennial Day	6th Millennial Day	7th Millennial Day	8th Millennial Day	
250 500 750 1000	1250 1500 1750 2000	2250 2500 2750 3000	3250 3500 3750 4000	4250 4500 4750 5000	5250 5500 5750 6000	6250 6500 6750 7000	7250 7500 7750 8000	
BMB - Before Messiah's Birth			BMB - Before Messiah's Birth	AMB - After Messiah's Birth			AMB - After Messiah's Birth	
4000 3750 3500 3250 3000 2750 2500 2250	2000 1750 1500 1250 1000	750 500 250 BMB	BMB BMB BMB	AMB AMB AMB 250 500 750	AMB AMB AMB 1000 1250 1500	AMB AMB AMB 1750 2000 2250 2500 2750 3000	AMB AMB AMB 3250 3500 3750 4000	
						reign	Day	

When Yeshua began preaching *"The acceptable year of the Lord"* (Luke 4:16-19), it was shortly *"...after that John was put in prison, [Yeshua] came into Galilee, preaching the gospel of the kingdom of God, and saying, The time is fulfilled, and the kingdom of God is at hand: repent ye, and believe the gospel"* (Mark 1:14-15). Yeshua preached to all those who heard him, *"repent ye, and believe"* (Mark 1:15). Yeshua said, *"The time is fulfilled."* Now what do you think that meant, *"The* _**time** is **fulfilled?**_" Even though this book is about "_**time**_," I am not going to touch that "_fulfilled prophecy_" with the proverbial, ten foot pole. Yet, for the inquisitive mind, I will attempt to provide a starting point for any supplemental studies, you just might want to conduct. Consider Daniel 9:20-27 and Isaiah 61:1-2. Anyhow - Onward. After Yochanan (_John the Baptist_) is imprisoned, Yeshua goes into Galilee preaching the _Kingdom of God_. No one could preach **The Gospel** better and with more authority than Yeshua. We all understand this. Yeshua also preformed miracles to compliment his message. He preached truth to all the Judean powers that were. Among those powers were the High Priest, his entourage and other envious influentials. They did not appreciate being called out in truth. After "_the acceptable year_" they murdered Yeshua. His gospel about the kingdom of YHWH found no place in them. It, and he was rejected.

How was it even remotely possible that such a wicked travesty of justice could ever occur in that time - when allegedly the Jews were looking for a Messiah to come? It was because they were not! The Jews were in the prophetic period prophesied by prophets Malachi and Isaiah. Listen; "_And the Lord, whom ye seek, shall suddenly come to his temple_" (Malachi 3:1). What this passage might reveal to all of us is this. YHWH has a set time for every prophetic event, whether we understand that it is occurring or not. Based on biblical passages, it would seem that Satan knows closely what time it is for him (Revelation 12:12). Demons also seem to have an idea when their time will end (Matthew 8:29). So why not man? <u>Why does man not know what time it is</u>? Here might be some insight to at least part of the reason why men have lost track of time as to understand with what urgency we ought to repent and believe the Gospel.

"Stay yourselves, and wonder; cry ye out, and cry: they are drunken, but not with wine; they stagger, but not with strong drink. For the Lord hath poured out upon you the spirit of deep sleep, and hath closed your eyes: the prophets and your rulers, the seers hath he covered. And the vision of all is become unto you as the words of a book that is sealed, which men deliver to one that is learned, saying, Read this, I pray thee: and he saith, I cannot; for it is sealed: and the book is delivered to him that is not learned, saying, Read this, I pray thee: and he saith, I am not learned. Wherefore the Lord said, Forasmuch as this people draw near me with their mouth, and with their lips do honor me, but have removed their heart far from me, and their fear toward me is taught by the precept of men: therefore, behold, I will proceed to do a marvelous work among this people, even a marvelous work and a wonder: (***YHWH's coming suffering servant in Yeshua*** - Isaiah 53) for the wisdom of their wise men shall perish, and the understanding of their prudent men shall be hid."

(Isaiah 29:9-14)

Yeshua was our witness to the truth of Isaiah's prophecy belonging primarily to those people of his day. Later in the year we are made aware that the blinding in part curse over Judah would be extended beyond their lifetimes, to the end of the age; when our fathers volunteered us to help shoulder the burden and blame for their wicked act of murdering Yeshua.

"***Then answered all the people, and said, His blood be on us, and on our children***" (Matthew 27:25). Every time I read that passage, I cringe and shake my head in dismay. How can hatred for one be so intense, the other would curse their own children? Thanks mom and dad! What is it? 1987 years later and all you guys are all dead! So we can't tell you how much we appreciate from your time our infamous, ancient, all-inclusive and self serving curse that shoulders your damnation. "***HYPOCRITES, well did Isaiah prophesy of you***" (Matthew 15:7). That curse of desolate *blindness in part*, was in Shaul's day and remains yet still today in ours.

> "Go unto this people, and say, Hearing ye shall hear, and shall not understand; and seeing ye shall see, and not perceive: for the heart of this people is waxed gross, and their ears are dull of hearing, and their eyes have they closed; lest they should see with *their* eyes, and hear with *their* ears, and understand with *their* heart," (Acts 28:26-27).

In one sense of the truth, time is fleeting. In another sense, time is everlasting. There is time that has passed. There is time in our present. And, there is time that has yet to arrive. With all the things Yeshua said that involved some form of time or another, two of the more important things we should know and treasure about time itself is this. We have the time to repent and the time to believe Yeshua's words about his kingdom are true. Being exposed to the "*Judeo-Christian culture*" we are all aware of the fact that we have all of the time in at least our human life to repent and believe theoretically. But on the other hand, two significant concerns are, most of us do not know how long the time we have is, or when that time period will end. Humankind as a whole has a predetermined amount of time also to repent and believe. But, those same concerns seem to be thorns in man's intellectual sides. How long is that time? When will that time end? And, how much of that time does man have left? It is amazing when we think about it. While prospects of knowing, scares us to death – *no pun intended* – almost every one of us, I suspect, is curious to some extent, about all the aspects of our time from the very beginning until the times beyond our imagination. We call it eternity. I may have some good news for you. If you can learn the lesson that so many in Yeshua's time **did not** learn. That requires we hear his word and grasp his perspectives. Those who do, will need to repent and believe. They will also need <u>to gain and sustain</u> **an absolute love of the truth**. While we are in the area, recall that belief requires faith. And, two frustrating things about faith is, "...*faith is the substance of things hoped for,* [and] *the evidence of things not seen*" (Hebrews 11:1). What makes faith so frustrating by definition? **Faith** (*the belief that something is true*) **is the substance**. I am hopeful, you will be able to grasp hold of what I would call a somewhat "abstract" concept. The definition for substance is, "*the real physical matter which a person or a thing consists of and which has a tangible, solid presence*"

(Webster Dictionary). So, in the spiritual sense; your faith has to be solid to the point of tangibility. It means the works of your flesh, supports the faith of your spiritual. What are you doing physically, to show that you believe by faith spiritually? I find it just as hard to grasp with clarity, the next concept. **Faith is also the evidence!** Now what is defined as the evidence? Evidence means, *"the available body of facts or information indicating whether a belief or proposition is true or valid"* (Webster Dictionary). In its more terrifying form, faith is the metaphysical act of stepping out on your productivity with your guarantee being, receiving in return absolutely nothing! It is like, from a high cliff you are stepping out onto nothing (*YHWH's word*), with everything (*your life*); for everything and more (*the promise of everlasting life*). Hence is the term, "Here goes nothing!" In our perceptible reality of things at least, we are hoping the thing (*physical works*) you are investing, will result in something more and not anything less – *and certainly not* – Nothing! Crazy right? That is most likely why when one steps out with true faith in YHWH, the reward has been promised to approach divine magnificence.

In plain words, your lawful works (*Substance without guarantee of a return*) is your faith in profession; while "they" at the same time show to others (*evidence*) that you indeed have that godly faith. I will try and give you an example. Let us assume I express a doctrinal matter you have yet to prove for yourself is true. At some point you will need to do your own study (*lawful works*) of that doctrine, to determine if my assertions have some merit. Does it make any sense to your spiritual sense? Based on my witness, do you think my matter can be truth? Finally, are you willing to do something to see if my witness is true? In the course of establishing if a matter has the initial air of truth; you may judge the motivations of the witness. For an example. Let us say - I believe YHWH has ordained man to rule his entire creation. However, YHWH must be able to trust man to dress and keep it properly. Not to ruin it, as he is doing the earth today. (Revelation 11:18) So I assert Eloah set up his temporal millennial week. This allows man time to prove - **if he will** or **will not** - obey Eloah's physical and spiritual laws. This, before YHWH glorifies man and gives him "...*the keys to the kingdom*" (Matthew 16:19 & Luke 12:32) - *The Full Creation* (Romans 8:21). **Do you believe it**? Whether you are sure or not, that is *substance*. If you study, that is *evidence* you want to know.

Hint: Why else would one think so-called nature (*In actuality it was YHWH*), has equally ordained, set up and fixed into place; the undeniable reality that in our human forms, man will never be able to reach beyond, to the stars. Similar to Moses' experience with the promise land, YHWH has allowed us to peak over into the creation - *just a bit* - but, we shall proceed no further. The lines have been drawn for us in the mortality and cosmic sands. For the life of us, we cannot go beyond them. YHWH says to have faith. If we obey his voice, the word given to Moses, the prophets and Apostles is that one day Elohim will give to us this entire creation; with full liberty to do his will. On the other hand, if even at the highest authority of carnal men's ability, man asked me to have that exact faith, apart from YHWH's authority; from my view it would be impossible to accept it at face value that man's promise was legitimate. My doubts are absolutely sustained when I understand man's limitations, when it comes to space travel and light speed. I have no faith in man's deep space travel ability. I know the limits to his frailty. I do not need to study. I need no further proof in my lack of faith. ***Example two***: It is only natural I would want people to purchase this manuscript. That is one of the primary goals of basically every author. If they sell books - they of course, can make a little profit, or a lot. If I were to tell you that making money was not my primary goal, knowing the nature of mankind, would you initially believe me? You probably would not. But, if you chose to step out on faith and purchased this book – *as apparently you have* – after you read it, you would determine based on the quality of the information and depending on how this book spoke to your spirit, that my intentions of getting good information public, was closer to the top of my list than was profit. You might appreciate that and in turn recommend, give or loan your book out to an associate or a friend. You could well decide to purchase additional copies for friends you believe would benefit from reading this book. In other words your faith was anchored by your works. When your works paid you dividends; your faith grew by reason of your tangible secondary purchases. When one obeys YHWH by faith, even while Satan is making war against him; YHWH establishes ways to converse with him at all levels; in order to let that person know our Eloah's ministering angels are standing by at his side at the ready. They are able to assist that person, if YHWH's intervention is warranted in his mercy or decreed by his grace.

YHWH will give man the keys to the cosmos. But, there is only so much time *at hand* for humankind (*for lost of better terms*), to qualify. YHWH has been forewarning us for some time now about that "*at hand*" time running out. YHWH has given us prophetic fulfillments and more than most would have imagined, when it comes to time spent and time left in prophecy. I did not write this book for fame and profit. With a real prophetic threat for our national financial collapse (Ezekiel 7:19) making profit with this book will only take me so far in these final prophetic minutes. And, *"so far,"* is not nearly far enough – if I am to "*know* [Yeshua] *and the power of his resurrection*" (Philippians 3:10). I was sent to deliver this truth. For whatever the reason (*I cannot tell*); YHWH wants this word of truth out. Because YHWH wants this book out and in mass circulation; I must make every effort and take every righteous path available and offered to get this book into the public eye.

Under normal circumstances, I might have said it would be nice to make a little bit of money; but these are not normal circumstances. We are in those last prophetic minutes. Many now think that money will fail like in Ezekiel. Come on now; do not pretend that you are blind to it all! Cannot you see it coming too? The Scripture has foretold, *"Men's hearts failing them for fear, and for looking after those things which are coming on the earth"* (Luke 21:26). *"For when they shall say, Peace and safety; then sudden destruction cometh upon them, as travail upon a woman with child; and they shall not escape"* (1st Thessalonians 5:3). Then too, The Scripture gives us this spiritual hope, in that the wise should know more than *apparently* they actually do. The passage then follows up with words of admonition, *"But ye, brethren, are not in darkness, that that day should overtake you as a thief. Ye are all the children of light, and the children of the day...Therefore let us not sleep, as do others; but let us watch and be sober"* (verses 4-6). I have a question for those of us who may see ourselves as wise and insightful by merciful revelation. If no one in reality can **see** anything definite as far as that final day coming, why then are we warned to "...**watch** and be sober?"

I would like to do something beyond the expected for YHWH's

people; since those future times are upon us. I pray that this book will do just that. I admit, at this moment, money is still of value to people and is a small part of my motivation. But, it is nowhere near being the most vital part. It is crucial that I get this information out. It is my calling from YHWH. I am convinced that Satan the Devil will do anything to keep it from the broader public. See, he knows that, It's Much Later Than You Think! Not necessarily because what I am saying, in this case, is right or wrong; but because if people read this book; it might get some of them to thinking a bit more freer and in the process learn things that by every right way, should have been given to them gratis. For this I am ashamed and - *I apologize* - for not having a large enough congregational backing to provide this information to you free of all charges. But as I said, It's Much Later Than You Think! and I do not have the luxury. Truly, partial proof of your faith, is this purchase. Hopefully, you will put together a picture with Holy Spirit logic. With the assurances of stated past times, existing times and declared future times recorded in the Holy Bible, and transferred into this book, will you independently evaluate to determine, free from denominational bias, if its findings are truth based and thereby at a minimum supported by firm research and study? If you can trust you are not being wickedly taken for a ride, do not be afraid you paid the fare of faith. I truly believe this book can help you get to the place you want to be. As far as this book and the information it holds go, I believe it is YHWH's blessing to you to "*see the day approaching*" (Hebrews 10:25).

So a couple of more things; remember faith means there is something that you are hoping for. In other words, what is being said here; you are hoping that it is reasonably true. Or, like many of the preachers I have approached concerning this matter, you are pretty much convinced that I am demonically insane. What you are essentially doing with this book - if you are leaning toward the latter is reading for entertainment; of which I am confident that you will get plenty of. But I must also believe many readers are curious to see how sensical my arguments will be, in making my points and assertions about knowing what time we are in. The subject matter could be for many readers, especially intriguing. Since it would appear presently that no one else knows. Some of you might be saying to yourselves, as you are reading through this book, "If no one else seems to know; how does this, insane idiot know?" Minus the "insane" and that "idiot" part I would have to say that is an excellent question. I would like to think that is why you are investing your time and money. You want to know that thing that has captured your curiosity. If you believe yourself to be a Bible student, it is likely you have already determined most of my future contentions will be based in error. Because you already know what Matthew 24:36 says. For you, the knowing time case is closed. To that mindset I will just say - keep on reading. We may prove to see what is in error or closed; my discernment of the times or that type of mindset?

For those of you who do not think you know enough about the Holy Bible to call me a liar or false prophet - yet, you may choose to hold your opinion and exhibit what the seasoned Christians might call faith. Blind though they think your faith might be. Rather than call your act of faith blind. I will be much nicer to call it a <u>curious mind</u>. After all you did buy the book. It is your faith for truth in future revelation; before you read it with your eyes. All of the acts you are doing at the present are not the very things. You are in faith hoping what you are about to read, at some later date will illuminate or make visible the things you are in the now pursuing. That is, compelling evidence of *what time we are really in and how much time we have left*. The two things I have yet to prove in your now. You may not even be close to confident the path you are taking will get you that thing you desire. But you read forward; because the faith of your desire, prompts you. If you want to be able to follow me through time, from the beginning, to the end; you have to be open to what I say for it to make any reasonable amount of sense. It must have a reasonable outcome and it must be with very little doubt - **<u>Holy</u> <u>Bible</u> <u>Sound</u>**. What I mean by that is this. I need to remind everybody again, <u>I do not know everything about anything</u>. Everything I think I know, I was taught. What you are about to read in this book about Bible time; it was taught to me by YHWH letting me glean information from others he had prior given it to. He gave me the divine insights to put their separate studies together to formulate revelations you are about to read. They themselves were either unable to get by a point of faith, were afraid to be seen in an unflattering light, while seeking peer respect; or to be called awful names. Of names that come to mind; false prophet, cult-leader and charlatan tops my list.

Hear me out. See if things fit your Bible puzzle. If your faith allows you to, throw out any old damned beliefs and start anew. The choices are totally up to you. All I ask is you take the time to read everything. If you get to that heated point; where I make you so mad with the things you are reading that steam starts to come out of your ears, stop for a moment. Put the book down and take a break. Once you have cooled down a bit, feel free to pick it back up; and then start back to reading it again. One more thing before we move on. This book deals with a subject in the Bible that **I do not think** has any sway on your, ""*chance*" **date**" (1ˢᵗ Corinthians 15:37) with the Lamb to his wedding feast. Still, I do feel understanding the contents herein; can enhance your passions to press ahead with more energy; as you maneuver in these last prophetic minutes of anticipation. Think about YHWH's ordained time for a moment. Since the Holy Spirit has shown unto me, what I am about to show unto you; I think about that

"<u>ordained time</u>" – all of the time. If you could know when the first day was; if you could know when the last day is, know what time you are living in at the present, not theoretically, but in actuality - your real time; if you trust the Holy Bible is true, you can literally know in your heart exactly to the year, to the day and to the hour, when the Messiah was going to return. Of course, I could also pretty much guarantee you that next to no one would believe you though. To be truthful, I asked YHWH if he would walk me up through time. When I thought about this recent task and path that YHWH allowed me to set my sights on, the thought of undertaking the time journey haunted me and it made me feel inadequate. When you are alone in a revelation and it seems no one else is claiming what you are claiming is the truth, or at least very few that we are able to identify; it can be quite unnerving. Actually to this point, I have not been able to identify **<u>one person or group</u>** with these newer perspectives. My presumed knowledge and understanding, which this book is filled with, made me feel a bit hesitant. That is another reason I needed to get this information published. With all of the Holy Bible vultures circling about to call me out; many of them with all kinds of resources at their disposal; it made for what is in my opinion, the perfect vetting machine. With all of the large groups no doubt having numerous assistants working in their organizations; most of them will no doubt be endowed with some kind of theological degree. All of them together would naturally have the ability and hopefully the knowledge and the wisdom to go in many directions of study; while their organization's leader could go in another. They could cover more ground of study on any given subject than I could dream of.

Why did YHWH choose me? It is a legitimate question. Why would he allow me to have a knowledge that perhaps no one else in the world at this moment possesses? Yes, I was afraid that I would be found wrong. But, I was not so afraid that I would not share this word with the world, if I could. If I am wrong, somebody will love me enough to let me know. But, if this book makes sense; eyes may see and ears may hear. Perhaps unsure hearts will obtain hope. I realize that an understanding like mine will attract that hardened yoke of ridicule with non-believers. No matter what I say biblically, some forms of condemnation from some direction is just par for the course. Believe **me** or not; those who read and believe the Holy Bible can sense we are in the last minutes of the last day. Today the likelihood for persecution of individuals who the wicked might even imagine to be a so-called, "*Christian*" is real; now even in the USA. The following reality is most terrifying for me, in our present environment.

Two times now the enemy has come into my forest. Each time he has cut down a tree and killed my sheep. But for divine intervention, there is no doubt Satan the devil would have sent my entire forest up in flames and every sheep would have been surely lost. I know in the last prophetic minutes, some of the righteous, some of the saints, must be overcome by the wicked one. (Revelation 13:7) I have to believe my family and I are as ready as we will ever be. Since I must trust you are also ready; I will proceed to show you as best I can, in similar fashion as to how YHWH guided me. And like me, you similarly and in sincerity, need to use your faith. One more thing along that line. I always in my mind try to weigh the cost of believing or not believing. I must continue to keep reminding you that in this book, there are some things I will write, whether you table them, believe them or not, they will have little bearing on salvation. At least, I do not think so and hope not. I will let you be the judge. Still, I feel knowing will help you focus on the big jig-saw picture. It will serve you well if you can use any or all of the things I will say. I pray this book is not promoting deceptions and evil (*twisted truth*) in any of the things I will say. Certainly, I am not being naive or arrogant in my thinking that I am 100% right in all my statements - with no chance for an error. Some things, I am still researching. Even though, I am confident. So, my total data is incomplete. I wished that I could be absolutely certain. But I am not in some areas. And, <u>I will say as much as often as I feel I need to</u> - as we proceed. If my comprehension is not complete enough to give you a discernible picture, I will try to mention it at least in passing, as often as I can in my writings overall. Before we start on our walk along the path of YHWH's revelation of time, there are a few effects on the reckoning of time that you will need to maintain in your mind as we go along as for as prophetic time and age are concerned. So listen closely to make sure you understand all of the following. <u>Do not let possibly inefficient descriptive abilities displayed by me, during our counting of time before or after the second Bible genealogy (*from Adam to the desolation of the first temple*) become confusing for you</u>. Take your time and read everything carefully.

If you will consider its possibility that my discernment on the subject of time is included in the mysteries of Eloah; and is being revealed by his Holy Spirit - today, but was withheld in the past from us, until these last few minutes of the last age, before Messiah's return; then walk with me from "*recorded*" biblical history through to "*revealed*" prophetic times, to conceivably an enlightened understanding of ***what time it really is and how much time we have left***, before his return. Not from man's view, but the Bible. As much as my dim eyes believe they can see, I will speak to.

*"For we know in part, and we prophesy in part...For now we see through a glass, darkly...[**so for**] now I [**can only**] know in part..."* (1st Corinthians 13:9&12)

Understanding, we are all as one looking through a "*glass, darkly*." I have discarded nearly all <u>guesstimations</u>, the <u>renditions</u> of evolution and <u>revelations</u> of time by men. So in the end, I must leave it to the minds of the objective readers of this book, as to how accurate my research is or is not; or how insightful my understanding of time and prophecy might be; or again, might not be. Even if readers conclude the probability exist that my understanding concerning the biblical record of time and my claims on prophetic declarations may turn out to be only partially told in these writings, I will be totally satisfied with their reviews. Get out the Holy Bible. Use the version of your choice. But for book matching, keep King James handy. Dust it off, if you need to. Get pen and paper for notes and to keep track. Most importantly, unlock your mind and keep it open. Get ready for perhaps the most thought-provoking walk of your life – to date! It is my retelling of my walk through time with the Holy Spirit as my guide. I pray you are called to discern this book's revelations of formerly hidden and unknown mysteries of YHWH. If you are, then you are truly blessed. If you have developed that divine gift to incorporate them into your life and keep them there until the end; **YOU** are more than blessed. I am confident that most of us are not, but I will say it anyway. **Do not be afraid**. **Be of good courage**. However, with every endeavor to find out YHWH's truth; we must all understand that there will be much deception lurking all about us. "False Christs" and "false prophets" are everywhere. This is especially true now, in these last minutes of prophecy before the return. That is a sure sign. **IT'S MUCH LATER THAN YOU THINK!**

CHAPTER 5

FROM ADAM TO THE FLOOD

By now we should all have our Holy Bible walking shoes on. I have said a lot in trying to prepare everyone for what is ahead. But I must be honest with you all and tell you the truth about our first leg. It is an uneventful journey through biblical history. Your biblical guide, should you have needed one, ***and you don't***; could have literally been a Holy Bible illiterate and only literate. And he still should have been able to pilot you through the first genealogy in Bible history - from Adam to the flood. The truth be told, you should be able to accomplish that feat by yourself. The only concern people might encounter an issue with is, "The Year One Error." That is, not taking into account there is no "*zero*" year. That means <u>date</u> counts, i.e. Hebrew years should start from year one and BC/AD years from 4000, not zero. I will ***try*** not to use many pages with these early years, from Adam to the flood. Personally, I cannot see many opportunities, apart from some accidental addition error for not knowing how many years there were from Adam to Noah. As far as I can see, all of the issues come after the flood. To the end, one of the main study tools that YHWH gave to me was this advice. "<u>Do not be afraid to be wrong!</u>" "<u>Do not be ashamed if you have to start over again and rebuild with truth - even from the very ground up</u>!" I was then reminded that even Elohim himself has done that – ***that is, start over*** – on at the least, some two occasions. One primary example cited is the Great Flood in Noah's day itself. That is the incident when YHWH Elohim started over again at the "second earth" from *nearly* the ground up, with his "second chance" opportunity (*if you will*) for humankind. He has given us this witness in the earth (*The rainbow*) and a witness in his word – The Holy Bible.

> "And God saw that the wickedness of man *was* great in the earth, and every imagination of the thoughts of his heart *was* only evil continually. And it repented the Lord that he had made man on the earth, and it grieved him at his heart. And the Lord said, I will destroy man whom I have created from the face of the earth; both man, and beast, and the creeping thing, and the fowls of the air; for it repenteth me that I have made them. But Noah found grace in the eyes of the Lord" (Genesis 6:5-8 & See: 9:8-16).

As Elohim, the divine godhead ordained; so it was 100 years later that YHWH started all over again with Noah, his three sons, and their wives. And, only as far as we know; that was the second time Elohim's divine executive authority has rebooted from some previous start. A scant 1657 years before that catastrophic flood, Elohim had started over for the first time with the first man Adam. The Adam event was after that great upheaval of disorder; in the rebellion, wreckage and the desolation of this entire earth by that wicked Devil Lucifer, along with the angelic forces under his command. (Isaiah 14:12-17) Take note: The creations of Adam and later Eve came only after what I would describe as unknown Millennia in years. This could have been perhaps billions of years. I, of course, like most everybody else, have all of my guessing on that matter. But that is about all it is. Now, from Adam to the flood is 1656 years. For optimal efficiency, we will do up that simple count. This is for those who have never performed such reckoning of times before. As I have stated it before, from Adam to the flood is an easy add. How most everyone who has ever done the count arrives at the "date" of 1657 is by using the basic mathematical practice of addition. Starting off with the Hebrew date of year one, add up all of the genealogies given to us in the Holy Scripture in chapter five (5) of Genesis. Then, with chapter eleven (11) resuming with the genealogies and the counting of Bible history in son's after the flood. Basically, the add count goes similar to this. We start in year one (1) with A. After five (5) years, we wrote B. After seven (7) years, we wrote C. And - three (3) years after that, we got bored and started writing numbers. Now we ask the question. "What is "the date" in years from the time when we wrote letter A, to the time we started to write numbers?" In this basic case, we simply add the numbers - "Starting from One." A is at one (1), plus five (5), plus seven (7), plus three (3) equals sixteen (16). However, understand this. While only fifteen (15) years passed from the time when we first wrote letter A, until the time we got bored and started writing numbers, **the actual date** is the year sixteen (16) – by us starting from year one (1) and not zero (0). For most educated people, solving the above word problem was elementary. However, I am acquainted with the fact some people have issues with word problems. In case you are one of them - ***no worries*** - you have me. So, things should be a snap! At least on our journey from the first man Adam up unto the flood – *I think*. And I also understand that many people in their counting start from zero. In essence, providing all things remain the same, they would only end up with one year less than my count. I ***suppose*** that (*the one year*) is an acceptable discrepancy. But, do not try holding me to that "***assumption***."

We do a similar type count in the time from the creation of Adam to the flood. Here is one for you. If we believe the Holy Bible, we do not need the erroneous theories of men or their archeological guesstimations, "*mucking up*" everything. *Yeah! I spelled it right!* - As in ***dirt;*** Most of you knew what I meant from the start. I will admit I was shaken a bit when I began to see the numbers after the flood; but, I went all the way to the end not knowing whether I would have to start over again or not. As it stands now, I will not. Assuredly, the numbers YHWH gave to me stand firmer than any other numbers I have yet to see in any study from the theological and biblical experts. I hope all of the numbers do for your faith, what they have done for mine. AMEN? If you do not already have them, get paper, pen and calculator out. Then add them up when you have the time. Easier than that, and without much objection on my part, merely look them up. They are literally plastered all over the internet. Various theologians will likely take exception to the second part of my next statement. However, in my study; the numbers bear out my claim. Adam was created on the sixth day in year one (1) or 4000 years BC - before supposed *"Jesus Christ's"* birth. Now let us see if we can actually uncover all of the 6000 years, to the affirmations of all my declarations concerning the millennial week; according to the history left to us in the biblical record. I have studied and examined several of the archeological and historical records. I have considered their findings, with my cautious optimism. I was hoping to view findings that made sense. What many of their studies insinuated, they declared with a good amount of confidence. However, when I tried to put practical applications with most of what they had concluded, I came out more confused than ever. In too many instances, when these *"experts"* spoke on the same subjects; while almost every one of them were trying to say some of the same things, in many discourses the one was consistently contradicting the other. They would say stuff like - he could have been born here, he could have been born there, we just do not know, there are no surviving records to verify a certain pundit's hypothesis, and let us not forget, this or that may or may not be true or ever happened, <u>no one can know the truth</u>. They usually say that last remark; only because they, **<u>do not know</u>**, "**<u>The Truth</u>**." And generally, if **<u>they do not know</u>** a certain thing; **it <u>CANNOT</u> be known - Period**. If the truth be told to me - by me; listening to all of the so-called, pundits was more confusing than **<u>BABYLON THE GREAT</u>**. Actually, I believe their philosophies, at least some of them, are in some ways a part of this world's modern **<u>BABYLON THE GREAT</u>** (*Who is the mother of many religious harlots in our world today* - **Revelation 17:5**). Truly, for me at least, their attempts to make *"sense"* of things just made my head spin. Yeshua said, if we continue (*trust and obey*) in his word, we are his disciples. Then we, "*<u>shall know the truth</u>*" (John 8:31-32). That truth will set us free from **<u>BABYLON THE GREAT</u>** – which is mass confusion.

In reading their studies, I began to think like a theological know-it-all. **<u>If I did not know it</u>. <u>It was unknowable.</u>** Few would admit to such arrogance. But some of my Christian friends could witness and assuredly tell you about me. I became a theological idiot. **Hold on!** I am not saying

I have it all figured out now; or anything like that. But, I will say I am

now learning how to believe the Bible over any of the oftentimes highly

acclaimed, but many times in the end, the non-sensical theologians and

historian giants. To Paraphrase an old saying, "Our historical records are

often manipulated by the winners of wars." The cleaner version of the

saying states, *"History is written by the victors"* (Robbins, Michael W.,

2012). It is often cited being authored by history's more notable Winston

Churchill, being among several others. (Lauterborn, D., 2016) Now on

the other hand, Scripture was spoken and recorded by the set-apart ones

called by YHWH. All of whom, spoke YHWH's truth to powers. They in

doing so, made YHWH's Word readily accessible to the scribes of their

powers; who preserved it as YHWH's witness. It is written, "...*prophecy*

came not in old time by the will of man: but holy men of God spake;

moved by the Holy [Spirit]" (2nd Peter 1:21). Later, the Scriptures were

translated into many versions as - **The Holy Bible**. I am persuaded this

inspiration also included the writings (i.e. Psalms), the instructions and

the histories. Even if we have let our familiarity with them die; with our

acceptance of our new depraved old progressive culture. Yet, if there be

any biblical thing still left in our hearts to recall; let us step up and speak

out with it in public, boldly as we dare. I think that is what I have done in publishing what I believe is this **thought-provoking** book of bold claims

- *no assuming* - I being warned by Yeshua of some professing believers.

> "...thou hast a name that thou livest, and art dead. Be watchful, and strengthen the things which remain, that are ready to die: for I [*Messiah Yeshua*] have not found thy works perfect before [Eloah]. Remember therefore how thou hast received and heard, and hold fast, and repent. If...thou shalt not watch, I will come on thee as a thief and thou shalt not know what hour I will come upon thee" (Revelation 3:1-3).

There is a very strong implication in the passage above. Does it not imply... no... It actually says it. "***If...thou shalt not watch,***" the thief thing and truth about not knowing the hour (*presume also the day*) would come into play. By opposition in omitting; does it not leave open in theory at least that if one was to "*watch*" YHWH might possibly offer or make known to him **the day and the hour**? I am only saying, "***Possibly.***" If we concede "***Possibly,***" what are the chances of "***Possibly***" being divinely upgraded to "***Probable?***" This book and journey through time is all about "***The Probable,***" YHWH has faithfully done just that. The remainder of this book - *for the most part* - is about wisely putting together in biblical chronological order, the completed history and future of the passage of our time. If we attain some new perspectives and communicate them well enough; I hope we can prepare every reader to experience that passage of time, through the illustration of a created spiritual jig-saw puzzle YHWH will help me to put together in their view. You got your calculator ready?

You might want to get paper and a pencil too.

At times, we may have to stop going from the beginning; and work our way back from the end. At times we may have to build a piece of the puzzle from the middle and set if off to the side until we establish the place where it fits. This will be a challenging walk. But, I know we can get to the end; if our faith to believe can prevail at the same time theologians are saying, "We do not think so" or "That cannot be right; because the history books say different!" I have just one test question for the theologians, the historians and some of their "history books." Who exactly did so many of them say for so many years discovered America? Yeah, I know – right? That is how really messed up many of our history books have been and can be. For those who know, I rest my case. And if any of ya'll ole codgers out there who think you know, blurt out and say "Columbus," I think I might upchuck! ☺ Seriously though, for the reader who have no clues about what many modern historians are saying about who really discovered the Americas; go to the local library or someplace official and do your own study and research on America's discovery; for your own historical perspective and confidence of mind.

Nevertheless, before we continue on, do not anybody get me wrong. I am not dumping on Columbus. Columbus was a great explorer. And, he did wondrous things in our history, to help us literally to broaden our horizons socially, economically and even spiritually. In times that existed when countless people in the world thought that our world was flat, Columbus was confident that the world was round. He was so sure; he was willing to sail off of the presumed edge of the world to prove that it was indeed not flat, but instead round. At least, that is one of the stories surrounding some of his exploits. ☺ When Columbus sailed out over the vast Atlantic Ocean, as with any sailor, he had so much food, so much water, so much time and so much patience by his crew to arrive at their desired location. That is, before a real possibility of mutiny occurred. In Columbus's case, that might have meant a return to Spain; quite possibly with no Columbus in tow. While our history books may have mistakenly credited Columbus with the discovery of the Americas; and in his honor our government gave to him his own honorary holiday, there's absolutely no doubt as to the importance Columbus made in our American history. Nevertheless, this book ain't no American History. So forget about it! It is time we put some **_subject meat_** on your spiritual plates. Some may feel it is past that time. That as it may be, while I feel what I said was serving a great foundational purpose well; no worries, your point is well taken.

Here are a few slices. Our subject's witness to history (*The Holy Bible*) declares that from year one, the first man Adam lived 130 years, before he "begat" his son Seth – who would be the continuation of the

Messianic bloodline that would eventually lead up to the birth of Yeshua.

We will follow that Messianic bloodline as far as we can, as long as the

bloodline remains on display to count. You see, if we believe the Holy

Scripture (*and I for one, do*), we can use its witnesses for time (*the*

bloodlines) to count up on a particular area of history in the process of

determining what time it really is. We do that by adding together their

respective succession of years, from the begetting or the birth of one

descendant to the begetting or birth of the next. So long as the bloodline

remain in what I would call "*transparency mode,*" the counting of years

to determine the passage of time, in finding out how much time we have

left remains easy math (*addition or subtraction*), with few questions and

little controversy. That way we will be able to verify how far in years its

processes will take us forward into time. Seth lived 105 years before the

bloodline continued. We simply add to one (1), Adam's 130 years, Seth's

105 years – and so on. Early on, you can see how this is going to work.

So far, we are up to the date year 236 out of the total 6000 years we need

to account for in biblical history and prophecy. Seth had a son named

Enos. Enos was the continuation. He lived 90 years until he had Cainan.

Cainan lived 70 years until Mahalaleel. Mahalaleel lived 65 years until

Jared. Jared lived 162 years until Enoch. Enoch lived 65 years until

Methuselah. Methuselah lived 187 years until Lamech. Lamech lived

182 years until Noah. Noah lived 500 years until Shem. From year one (1), we just add on Adam's 130 years, Seth's 105 years, Enos's 90 years, Cainan's 70 years, Mahalaleel's 65 years, Jared's 162 years, Enoch's 65 years, Methuselah's 187 years, Lamech's 182 years, Noah's 500 years and we have began the walk. In total time we are at the year 1557 and the BC time is 2444. Strange enough we have 4444 years still remaining we have to account for. I am sure those uncanny numbers mean something. Honestly though, I have no idea what that something might be or if it has relevance. But, in comparison and for our perspective; 1557 years is the age of the United States of America more than six (6) times over.

I need to stop for a second to state an unusual belief. Some biblical students and theologians have thought Shem, Ham and Japheth to be triplets. I do not hold to this premise. The words are strikingly different from the other genealogies in the line. I believe it was said this way for good reasons. In my own words, which are usually inadequate, I will just say it this way. YHWH is preparing to lay the spiritual underpinnings for sealing up prophecy from the upcoming wicked generations. I am saying Genesis 5:32 was written as it was for reason; and only meant to reveal Noah was at 500 years old and had three sons, when YHWH made the divine decision to destroy man from off the face of the earth with a flood. YHWH's judgment was revealed to Noah, most likely right at or right after Shem's birth. It was for Holy Bible revelation that YHWH inspired Moses to mention in solitary and by an, "***incidental commentary¿*" only** Shem, was at 100 years old when the flood came (Genesis 11:10). This passage is given for insight. My belief of this *insight* is a stance that is for many, not beyond their disputations in debate. You yourself might find fault with my perspective; and I am okay with your dissent. I am hopeful as we continue; I will be able to illuminate your mind to the strong possibility of my correctness. Whether I am successful in my attempt to get your tentative consideration to my accuracy of insight or not; before you come to any dogmatic and irreversible rejections of my insights through your dissent, before the fires of debate rage hotter than the fiery blaze in the furnace oven of King Nebuchadnezzar, ask yourself this question. Why is it or what is it, that makes any questions that we could have over the subject matter of Noah's sons so important; that you or others who might or even will stand up in opposition to my "insights" on Noah's sons not being triplets, must be right and my insight be wrong and without understanding? If I am right and I am convinced that I am. What is the worst thing that could be incurred by or derived out of the circumstances - *if I am right about the situation of Noah, Shem, Ham and Japheth*? It is for good reason, I am making this position statement now; because in its shadow, there will be another just as important revelation later - in our walk along the Messianic bloodline. I will not attempt to lay out all of the reasons and nuances as to why my position on Noah's sons is as it is. For the longer walk, your *tentative* concession to my assertion would be notable and is of value in the overall process to soften possibly diverse mindsets, for the consideration of, and/or the receiving of other conclusions and better fits to the truth of YHWH. Even so, less we lose vision; the prime focus of this section is to account the accurate passage of time and the culmination thereof – from Adam up until the times of Noah. However, if you wish, you can respond to my claims with your questions in an email or write me and enclose a SASE and I will try to give you a more complete reply. My contact information is on Roman number page fifteen (xv). Funds to help our printing cost is appreciated. Since it's just a letter, $5 should do fine. Now where did we stop in time?

We are at the year 1557 and Shem is born when Noah is 500 years old. Then for the next 100 years, Noah preaches to everyone around him. (2nd Peter 2:5) While he was building on the ark, the news no doubt of YHWH's coming judgment spread abroad with the ramblings of that, "*madman,*" in Noah. And I do use that label, affectionately. We see from before the days of Noah, all the way back to Adam, water did not fall from the sky. (Genesis 2:5-6) So what Noah was predicting was in fact, an ecological impossibility in the minds of the people in his day. Even so, right after Noah had finished building the ark, YHWH informed Noah, "***For yet seven days***, *and I will cause it to rain upon the earth forty days and forty nights; and every living substance that I have made will I destroy from off the face of the earth*" (Genesis 7:4). **Noah knew the day and hour "seven days" before the flood came**! It is now year 1657 or 2344 BC. I contend, YHWH's divine notification to Noah is the prophetic shadow picture in ancient days for our end time modern years.

YHWH fulfills what was then a 100 year old prophecy by Noah. The windows of heaven, which YHWH clearly had closed to hold up the sky water during the time Noah built the ark, are opened wide. And the supposed impossible occur. It starts to rain... and it rained... and it rained... and it rained some more. For forty days and nights the Holy Scripture witnesses to us concerning the event. In many similarly social and spiritual ways; as it was in Noah's time with the rains and the flood, our disbelieving minds today cannot with clarity truly comprehend or apprehend the gravity of our own impending date with judgment. **JUST A SIDE NOTE**: I really do not think that I need to remind anybody that our judgment will not be nothing-nowhere near as cool as rain water. Our judgment will involve the purging of all - the heavens and the earth with the unquenchable Eternal fire from YHWH. We have as its microcosm an example and ensample with the event of Sodom, Gomorrah and the cities in the plain (Genesis 19:1-25, 2nd Peter 2:5-6 & Jude 7). We also have of its macrocosm with us in similarity - as far as catastrophic worldwide events - in the Great Flood.

> "And all flesh died that moved upon the earth, both of fowl, and of cattle, and of beast, and of every creeping thing that creepeth upon the earth, and every man: all in whose nostrils *was* the breath of life, of all that *was* in the dry *land,* died. And every living substance was destroyed which was upon the face of the ground, both man, and cattle, and the creeping things, and the fowl of the heaven; and they were destroyed from the earth and Noah only remained *alive,* and all they that *were* with him in the ark" (Genesis 7:21-23).

The great flood was on the earth for a year. (Genesis 7:11 & 8:13-14) Noah is now 601. Shem is 101. In date years, it is 1658. Theological wise – *if the Bible is true* – it is 4343 years until man's rule ends and before The Day of YHWH (*The Millennial Reign of Messiah*). In the BC, BCE and AD, CE equivalences of time it is 2343 BC (*Before Christ*). Here, we might be at one of those points where some Holy Bible students allow themselves to get caught up in what I could term as "*Exactivity.*" I had to add that word to my word processor dictionary. I heard when people do things that carn them a doctorate degree; they sometimes get to make up words for themselves. I suppose somebody's been taking literary liberties and indulging in the writing art of "*Wordorgy¿*" Yeah... I wondered who made that one up too. Although, if I might say it so myself; I think those two "*not-a-words*" define themselves by themselves.

What I believe YHWH has taught me concerning the sickness of Exactivity is this. If you are absolutely confident, then so be it. If you are unsure, then note it so. Then move on as best you can, or until other illuminating events or information of value avails itself to you. Then you make the proper adjustments or rebuild; whichever one is judged most appropriate by the inspiration of YHWH's Holy Spirit. As to the Shem timeline, simply add them up, have faith and move on. Consider all its aspects, "What is the worst that can happen if you are wrong?" You are off by one year. If so, have faith that YHWH will get you back on track later on, if he so chooses to. Take note; and remember this distasteful lesson of rejection I had to learn. To millions and perhaps billions, it is not given to know the mysteries concerning the Kingdom of Eloah. (Matthew 13:11) I know it is disconcerting – if we consider that we might be in that number of the unblessed and uncalled, but consider the odds that we are not. Think, the Holy Bible witnesses that in the last days Satan will trick the "whole world" (Revelation 12:9). The odds are not good. And, if we are in that deceived number, in all honesty, as far as us knowing and understanding the truth of YHWH that will lead us to eternal life; guys it is not going to happen for us. However, I do want you to know. There is real hope for those of us who are not among the number of them whom Yeshua speaks and reveals to.

"I saw a great white throne, and him that sat on it...And I saw the dead, small and great, stand before God...the books were opened: and another book was opened, which is *the book* of life: and the dead were judged out of those things which were written in the books, according to their works... **[but]** whosoever was not found written in the book of life was cast into the lake of fire"
(Revelation 20:11-15).

I shudder to think and/or say, concerning you or myself; if we cannot hear the word of YHWH through Moses and the Prophets or Yeshua and the Apostles, there is a truth reason to our condition. We were not called. May YHWH Elohim have mercy on our souls? To know "**The Truth**" is not enough. The five foolish virgins can attest to that. (Matthew 25:1-13) Though I claim YHWH have revealed to me holy things for you to glean from; I have not yet attained the prize. Though I may know things; even preach the things I know; I have no guarantees beyond faith. There is a strong charge before me that I should keep my "*spiritual wits*" about me and be ever conscious of the real possibility of my falling short, "*lest that by any means, when I have preached to others, I myself should be a castaway*" (1st Corinthians 9:27). Naturally and spiritually, we want to be sure in all our facts; but, not so rigid and foolish to the point, we cannot discern change demands when YHWH reveals new altering things to us.

"The Lord will come as a thief in the night [*To the wicked and ungodly, the foolish and the deceived*] in which the heavens shall pass away with a great noise, and the elements shall melt with...heat...**seeing**...that all these things shall be dissolved, what manner ought ye to be in <u>holy conversation</u> and godliness **looking for**...<u>the coming of the day of God</u>, wherein the heavens being on fire shall be dissolved, and the elements shall melt with fervent heat? Nevertheless we, according to his promise, **look for** new heavens and a new earth...beloved, **seeing that ye look for such things**, be diligent [*attentive*] that ye may be found of him in peace..." (2nd Peter 3:10-14)

There are so many passages of scripture that continually hint at the idea that we should know more than we actually know. Apostle Shaul is purported as saying, *"And if any man think that he knoweth any thing, he knoweth nothing yet as he ought to know"* (1st Corinthians 8:2). I think scholars say he also said this. *"Awake to righteousness, and sin not; for some have not the knowledge of God: I speak this to your shame"* (1st Corinthians 15:34). With these; and others of the scriptures I have read and studied over the years; I am convinced we should know more. That is why I asked YHWH, for more. However, I asked him for information that others, it appears did not. Maybe they thought it had no value. For an example, what purpose does it serve to know the date of your death? It will not change your character. If you are wicked – most likely you will be wicked with the knowledge. If you tried to be otherwise, psychiatrists contend that such a person would condemn self for not being true to their nature and is only trying the change natures due to new facts of knowing their death date. If you think about it; it makes sense. Self-condemnation is common with the guilty. No matter how we act on the outside – the heart is where true cleansing needs to occur and true guilt will not allow for such a grand conversion to the good. Yeshua says, *"That which cometh out of...man, that defileth the man...out of the heart...proceeds evil thoughts"* (Mark 7:20-23). Self-blame and sin parts us from Elohim. (Isaiah 59:2) He speaks and we cannot hear. He reveals, but we cannot discern. Still, I believe this book is YHWH's special divine grant to those who have requested this type of knowledge. I feel its insights are visibly simple. Its math applications are well established and recognized. So, to whatever end we come to – you can know the truth of this book.

CHAPTER 6

THE BABEL EFFECT

Babel (*Babylon*) literally represents almost everything appalling and wicked in our modern world today. The Holy Bible calls Babel in the last days, "**GREAT**." (Revelation 17:5) It reveals that, "*the inhabitants of the earth have been made drunk with the wine of her fornication*" (Verse 2). Babel has intoxicated the souls of untold billions over 4300 years. She has survived the many centuries by seducing all wayward souls with her progressive seductions and **THE GREAT DELUSION**. Her temptress feminine scent is the beguiling allure of a carefree non-responsible non-accountable social life. Her **GREAT** delusion is the *mystery of iniquity* at work, in the children of disobedience. Babel consummates that deception intimately inside all of their spirits financially, socially, psychologically, scientifically and spiritually. Her haughty bouquet of debauchery, her social appetite for any and all things wicked and sensually imperious wets the wanton pallet and has polluted our world and modern times as well. Babel facilitates social warfare and resistance to Eloah in **GREAT** rebellion to divine law. She disguises her rebellion and loathing of Eloah with her **GREAT BABEL MYSTERY DOCTRINE**; which teaches a... "*Righteous Lawlessness.*" Finally, Babel wraps her evil disgust for and rejection of YHWH's authority over her, with her **GREAT** deceiving façade of "***Unconditional Adoration***." The **Lie** of **BABYLON** is **THE GREAT RELATIONSHIP**. "*He that hath an ear, let him hear what the Spirit saith unto the churches*" (Revelation 2:7). This is a sad truth. Few of us have the divine ear to hear the words of this paragraph. For the rest of us Eloah left tangible data, much easier to hear and see. We will not need divine ears to hear or divine eyes to see. All that is required is a little faith and literacy.

We will read Bible years and see the time we used versus time had. A key reason the Day of YHWH will come as a thief to the world is the ancient influences of King Nimrod and his rebellious Empire of Babel. (*Genesis 10:7-10*) In biblical Babel history, we continue to witness the ungodly results of man's interaction with the Serpent. (*Genesis 11:1-9*) Even though YHWH scattered the citizens of Babel "*abroad upon the face of all the earth*" her spirit survived, evolved and thrived. Over time

Babel's curse of confusion found facilitation in the secret places of societies' civil and religious orders. Today Babel is a social, economic and religious behemoth. Babylon has become otherworldly, "**GREAT**." (Revelation 17:5) The purposeful engineered unfinished appearance of The European Union Parliament Building is "*absolutely*" more than a coincidence; and, it pays more than blind praise to Nimrod and his tower. In the union's haughty wickedness, they think to mock YHWH with their modern finished-unfinished rendition of that infamous biblical erection.

The European Union's Parliament in Strasbourg / The Louise Weiss Building | Photo by: ID 107216670 © Leonid Andronov | Dreamstime.com

Arial view: The European Union's Parliament in Strasbourg / The Louise Weiss Building | Photo by: Jacky Hénin | Flickr.com

The Tower of Babel - Artist: Pieter Bruegel the Elder - 1563 | Photo by: Eduardo Urdangaray | www.flickr.com/photos/bancoimagenes

You can see more **imaginable** renditions of Babel's blasphemous structure with an internet search. You merely type in the search box, *European Union Parliament Building*/images. You will be able to view them at your leisure. Believe it or not, even in our time Nimrod's ancient Babel (*Babylon*) culture effects and influences more things than most understand. It has reached across barriers of time, space, science, religion and more. I contend in some ways Babel has influenced parts of the Holy Bible. Nebuchadnezzar, the king of Babel roughly 1800 years after the tower, was privileged to write his witness to YHWH's authority inside the pages of the Holy Bible. (Daniel: Chapter 4) It is evident however, those 1800 years earlier that Babel, her people and the culture round about, became the product of a curse. Her societies are permeated with unparalleled sins, corruption and wicked abominations. No matter how **GREAT** she appears, her fate is seal by YHWH. Her time of glory will end just prior to Yeshua's return. The cultural system of Babel is under an everlasting curse. If you recall that infamous event after the flood, for which this section is named; we can pinpoint the curse's roots by reading Genesis 11:1-9. **We,** attempted to build a tower into Heaven. YHWH cursed us with different languages to stymie any future, beyond our limits, interactions. Different languages in our reality, is a curse. It is a formidable barrier to a trusting and lasting cooperation. It is a constant reminder that no matter how hard we try to be one again; there is always looming, the psychology of our misgivings due to our diversity in the vernacular. And, time is fast running out for our peace to survive. Divine judgment declares Babel's glory will see ruin. "*Babylon...is fallen... and is become the habitation of devils and the hold of every foul spirit...*" (Revelation 18:2).

Are we Babel drunk? What do we know? My fear is, we do not know as we should. Do not get me wrong. I guess I am a fairly intelligent guy. But, I am far from being a rocket scientist. Yet, for some reason YHWH called me and chose to reveal to me part of his formerly hidden end time knowledge. Then he told me to get the word out to His people; and they can do with it as they so please. I tried going straight for the head. That was mostly a waste of time; except for the witness that was left behind in their spirit of my testimony. I am not even sure that my information got to the top. Most of us know how that works. When people are important, they tend to get the busy bug. Busy people rarely give time to no names that show up at the door offering good intentioned, but often ill-informed religious words; especially if one is not in their group. It is difficult for leaders to fairly judge potential spiritual insights from the outside. I mean when you know you know. **WELL**, **You Just Know**. There is no need to be taught anything by anybody you might view as, biblically inferior. It is not hard to identify why the Kings and High Priests of Israel and Judah rejected and murdered all of the prophets. All... you may ask! Okay, you tell me, "*Which of the prophets have not your fathers persecuted? and they have slain them which showed before of the coming of the Just One*" (Acts 7:52). If you say Enoch (Genesis 5:21-24) and Elijah (2nd Kings 2:11-12) ...let me simply state; there is more to their stories than meets traditions' eye. And, if somebody tries to squeeze Noah into the midst; just know that Noah was "*a **preacher** of righteousness*" (2nd Peter 2:5). One can argue, Noah did ***prophesy*** in regards to the flood. Theologically debatable as that might be, even if I conceded Noah. Just look to what extremes YHWH had to go to, in order for him to preserve Noah's life. I have little doubt had Noah remained in the world before the flood; today, he too would have his place in our "***Prophets' Hall of Shame***" by being murdered for relaying YHWH's word concerning an impending disaster.

Now from the bottom to the top, let us take a look at the preaching of

Yeshua. Why did not most of the devout leaders of Judah believe him? Yeshua preached truth. Yeshua did all kinds of miracles. Yeshua did so much Yochanan was moved to write a witness, "*there are...things which Yeshua did...if they...be written...the world...could not contain the books. Amen*" (John 21:25). I am aware Yeshua spoke of his disciples that they would do greater things than he. (John 14:12) Still, who could preach or teach clearer than Yeshua, when he chose? Some leaders and people did not believe him! So then, if it is a truth that some did not hear him, who am I? And please, do not look to your brethren; to see their reaction to this book. Had the wise virgins done that, they might have in error, shared their oil. Think for yourself this time. Answer this important question for yourself. Has what I have said so far made *fairly* good sense to you? That is one of the reasons I did not envy a prominent reviewer and forwarder of this book. I have always known in my articulation, especially when I get very excited concerning the subject matter that I am discussing, I struggle sometimes with details and certainly with clarity. I could not get through to the leadership of those who say they are responsible to feed the sheep. So then, I am forced to present to the sheep themselves. I hope this book's witness will aid the sheep. And, I pray my fervor does not get in the way.

Let us proceed by considering a key part for one being able to walk with me in the pathway of ordained time. It is imperative that you understand what YHWH has taught me on the subject of numbers in the Holy Scripture and what methods of counting we should use as it relates to their context in our adding up of time. I am not talking about some crazy, cockamamie method I just made up to make the numbers turn out right for my narrative; in order to sell the reader a bill of goods and is simply sensationalism up for sale. I am sure there are enough religious charlatans out and about that my name and work does not need to be named with their financial and religious scams. I do not pretend to know all. But, what I feel I have discerned from YHWH, I speak. Look at two typical Bible texts. Discern their secrets to put a pivotal piece into its place on YHWH's enigmatic puzzle of time.

- "And Arphaxad lived five and thirty years, and begat Salah" (Genesis 11:12).

- "Jehoshaphat *was* thirty and five years old when he began to reign" (1ˢᵗ Kings 22:42).

I had read over these two passages for, for ever in the Holy Bible. Arphaxad was five and thirty (35) years old when he had Salah. Jehoshaphat was thirty and five (35) years old when he began to reign over Judah. They are very plain observations and there is really nothing to see here. I placed my arrogant understanding out there just to highlight some indirect insights. One of which is this. If YHWH does not reveal to

Timothy B. Merriman

us, our intellect and discernments will not go beyond the simplicity of a carnal human. I mean seriously. I think most readers have heard of this before, and it is true; or at the least, debatable. When it comes to the resurrection of Yeshua, consider this. I would like to have thought it was as simple and obvious as ABC, when it came to his resurrection. But, here we are, purportedly 1987 years after Yeshua's tragic, but ordained **murder/sacrifice**. Even with his personal testimony – first telling us he would be killed, then resurrected <u>after</u> three days. (Luke 24:7) Then, foreseeing that in our time, we would have trouble with numbers – not knowing exactly how long the three days would be or how much time they would cover; he said it as plain as I think anyone could. He told us straight, *"For as Yonah was <u>three days and three nights</u> in the whale's belly; so shall the Son of man be <u>three days and three nights</u> in the heart of the earth"* (Matthew 12:40).

If people have any denominational doubts as to where, *"the heart of the earth"* is; we have Yonah's witness to experience what was it like for Yonah himself; while he was on the insides of the great fish's belly? Read a part of Yonah's agonizing testimony; then answer yourself. Is there any legitimate debate as to where Yonah was comparing himself to be or how long he was there?

"<u>Yonah was in the belly of the fish three days and three nights</u>."
(Yonah 1:17)

109

"Yonah prayed unto the Lord his God out of the fish's belly, and said, I cried by reason of mine affliction unto the Lord, and he heard me; <u>out of the belly of hell</u> [**sheol -** *the grave*] cried I, *and* thou heardest my voice" (Jonah 2:1-2).

As amazing as it may sound to many readers who have ears to hear; as I mentioned before, even with us living about three Millenniums later, there are still literally millions and perhaps billions today who believe that ***unlike*** Yonah, Yeshua was in the grave for **less than one day and a half!** For some reason, people have believed the false narrative, from Friday evening just before sunset (Mark 15:34 & 42-43), until Sunday morning before sunrise *"while it was still dark"* (John 20:1), versus Bible. Our own sense of time - *if we use it* - should tell us at the most, <u>tradition is working with a day and a half</u>. But this same time period was transformed into three days and three nights with the cooperation from Catholicism and Christendom overall. Not to place any blame, only to identify a root and a branch for its acceptance and growth; which I say from my viewpoint, is bewildering. At some points one has to imagine; if otherwise functionally intelligent people are having trouble counting up to three, there is substantial opportunity that an error will be encountered before they reach a sizeable count; say like five and thirty or thirty and five. I'm just saying! Of course, I can understand how that might happen to some people, but "I" am not quite so simple; so be assured, that would never happen to moi. Math is not my strong suit. But even with my own limited skills sets in the more advanced methods of our mathematical computations, I knew there was something **not right** with that traditional narrative. It just does not smell right. Can't you smell it too? Three days and three nights infer a seventy-two (72) hour period; of which Friday twilight until before sunrise on Sunday morning does not approach. I am certain there is a logical explanation as to why; "*Jesus*" himself did not know how many hours were in a day. **Oh Snap! Wait a minute!!**

"*Jesus*" did know! Actually, "Yeshua" spoke it and left it as this, dare to believe. It has endured almost two millennia, for our eyes these last few minutes. "*Are there not twelve hours in the day* (daylight)?" (John 11:9) Because there are three watches in the night, covering an equal length of time; Yeshua goes on to describe a complete day in association with the daylight and the shadow by their contrast; saying, "*If any man walk in the day* [a twelve hour time], *he stumbleth not, because he seeth the light of this world* [Sun]. *But if a man walks in the night* [also twelve hours], *he stumbleth, because there is no light in him* [The sun is gone down, we are in the shadow and the sun will not rise again for another twelve hours]" (Verses 9-10). I know some will still insist this or that in their attempts to justify tradition's error; and that is okay. At this point, I am not demanding yours or mine. I am just stating what I feel "*should be*"

111

evident in our standard counting. Yet, being that we are over 2000 years removed from the culture of, *"Jesus Christ"* and his direct teachings, every individual will need to put it together for themselves, or with the assistance of their group, what has now apparently become a biblical jigsaw mystery in YHWH's truth. In doing so, they/we must try to attain as much clarity with our new discoveries for any new spiritual perspectives as we all can. In the event you do not already know and you would like some assistance in your quest to understand the, *"three days and three nights"* mystery, there was a good article in booklet form (*If it is still in print*); that perhaps will help explain why tradition is in error. That book offers a more plausible Biblical explanation regarding the resurrection of *"Jesus."* The book is called, *"The Resurrection was not on Sunday."* You may be able to find it in PDF with a search of the internet. Make a search for it and if you find it, obviously I consider much of the information contained within it would be very beneficial to your spiritual growth. Notwithstanding, in the end, we must all run in our own races and we must all finish our own courses. May the best blessed man person win; because, as we should all know, if just in symbolism alone; all run the race, *"...but one receiveth the prize"* (1st Corinthians 9:24).

I wanted to express that idea the best as I could; to show the kind of thoughts that runs in my head. I wanted you to know too, how I have had my struggles with denominationalism and what I have called the _worldly_

portion of Christianity and its general trappings of religion overall for the

lost¿ parts of my life. It appears to me as if the powers that be, in certain

groups, do not want their subjugated converts or parishioners to do any

logical spiritual thinking on their own. And, if anybody did have enough

nerves to ask weird or challenging questions on subjects such as what we

have only touched on in this book; it is often treated as if that member

did some act of mutiny against church authority and for this they must be

made to walk the plank of shame. And, if there is not a ceased and desist;

then ouster (_protestant excommunication_) will likely follow. Me... I am

use to that hostility. But, getting to that point took prayer and patience. I

asked because I wanted to know. I am amazed how it is sometimes. How

we are asked to **not think** and believe without question, anything certain

church authorities might teach. I wanted to be able to ask any question I

had concerns about and get legitimate answers without the animosity that

often go along with people's disagreements in debates over their political

issues, social matters and spiritual doctrine. Eventually, I went to YHWH

for help. I am absolutely confident and truly believe YHWH honored my

request. Among many things - I asked YHWH to help me in anyway his

Spirit willed; so I might fulfill his calling for election to the highest level.

You see, at that specific point in my life, I understood though

YHWH's mercy, grace and revelation, that quite frankly, **I** did not think right. Even though I did not realize it at the time, what I was truly asking was for YHWH to give me a clean heart and restore in me the right spirit. (Psalms 51:10) Eventually and over time, my Eloah began to open up my mind and clear out my eyes to truths that to this day, I am truly unworthy to understand. Miserably and to my shame, I am so far removed from the behaviors of our righteous fathers that I am only able to receive truths in limited fashion. In truth, I am unable to bear their spiritual weight. I wish this was not the truth, but it is. Saul spoke related words to one fledgling church he minister to. "*I have fed you with milk, and not with meat: for hitherto ye were not able to bear it, neither yet now are ye able*" (1st Corinthians 3:1-2). One in another place spoke regarding our unenviable state saying we, "...*should earnestly contend for the faith which was once delivered unto the saints*" (Jude 3). Once I recognized my condition, I believe YHWH authorized his ministering angels to reveal to me some basics, then later some intermediate and formerly hidden pieces of his knowledge for my perception. I am now sharing what portions of those perceptions I am able to explain clearly enough to be received. YHWH's ministering angels started to make me notice things in my reading of the Holy Scriptures that I had previously just read over with only a glance of curiosity. YHWH's ministering spirits began to ask me questions; which many years ago I had been shamed and ridiculed so bad for that I stopped asking them aloud. Eventually they settled in the back parts of my mind. Now/then those, *"uncouth questions"* were back at the forefront of my mind and seeking real answers that made good sense, no less. And do not let anybody fool you. I was really terrified at the possibility, and perhaps the probability; that I had gone and asked of YHWH, for the answers to questions that I really might not be able to receive with my self-assumed, readiness of spirit. Before I forget, I likely do not need to tell all readers, but I do feel I need to remind some. The Holy Bible is not "literally" the Word of YHWH. It is merely the translated, and in some instances, the transliterated Word of YHWH. Because oftentimes it is fact. Different, exact, proper and clear meanings get lost in the Bible's many translations and transliterations. Know sometimes, we need to go back more into the original tongue and culture when confusion is prevailing and our deeper understanding is require.

For my examples: Are you aware that YHWH created the realms of physics and mathematics? That was rhetorical. Of course you are. I have already said that. I only said it again to reintroduce you to his numbers. Eloah created all: addition, subtraction, multiplication, division, with the processes involving conversions, overlaps and so on and so on. The Holy Bible contains aspects and examples of many forms of math. Like I said,

I am not telling **you** a thing **you** do not already know. Atheists and some scientists are different stories. But, in order for **you** to follow me where I want to direct; whether you feel the things I am about to show you have merit or not, you need to at the least, understand where it is I am coming from. This brings me back to my "*unquestionably*" opened and shut case.

- "And Arphaxad lived five and thirty years, and begat Salah" (Genesis 11:12).

- "Jehoshaphat *was* thirty and five years old when he began to reign" (1ˢᵗ Kings 22:42).

I don't remember "*exactly*" how I got on this trail. It could have been a number of ways. It was most likely a combination of different pathway scenarios. The one that straightway comes to mind and perhaps got me leaning toward the way I got wind to my perceptions, is when I read the parable of, **"The Rich Man and Lazarus."** (Luke 16:19-31) During my study, YHWH's Holy Spirit nudged my spirit; when I read the counsel Abraham gave the rich man regarding his five brethren. If you will recall then, after the rich man had given up on the hope of his own pardon for everlasting life; in an act of what could be called sibling selflessness, he shifted his focus on to his brothers, presuming they were still existing carefree in the physical realm of earth. And like the rich man, was most likely oblivious to the possibility of any kind of upcoming damnation in judgment. He frantically begged Abraham to allow Lazarus to go back to his father's house and testify to his brothers. Abraham's reply is made up of words; which elements of our "modern-day" Christendom would haul him over the coals with a severe rebuke for actually declaring it. I hope no one is offended when we return to that passage in parable history to reacquaint ourselves to those words spoken by "*Jesus Christ¿*" himself. When those words are spoken by others today, they are treated literally by most Bible teachers in the Christian world as blasphemous. However, we gain our access to their truth by the Holy Spirit through the revelation of Yeshua our Eloah and Messiah. Recall, this was after the rich man had given up on all hope for any kind of personal redemptive judgment. As many Christian organizations assume and teach, the rich man **is not** in a holding site before "*Judgment Day.*" It is Judgment Day! "...*in hell* [from Sheol, the grave] *he lifted up his eyes* [is resurrected], *being in torments*" (Luke 16:23). He saw the reward of his deeds (*fire*) and end of his life.

> "Then he [*the rich man*] said, I pray thee therefore, father [*Abraham*], that thou wouldest send him [*Lazarus*] to my father's house: for I have five brethren; that he may testify unto them, lest they also come into this place of torment." (Verses 27-28)

Now hear what Yeshua said in this parable through Abraham in reply not only to that rich man, but to all of us; whom today would deny his words to live in error. Because we fail to see their truth and wisdom; as ignorant protest, objection and denials among a diversity of Christian theologians, preachers, evangelists and some of us who seek alternatives to its truths; dance and rejoice in our demonic deception at the edge of blasphemy.

> Abraham [*Theology wise; **it was Jesus;**] saith* unto him [***the rich man, the people of his time and also to us today***], "They [***we***] have **Moses and the prophets**; **let them hear them**" (verse 29).

First let me say this. I have simply repeated. Do not be angry and kill me. I am just a messenger. Next, "...*let them,*" would include not only the rich man's brothers, but anyone else; who wanted to escape ending up in the same dilemma that the rich man found himself in - believe it or not. The name, "Moses" is synonymous with the given law – besides it being divinely odious to many "*Christians*" and their so-called "*trained leaders and theologians.*" And the title, "Prophet of old" was that witness to the Testimony of Messiah; for Yeshua testified, "*Search the Scriptures; for in them ye think ye have eternal life: and they are they which testify of me*" (John 5:39). Also, Messiah Yeshua spoke in another place.

> "O fools, and slow of heart to believe **all** that the prophets have spoken: ought not [Messiah] to have suffered these things, and to enter into his glory? ...beginning at Moses and all the prophets, he expounded unto them in all the Scriptures the things concerning himself" (Luke 24:25-27).

Let us go back to the parable of the rich man. So as not to feel totally rejected, the rich man made a last desperate effort. The rich man actually rebuked his forefather Abraham saying, "*Nay, father Abraham: but if one went unto them from the dead they will repent*" (Luke 16:30). We have to admit, desperation will make one persistent. And one might think in our modern-day and age that the rich man was making a really good point with his arguments. Having somebody come back for you from the grave to testify to you about impending judgment, one would have to imagine, has to be a pretty strong testimony and deterrent - right?

With our *modern progressive* theology of today, I can imagine if **we** were the rich man we might likely snarl expletives back at Abraham after his last reply. I will give you a PG-Rated version. "Screw you Abraham! My "**Pastor**" told me I do not have to listen to any of that Old Testament Crap!" In seriousness, I would like us to reply to that parable's challenge in our own minds. How would *church doctrine* had us reply to Abraham? Wait! It's really not Abraham speaking is it? *In our Christian theological reality, it's really Jesus Christ, right?* So truly, it's after "*Jesus Christ's*" divine reply to the rich man's plea for sibling mercy. Because this is how "*Jesus*" replied to that send Lazarus back nonsense. "*Jesus*" said to the rich man and by the way, **all of us today**, "*If they hear not Moses and the prophets, neither will they be persuaded, though one rose from the dead*" (Verse 31). Yeshua himself being by faith is the living proof to that; isn't he? In truth, I confess in studying this parable, many of the "concepts" I am citing to you, I have already adopted as part of my theology. I believe their lessons help me run my race to finish my course. Though it is sad to say, at one point in my learning; I was more afraid of how many people there were who did not see the parable my way, than I was thankful with the truths I received by its revelations. In any case, it was the Spirit that *suggested* I go back to study Moses and the prophets, in review. This was just in the case there were some other significant findings or insights and revelations that my theologically trained intellect may have missed. <u>Bear in mind, this is the same brilliant mind, which at one point in my spiritual life, was **"absolutely"** unable to account for the three days and nights of Yeshua's burial</u>. So, I lazily accepted all of our traditions' words and I "*assumed*" it was me not understanding things. I think that realization pretty much sums up how absolutely clueless I am, without the revelation of YHWH's Holy Spirit. So, with no real and deep expectation to look forward to, you see - *for the most part* - I had read *most* of Moses and the prophets. In my "brilliancy," I had to skip past all of the "impossible" to pronounce names and places. I could imagine most all of my seminary lecturers may have been shamed to claim me as one of their students; in calling me lazy, literarily lethargic and biblically apathetic. Considering all of my spiritual arrogance in my assurances concerning my presumed biblical knowledge, those labels fitted me very well. But in my mind, I had no worries; it was just an Old Testament refresher. <u>I guess God felt I needed it</u>. In my old spirit I was a bit arrogant. Today I am just confident.

Still, I began again from the very, "*In the beginning*" of <u>Genesis 1:1</u>.
I read through the genealogies, Abram, Isaac, Jacob and the prophets. In
many places there was numerical wording that was correlated with texts.
Somewhere between then and I don't know where, the Holy Spirit asked
me the question that might or might not have been the beginning of my
journey in a completely "new" direction. That is, when it comes to these
unique discernments now a part of my biblical jig-saw picture. Like most
everyone, my picture is not complete. Despite, the eye-opening question
asked; focused on the order of the numbers as I read. Years ago, the Holy
Spirit asked me why did people believe so many untrue things about the
truth. He asked me why could not people see, simple non-commonalities.
I had no suitable answers; especially not back then. Now all of a sudden,
decades later; the Holy Spirit brings those questions of thought back into
the forefront of my mind and answers them. He said this is why people
cannot see certain things. It is because they are afraid to ask themselves
Bible difficult questions and expect make-sense answers for themselves
through and from the Holy Spirit of YHWH Elohim. Paraphrasing the
event and substituting one of YHWH's original passages he gave me, for
another text, to get the same effect easier. He said to me, "Read here." As
far as new knowledge he wanted me to discern, this is what I read.

- *And Arphaxad lived five and thirty years, and begat Salah.*"
                                                            (Genesis 11:12)

Then YHWH took me along the Scriptures and said, "Read there." And, this is what I read.

- *"Jehoshaphat was thirty and five years old when he began to reign."* (1ˢᵗ Kings 22:42)

Then the Holy Spirit asked me that question, "Why does one passage say *five and thirty* and the other says *thirty and five*?" Me, being the spiritual giant I thought I was, after a little intellectual jousting with the Holy Spirit, I said - *patting myself on the back* - "Because in mathematics order does not matter!" Holy Spirit replied, "Are you sure? Look it up." Picture in your mind this serious *"back and forth"* I was having with the Holy Spirit. I told my wife. She says, "Really?" I said, "Yes, really!" She didn't have to be snooty about it. I already knew I was not going to win. Anyhow, I looked up mathematics and this is what I officially discovered yet again. I knew it once before. I had just forgotten it for the time being.

Mathematics is the abstract science of number, quantity, and space. Mathematics deals with the logic of shapes, quantities and arrangements. Mathematics may be studied in its own right (*pure mathematics*), or as it is applied to other disciplines such as physics and engineering (*applied mathematics*). Mathematics includes the study of such topics as quantity, structure, space, and change. Mathematics seeks and uses patterns to formulate new conjectures; it can resolve the truth or falsities of conjectures by mathematical proof. [Mathematics]...includes arithmetic, algebra, calculus, geometry and trigonometry.
(Vcoit, 2016 & Encarta Dictionary, 2019)

In my re-reading, I re-realized its order <u>does not</u> matter when adding; <u>but it matters</u> in other aspects of science and math. <u>I knew that</u>! After my re-discovery YHWH said, "Tell me; are both passages you read adding?" Confidence shaken; I replied, "I don't know." There was this truth in my confession. I would have it many times over in the following months and years to come. More often than I would care to acknowledge. YHWH asked me did I recall what **"<u>Roman Numbers</u>"** are, how they work and had I ever thought about what they would look like, if they were written down in words form, versus being deciphered through their traditional symbols, as they are generally viewed by today? YHWH asked me if I knew where the Roman Numbers' concept came from. I had no real idea until he asked me to think. Then, I think I understood through deduction; that is how addition and subtraction likely formed in Babel's beginning. Then the Holy Spirit said something to me; which will stick with me for the rest of my life. I am paraphrasing this. Still, YHWH said to me, if I was afraid to believe, because I was afraid to be wrong and I would have the need for repentance; I would not be able to establish the kind of truth I would need to know and live by in order to perhaps get my opportunity to go to the Bridegroom's wedding feast as part of the glorious five wise virgins. In a moment of clarity, I understood the truth of my situation.

When the Holy Spirit of YHWH conveyed to my spirit the idea of

Roman numbers being part of the Holy Scriptures, I was afraid to trust it. Simply because I have never heard any theologians or any Bible teachers and certainly not any television evangelists, speak to that concept. I had certainly not entertained in my own theology, any doctrines that would suggest the concept of Roman numbers being part of the Holy Bible - not in my wildest Bible dreams. Thinking back now though, I ask myself, "Why in the world not?" Everyone who studies the Holy Bible seriously, knows that the Roman Empire is a prophetic descendent from the ancient Babylonian Empire. If you are not sure, do a study on the second chapter of Daniel. Then you might prove to yourself, the conclusions that I came to. Then you might say like I did. Why would the modern Roman culture not retain portions of the ancient Babel culture? And why would Roman numbers not be part of the Babylonian/Roman's retention culture? It all made reasonably good sense to me. Then again, I said to myself; what if I do not believe this spirit that is speaking to me or what if I spend all my time researching with this spirit and come to a dead end? YHWH said to me, 'Do not be afraid. This is all part of the learning curve. Every sincere spiritual investigator will have to overcome it - if they have any realistic intention of winning The Prize of Eternal Life.' YHWH said, 'Besides all of this, I have already said, "*believe not every spirit, but try the spirits whether they are of God*" (1ˢᵗ John 4:1). What do you think I means? Do you not think that *"try"* action would take time? And, do you think such actions is a waste of your time? Do you have something more valuable to pursue or some other place you would rather be?' YHWH said to me, 'Treat the truth like a puzzle. Put the pieces in place the best you can. If you have to remove a piece - do it. As with all jig-saw puzzles, you know there are some shape patterns that repeat themselves. They might seem to fit or they may even fit. But, you will find out later that they were in the wrong place that entire time you **"KNEW!"** they were in the right place. I will show you. If you are willing to follow me wherever I go, no matter what. <u>Because if you want life, that is what it will take</u> - **and more!**'

'So now tell me,' YHWH said, 'Why do you think the devise of Roman numbers were in the beginning?' I said because my studying has taught me modern <u>Rome is an end time descendent</u> of Nebuchadnezzar's Babylonian Empire; **politically, socially and religiously** (Daniel's 2nd Chapter). It is a Holy Bible fact that the same Babylon is connected to Nimrod; who became quite infamous after the flood as the *mighty hunter* before YHWH [*The great adversary against YHWH*]. Yes! **Nimrod was wicked.** The beginning and foundation of Nimrod's kingdom was Babel (*Confusion*). It would be religiously expected - in Nimrod's hatred for YHWH - his kingdom would establish ideas in science and concepts in math that conflicted with or would mystify YHWH's created order and way on earth. <u>Does this sound in any way similar to the way science and the social orders are walking in today</u>? Corrupting YHWH's way in the earth, i.e. **<u>The Big Bang Theory and Evolution</u>** (*The origins of life and development of species, without a creator/YHWH*), <u>Abortion</u> (*On demand - Really?*), <u>Gay marriage</u> (*Don't get me started on that twisted ideology - **<u>as if such an act was even possible</u>**! You see pretending, no matter how hard you make believe and no matter what type of "**<u>Law</u>**¿" you write or construct, does not make it genuine or truth*) (<u>Leviticus 18:22 & Romans 1:26-27</u>). What about our generalized socialized suppression of all of the Commandments of Elohim? And the list of our unrighteous, unholy and ungodliness could go on and on. It was for these reasons and more that caused YHWH to destroy the earth with the flood only about three generations earlier in the first place. (Genesis 6:12) And, it will be for these reasons YHWH will destroy the earth yet again in a little over two days "*Millennial Future Days*" distances. But, that is enough talk of that kind for a while. Besides, most of this book's readers already know about our impending dates with honor and glorification or with judgment, mercy and/or damnation. Besides the "*occasional*" drifts into righteous implications and assertions; at length, that is in its finality what this book is truly about. It is about finding a, the, that, our discernible date with destiny and eternity. But right now, as we speak and where we left off, we are in YHWH's Adamic base year 1658. It was in that year all of the flood waters subsided from off the face of the earth. Then Noah, his sons and their wives, along with all air-breathing animal life came forth from the ark. Admittedly, that is still quite a few years away from our biblical target date of 6000. Shem's son Arphaxad, who was the continuation of our Messianic bloodline, would not be born for another two years; in YHWH's Adamic year of 1660 or 2341 BC. (Genesis 11:10) From the year of 1658, there is still 4343 years of Bible time to account for before Messiah is expected to return. So I guess we need to get on with it a bit more by continuing with our journey and walk through time.

YHWH said, 'Run with that. I want you to run through history. See can you start from day one physically and spiritually and continue on to the last great day physically and spiritually. Keep in mind the lesson you learned as far as Roman numbers; when you entertain the age of men and the times of prophecy. In doing so, you will understand and discern that Arphaxad's "*five and thirty years*" meant that he was twenty-five (25) years old – versus the presumed thirty-five (35) years of age when he begat Salah. YHWH alerted me to the fact that this was the process with the rest of the biblical genealogies immediately after the flood. I wonder if you can imagine how afraid I was of the theological embarrassment I would have to endure; if I ended up being wrong. Still, I continued on with the journey anyway; not sure where I would end up. And, the discoveries were nothing short of eye-opening amazing for me. They gave to me very different perspectives in my biblical understanding. In this life I will likely never know to appreciate in truth, everything I could have known or should have known as far as spiritual truth. Nevertheless, I am humbly grateful for the inspiration and the chance for Bible insights YHWH's divine processes of Discovery and Perspective has given me.

With all of that said, the easiest way to appreciate what you are about to read in order to get through this time walk; is for you to understand the mixed counts in the similar way that you understand those basic Roman numbers. The main difference is that numbers in the Holy Scriptures are recorded in words versus in symbol; i.e. #25 (twenty and five, instead of XX-V) or #15 (five and twenty, instead of V-XX). Admittedly, over the centuries and Millennia, cultural changes with usages have occurred and affected Roman numerals in subtle ways. In certain ancient days, of the above when we said "twenty and five" it was twenty-five (#25); but for some unknown reason, at a different time in history "five and thirty" was also determined to be that same twenty-five (#25); i.e. the following.

$20 + 5 = \underline{25}$; then again, minus 5 or 5 from 30 = $\underline{25}$ (*Babel/Roman*)

Now, as far as Roman Numbers in the Holy Scriptures go; their basic functions of operation remains the same. At one point, I hypothesized the reasons for recording numbers in that fashion was to hide the age and to help ensure the survival of their patriarchal lines and for the life of too young kings. So their enemy would be less tempted to take advantage of their tribe and kings' youthful vulnerabilities before their kings came into maturity to lead his people. In other ways and for other reasons, I thought the Roman Numbers system of counting was used so a tribe could keep their enemy in the dark and deceive them concerning troop count or other tactics of war. Every one of these reasons mentioned, were crucial for the survival of a leader's linage and his people in ancient and arguably more barbaric times. However, in the end, I am not contentious with anyone; if they do not accept my thoughts. Because, they are simply theories. I have also considered the Babel nations in their times may not have been trying to hide a thing. Maybe our societies of today, like with time, simply lost some of our relationships and the understandings we had of those ancient cultures through chance mergers of unalike cultures, by war and peace or changes in its social usage. Systems, i.e. Roman Numbers are sometimes altered in use by their social misuses by generations of peoples over the centuries and millennia. Notwithstanding, on the next page over is your modern standard Roman Numbers chart from one to 100. It is for your viewing, reviewing and understanding. It should help you, as we make this sectional journey in our pathways up from Adam on through to the patriarchal lineage immediately after the great flood. Then we will go on

to Abram. And again, even though we will not need and use it during our

walk through time, I am persuaded that the Roman Number concept was

adopted in the formulation of prophetic computations for the purpose of

sealing prophecies. This is a truth you might witness for yourself in your

own pathways to "Discovery and Perspective." That is, if you should

decide to adopt or consider the Roman Numbers concept in your own

biblical studies and with divine revelation from YHWH's Holy Spirit.

Roman Number 1 to 100

1. I	21. XXI	41. XLI	61. LXI	81. LXXXI
2. II	22. XXII	42. XLII	62. LXII	82. LXXXII
3. III	23. XXIII	43. XLIII	63. LXIII	83. LXXXIII
4. IV	24. XXIV	44. XLIV	64. LXIV	84. LXXXIV
5. V	25. XXV	45. XLV	65. LXV	85. LXXXV
6. VI	26. XXVI	46. XLVI	66. LXVI	86. LXXXVI
7. VII	27. XXVII	47. XLVII	67. LXVII	87. LXXXVII
8. VIII	28. XXVIII	48. XLVIII	68. LXVIII	88. LXXXVIII
9. IX	29. XXIX	49. XLIX	69. LXIX	89. LXXXIX
10. X	30. XXX	50. L	70. LXX	90. XC
11. XI	31. XXXI	51. LI	71. LXXI	91. XCI
12. XII	32. XXXII	52. LII	72. LXXII	92. XCII
13. XIII	33. XXXIII	53. LIII	73. LXXIII	93. XCIII
14. XIV	34. XXXIV	54. LIV	74. LXXIV	94. XCIV
15. XV	35. XXXV	55. LV	75. LXXV	95. XCV
16. XVI	36. XXXVI	56. LVI	76. LXXVI	96. XCVI
17. XVII	37. XXXVII	57. LVII	77. LXXVII	97. XCVII
18. XVIII	38. XXXVIII	58. LVIII	78. LXXVIII	98. XCVIII
19. XIX	39. XXXIX	59. LIX	79. LXXIX	99. XCIX
20. XX	40. XL	60. LX	80. LXXX	100. C

There are basic rules with regard to the use of modern Roman numbers. Among them are, they do not use the same symbol more than three times in a row. When it comes to subtracting amounts, only powers of ten are used to subtract from. There is also the rule that you cannot subtract a number from a number that is more than 10 times greater. For larger numbers in the thousands, a bar [–] is placed over the tops of the letter or string of letters. It multiplies the numerals' values by 1,000. The number desired is formed by combining its requirement in various letters and finding their calculate value. The basic Roman Numeral symbols "I" (1), "V" (5), "X" (10), "L" (50), "C" (100) and "M" (1000) are placed in line from left to right in choice order and according to Roman Numeral rules, depending on the final number sought. The order of the numerals would determine whether one adds or subtract values. But, if one or more letters are placed after a letter of a greater value and each of those numbers in succession are equal or of a lesser value, the action taken would be to add all of their sums. If a letter of lesser value is placed before a letter of greater value the action taken would be subtraction. For examples: "VI" = 6 because "V" [5] is higher than "I" [1]. But "IV" = 4 because "I" [1] is lower than "V" [5]. In the grouping where both adding and subtracting are involved, subtraction is always the "priority" action in summing up.

(livescience.com/32052-roman-numerals.html. - paraphrased)

Note the concept in structure when adding and subtracting on the chart. If a lesser number is to the left of a larger number (*In letters or in texts*), "**Subtraction**" is the "priority" mathematical action taken. In the larger numbers, an action similar to the process of conversion sometimes takes place. Consider now, when a Roman number equation, say with three numerical symbols is employed. If a lesser number symbol is located to the left of a larger symbol, as with the Roman number of "XIX" (19) we must prepare the set to add on to its base symbol(s) "X" (10) to the far left. To do this, because there is a lesser number symbol followed by a greater number symbol, we must first convert (*subtract*) those two to the right of the base "X" (10); the "I" (1) from the "X" (10). Our illustration follows a distinct pattern. We have a base symbol for ten; the first "X" for which we will add to, after the equation is prepared or converted. When we subtract the symbol for one "I" from the second symbol for ten "X;" it is easy to see we get the numerical value of nine (9). Now the equation is ready for its final action of addition. Simply add nine (9/IX) to its base ten (10/X) and we get the understood value nineteen (19) or (XIX). Remember. In the Roman Numeral system, if symbols from left to right are equal or lesser in sequential value, only the adding process takes place; i.e. thirty-eight (38 or "XXXVIII). That was harder to explain than I first thought. I hope you got it.

As I am not fluent in any second language, let alone being an expert in the ancient Babel number system. I cannot attest to all the rules from that ancient age. Yet, based on all I trust YHWH has revealed, to include Roman Numbers in the King James; I stand by it. It is the version I used. I just followed along with what YHWH told me to do in the KJV. I did not know where I was going to end up. The information I will give you is how the numbers came out. **Note:** This method is by no means foolproof on all fronts. There are instances recorded in the Holy Bible as pertaining to the everyday counting in the days of the months, where in fact <u>one and twentieth</u>, <u>two and twentieth</u>, <u>three and twentieth</u> and <u>four and twentieth</u> meant <u>21</u>, <u>22</u>, <u>23</u> and <u>24</u> respectively – <u>in the days of the month</u>! (1st Chronicles 25:7-18). Nevertheless, according to my instructions from YHWH, in those certain places where the Holy Bible dealt with ages and prophecy, "**five and thirty years**" meant <u>twenty-five years</u> (*25yrs.*) (Genesis 11:12 & Daniel 12:12) and then too, "**two and thirty years**" meant <u>twenty-eight</u> (*28yrs.*) (Genesis 11:20), respectively. In all of these cases, whether it was the person's age or the seal over a prophecy, it appears from my perspective, the shadow and concealments were, or at least became over time, their significant results or prophetic intents and objectives. But then, as I have said before, all of our misunderstandings could be attributed to our loss of culture through generations of sin and rebellion against YHWH. And this should be clear to us all. Sin makes us unwise. This is conceivably why YHWH has linked our deception to our wickedness and not to our *"Intelligence¿,"* Hence, based on our pathetic abilities to not be able to discern YHWH's truth from an **obvious** lie; it is with our end time generations, as it was written to those of old. Sadly, it appears many of us are part of the ones to whom the prophet now speaks.

> "For the Lord hath poured out upon you the spirit of deep sleep, and hath closed your eyes: the prophets and your rulers, the seers hath he covered. And the vision of all is become unto you as the words of a book that is sealed, which *men* deliver to one that is learned, saying, Read this, I pray thee: and he saith, I cannot; for it *is* sealed: and the book is delivered to him that is not learned, saying, Read this, I pray thee: and he saith, I am not learned."
> (Isaiah 29:9-13).

I think I have said something similar, prior to. It is because I do not speak or write ancient Hebrew or any foreign languages as far as those matters go, I have only perhaps a few completed and incontrovertible answers of surety that are now readily available in their entirety on the matter of the history of the Roman Numeral revelation; which has not already been established since our Middle School taught years. That is one of the reasons I was enthusiastic, yet apprehensive at the same time, in publishing this matter for the Christian community's broader scrutiny. The matters I was able to make the connections to as far as the functional use of Roman Numbers in the Bible was in the cases of prophecy, post flood genealogies and age concealment. By not being familiar with the ancient cultures history wise, all Bible numerical uses are not clear to me. Nevertheless, I have seen this Roman numbers concept, far as having used them in a system; work consistently all throughout the Scriptures. As with any one or all of the subjects I will speak to, if you can see any resemblance of validity in my madness, please take the spiritual logic in my perspectives and use them for what they are worth to you; if you can use them at all. Remember, I am writing this to help all those who want to be helped. If I can do it by declaring what I judge to be the truth; or by helping you to prove for yourself what I have written is as false to its core as Satan is with his deceit. We are all aware that Satan's outward show is to look like **The Truth**. His attempts to palm himself to be good, righteous, holy and even godly, he retains in infamy. (Isaiah 14:12-17)

May Eloah bless you to see past any and all falsehood; so that you may, "*hold fast to that which is good*" (1st Thessalonians 5:21). To help you better accept what I will speak, consider the following foundations for, "My walk through time." Actually now, it is more properly, our walk! Most understand that the millennial day consist of 1000 years. "...*beloved, be not ignorant of this one thing, that* [in prophecy] *one day is with the Lord as a thousand years, and a thousand years as one day*" (2nd Peter 3:8). At this moment of our walk, I feel that it is good to remind you again in mentioning that very important concept; to keep with you during our walk from the creation to the immediate time; and beyond to the everlasting. Just as a reminder... please read it once more.

> "[*Apostle*] Shim'on Kefa (*Simon Peter*) was speaking the very same thing that the Hebrew [*Jewish*] Rabbis have taught for thousands of years. In that God created the heavens and the earth in six days and on the seventh-day he rested; what that means [*In Hebrew and Jewish theology*] is that man will have his time of rule and reign on the earth for six thousand years. The Messiah will reign in the seventh or the Sabbath Millennium -The Day or the Millennium of the LORD."
>
> (Rood, M. J., 1999 – *Prophecies in the Spring Feasts*)

I believe a majority of you reading; can understand this Hebrew premise and that you can receive the basis of the concept itself as spiritually true. It is a deeply rooted belief that was handed down from generation to generation through the oral traditions long before it was scripted down by any High Priest or Rabbi's scribe in any scroll or Talmud. Though it is not included in the canonized books of the Holy Scriptures, the Book of Barnabus speaks of the millennial Sabbath of YHWH.

> "The idea that God has a 7,000 year plan is not a new one. In fact, it has been around for many centuries. The Epistle of Barnabas taught it in the first century A.D. by stating that "*in six days, that is, in six thousand years, all things will be finished...This meaneth: when His Son, coming [again], shall destroy the time of the wicked man, and judge the ungodly, and change the-sun, and the moon, and the stars, then shall He truly rest on the seventh day.*" (Epistle of Barnabas, XV verses 4-6)
>
> (Melton, James L., 2010)

As a point of disclosure, I do take issue with Barnabas' chronological order of events. The fact is, it appears he believes Messiah will, *"judge the ungodly, and change the-sun, and the moon, and the stars"* before His Millennial Reign, is at present unacceptable to my theology of truth. Maybe Barnabas did not have access to Apostle Yochanan's book of Revelation. For me, it clearly states it was not until after the 1000 years have expired will these events occur.

1. Satan will be loosed for a little season. (Revelation 20:3 & 7)

2. In that, he will go and deceive Gog and Magog. (Revelation 20:8)

3. Once deceived, they will attack Jerusalem and the saints camped around. (Revelation 20:9)

4. After their defeat, Satan is cast into the lake of fire with the beast and false prophet. (Revelation 20:10)

5. The Great White Throne Judgment (*1000 years in duration*) (Revelation 20:12-13)

6. New Heaven & Earth (*Changes Barnabas felt would occur over 2000 years earlier*) (Revelation 21:1)

I want to think my point has been made. A 7000-year God-plan was seen as valid dogma. It is odd that most professing *Christian* rejects a weekly Sabbath. Which YHWH appears to have made a part of earth's basics for time. (Genesis 2:2) We do still have a seven-day week... Don't we? These same *Christians* for the most part, trust *Jesus* to rule 1000 years to fulfill what the rejected weekly Sabbath seems to represent in shadow picture - the _Sabbath_ _Millennial_. The quotes written above and below are taken from the Bible Baptist Publication group. Within their denominational pages, they defend the concept. They believe God indeed has this 7000-year plan for man. In so believing, these Baptist at least accept as truth; time as we know it will end after "_Jesus'_" _Sabbath Reign_.

> "Irenaeus taught it in the second century, Commodianus in the third century and in the fourth century Lactantius wrote that, "_the world must continue in its present state through six ages, that is, six thousand years...at the end of the six thousandth years all wickedness must be abolished from the earth and righteousness reign for a thousand years..._" (The Epitome of the Divine Institutes, Chapter 70)" (Melton, James L., 2010).

This is why so many professing _Christians_ believe, "_Jesus Christ_" is coming – any day now! The 6000 years many of the _Christian fathers_ taught, past by twenty years ago. Christians declare they trust in _Jesus_. Clearly, I too feel Messiah Yeshua's return is very close. It is in the wind of my breath. By this, I mean the scope of my presumed normal lifetime. In AD 2020, I will be 61. That might say something to what I think. It is highly unlikely, I will live to see 100. Still, if I could in some way cope and survive another decade; I might see that amazing, yet terrifying to some event.

Presuming that you accept the concept of a millennial day being a 1000 years, I want you to consider these next things as common spiritual logic or steps to knowledge and discernment in our walk through time. And understand this also. Not only do I want us to believe and know that the Holy Bible walks us through this time I speak of, but it also reveals to us, the exact year as to where we stand in time today and at this very moment. For me, not only is that exciting; but, it is also extremely frightening. That is, if one can believe that any human being can know the hidden things. If you believe that humans are living in the total time period of a millennial week and six millennial days before the return of Messiah Yeshua; and you feel that we are close to the end of the sixth day of that millennial week, then you accept through biblical revelation that each day is equal to 1000 years. As it is written right now, this book is a hard sell for many. I, more than you know, understand some readers opposing sentiments deeper than they might think. Nevertheless, in absence of faith over my contention of YHWH's ordination of the times, if the thousand years for a day and the millennial week foundation is rejected; quite frankly, I feel that I am at a loss as far as being able to assist anyone with time recognition as the Bible records it. Let it be noted for now, to anyone who has received and embraced their faith concerning the millennial days and week. We are armed only with our knowledge of standard counting procedures and the Roman numbers concept; which we will be using to resume our count through time. We began this walk basically to see how far we could count up. Remember, YHWH created numbers and time. Humans have only been allowed to borrow them and to use them as best we can. So then... shall we find out if or whether the Holy Scripture can account for all of the time we need to find – without having to contend with the oftentimes great confusion and uncertainty of certainly man's more ancient recordings of human history? As the Holy Scripture has admonished us in the past, let us also remember and retain its lessons now; and into the future time that is remaining for intellectual humans. "Let God be true, but every man a liar; as it is written, that [we] mightest be justified in [our] sayings and mightest overcome when [we] art judged" (Romans 3:4). If it is not written, we risk a walk in deception.

Keep in mind throughout our walk and count, we need to account for not only the first six millennial days, but also for Messiah Yeshua's Sabbath millennial reign and that Last Great Day of Judgment. That is a total of no less than eight thousand years. We could easily account for the millennial Sabbath and Judgment Day. It is because these have not occurred yet. We can just put them neatly at the end of our time table jig-saw picture for now. Take a look for your convenience.

1st Millennial Day				2nd Millennial Day				3rd Millennial Day				4th Millennial Day				5th Millennial Day				6th Millennial Day				7th Millennial Day				8th Millennial Day			
250	500	750	1000	1250	1500	1750	2000	2250	2500	2750	3000	3250	3500	3750	4000	4250	4500	4750	5000	5250	5500	5750	6000	6250	6500	6750	7000	7250	7500	7750	8000
BMB - Before Messiah's Birth														BMB - Before Messiah's Birth	AMB - After Messiah's Birth																AMB - After Messiah's Birth
4000	3750	3500	3250	3000	2750	2500	2250	2000	1750	1500	1250	1000	750	500	250	AMB 250	AMB 500	AMB 750	AMB 1000	AMB 1250	AMB 1500	AMB 1750	AMB 2000	AMB 2250	AMB 2500	AMB 2750	AMB 3000	AMB 3250	AMB 3500	AMB 3750	AMB 4000
BMB	BMB	BMB	BMB	BMB	BMB	BMB	BMB	BMB	BMB	BMB	BMB	BMB	BMB	BMB	BMB																

Since those two final millennia ordained for intellectual man are yet to come in the great days of prophecy; in general theory, we only need to account for six millennia or 6000 years and then we add the latter days back on; to get the broader more complete picture of YHWH's grand design. I thought that plan sounded simple enough. At least it did in my head. I sat out to review the Holy Bible (*King James Version - KJV*). It was through that KJV of the Bible, that YHWH tipped me off to what I will right now call or label the Adamic/Noah/Nimrod/Babylonian/Roman Numbers System. I understand that I left out YHWH and Moses, but the involvement of those two seems rather obvious. Since we are using the words translated directly from their spiritual instructions and historical writings. After the Towel of Babel, cultures changed with languages. The evolution and the modernization of the Babel/Roman numbers structure would have expectedly taken place over time. But its basic rules are still in place today. Difference today, we only see them illustrated in their symbol forms and we never see them in words for discernment. But, that is how we find them recorded in the Holy Bible. That point is for those who will at the least, consider my witness as *possible* truth revealed.

Take a moment to review the base chart above of the total years of intellectual man. You should notice that there are four rows, with eight major column headings, containing the eight millennia. The second row is made up of the numbers representing the total of cumulative years from one to 8000. As you should see, the numbers start in the first cell at 250 with 1-250 being implied. Then the years advance in 250-year increments, until they reach the 8000th year. The third row denotes times Before Messiah's Birth (BMB) and After Messiah's Birth (AMB). BMB and AMB are my own creation for the chart; and are equivalent to the more conferrable BC or BCE and AD or CE. The years in each era is noted beneath their respective color schemes. BMB is underneath black print and grey background. AMB is underneath the red print, yellow and red background. Notice that the chart starts with the year 4000 BMB. Regardless to what the so-called expert theologians have concluded, my research determined that number to be absolutely *precise¿* **If** you do not step into one of a few potholes of disbelief on our way to 6000, we may see eye to eye at the end. Since we do not need those last two days right now, let us simply cut them off for training and teaching purposes - just for now. Then hopefully, we can make a smaller chart larger and easier to see and work with. If we end up needing them, we can easily add them back on to the chart – right? So, let us take a look below at our *"New and Improved,"* really *bigger* viewing chart of YHWH's first six millennia.

1st Millennial Day				2nd Millennial Day				3rd Millennial Day				4th Millennial Day				5th Millennial Day				6th Millennial Day			
250	500	750	1000	1250	1500	1750	2000	2250	2500	2750	3000	3250	3500	3750	4000	4250	4500	4750	5000	5250	5500	5750	6000
BMB - Before Messiah's Birth														BMB - Before Messiah's Birth	AMB - After Messiah's Birth								
4000 BMB	3750 BMB	3500 BMB	3250 BMB	3000 BMB	2750 BMB	2500 BMB	2250 BMB	2000 BMB	1750 BMB	1500 BMB	1250 BMB	1000 BMB	750 BMB	500 BMB	250 BMB	AMB 250	AMB 500	AMB 750	AMB 1000	AMB 1250	AMB 1500	AMB 1750	AMB 2000

Timothy B. Merriman

Prior to starting my research in depth, I felt somewhat isolated; when it came to my spirit as not to be a stumbling block to anyone. There are many individuals and organizations in the public that offers information which is intended to help people understand existing life. They also try to help people find what their spiritual purpose and destiny might be. That said, I am not dismissing what Yeshua stated when he warned us about if the blind is allowed to lead the blind, "*both shall fall into the ditch*" (Matthew 15:14). This is also true in our modern era. We must all be, vigilant. With the invention of the computer, development and growth of the worldwide web (*internet*), a massive amount of information has been made available and is at most of our fingertips. The only warnings I can think of at the moment are these. Make sure that any information you receive as truth, is thoroughly vetted. And, make as sure as you can that if you do not believe you know the actual truthfulness of a given answer; or if there is a possibility of you being deceived about said information, make sure as possible – not knowing – has no effect on salvation. From my Perspective, whether you know who was alive and possibly knew each other in ancient times, might be interesting; i.e. Lamech – Noah's father likely knew Adam. If we think about the possibilities of – who knew who – it could make for real stimulating discussions. Nonetheless, I do not think that it will play a significant role in whether we get into the wedding or not. I mean truly now; the demons knew the Messiah - right? (Matthew 8:29) Certainly, some of the things I have said will have some bearing on your salvation. Indeed, others most certainly will not. Choose wisely. Truly, everything I have written in **IT'S MUCH LATER THAN YOU THINK!** is meant to divinely encourage you to the way beyond. I wrote so that I may help you and myself to flee from the darkness; which is deception and wickedness.

Any and all truth is light. Any and all light helps. Here is one more thing before we move on. Any darkness that you are able to identify, whether it comes from me or some other source; it will help you to flee spiritual corruption and death. And, after I have said everything I will say inside **IT'S MUCH LATER THAN YOU THINK!** - YHWH as my witness - **The Truth** is all I pray you are blessed with - and that YHWH given gift to spot a lie; whether it is given to you intentionally; or by the accident of blind deception. Last, make no error. If spiritual truth cannot be established as truth exclusively from YHWH's word; it is and should be unquestionably labeled a lie. Come on you guys and gals, don't insult yourself. It does not take a rocket scientist to understand where **Every Spiritual Lie** originates from. (John 8:44) While you may not know his reasoning or strategy, you know **who** it is coming from. And you should know that he has a reason and a strategy. Finally know this. His ultimate strategy is intended to end with your death. If you are wise, you will <u>Flee From It</u>! Certainly, you will be better off and immeasurably blessed for your actions. I believe rejecting all things one has determined to be a lie is a strong testimony in making one's continued spiritual growth vibrant and their divine maturity without any doubt or delay, imminent. May our Eloah grant to his faithful such a blessing at this time and inspire the reader, as they read the rest of this book. I pray your study considers objectively and in proper contexts, every number we have given from the Bible's history and prophetic designation; which we were able to receive from YHWH's tender mercy, revelation and discernment. <u>In researching</u>, whatever the numbers were we had, we gave. We have determined them all to be enlightenment. We pray you do too; as together we look through what is oftentimes, the darkened glass of history and prophecy.

CHAPTER 7

FROM SHEM TO TE'-RAH

Yeshua's line – *as we understand* – is carried on by Noah's son Shem two years after the flood. (Genesis 11:10) Shem's son Arphaxad is born year 1660 or 2341 BC. Here we must pause for an unconventional, but central review study. I need you to consider objectively, what YHWH revealed to me after he instructed me to review and compare the two Messianic bloodlines in the fifth chapter and the eleventh chapter of Genesis – *its continuation after the great flood*. YHWH moved in spirit to give his "*Roman Numbers*" revelation to me, divine weight. Reading with a bit of scrutiny I was able to see in a new light, there was a subtle variation in the two declarations. In the fifth chapter of Genesis "total years" are recorded with the years of every patriarch's life. It is their number - *if you will* - how old they were when they died. I would also have you to take notice that this "total number mark" is *for no apparent reason*" missing or omitted from Moses' records in the second part of the bloodline's affirmation from Shem leading up to the birth of Te'-rah. We bear in mind or gather that it was supposedly the same person [*Moses*] who at the least oversaw to record and thus bear witness to both sections of the genealogy in only a mere six chapters or 128 years of history.

From YHWH allowing me to spiritually discern it to my viewpoint, it is well worth noting that interestingly enough, out of nowhere and for no apparent reason again it seems; with Te'-rah and the generation of Abram (*Abraham*) - *for those brief generations leading up to the Egyptian slavery* - the totality of years in the genealogies are resumed. Consider the years of Abraham and Isaac. Abraham's age was listed at 100 when Isaac was born (Genesis 21:5) and Abraham's total years at the time of his death is listed at 175. (Genesis 25:7) Also the age of Isaac when he begets Jacob (Israel) was sixty (60). (Genesis 25:26) Isaac's total age at the time of his death is listed at 180 years. (Genesis 25:28) Even Moses – who is not purported to be part of Yeshua's Messianic bloodline, even in his record is a totality of years. Moses is listed at 120. (Deuteronomy 34:7) So, why not the sons immediately after the Great Flood of Noah's day? Why is there this variance in the bloodlines? After Jacob - as far as the Holy Bible is concerned, a birth shroud covers the total years and ages of the Messianic genealogy from Jacob's generation on; with the exceptions of Joseph (Genesis 50:22) and Joshua (Joshua 24:29). Moses did not give the same genealogical pattern for sons in Genesis' eleventh chapter, as he did for sons in the fifth chapter? Again, **If Not**. **Why Not?**

Why did Moses resume these "*age totals*" from the generation of Te'-rah (*Genesis 11:32*) into Egypt? It is simple to compare the fifth chapter of Genesis with that of the eleventh chapter. Read the following Biblical texts and see, "...*and all the days that Adam lived were nine hundred and thirty years: and he died*" (Genesis 5:5). <u>Do you see it</u>? We have a total there. Recognize the point I am trying to establish here. If one had cause or need to validate in that passage (**and for the greater confirmation in this book – we do**), that only the mathematical processes of **addition** was employed there; we merely read the supporting <u>verses three and four</u> to clearly see the add process at work. <u>Notice now</u>. "*Adam lived a hundred and thirty (130) years and begat a son...and called his name Seth:*" After Seth, he lived 800 years, "...*the days of Adam after he had begotten Seth were eight hundred (800) years:*" Then Moses "<u>adds</u>" up the two, "...*all the days that Adam lived were nine hundred and thirty years*" That verse makes it clear to see that Moses was adding. 130 years plus 800 years is equal to 930 years. It was simple addition, ABC-123. On the other hand, for the after-flood bloodline witness in chapter eleven; the tallies are not as clear. And in my opinion, when we assume, we risk error. But, almost

everybody I have ever encountered, whether they were simple laypersons

or one of the vaunted theologians, most all have basically assumed that

the process of addition was at work. I confess. I was among those many

assumers for many years; before I earned my theological degrees. Truth

be told, they made no differences. No matter how smart we would like to

believe we are; YHWH has to reveal to us his truths or we will remain

blind and lost. My trek to Roman numbers absolutely was no different.

> "...it is written, Eye hath not seen, nor ear heard, neither have
> entered into the heart of man, the things which God hath
> prepared for them that love him. But God hath revealed *them*
> unto us by his Spirit: for the Spirit searcheth all things, yea, the
> deep things of God...the things of God knoweth no man, but the
> Spirit of God...we have received...the Spirit...of God; that we
> might know the things that are freely given to us of God. Which
> things also we speak, not in the words which man's wisdom
> teacheth, but which the Holy [*Spirit*] teacheth; comparing
> spiritual things with spiritual...the natural man receiveth not the
> things of the Spirit of God: for they are foolishness unto him:
> neither can he know, because they are spiritually discerned."
>
> (1st Corinthians 2:9-14)

So, when the Scripture said in Genesis 11:11, ***"Shem lived after he***

begat Arphaxad five hundred years and begat sons and daughters" the

Spirit tapped my brain and asked me why did Moses not record the totals

in years there; like he recorded in Genesis chapter five? [Granted, we can

reason out Shem's age simply by adding his 100 years of age at the time of the flood, to the one year that the flood was upon the earth, to two year later at the birth of Arphaxad and the 500 years that Shem lived after he begat Arphaxad. Their totals give us Shem's total years at the time of his death as 603 years of age. However, we cannot assume such is the same scenario with the rest of those genealogies immediately after the flood.] Review it for yourself. Do you see it? There are no totals in the years of the Patriarchs from Shem until Te'-rah. (Genesis 11:32) The Holy Spirit needed to reveal when Abram was born to Te'-rah. It is error to presume. By then the mysteries within the count (*subtraction*) had possibly already been sealed and hidden from the wicked eyes of the ensuing generations. It appears that mystery held firm up until our generations. Late into our sixth day's latter minutes, I am called to declare they have been revealed.

This was the place and time that YHWH opened my understanding to his formerly hidden truth that (*Babel*) Roman numerals had in reality been used in the Holy Scripture. Moses left off the total of the Patriarchs' years in Genesis eleven on purpose! Yes, I can prove that! Although I am not sure whether it was on purpose or not has any relevance. The fact is, most of us did not know it. And the fact remains, most of us still do not know. And what has the potential to make this situation really bad is this. A majority of the people who YHWH has revealed this Roman numeral shocker to so far, still do not believe it is true. I guess it goes back to our sometimes arrogant and narcissistic attitudes. That being, we sometimes think our modern generations are the only really smart ones. We claim we are smarter, because of our modern technologies and cool inventions. Whether any will go with my *premise* or not, it does not matter. But, before you shoot me down completely as being false; ask yourself a few ***thought-provoking*** questions of debate in the possible context as to <u>what was meant</u> and <u>how was it done</u>.

1. "When YHWH says a book is sealed to the learned and the unlearned (Isaiah 29:11-12).

2. How does a prophet respond in actions when YHWH tells him to, "*shut up the words, and seal the book?*" (Daniel 12:4).

3. What did YHWH do to scripture when he declared, "*the words are closed up and sealed till the time of the end?*" (Daniel 12:9).

4. What methods does an Apostle employ to come into compliance when instructed by The Angel of YHWH, "*Seal up those things which the seven thunders uttered, and write them not?*" (Revelation 10:4) [Meaning in this case - put the message of the words in the book, but do not write the words per bedim. Remember, Yochanan was first told to write what he saw (*and heard*) down; then send it to the seven churches in Asia (Revelation 1:1-11).

5. His book is called ***Revelation***; which means ***to reveal***. But in case Apostle Yochanan did not completely understand and to keep him from sealing up the entire book; the supposed angel, who turned out to be one of his unidentified, "*fellow servant, and of [his] brethren the prophets*" (*A talk for another time perhaps*), instructs

Yochanan on the overall matter, *"Seal not the sayings of the prophecy of this book"* (Revelation 22:10).

Look, all I am implying is this. Why could not the term, *"seal up"* very well include what we might call *misdirectional* plays in the forms of *misdirectional* words or phrases and so on. So that only the writer and to whom he chose to revealed his secrets keys to, would understand! Is this so unreasonable? Is my hypothesis so outlandish that it does not deserve serious consideration? I do not think so. While my narrative to *"seal up"* may not be that spot on, I am more than convinced it is because YHWH wanted Moses to stymie the ability of wicked men to calculate out what I would term as their accurate accounting of time; that YHWH instructed Moses to mix in the use of Roman numbers in the second genealogy. That is, until such time in YHWH's plans that he would reveal it again. I believe this <u>was done</u>; to offer the ability for determining correct time to the part of his saints who he extended its wisdom to. It would also be the fulfillment of <u>Daniel's</u> prophecy in his <u>12th chapter</u>. For the wise to know how close to the end they were truly living. For those who have enough faith to believe it, I will declare to you that this knowledge is reserved only for those who are developing within themselves, **the Absolute Love of the truth**. That is <u>absolutely</u> required. That is, if we want a real chance to meet, greet and to go into the wedding feast with the Messiah on his return. You see now, if Moses had recorded the "**totals**" number for the

Patriarchs in that eleventh chapter of Genesis, every literate person on the earth - *whether wicked or wise* - would have been able to **_unseal_** and **_easily discern_** that which would have been made obvious in the giving of their tallies. It was **subtraction** that was in play during the second listing of the genealogies. That is, if YHWH had instructed Moses to use that same pattern in the eleventh chapter, as he did in the fifth chapter. In the *nullification* of his **subtraction seal**, I am sure Moses would have used, and had us read the following words, just as I have typed them.

> "And Arphaxad lived five and thirty years, and begat Salah: And Arphaxad lived after he begat Salah four hundred and three (403) years, and begat many sons and daughters: and all the days of Arphaxad were four hundred twenty and eight (428) years: and he died." (*Revealing Moses subtracted the five from the thirty*)

...or to the contrary of my claim, Moses would have said this.

> "...and all the days of Arphaxad were four hundred thirty and eight (438) years: and he died." (*Meaning Moses added the five and the thirty*)

However, Moses did in fact, write neither. I say again. **MOSES DID NOT ACTUALLY WRITE EITHER!** Because YHWH did not inspire Moses to write either phrase, it is absolutely understandable why every person I have discussed this issue with, stands with the more prominent biblical theologians – saying there is no credible reason to believe that Moses was hiding anything; and especially not, that he was subtracting rather than adding; and here I am with just a claim "God revealed!" Mine may not be a compelling case. But, I thought this Roman Number thing might be a hard sale. Particularly in view of the thousands of people alive today who take liberty to speak in the name of YHWH who oppose me. I just love how they throw out that discrediting phrase at me, "No credible reason." I encourage everyone to bear me out to the end. My standing is still firm as far as my proof goes. As far as whether Moses was adding or subtracting, my claim is that YHWH has revealed to me which. When Moses recorded, "*Arphaxad lived five and thirty years*" (Genesis 11:12), he was subtracting that five from the thirty base in true Roman Numeral fashion. So then for all of our far into the future wicked generations, that originally simple Babel or Roman Numbers concept, developed into the formidable seal and hidden component of "***minus***" that it is today; rather than our ***generally*** presumed "***adding***" process; which is inspired by the spiritual urge of our Satanic greed. So the age when Arphaxad, "*begat Sa'-lah*" was the age of twenty-five (25), rather than thirty-five (35); as it has been believed for likely hundreds - perhaps thousands of years.

If one accepts this, it should become transparent in reasoning why Moses under YHWH's instructions, omitted the total age numbers of the chapter eleven Patriarchs. Regardless to whether you can receive this as an eye-opening truth or not - keep reading. Hopefully, the proof of it will come to you by the end. Nevertheless, for instruction purposes, we will continue from Shem to Te'-rah, using the Roman numbers system. If we have been taking notes in our walk, we know according to our present count, we are in Adamic year 1660 or 2341 BC. And, we are at the birth of Shem's son, Arphaxad. Follow closely. View the second genealogy carefully. Take good notice in those subtle places where it is critical for accurate time-keeping - where the Roman Numeral concept is utilized. Because those key scripture were written in such a manner; in effect, no one could come provable close to revealing *what time we are really in and how much time we have left*; until our more modern times with their mass printing of the Holy Scriptures and perhaps other holy manuscripts.

This is YHWH's Roman Numeral revelations. Read and understand. Arphaxad lived, *"five and thirty years"* or (five subtracted from thirty); which is twenty-five (25) and begat Salah. Salah lived, *"thirty years"* (30) (Self-evident) and begat Eber. Eber lived, *"four and thirty years"* or (four subtracted from thirty); which is twenty-six (26) and begat Peleg. Peleg lived, *"thirty years"* (30), (Again – this is self-evident) and begat Reu. Reu lived, *"two and thirty years"* or (two subtracted from thirty); which is twenty-eight (28) and begat Serug. Serug lived, *"thirty years"* (30), (Self-evident) and begat Nahor. And Nahor lived *"nine and twenty years"* or (nine subtracted from twenty) which is eleven (11), and begat

Te'-rah. (Genesis 11:12-25) There are ninety (90) years in the Roman numeral count (*25, 26, 28 and 11 = 90*); and there are ninety (90) years in the standard addition count (*30, 30 and 30 = 90*). This is for the total of 180 years.

"**Eleven¿**" I admit that last Roman Number was problematic for me. I doubted my, "*Roman Number hypothesis¿*" now; and what spirit was actually speaking to me. If Nahor was really only eleven years old, was he even old enough yet to be able to impregnate a fully mature woman? David said, "*O taste and see that the Lord is good: blessed is the man that trusteth in him*" (Psalms 34:8). It was about then YHWH told me, I might try following some of the same advice I am "*occasionally,*" in my sanctimonious attitude, admonishing others to do. YHWH said, "*Prove it. – Prove all things.*" If it is possible and probable, walk on with it, by faith. So that is what I did. I researched the matter on the earliest age that a young man could impregnate a woman. I found out according to our modern medical science, the time was right about eleven to twelve years of age. Theoretically, it could be as low as age nine (9) (kidshealth.org). The following is presented as evidence in an excerpt from a modern-day example of a young man impregnating a woman and/or fathering a baby. While in our present time, it is considered a sexual crime of deviancy. In generations following the flood, it was most likely or may have been considered an act of survival. And in more desperate times, it might have been considered the family's assurance, or at the least its insurance of the continuation of family, tribal or Patriarchal bloodlines.

11-year-old Auckland boy fathers child

"A woman is to appear in court after she gave birth to a child with a primary school aged boy. A Child, Youth and Family Services spokesperson today confirmed CYFS was involved with the case and the 36 year old woman was facing criminal charges. However, because of the sensitivities around the case CYFS would not confirm details or even the charges the woman faces. The boy, from Auckland [*New Zealand*], is understood to have been 11 when the woman had sex with him and is now 12. It is understood the boy was friends with the woman's son. The woman coerced the boy into repeated sexual encounters over a period of time before becoming pregnant." (Gadd, D. 2013)

I simply thought I needed to show this information to readers; like I had to show it to myself - when I was initially being directed by YHWH. It should satisfy most. So then let us add to the base years, those of Shem to Te'-rah. From our cumulative base of 1660 (*2341 BC*), we just add on Arphaxad's 25 years, Salah's 30 years, Eber's 26 years, Peleg's 30 years, Reu's 28 years, Serug's 30 years, Nahor's 11 years and also add Te'-rah's 70 years (Genesis 11:26). We come to the year 1910 or 2091 BC.

Now we come to that place in Holy Bible history, where my stance opposing the premise regarding Noah having triplets in Shem, Ham and Japheth, was meant to soften up any dogmatism that Te'-rah had triplets in his sons Abram, Nahor and Haran. Which by the way of discovery and perspective; I contend this **was not** their case at all. Now, here we find

ourselves again, it seems. We have this aberration. It could be described

as a biblical seal. That is, when the Holy Bible cites the years in age of

Te'-rah with his sons Abram, Nahor, and Haran. It is a misread, a critical

misunderstanding and the presumption of a second set of biblical triplets.

However, surface appearances are not always the reality underneath. As

it often allows for people to believe what they will at the outset. With an

objective mind, this might become evident as we read over that surface

from the translated manuscript (*The Holy Bible*); but discern from the

deep - *the Holy Spirit willing* - concerning the triplet viewpoint. Let us

see if we can look close and gain some clarity concerning the situation

behind Abram and the continuation of the Messianic bloodline. For his

light of insight to shine into my darkened mind, YHWH put a pin in; and

stopped me where I was at his Adamic year 1910 or 2091 BC. YHWH

began to build other parts of my spiritual jig-saw picture. To be honest,

the spiritual pathways I actually walked are too complicated in my mind;

and I do not have that true narrative ability to articulate them in the way I

would need to, in order to walk you along the same trails as YHWH had

me to travel. I can only say this. Follow along with me the best you can;

and then ask YHWH to please fill in any blank spaces I by my spiritual

incompetency might leave bare to a free imagination. If you can hold to any of the things I say, I trust YHWH to set you on a path that best suits your spiritual fight and race. If like me, you hit a few dark spots with some of the information in this book, I have only the best hopes for your patience and understanding; as I continue the effort to walk you through the biblical history and the night of prophecy with YHWH's divine light.

YHWH coached me as far as how I was to proceed. However, my mind was darkened a bit by several traditions and elements of modern *"spiritualized"* Christianity, as it exist and functions today. It was similar to that of the divine mystery surrounding Yeshua preaching and teaching. The people heard it, but they could not understand it. The people saw it, but they could not perceive it. I wanted, or at the least, I thought I wanted to understand and perceive. I even knew and understood YHWH's truth was available to understand and perceive; sitting right here in front of my face. Nevertheless, I had to confess to YHWH. I could not see His truth, unless He wanted me to see it. It was similar to that of a rocket scientist explaining to the base mindset concerning the complicated mathematical calculations of going to the moon or deeper space travel to Mars, or even someplace further. You hear it. But then again, **You don't hear it**. That was somewhat the way it was when YHWH's Spirit was teaching me on this subject of time. So believe it or not, this is what YHWH told me to do. Keep on going with it. So that is what I did. YHWH had made me to recognize that something was off, by putting in my spirit an uneasiness surrounding the age of Te'-rah with the birth of Abram; and his brothers Haran and Nahor. I heard all of what YHWH was saying; however at that time, I just did not have the spiritual roots for a discerning foundation to understand YHWH's words I was hearing. I suppose that is why YHWH instructed me just to continue. YHWH had to build my foundation. I was somewhat encouraged when YHWH reminded me, **even Daniel** did not understand everything that he was shown and told about. (Daniel 12:8) Absolutely, I am not in the same league with a Daniel, in terms of his knowledge, understanding and wisdom. But, I also know a Daniel would have no idea what to do with our "modern technology." It is a different knowledge for a different people. While Daniel would not be expected to "*Instantly Engage*" with our hi-tech toys and gadgets; certainly he could learn. Even as we at some point had to learn. Granted, it is a technology that we grew up with. Though we must contend for the ancient truths of YHWH today (Jude, 3); because our time and cultures are so far apart. In a similar sense, YHWH's wisdom, knowledge and understanding, though "*a little thin*" in our day; we are still "*without excuse*" (Romans 1:18-25).

Even some 2500 years after Daniel, we should - **all of us** - be much more familiar with YHWH's word than most of us are. This is obviously, not the case with our familiarity. I would like to think that we could have been, had it not been for our lack of belief and brazen sin. All the same, our situation and circumstance regarding our sins, is what it is. And, we have all played our parts, in our own spiritual demise. I can give you no logical reason why YHWH has chosen me to relay this portion of his knowledge and understanding to you and the world. But here I am. Here you are. So then, we must continue on to whatever end we come. During our walk through biblical history and prophetic time I hope you are being patient with me and prayerful to our Eloah that YHWH, in his mercy and grace, will ordain for us that we should see more revelations of his truth, discern their places in our spiritual lives; therewith incorporate them into our daily arsenal, for our own personal spiritual warfare. If we differ on an issue, the cause may just be we are at different spiritual growth places. Who knows, we could well be witnessing to the same truth, merely from a different angle. We do not have to hate each other or betray each other and call each other awful names. Minimally, we in our faith need to just keep going with it. Until YHWH reveals to us the deeper understandings we need to perhaps come together as one. If that be his will.

> "For we wrestle not against flesh and blood, but against principalities, against powers, against the rulers of the darkness of this world, against spiritual wickedness in high *places.* Wherefore take unto you the whole armor of God, that ye may be able to withstand in the evil day, and having done all, to stand" (Ephesians 6:12-13).

CHAPTER 8

MY ISAAC SHIFT AND TE'-RAH ERROR

In an abstract way, given the heading of his section, it sounds like I was trying to do some sort of a spiritual dance of deception with the devil or something. In truth, on a more serious note, that is sort of what it felt like I was doing. Not knowing a thing can many times make people feel like they are waltzing in deception with a demon. One would think all we as "believers" needed to do, was read the Holy Bible. Then things would change for the better. If we believed it and lived by it. Sadly, the truth is; most would be shocked, if they knew the condition of the people's ability to read - right here in America. Maybe that is why so many of us have so much trouble reading, understanding and therefore believing the Bible.

"...Approximately 32 million adults in the United States can't read, according to the U.S. Department of Education and the National Institute of Literacy. And, the Organization for

Economic Cooperation and Development found that 50 percent of U.S. adults cannot read a book written at an eighth-grade level... If you are reading this, then by definition you don't have a problem that more than 20 percent of the adults in the nation's capital struggle with every day: illiteracy" (Strauss, V., 2016).

Nonetheless, when it comes to reading and understanding the Holy Bible, even the so-called "literate person" seems to have trouble discerning its truths. So then, I hope you can appreciate why I, sometimes we, all may need to re-ad and re-re-ad, re-cant and re-pent, if needed. For me at least, when re-ading the Holy Bible, the **"Re"** tool is one of my most valuable resources. So, when YHWH's Holy Spirit instructed me to pause at his Adamic Hebrew year of 1910 or 2091 BC; I was a bit fretful. But, I was not yet in a spiritual panic. So, let us continue on from there – shall we?

We are in the year 1910 or 2091 BC. Te'-rah is seventy. And, if we can presume Abram is just now being born we will move forward; unless YHWH shows something different. Remember, I am just showing you as closely as I can remember, the way YHWH lead me in my walk through time. So, as the Messianic bloodline moves forward; Abram (*Who would later become Abraham*) was at 100 years of age when Sarah gave birth to Isaac; and Isaac was **forty (40) years old** (Genesis 25:20-21), when he begat Jacob (*Who later became Israel*). I know – I know. I misread it. Give me a break! I am merely trying to show you the paths that YHWH walked me along on my journey to deeper insights of his hidden truths. If you read over the following - late at night into the early morning, tired, sleepy and after all the numbers had started to run together - what might you have thought?

> "And Isaac was forty years old when he took Rebekah to wife, the daughter of Bethuel the Syrian of Padan-aram, the sister to Laban the Syrian. And Isaac entreated the Lord for his wife, because she was barren: and the Lord was entreated of him, and Rebekah his wife conceived" (Genesis 25:20-21).

I am showing you this to demonstrate how YHWH can allow one to proceed on forward, and to not know a thing – *while he builds one the spiritual foundation* – in order for one to be able to receive the truth of that thing at a later date. I am simply saying. That is what happened to me. So before we go forth speaking and determining who is going to hell and who is not, *based on whether they agree with us or not*; know in my opinion, that is spiritually judgmental and premature. I feel if a particular individual is making every effort, in all humbleness, to understand and to live accordingly, to YHWH's Word of Truth; YHWH knows and he will judge justly; whether you and I are on the same page with that person or not - Capeesh? I say it is a good thing many of us will not be judging in the judgment. If that were the case, your so-called *"heaven"* would be an awfully lonely place for us. That is enough of that. We will now walk forward in my present error. Because, that is the way YHWH led me.

Jacob was 130 years old when he went down into Egypt. When we add to the current year of 1910 and we subtract from 2091 BC, the totality of Abraham's 100 years, **Isaac's 40** years and Jacob's 130 years (Genesis 21:5, 25:20 & 47:7-9), we march forward in time to the Adamic year of 2180 and count down to the year 1820 BC. If you want, use terms BCE/CE. **My Disclaimer**: Isaac was in fact, **60 years old**, when he begat Jacob (Genesis 25:26); but you have already been given wind of that shift. The Holy Spirit will prove us out on that matter before too long. Just notate it. Also know, now that Israel is in Egypt, and will eventually be put into slavery – those Egyptians deciding to, "*deal wisely with them*" (Exodus 1:10); their Patriarchal record-keeping would now tend to suffer somewhat. Israel's Egyptian slavery would no longer allow for a thorough record-keeping of the time through the Messianic bloodline. Of course this is only true as far as I understand, as far as the Bible's records of time are concerned. Because of the Egyptian slavery, we are forced to use other means to keep track of time. These other means/methods must help us to eventually account for and count off as much time from the historical and prophetic calendar as possible. And, the Bible from my perspective, does just that. It provides us with those believable and accurate measures of time. At least I believe so. Over time as you read this book, I have every confidence that you will believe too. And you have my permission to consider that - a challenge!

CHAPTER 9

FREEDOM, JUDGES AND KINGS

Where we left off, according to our last count, we were at the year 2180. When we do the corresponding BC/AD dates, we find ourselves at year 1821 BC (*Before Christ*). Jacob and all of his children have just gone down into Egypt. Bible students understand Joseph was already there. Things went well at first. However, some thirty years later, with Joseph's retirement, the death of the old Pharaoh and the ascent of a new Pharaoh, things began to grow sour. The generation later (*40 years*) after the death of Joseph's brothers, their generation and even Joseph himself, another Pharaoh ascended the throne that did not know Joseph, nor did he respect his accomplishments or what he did for Egypt. Not long after, under that new Pharaoh and with a new generation of Egyptians, slavery ensued and things just got *bitter*. (Exodus 1:13-14) According to biblical prophecy, Israel was in abject slavery for 400 years. (Genesis 15:13) Israel was in Egypt for a total of 430 years. Most all of us know that the Children of Israel departed from Egypt under Moses when the era of the Judges began. (Genesis 18th chapter) Judges cover Israel's forty years in the wilderness and the next 410 years after they had entered into the Promised Land. In fact, Judges lasted 450 years; as did the **net** years of kings. Judges to kings has an overlap time with Samuel, Sampson, Saul, Ish-bosheth and the first fourteen (14) years of King David's reign. True Kings began in 3043 (*958 BC*) with Saul when the Judges were still very much prominent. It was Israel's final judge of prominence Sampson and he was in the third year of his twenty-year term. Some find that hard to believe. Others never thought about it. Maybe that is why Eloah had me write, to evoke, "***Never-thought***."

Years after David's sin *with Bathsheba*, with the death of Israel's last great judge in Sampson and arguably with the birth of Solomon, the **net** years of kings began. The **net** years of kings from the death of Sampson until the desolation of the first temple raised by King Solomon lasted **450 years**. I carried out what I felt like was an exhaustive biblical research and accounting of both those eras. And even though I am confident in my findings; to satisfy any detractors, I will say it is possible an error could have been made. I will also say, I invite critics and anybody else as far as that matter goes, who would find fault with my lecture and distrust my findings, they are very much more than welcome to examine the biblical record for themselves. Upon such an effort, should anyone find fault with my conclusions; please feel free and be so kind as to write me with your information for my own personal review. In doing so; if I can determine the validity of your critical review, I can acknowledge my false findings published in error, but truly unintentionally. (*Contact information - p. xv*)

Now where were we? Oh yes. We are in the year 2180 or 1821 BC. Israel has just moved down to Egypt. In order for us to carry on with our walk through the time of intellectual man, we will have to add the years we have just discussed. When we add on the Egyptian slavery years of 430, the wilderness travels of forty (40) years, the 410 years of judges and **450 net** years of kings to 2180 (1821 BC). We find ourselves at the beginning of YHWH's Adamic year 3510 or 491 BC. It is the collapse of Jerusalem "*on the ninth day of the fourth month*" (2nd Kings 25:3) and "*in the fifth month, on the seventh day of the month*" (Verses 8-10) the city's defense (wall) is torn down and YHWH's temple is burnt to the ground. This desolation was carried out in a siege and violent attack by the then *ruthless* King Nebuchadnezzar of Babylon. I meant to say this earlier. If you feel it is more appropriate for you to use BCE/CE dates, feel free to do so. BC and AD are merely my preferences inside this book. That said;

also know that I have provided for your viewing the chronological record covering that full period and terms of the Judges; with servitude and liberation years listed from the Bible. I started from the exodus, which is Adamic year 2610 – corresponding with 1391 BC. Please take notice here. From YHWH's Adamic Hebrew year of 2180 or 1821 BC, when we add on the 430 years of the Egyptian slavery period, we come to that year; which is my exodus notation. That is the true Hebrew year 2610 or 1391 BC. So then, let us continue with the affirmation of the numbers in our effort to account/recount the complete witness of biblical history and its future prophetic times. I want to remind everybody to continue taking good notes. This is so if you want to, you can do a review at any time. Now from 2610 (*1391 BC*) we add on or account for the following years.

1. **The Exodus**/time in the wilderness (*Exodus 16:35*). .... **40 years**
   Judges begins in the wilderness (Exodus 18:13-26)

2. Chushan-rishathaim / Mesopotamia - Served (Judges 3:7-8).... **8 years**

3. **Judge Othniel** - The land had rest (Judges 3:9)..................... **40 years**

4. King Eglon of Moab - Served (Judges 3:12-14)..................... **18 years**

5. **Judge Ehud** - The land had rest (Judges 3:15-30)................. **80 years**

6. Jabin king of Canaan - Mightily Oppressed (Judges 4:1-3) .... **20 years**

7. **Judge Deborah** - The land had rest (Judges 4:1 - 5:31) .... **40 years**

8. The Midianites - Prevailed against Israel in war (Judges 6:1)... **7 years**

9. **Judge Gideon** - The country in quietness (Judges 8:28) .... **40 years**

10. Abimelech - Reign of whoredom (*Judges 9:22*).....................3 **years**

11. Judge Tola - Defender (*Judges 10:1-2*)...............................23 **years**

12. Judge Jair - Judged (*Judges 10:3*)..22 **years**

13. The Philistines - Oppressed (*Judges 10:6-8*)..........................18 **years**

14. Judge Jephthah - Defender (*Judges 11:29 - 12:7*) ....6 **years**

15. Judge Ibzan - (*Judges 12:9*)..7 **years**

16. Judge Elon - (*Judges 12:11*)..10 **years**

17. Judge Abdon - (*Judges 12:13-14*)...8 **years**

18. The Philistines - Oppressed (*Judges 13:1*) ....40 **years**

19. Judge Sampson - (*Judges 13:25 - 16:31*)..............................20 **years**

Total years of Judges .... **450 years**

Because we are dealing with two nations, the Northern Kingdom of Israel and the Southern Kingdom of Judah; Kings was a much more complex chronological challenge than Judges. While I was looking for the chronological link from year 3060 (941 BC) into the future; I came to what I saw as an impasse. **I could not find a connection date**. I could not find a date for King Saul's birth. I could not initially find the date for King David's birth. I could not even find the date for Samuel's birth. The Bible reveals to us David's age when he became **The King** and how long his reign was. The Bible tells us how long David's reign was in Hebron and it tells us how long he reigned in Jerusalem also. (2nd Samuel 5:4-5)

Also because of biblical vagueness, I could not determine when Solomon was born. I also could not confirm - without reasonable debate - what age Solomon was when he ascended to the throne of Israel. I believe that my dates are extremely close. But in the end, I must admit a small part of it was my guesswork. I was determined not to be tempted to use the more confusing theologians' and historians' routes. I wanted YHWH to allow me to go as far as he would, by using only the biblical record. When I hit what I felt was a biblical brick wall. I got a bit worried. And for a little while, I thought the end of Judges was it. It, as far as my book being able to reasonably support the idea that we can know *what time it really is and how much time we have left*.

To make what was for me a complex, but intriguing journey, a bit simpler for you; let me say this. I suppose YHWH did not need to take me through the longer route of the judges. However, in review of what I learned, I suspect for a clearer jig-saw picture and easier remembrance; YHWH wanted me to know judges ended after exactly **450 years**. Then from judges to the destruction of the first temple was exactly **450 years**. That is easier for people to keep in mind, than all of the numbers I used; when I counted out on paper the passage of time during the two periods. However, the status of knowing or thinking you know a thing and being able to reasonably prove it, are two wild animals, difficult to tame. To be honest, I believe YHWH had me running to and fro, all over the Bible; looking to find some specific text that would give me an indication as to when Samuel, Saul, David or Solomon was born, was for my training. As time has progressed and my divine learning has increased the Holy Spirit has allowed me to recognize, some omissions are by design. One could deduce the obscurity in knowing the age was especially important with a young king. As it was in the case of Solomon. Had Solomon's enemies knew of his young age and his total lack of war experience, things might not have gone as well - *in theory* - as it related to his long and prosperous reign. Even Solomon himself realized his "*state of affairs*" as far as his "*inexperience*" was concerned, when he testified as much to it. (1st Kings 3:7-8) So it was reasonably easy for me to conclude that the age of King Solomon was likely kept back from the eyes of the broader public; until such time he would be able to hold his own among the more treacherous entities and elements in, and around his newly acquired kingdom. I still believe there are many insights and revelations - *unknown at this time by yours truly* - that remain to be learned. It is possible I am *similarly* in this way to Yeshua's disciples not long before his crucifixion. Yeshua said to them, "*I have yet many things to say unto you, but ye cannot bear them now*" (John 16:12). My eyes are no longer as dim to Bible truth as they were before. So note; although not without debate, I am comfortably sure

King David was born in Adamic year 3016 (*985 BC*). It is also *somewhat* likely that King Solomon was born in the Adamic year of 3060 (*941 BC*). Other studies could make these dates and witnesses of some significance.

I have already stated it. But, what had to be the most sobering of the new perspectives in light of the Holy Bible's silence on the matter; is that interesting truth I learned from my study of the times during judges and kings. That is, there is a significant overlapping of the two periods. What I mean is, the Seer Samuel, King Saul, King David and King Ish-bosheth (*He ruled the northern Kingdom of Israel briefly for two years before his assassination, while David only ruled the southern kingdom of Judah*) all four likely knew Sampson. Sampson was actually judging Israel during the **three years reign** of King Saul and the **first fourteen years** of King David's reign, according to biblical revelations. And from me, the Bible was careful to hide it. But most likely, Solomon was about five and thirty (25) to three and thirty (27) years old, when he ascended to the throne of Israel (*In my tally, Roman Number subtraction is at work*). I was also able to note, during 3044-3060 or 957-941 BC of Israelite history, there existed simultaneously Kings (*Saul, David & Ish-bosheth*) and Judges (*Sampson*). The truth is, when YHWH showed me what he did, I was forced to consider all of these things. I was unsure what I was looking at. Because, I had never heard of anyone else, saying these things from such an angle. Personally, I find it bizarre how we as people oftentimes react when it comes to the possibility of controversial, or debatable, **"<u>NEW</u>"** knowledge; when there is no one else espousing it. You would think, the person (*myself in this particular instance*) would understand the principle of the term, **"<u>NEW</u>."** But, there I was; doubting what it was that I was so clearly looking at. I was afraid how my critics might react. I expect I was more afraid that they would prove me wrong. In case you did not know; it is a whole lot easier to tear most things down, than to build them up. I was afraid of being torn down spiritually. But in truth, that is how we learn. That is, if we are not too afraid of being torn down and having to build over again. We might end up needing to rebuild a meaningful part of our spiritual underpinnings. From personal spiritual experience, I can testify. That is faith-shaking terrifying. If you have never had to discard a long-held doctrine after you found it was error; but prior, to you <u>believed</u> the Holy Spirit had revealed it as <u>Truth</u>; you might be one of the few and the proud. Hey! You might even be a Marine! NO? But seriously, I think most of us have done that; or at the least, something similar to that. By this time, I was beginning to get over my, *"might be wrong syndrome."* I was surely determined to put what I contend YHWH has revealed to me, on the line. I am okay to let readers and the critics judge it - good or bad.

However, I will not deny it. I really wanted to know what years were

David and Solomon truly born. For a long time, I did not think I could know. After a truly exhausting study over the years of Samuel, Saul, Ish-bosheth (*Saul's son*), David and Solomon (*David's son*), I was really only able to establish what I would critically describe as debatable and controversial conclusions. And, with all of the controversial things I have already said in this book; I was pretty confident, that type of win was not going to fly with most of the haters and actually fair-minded detractors. I was feeling a little despondent about that time. I did not see the pathway forward. That is when YHWH gave me the "**big break-through**" on my impasse. As it turned out, I did not need to know the exact dates of David and Solomon's birth. I did not need to know how old he was – *in the case of Solomon* – when he ascended to the throne of Israel. I did not need to know any of those "**unknowns**" I had for any of the persons in question. As I said before, YHWH took me, "***The Long Route***" to help me in developing his spiritual jig-saw picture inside my mind. And, it has absolutely helped me, in the long run. Perhaps one day, YHWH will take me back and reveal to me exact dates for the things I yet have questions about. Far as this book's focus, I do not need that knowledge to gain the understanding of *what time it really is and how much time we have left*. I merely needed to know and understand, what the Holy Bible ultimately provided. That was an exhaustive record of all of the kings of Judah from

Solomon's forth year, when he began to build YHWH's house, until the destruction of the same. <u>That record is absolutely inside the Holy Bible</u>! Only thing, along with the record we needed a chronological year to date match: i.e. Ahaz's reign began in YHWH's Adamic year 3363 (638 BC). Such a record was needed in order for us to continue our <u>chronological walk</u> in Bible history with accuracy. As I argue, we have done so far – in accounting for our, declared dates. Understand though, the kings' line of **True Israel (<u>The 10 Northern Tribes</u>)**, was lost to the eyes of history in infamous fashion. They became the prophetic victim of displacement and attempted disbanding by the Assyrians. With Assyria's fall, Israel further experienced ruin in YHWH's fated hostile times of, <u>2nd Kings 17:21-23</u>.

YHWH showed to me what it was that I truly needed to know in his revealing fashion. And, most Bible students will likely know this route. However, when the mind is so focused on the numbers of time, it is easy to get lost or overlook those simple things recorded in the biblical record. That is kind of what I did in this instance. Mercifully, YHWH helped me get where I needed to go. Even if you are not a Holy Bible student, you need not have any worries. I am going to show you; that revealed route. That invaluable chronological time anchor in history, is exact in its years.

> "...it came to pass in <u>the four hundred and eightieth</u> (480) year after the children of Israel were come out of the land of Egypt, <u>in the fourth (4th) year of Solomon's reign over Israel</u>, in the month Zif, which *is* the second month, that <u>he</u> [*Solomon*] <u>began to build</u>

the house of the Lord" (1st Kings 6:1).

There it is! That was all we needed to get pass the impasse and take a giant step forward through biblical history. In case one cannot see it. Let me explain it in detail. We have the date of the exodus. That occurred in Adamic year (*From year one when Adam was created*) 2610 or 1391 BC. From there, we simply count forward 480 years; and, we come to the Adamic year of 3090 and 911 years BC. We are back on track! As I said at the start of this book, most of our walk through time simply involves elementary mathematics. All of the time leading up to the destruction of the first temple, in my study of that count, is meticulously recorded in the Holy Bible. The Bible speaks in precise fashion as it switches back and forth from the Northern Kingdom of Israel to the Southern Kingdom of Judah. That is, when it came to when or who was ruling in one kingdom when another king was ruling the other kingdom. But, after the Assyrians carried away Israel (*The Northern Kingdom*); and they were lost to the view of world history - *out of the eyesight of carnal mankind* - the Holy Bible continues with decipherable language; revealing Judah's kings and their time in years leading up until its last king Mattaniah's overthrow by Nebuchadnezzar's Babylonian siege. To be precise, thirty-six (36) years later, with the end of Solomon's reign (*Solomon reigned was a total of forty [40] years; and those 480 years after Israel's Exodus from Egypt in the Adamic year of 2610 is witnessed by your Holy Bible to be the fourth year of King Solomon's reign*); <u>there is that witness in the Holy Bible's records</u>. There were 384 years to go before we came to Judah's infamous Jerusalem and First Temple destructions; which takes us forward into the Adamic year of 3510. We have said this before - but our proof from the Bible might have been viewed as "**_suspect_**." We can now state with good faith that the destruction of YHWH's first temple took place in the fifth month of Adamic year 3510/491 BC. I find this knowledge exciting now, but not then. Because then, I did not know what significance it was that the date carried - if any. I did not know where I would end up Bible wise. I was simply going along for the ride of my life. Recall, according to my, "*hypothesis¿*" - *if you will* - I only have 6000 years in which to work with. If I go past that mark, in my accounting and current understanding, I call my Messiah Yeshua a liar. And absolutely, my Eloah forbid any such unsavory scenarios.

CHAPTER 10

THE BABYLONIAN STINT

What do you think so far? That is, as far as me claiming that I have a wholly Holy Bible based, factually correct account, of biblical history to this point. Based on all of our supposed to be kept notes, do you feel I am even close? Forget what everyone else might think. What do you think in your own heart? Come on guys. I have not really asked for you to believe anything, "*Outrageous!*" - at least - not yet. That is, as far as the numbers themselves are concerned. If anybody runs into what they may perceive to be potential doctrinal matters, if you feel you must and if you feel you can, push them off to the side in favor of the numbers of time. After all, they are the main focus of this book. In their contexts and to their points, I have only asked my readers to consider the acceptance of three things. Just in case you have been wondering. In my case, I can accept the term "hypothetical," in order to tune down offense - if we must. Then perhaps, the odds are better in my favor as it relates to an ability to possibly prove any one or perhaps all of my *revelations* to readers as truth from YHWH. Like I said, there are only three things thus far and the first two are just reminders of things any believer <u>should</u> already be able to accept as true.

1) Let YHWH (*The Holy Scripture – the Bible*) be true and <u>every man</u> (That means you, me, theologians, historians, rabbis, evangelists, the Doctors of divinity, your brother, sister, your daddy and your momma - whomever) a liar. Do not forget what Messiah Yeshua declares. "*He that loveth father or mother more than me is not worthy of me: and he that loveth son or daughter more than me is not worthy of me*" (Matthew 10:37) & (Romans 3:4).

2) Even though, **I do not think** it is of an absolute necessity; I have asked you to consider my assertion or if you will, my "*hypothesis*" to the possibility that Shem, Ham and Japheth; also Abram, Nahor, and Haran were not triplets. That is, unless you never thought that they were from the start. Anyway, if you still suppose they are, no worries either way. You could review, "*From Adam to the Flood.*"

I do not have to suppose on the next identification. <u>To this point</u> my third call-on for you to consider as true is – "**The Big One**" – <u>To this point</u>.

3) I have asked you to recognize from my *insights*, **written** Roman numerals were used four times in the genealogy after, <u>The Flood</u>. Possibly and in my opinion, ***likely*** to help ***seal up*** the accurate knowledge of time. (Genesis 11th chapter) <u>Special Note</u>: *YHWH revealing, I was able to discern Genesis is not the solo account.*

If you kept good notes you may noticed. I have only saved (*reserved*) in theory, <u>forty (40) years</u> of time. You might ask, "What is the big deal? Why is the third (3rd) "*insight*" so important to you?" Or, "Is there a dogmatic bone of contention here?" Do not bite the messenger. I am just showing you the route I claim YHWH took me the best I can. There is no direct harm done to me, if you do not believe me. So please, continue to try and enjoy this walk as much as you can. And, like I said before; if anyone perceives any doctrinal miscues or insults, if at all possible, push them off to the side for the numbers sake. Because whether you believe nothing else in this book, you can trust this. **It's Much Later Than You Think!** I pray that the numbers will prove themselves out invariably and undeniably; or at the least *"reasonably so"* by the end of this book.

Let us think about this. In the genealogy after the flood, we have the four instances where we used the Roman Numeral concept. It was with Arphaxad's <u>five and thirty years</u> (we saved ten [10] years), in Eber's <u>four and thirty years</u> (we saved eight [8] years), Reu's <u>two and thirty years</u>, (we saved four [4] years) and last, Nahor's <u>nine and twenty years</u> (where we saved eighteen [18] years). *In our modern time, one can see why they would keep his youth under wraps.* That makes a total of forty (40) years. <u>My read error between Isaac and Jacob causes a twenty year discrepancy</u>. Please bear with my mind's meltdown. Trust me when I say this. YHWH will save the integrity of my count ahead. The grand total of years saved in time to this point is **a very significant forty (40) years**. And, a grand total of the time lost is twenty (20) years. *Try not to get confused*. Simply stay with the present count at YHWH's Adamic Hebrew year of 3510 or 491 BC. One may be able to easily see the great potential for numerical disaster in my accounting of the times. But, as YHWH told me earlier; keep on going with it. We will see how major the sixty years are later in this book. Even with my twenty year mishap (*Isaac error*), what was so amazing and such a spiritual morale booster in supporting my faith that YHWH was leading me, was how he kept me on track with my years despite my misread. For me that was huge. We will discern later why the years turns out to be immeasurably significant in terms of their Scriptural integrity. That is, provided in this case we do not all discard our spiritual common senses, for denomination or traditions' sometimes irresponsible convenience. Let us all pray to Eloah that we not be found guilty of that error. Truly, I do not mean to be offensive. But, if we are all being honest with ourselves and each other; we can acknowledge there are elements in Christianity that seems to at times, flagrantly ignore clear Bible teachings and they instead opt out of truth. YHWH says, "*...in vain they do worship me, teaching for doctrines the commandments of men*" (Matthew 15:9).

However, persuading people to believe my insights, which I claim just like everyone else, **_YHWH revealed to me_**; is not my aim. In earnest I just simply want to get this **"Word of Revelation"** out for the broader or general public of professing Christians, Messianic Believers and Jews;

182

and to those who claim no alliances; but are simply seekers of truth they believe is found inside the Holy Bible, or Holy Scripture; whichever they choose to be their authority. So, I am not really trying to prove anything "*necessarily*." Because as always, every time, every individual must or at least, needs to prove things for themselves. That said, make a note. With my twenty years error, we are in effect sixty year **less** into the future than we would be, if we were using the expected traditional counts. I would have you know though; Eloah will take us where we need to be. I would have liked to think what we have already gone over is the hardest parts to receive as truth. However, knowing prophecy is what we will be dealing with shortly, I am certain it was not. One would think with prophecy, it is a matter set in divine stone. On the other hand, I will acknowledge the Holy Bible does give us stark warnings, "...whether *there be* prophecies, they shall fail..." (1st Corinthians 13:8). But to be honest, I am quite sure the prophecies we will be examining, will not fail. Not only will they not fail, but I argue in chronological accuracy, these prophecies will take us in discernible years to Messiah's coming (*Jews*), Yeshua's long-awaited return (*Many Messianics*), "*Jesus*'" return (*Most Christians*) and beyond.

Now! I want to be as clear as possible, as we restart our years count. In YHWH's Adamic Hebrew count, we are in the year of 3510 or 491 BC. From year 3510 (491 BC), I would love to be able to make the rest of our walk as theologically painless as possible. But, I know with all of the theological difficulties and the prophetic arguments on the biblical horizon in this book; which I am positive will spark debate; I will not be able to pull off the ideal ending with ease. In our reality show that is sometimes called Christianity I can imagine it will be next to impossible. But, I also feel that I am divinely obligated to give things my very best effort. So, here goes nothing! Practically, every Holy Bible student and theologian acknowledges Judah's Babylonian captivity came to its High Priest, the Jewish leadership and likely a limited number the people as no real surprise. At this point, I feel the need to tell some of you and remind others that Adonai YHWH will do nothing, commit no divine act, will do nothing, unless he first tells at the least, one of his prophets, or Apostles, or someone that stands within his mercy and blessed Grace. "*Surely the Lord God will do nothing, but he revealeth his secret unto his servants the prophets*" (Amos 3:7). Now you have read it (*again!*). Do you (*still*) believe it? For the ones who say your answer is still, "yes." I will make every attempt at reminding you; and will hold you to that confirmation of your faith in the Word of YHWH; when we tackle the other, most likely more divisive positions of this book's perspectives. Because, just like the Babylonian captivity was no surprise *to the ones who received and then believed the prophet Jeremiah;* other things YHWH might do should be no surprise; to those who believe it when he reveals it to them. With the siege and the overthrow of Jerusalem at the hand of Nebuchadnezzar, the King of Babylon; Jeremiah had a letter sent to those of the captivity. Its contents are preserved for us in <u>Jeremiah's 29th chapter</u>. At that time and throughout Judah's history, the people and land had its fill and overflow of false prophets. These prophets took liberties and spoke in the name of YHWH; when in truth, YHWH had not spoken to or sent them. Jeremiah sent the people of the captivity a letter; to tell them no miraculous release was coming anytime soon; no matter what their lying prophets who were among them might have been inclined to tell them. Listen carefully now, to what Jeremiah the prophet said to the Judah captives in Babylon.

> "Thus saith the Lord…the God of Israel, unto all that are carried away captives, whom I have caused to be carried away from Jerusalem unto Babylon; Build ye houses, and dwell in them; and plant gardens, and eat the fruit of them; take ye wives, and beget sons and daughters; and take wives for your sons, and give your daughters to husbands, that they may bear sons and daughters; that ye may be increased there, and not diminished. And seek the peace of the city whither I have caused you to be carried away captives, and pray unto the Lord for it: for in the peace thereof shall ye have peace. For thus saith the Lord of hosts, the God of Israel; Let not your prophets and your diviners, that be in the midst of you, deceive you, neither hearken to your dreams which ye cause to be dreamed. For they prophesy falsely unto you in my name: I have not sent them, saith the Lord. <u>For thus saith the Lord, That after seventy years be accomplished at Babylon I will visit you, and perform my good word toward you, in causing you to return to this place.</u>"
>
> (Jeremiah 29:4-10)

It's Much Later Than You Think!

Jeremiah's word of prophecy from YHWH – *from my perspective* – clearly identifies the time span of the Babylonian captivity; declaring that Judah would remain in Babylon for a full seventy (70) years. After which Judah would receive a visitation from YHWH, authorizing their return to Jerusalem. (Jeremiah 29:10) We go on with our walk, from where we left off. We are in the year of 3510 or 491 BC. When we add on the seventy (70) years of Jeremiah's prophecy - *which were fulfilled* - to our walk, we advance in history and arrive at year 3580 or 421 BC. <u>3510 years plus 70 years equal 3580 years</u>. Looking in terms of its length, the Babylonian stint was considerably short. Even so, challenges to the Jews with kings from Nebuchadnezzar to Cyrus were of significance. The experiences of Hananiah, Mishael, Azariah (*Their Babylonian names were: Shadrach, Meshach and Abednego*) and Daniel (*Daniel's Babylonian name was Belteshazzar*) illustrates the inherent dangers that could have beset them at anytime in Babylon's potentially lethal environment. Where often, for the entirety of Judah's stay, they were considered as less than first-class citizens. Apart from Israel, Judah found themselves once again in slavery because of sin. As cited, the captivity ends in year 3580 (*421 BC*); except this displacement in the time of the Jews sets up an even more perilous period in their history. It is desolation only rivaled and surpassed by their *almost unspeakable* experiences in the Nazi death camps during WWII.

CHAPTER 11

DANIEL'S AMAZING SEVENTY WEEKS

Our next important step is prophetic and spiritually multidimensional (*complex*). This implies for the average mind like mine - it will be next to impossible to explain them in their fullest of terms. *Being full of wisdom*, I will make no such attempt to do so. But, I will make an effort to remain within the duality of any event's fulfillment or time count, and leave the rest of them alone. Besides, you will not actually need the other parts and dimensions to understand where you stand in time as far as our past, and how many years still awaits us in the prophetic pathways of man. Those other aspects are perhaps given to our simple level of understanding to the confirmation of certain dates and of times, to build up our faith and confidence toward our purposes. Since, if we have enough faith from the outset, we may not *necessarily need all* of the other Bible confirmations.

With all of that said; let us take the next steps in time to and through the well-known, the well-read; but to the unwise, the well-misunderstood and therefore a well-misinterpreted prophecy from the Prophet Daniel. It has been named with their consensus by the old guards of theology, "***The Seventy Weeks Prophecy***." Which according to Jeremiah 29:10 and the Archangel Gabriel; was to be fulfilled on Judah, Jerusalem and the next temple over the next 490 years immediately after the Babylon captivity. Some may take issue with my chronological findings. That is okay. So long as they and everyone reads this entire book. That is my main goal.

Most Bible students who read the seventy weeks prophecy agree that it has enigmatic properties. But, most do not know to what depth. Sadly, besides this book and possibly a few others; it appears many believers imagine the seventy weeks prophecy is broken into sixty-nine (69) weeks and one (1) week. Their thoughts are that the last week fulfills the final seven years of time. If one is pre-tribulation, then before the seven years "*Jesus*" returns and then raptures the church into heaven. Of course, we all know there are the mid and post-tribulation rapturists; who in turn believe variations of the rapture. "*Jesus*" will either do it in the middle of the seven years, or he waits until they are finished; and then he comes to save Christian and Jewish converts just in time before they are wiped off the face of the earth. Then, he sets up a millennial reign of some sort. I can't keep up with all of the varying scenarios. So, I suppose me adding a scenario will not make much of a ripple in water full of interpretations. I have to say it is left up to the reader to determine which scenario makes the most sense to them for their biblical spiritual adoption. As we all may know and could be a witness to, the Holy Bible records that there were many who did not accept Yeshua's preaching or doctrines well. Most did not understand Yeshua's parable teachings at all. Of course, that was by design. But, still again, if Jewish leaders did not believe Yeshua and <u>His</u> **"*Interpretations*"** of <u>His</u> <u>Scriptures</u> and <u>prophetic renderings,</u> how much less so, will people be likely to believe me? Minus the strange idealistic antics of some antichrist in the last seven years of time, few if any detect and believe, laying within the seventy weeks prophecy of Daniel are key revelations that take us chronologically to the end of our age. Most have read <u>it</u>. But for some reason when they read <u>it</u>, they read right over <u>it</u>. Let us take time to read <u>it</u> again. Only this time, we will read <u>it</u> together; and also this time a little slower, with a bit more scrutiny. I will **<u>underline</u>** it!

> *"Seventy weeks are determined upon thy people and upon thy holy city, to finish the transgression, and to make an end of sins, and to make reconciliation for iniquity, and to bring in everlasting righteousness, and to seal up the vision and prophecy, **<u>and to anoint the Most Holy</u>**"* (Daniel 9:24). [I am afraid <u>it</u> is not talking about a third physical temple being built]

So, what do you think <u>it</u> means? I will give you a hint. **<u>Who</u>** do you think it means? You're is right! It means Messiah comes (*Jews*), Messiah Yeshua returns (Messianics) and "*Jesus*" returns (*Christians*). Guys - you have to know Messiah Yeshua has not yet officially been or should I say divinely anointed, "*King of kings and Lord of lords*" (1st Timothy 6:15). It is only by faith we call him that today. At this point in prophetic time, Messiah Yeshua has no kings or lords under his command; because quite literally spiritually, the resurrection has not occurred yet ...Capeesh? That official divine coronation will not come to pass until after we see Yeshua coming in the clouds "*with power and great glory*" (Matthew 24:30). Once Messiah Yeshua sends his angels to gather in his elect, then those prophetic words in Daniel 9:24 will be fulfilled. We also have a witness in Yochanan, where he testified to this vision from Revelation 19:11-16, "*He hath on his vesture and on his thigh a name written, King of Kings, and Lord of Lords*" (Verse 16). Sometime soon, reread that entire book.

Several years earlier, in the first year of King Darius of the Medes, Daniel had a Discovery. He; "*Daniel understood by books the number of the years, whereof the word of the Lord came to Jeremiah the prophet, that he would accomplish seventy years in the desolations of Jerusalem*" (Daniel 9:2). [Daniel's incident of discovery confirms my original claim that Jeremiah's letter regarding the seventy years was suppressed by the High Priest and false prophets among the people. It never truly reach the general Jewish public. The fact Daniel himself had to discover YHWH's judgment through books is proof of the situation] I suppose at this point, it is important that we all have a clearer understanding of exactly what "*desolations*" mean. If one is an average Bible student, they know one of the big issues with Bibles are meaning, matter and substance sometimes get lost in its many versions of translation. This fact in turn often present problems of perception. This is especially true when we read key words in Bible passages. When we read a key word in the Bible, we get one generalized meaning or implication. Take the root word "*Desolate*" and two of its variations "*Desolation* and *Desolations*" translated in the KJV.

From surface reading, somebody from our culture might view the three words in similar fashion as we refer to the trio of words in apple, apples and many apples. But, when it comes to the three words *desolate, desolation and desolations*; instead of one basic meaning, they share roughly, twenty-five (25) different Hebrew words that describe them in The Old Testament Hebrew Scriptures. Between desolate and desolation in the New Testament, there are four different words. In terms of study and understanding, it behooves us to check on some of these words from time to time. This is especially true when we feel a word or a phrase may need special thought or attention. Controversy is hard to comprehend and difficult to articulate. So, at the Spirit's behest; I took a closer look at the word, *"Desolations"* in Daniel 9:2.

> The Hebrew word for *"desolations"* is **"chorbâh."** It is
> pronounced *"khor-baw';"* proper: *drought*, i.e. (by implication) a
> *desolation* - decayed place, desolate (place, -tion), destruction,
> (laid) waste (place). It is feminine of 2721 - **chôreb**.

> 2721. **chôreb**, *kho'-reb; drought or desolation* - desolation,
> drought, dry, heat, x utterly, waste. It is a collateral form of
> 2719 - **chereb**.

> 2719. **chereb**, *kheh'-reb; drought;* also a *cutting* instrument
> (from its *destructive* effect), as a *knife, sword,* or other sharp
> implement - axe, dagger, knife, mattock, sword, tool. It is from
> 2717 - **chârâb** or **chârêb**.

> 2717. **chârâb**, khaw-rab' or **chârêb**, *khaw-rabe';* **a prime root**;
> to *parch* (through drought) i.e. (by analysis) to *desolate, destroy,*
> *kill* - decay, (be) desolate, destroy (er), (be) dry (up), slay, x
> surely, (lay, lie, make) waste.

From my perspective, when I take on the deliberation of Daniel's 9:2

"desolations" alongside of its corresponding Hebrew word and trail of

connected Hebrew words with their meanings, I have no problems in my

surmising that Gabriel was revealing to Daniel that an angel, *perhaps it*

was Gabriel himself; was given his authority and held responsible by

YHWH himself, for making absolutely sure that the conditions of the

Jewish captivity in Babylon remained in place. Jerusalem and her temple

also - were to remain in the ruin of utter disrepair - for the duration of the

seventy years. However, even though the actual Hebrew word is **kᵉruwb**

/ker-oob'/; the Bible translators saw it *meet* or somewhat right to use the word **cher'-ub** (*coincidentally implicating him¿*), when referencing the wicked former archangel Lucifer. (Ezekiel 28:14) Perhaps Lucifer was place as the overseer. Clearly **"ruin"** would have been right up his alley. (John 10:10) Certainly, it would not be the first time YHWH has given Satan limited reign over a given situation. (Job 1:12) Think about that basis connecting the words for a moment from my perspective. Clearly again, salvation is not on the line to agree or disagree. So we can advance without controversy. As we look to the Seventy-weeks, we again see the word "*desolations*" and "*desolate*" twice. They are in Daniel 9:26-27. However, a different Hebrew word is used in this case for "*desolations*."

> 8074. **shâmêm**, *shaw - mame';* a prim. Root; to *stun* (or intr. Grow numb), i.e. *devastate* or (fig.) stupefy (both usually in a pass. sense): - make amazed, be astonied, (be an) astonish (- ment), (be, bring into, unto, lay, lie, make) desolate (-ion, places), be destitute, destroy (self), (lay, lie, make) waste, wonder. (Verse 26; and first, "*desolate*" cited in verse 27) The second, "*desolate*" cited in verse 27 in a different contexts is: 8076. **shâmêm**, *shaw - mame';* from 8074; *ruined*: - desolate.

I did the *desolate* definitions to stress a shocking revelation for pious Jews. It is an unbelievable and so a rejectionable claim. Jews are being *misled* by Jewish religious leaders, who give out their third temple hopes. According to Gabriel's illuminations, "There will not be a third temple!"

"THAT'S RIGHT! I SAID IT!"

It's Much Later Than You Think!

I imagine I have raised the ire of most every prophecy gurus with such a claim. I know there are those who believe there must be a third temple, in order for "**the Antichrist**" to do his thing. But, for other Bible minds, I have no idea why there must be a third temple. Maybe the same reason. I will study it to get my own confirmation. How about this? How about we try compromise? I will say this. There cannot be a third temple built until past YHWH's *three* consecutive adjoining/overlay desolations. To date, those desolations have continued for almost 1950 years after the destruction of the second temple; **with no end in sight**. Why? Because, there was in addition to those 490 years. Some *"poured upon"* period that comes on after some mysterious *"consummation"* (Daniel 9:27); however long that is going to be – **_believe it or not_**. So then, in naming those *three* desolations, I claim to the reader; we have them in the following.

1. The Second Temple is destroyed (*Is laid waste and made desolate*)

2. The time period between or up *"until"* the consummation (*Remains in desolation*)

3. The *poured upon* time marking the length of the consummation (*Continued desolations*)

Desolate basically defined, is to lay in ruin and to remain in utter disrepair. With events going on in Jerusalem in our time, the ever tense so-called Palestinian dilemma, the Dome of the Rock - with many Jews desiring to build a third temple, hostile enemies all around and to hear the United Nations speak - another enemy of the Jews; there should also be this hostile enemy state **_within_** the Jewish state (*A _Palestinian state_ if you will - _REALLY?_*). Now, how **"IDIOTIC"** of the Jews would that be? But the facts are, the second temple is still in ruin. The "Jewish state" at this moment, along with its capital city Jerusalem, is very much a divided state and city. Even though at present, there are many Jews in the city of Jerusalem, there are also many Gentiles, "*trodden under foot*" the Holy City; while they do so in despisement of the Jews. Up until AD 2020 at least, Gabriel's prophecies to the conditions of Jerusalem and the temple hold true - **desolations!** So, let us go back to where we left off. Then we can go forward to where we need to be. We are in year 3580 or 421 BC.

I do not know if many taken to Babylon knew how long the captivity would be; the priests, prophets and elders were all hostile to Jeremiah's words (26:8). Lying prophets and "*holy men¿*" (*diviners to sorcerers*) misled the people. (Jeremiah 27:9-10) It is likely after Judah was taken to Babylon, Jeremiah's letter reaffirming their seventy years, like his first declaration, did not reach the greater numbers in the public. Even Daniel himself had to discover it and believe it by books (9:2). On the exact day in fulfillment of the seventy years, Daniel prayed with great expectation. And he received a visitation from the Archangel Gabriel with spiritual intelligence from YHWH. Gabriel declared, "*O Daniel, I am now come forth to give thee skill and understanding*" (Verse 22). YHWH greatly loved Daniel because he was meek and obedient to YHWH's divine law of righteousness and holiness. We should all recognize as Daniel and in a time before, even King Nebuchadnezzar himself. We are all mortal men. Some will have more authority physically, socially, government wise and spiritual wise than others; but in the end we are all plain, simple, delicate, weak mortal men. Daniel testified to Nebuchadnezzar of that fact in this following reality check for the king when he interpreted a dream for him.

> "The secret which the king hath demanded…the wise men, the astrologers, the magicians, the soothsayers, [*cannot*] show unto the king; but there is a God in heaven that revealeth secrets, and maketh known…as for me, this secret is not revealed…for any wisdom that I have more than any living," (Daniel 2:27-30).

I absolutely concur with Daniel's acknowledgement. His assessment comes home for me through the writing of this book. I believe I can by and large identify with that humble attitude in Daniel. So for wisdom and revelation sake, do not be offended if or when YHWH does not reveal to you directly. That is clearly a decision that is under his divine executive authority to make. If we will humble ourselves, then set our faces toward absolute truth and have faith; I believe that in due time of prophecy, YHWH will have mercy and heal our deceived hearts with his wisdom, knowledge and understanding. We see examples continually throughout the Holy Bible and the book of Daniel is no exception. One of the first things Gabriel told Daniel during his visitation was that from the start of his prayers of supplication, YHWH's fulfillment of Jeremiah's prophecy was declared. This officially ended those seventy years. Cyrus's royal commandment was decreed authorizing chosen ones of Judah to return to Jerusalem and rebuild her walls torn down by king Nebuchadnezzar, and rebuild her temple, which had been totally burned down in YHWH's Adamic year of 3510 or 491 BC. (Daniel 9:23)

> "Now in the first year of Cyrus king of Persia, that the word of the Lord spoken by the mouth of Jeremiah might be accomplished, the Lord stirred up the spirit of Cyrus...that he made a proclamation throughout all his kingdom and put it also in writing saying, Thus saith Cyrus king of Persia, all the kingdoms of the earth hath the Lord God of heaven given me; and he hath charged me to build him a house in Jerusalem, which is in Judah. Who is there among you from all his people? The Lord his God be with him, and let him go up."
> (2nd Chronicles 36:22-23)

From that point during Daniel's visitation, the Archangel Gabriel began what has become for assorted theologians and Bible students, the encouraging building of the second temple declaration, the now infamous Messianic *"cut off"* sacrificial revelation and afterwards, ultimately that disheartening edict in the destruction of the Holy City and that very same temple which had been prophesied in that very same prophecy - through Gabriel's first proclamation. There are also those invaluable, once hidden and now revealed enigmatic gems most theologians, Bible students and everyday Christians of this age had no idea existed. They offer up divine confirmation for what was once unknown and only wondered about. We will reveal some and discuss them - shortly. So then, we can step up from YHWH's Adamic year of 3580 or 421 BC, and forward into their future history - using Daniel chapter nine; the Archangel Gabriel announcing in his confirmation, "***I am come to show thee****; for thou art greatly beloved: therefore understand the matter, and consider the vision*" (Verse 23).

> "Seventy weeks are determined upon thy people and upon thy holy city, to finish the transgression, and to make an end of sins, and to make reconciliation for iniquity, and to bring in everlasting righteousness, and to seal up the vision and prophecy, and to anoint the Most Holy. Know therefore and understand, that from the going forth of the commandment to restore and to build Jerusalem, unto the Messiah the Prince, shall be seven weeks, and threescore and two weeks: the street shall be built again, and the wall, even in troublous times. And after threescore and two weeks shall Messiah be cut off, but not for himself: and the people of the prince that shall come shall destroy the city and the sanctuary; and the end thereof shall be with a flood, and unto the end of the war desolations are determined. And he shall confirm the covenant with many for one week: and in the midst of the week he shall cause the sacrifice and the oblation to cease, and for the overspreading of abominations he shall make it desolate, even until the consummation, and that determined shall be poured upon the desolate" (Daniel 9:24-27).

Not that their nod of approval is needed for stuff to be true or their scornful ire for stuff to be false; yet, I find it odd they believe the following, due to timing. Most theologians believe and recognize that each day in the seventy weeks prophecy revealed to Daniel, represents one year of time off the prophetic clock and time of man. You will see what I mean by odd later. But to start, allow me to explain the concept, prove it the best I can and as briefly as possible - before we step forward in moving on. Understanding and recognizing the concept of one day being synonymous with one year is an insightful key when we study the passage of time and numbers in the Holy Bible. To make a sometimes complicated concept simple as I can, a common example often used to denote the day for a year is found and determined to be when Moses sent twelve spies into the Promised Land of YHWH, right before the children of Israel were supposed to have entered into to take the land. They spied out the land for forty (40) days and then they returned with an evil report. When they stood before Moses, Aaron and before all of the congregation of the children of Israel, they did not care to remember any of the words that YHWH had spoken to them. When they saw the land and the giants that inhabited the land, they forgot the wonders YHWH worked for them before the Egyptians. Listen to their faithless testimony before YHWH.

> "We came unto the land whither thou sentest us, and surely it floweth with milk and honey; and this *is* the fruit of it. Nevertheless the people *be* strong that dwell in the land, and the cities *are* walled, *and* very great: and moreover we saw the children of Anak there. The Amalekites dwell in the land of the

south: and the Hittites, and the Jebusites, and the Amorites, dwell in the mountains: and the Canaanites dwell by the sea, and by the coast of Jordan" (Numbers 13:27-29).

In so many words, those spies were saying, YHWH brought us all the way out here from Egypt and across the great wilderness of Sin for nothing. The peoples are too strong for YHWH. They felt that even with YHWH at their side, they could not take the land. Only Caleb and Joshua said otherwise. For their treachery to dishearten the children of Israel - which they were successful in doing so – to the point that the people threatened mutiny against Moses, Aaron and *YHWH,* saying, "*Let us make a captain, and let us return into Egypt*" (Numbers 14:4). They were actually going to stone Joshua and Caleb (Numbers 14:10) for their effort in urging the people not to rebel against YHWH. YHWH had a mind to destroy virtually everyone of them and make Moses' seed a mightier and greater nation than that which the Children of Israel had achieved. After Moses interceded, YHWH pardoned the people and only punished them; as compared to their complete annihilation. Their sentence was that they would have to wonder in the wilderness until every person twenty years and older who rebelled against YHWH would die in the wilderness. They would not enter into the Promise Land; but rather, they would wonder in the wilderness and ultimately die in the wilderness.

"Your children shall wander in the wilderness forty years and bear your whoredoms, until your carcasses be wasted in the wilderness. <u>After the number of the days in which ye searched the land, even forty days, each day for a year, shall ye bear your iniquities, even forty years</u>, and ye shall know my breach of promise" (Verse 34).

We gain discernment as to whether it is a literal or symbolic day or a prophetic day by the way of the context that day, week or year is used in a sentence. In other words we can understand if we have the ability and the faith to use our spiritual common sense when reading. Of course as always, YHWH's revelation is absolutely essential. Without it, we have no opportunity for a true understanding. Here is an example. Yeshua said he would be in the grave for three days and three nights. To think he meant three years or three thousand years would have been intellectually on a level with insanity. His body would have long before the elapsing of the time, seen its corruption and moldered away. Literal, days are the only option. That is called, spiritual common sense. We must use that same spiritual common sense, when we consider, Daniel's seventy weeks. Seventy literal weeks are not feasible if we consider the events that must occur in the time span of under a year and a third (490 days). Even if we discounted the reality that we today have an advantage of 20/20 hindsight view; we should be able to read Daniel's vision and understand the ancient times to know, we could not construct <u>a temple for YHWH</u> in forty-nine (49) days or as Prophet Daniel was informed by

Gabriel, seven weeks. It is extremely improbable that the days referenced 1000-year intervals or a millennium. Honestly, which one of us would imagine YHWH sending an angel and speak to, proclaim, or prophesy to a human concerning a future event that would not happen for another – let us see – seventy weeks – 490 days times 1000 years is equal to almost one-half million (*490,000 exactly*) years. Theoretically it is possible, but like I said before, it is extremely improbable. Utilize your own spiritual common sense. Since, I am confident in the day for a year concept and scenario – *at least in this circumstance* – even if you are not sold on the idea, humor me and continue to journey with me in our walk forward with that perspective; just to see where we end up at. Who knows, you may have fun with my, "*biblical error and theological foolishness.*"

For effect sake, open your Bible and scrutinize with me Daniel 9:24-27 again. Then, walk along with me as we divide up the weeks according to my revelation and perspective. Remember now, we have come to the end of the seventy (70) years and we are at the year of 3580 or 421 BC. Here is the place where most of the time I lose people to indoctrination. I asked earlier to humor me and read on to the end. Hopefully, you will at the least see where I am coming from. YHWH revealed to me five (5) distinct declarations in Daniel's seventy weeks at their face value that I would like for you to consider, based on my revelation and perspectives from the Holy Spirit. The five divisions are:

1) The Second Temple
2) The cutting off of Messiah
3) The coming people of the Prince
4) Covenant (Part I)
5) Covenant (Part II)

From YHWH's Adamic Hebrew year of 3580 or 421 BC; we can, or at the least we ought to be able to easily count up. Nevertheless, my non-traditional declarations will not suit many of the dogmatic traditionalist tastes out here, as far as their spiritual pallets go. But still, bear with me. Set aside what many churches through the dimmed eyes of the vaunted historians and theologians have speculated on and espoused concerning, for... for ever! But seriously, and more accurately, we are talking about at the least hundreds of years. We are covering a time period of thousands of years. Let us lay out those divisions by the insight I declare YHWH in his mercy revealed to me. Follow along with the account as it displays a non-traditional perspective. It is really quite simple if one is able to apply a bit of faith. You could ask yourself questions similar to the following before going on to challenge yourself whether you want to believe or not.

1. If the divisions are right and I believe them, how will it transform my spiritual picture?

2. If the divisions are wrong and I perceive it; what can I do and will I do to warn others?

3. If the divisions are wrong, but I believe them; can it and will it affect my chance at salvation?

4. If the divisions are right, but I do not believe them; can it and will it affect my chance at salvation?

5. If the divisions are wrong and I believe them; what spiritual perspective and growth, have I lost?

6. If the divisions are right and I believe them; what spiritual perspective and growth, have I gained?

As a rule, I feel it is usually safer to evaluate the consequences for an action or a decision, before doing or making it. We all know this practice to be prudent. But some of us tend to ignore this wisdom, at times. Then when we proceed, it is often to our own detriment. Then there are the times we just forget to proceed with caution in our rush to gain perceived new knowledge and need to be reminded. Consider the questions above as your official reminder and advisory to thoroughly evaluate any and all so-called new spiritual pathways claiming to advance new perspectives of and into biblical truths and revelations. Now, let us continue.

1) Rebuild the wall at Jerusalem and the Second Temple - seven weeks or forty-nine days.
   a. These forty-nine (49) days in this prophecy are equivalent to forty-nine (49) years.

From 3580, we walk forward in time 49 years and we are at year 3629 or 372 BC. The city walls of Jerusalem and the Temple have finally been finished - despite the five decades full of all types of social and civil adversarial undermining and violent turmoil.

2) The Messiah (*Yeshua*) is cut off after <u>threescore weeks</u> (**NOT THREESCORE AND TWO!**). The "*and two*" is reserved for, "*the people of the **Prince***" [**WHO IS NOT MESSIAH!**] rather he is their brethren - to the emissaries that came forth to Jerusalem to negotiate the "<u>weak</u>" one-week <u>covenant</u>. **Note:** Revealing it out at threescore weeks at seven days in the week comes up to be 420 days. It is not "*threescore and two weeks*" or 434 days; which would make for 434 years before Messiah would be cut off. The reason why this is very important as far as my perspective goes, will become apparent. And, people should be able to see what I consider to be likely an honest, but a crucial careless assumption in the accountability of truth in unbelief by the translators - shortly.

   a. Threescore weeks (*A score is 20; then times 3 and times 7*) is 420 days or (<u>420</u>) years.

From here – *but not without some debate* – we are told by Archangel Gabriel through Daniel that from the Adamic year of 3629 it would be 420 years before the Messiah is "*cut off*" (<u>put to death</u>), "*after threescore* [~~and two~~] *weeks shall Messiah be cut off*" (Daniel 9:26). If you recall from YHWH's revelation; or my perspective, the "*and two*" should have been assigned by the translators of the Holy Scriptures to, "***the people of the prince** that shall come shall destroy the city and the sanctuary*" (Verse 26). From that perspective, Bible history bears out my insight in Messiah Yeshua's prophecy, "*See ye not all these things*?" [Yeshua meant the buildings of the sanctuary]. Then he made what then had to seem like an almost unbelievable prediction of prophecy. He said plainly to his awed disciples hearing and all of us reading from the Bible record,

"*Verily I say unto you, There shall not be left here one stone upon another which shall not be thrown down*" (Matthew 24:2). This prophecy was fulfilled when Rome totally obliterated YHWH's second temple at Jerusalem. More on that in a bit; but for the moment let us keep the focus where it belongs. It is year 3629 or 372 BC. We are asked to displace the words "*two weeks*" from Daniel 9:26, by what we have determined to be translator error, through my claim of divine revelation. We have in turn, assigned the "*two weeks*" where they rightfully belong. That assignment is to, "...*the people of the Prince that shall come.*" So then, from year 3629; we add on the 420 years of "*three score weeks*" to discern the true year in which our Messiah Yeshua was, "...*cut off.*"

What I am about to say next, most will not accept. I only ask that you consider it, do your own study to come up with your own conclusion. It is common knowledge that many theologians feel that Messiah was born somewhere between those years of what many of them term as 6 BC and 4 BC. Some broaden the birth net and state between 7 BC and 2 BC or BCE. Whichever one they choose, it makes no difference to me. Most theologians and Bible students that I have heard, write and speak on the subject of Messiah Yeshua's birth, will have comments that go along the lines that nobody really knows exactly when - "*Jesus Christ*" was born. If that is their stand, I reason then none of those "*Bible experts*" will care much when I contend <u>Yeshua was born in year 4000 or 1 BC</u>. In this case <u>1 BCE</u> is better stated. But in order for anyone to believe that of me, they would have to *entertain* other beliefs that virtually all biblical pundits in Christianity would call insane. Nevertheless, I am going to lay my cards right on the table. So, here is the deal. From the year of 3629 or 372 BC, when we add on the 420 years; the years that I have declared the book of Daniel indicates or culminated with - *according to Daniel* - the year that our "*Messiah be cut off*," we come to the year of 4049 or 49 AMB (After Messiah's Birth) (AD or CE). 3629 plus 420 is 4049. It is a simple case of addition. If those who hold to tradition, dogmatically cite "*Jesus*" was born in or between the years of 7 BC to 2 BC, then provided that I am even fairly close to being accurate concerning the year that the Babylon captivity commenced was in the year of 3510 - then too, if we accept the <u>threescore and two</u> is joined, then "Jesus Christ" would of necessity been between <u>sixty-four</u> (64) and <u>seventy</u> (70) years of age - when he was crucified. Do the math for yourself. The Bible itself argues that such a logic is to be viewed as error. When Messiah Yeshua was in the last year of his life (Luke 4:14-21) he was, "*not yet fifty years old*" (John 8:57). And, to accept the "*threescore*" and the "*and two*" of Daniel nine (9) belonging together should fly into the face of all of our reasoning. From my perspective, I have concluded, at least on this point, the translators did not visualize the wayward implications or difficulties regarding their translation of the passage. This is just where I stand for myself. At this particular point in my learning and in my quest for understanding, I can see no other spiritually logical determination for any different scriptural conclusion. I have used this Bible quote before, "…*let God be true, but every man a liar*" (Romans 3:4). As far as I can see, there is really no need to speculate on the issue. But, we all must consider the spiritual ramification to our own long-held doctrines for ourselves. If you counted yourself and considered my conclusion; it is exactly as many at this point are thinking that I am implying. With almost certainty, not a year of what I would label as, "wiggle room;" Messiah Yeshua was much older than almost all of the theologians have believed and taught. <u>Messiah Yeshua was forty-nine (49) years of age when he was crucified and his adult ministry covered nineteen years</u>!

<u>"THAT'S RIGHT! I SAID IT!"</u>

It is likely why Yochanan was inspired to record these words in <u>St. John 21:25</u>. "…*many…things* **Yeshua** *did, the which, if they should be written every one, I suppose…the world itself could not contain the books that should be written.*" It is reasonably unlikely Yeshua did so much in those three and a half years he is purported to have carried out his ministry.

Not only do I make my forty-nine (49) years old claim, concerning

Messiah Yeshua's age at the time of his crucifixion; by necessity this demands, since Yeshua was beginning *to be about thirty* (Luke 3:23) when he was tempted in the wilderness forty days by the Devil and afterwards, he returned to Galilee and Nazareth and began his, "adult ministry" (Luke 4:14-21) - If all of this is true, and at this point, it would appear to be reasonably so; Messiah Yeshua's total ministry in his adult years, including the last year of his life, which was, "*the acceptable year of the LORD,*" was nineteen (19) years - believe it or not! Nineteen has a shadow I will not be able to address in an understanding manner in this book. So, let us carry on. In case it was not noticed, I said in his adult years; which implies that Messiah's ministry in total, started earlier. That much is recorded in the biblical witness concerning Messiah when he was close to twelve (12) years old, "*How is it that ye sought me? wist ye not that **I must be about my Father's business**? And they understood not the saying which he spake unto them*" (Luke 2:49). It is evident; most of us do not understand it or believe it even today. Minus any miracles, that is when Yeshua began to minister. Bible students know Yeshua's first miracle came after he reached age thirty. (St. John 2) Still, close to the age of twelve he returned with his parents to Nazareth "*and was subject unto them*" (Luke 2:51). Meaning while his ministry began, he limited its scope ***somewhat*** due to his "*lawful*" responsibilities to his parents. And know this as fact. Being around age twelve, Yeshua still had to **LEARN**. He had to grow in wisdom, just like us and everybody else (Verse 52). Recognize this also. One does not grow "*in favor with God and man*" gaining no wisdom and having no works. Yeshua's *ministry* was well underway by the time he reached the "rabbinic" age of thirty. **"What!?"** None of us in reality believe Yeshua lived like a spiritual hermit (*That would have been Yochanan – the baptizer*) or in a vacuum and once he reached the age of twenty-nine (29), he cut on the divine switch, did a couple of kick starts and said, "Let's Ride!" It seems like even with our Bibles for our 20/20 hindsight; we find YHWH's truth too difficult to understand and believe. Believe it or not, I pray your spirit is provoked enough to continue on with your reading of this book; with the option to write me over any concerns you might have. So then, as you continue your reading, consider the following in the mean while. It is a visual of events we have covered so far in our study of what is now Bible history.

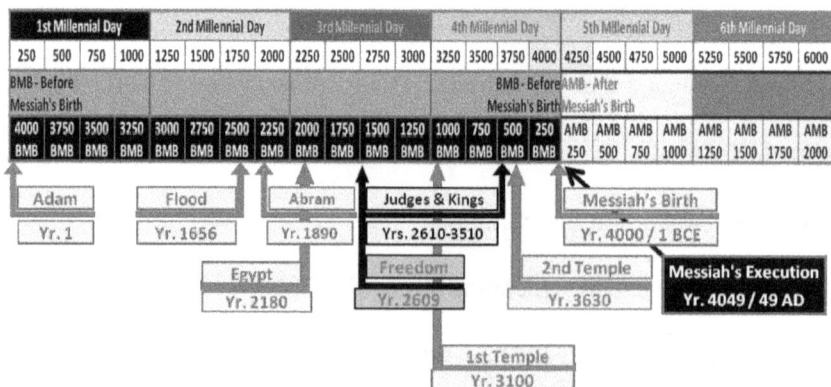

1) Adam was created in year one (1). That is 4000 BC (BMB - *Before Messiah's Birth*).

2) The great flood of Noah's day was 1656 years later in year 1657 or 2344 BC.

3) The birth of Abram was in the year 1890 or 2111 BC.

4) The Israelites began their time in Egypt in the year 2180 or 1821 BC.

5) The Israelites departed Egypt in the year 2610 or 1391 BC.

6) Judges (which included the 40 years wilderness trek) began in year 2610 or 1391 BC.

7) Judges ended in the year 3060 or 941 BC with a net overlap of kings totaling 450 years. Kings began theologically in 3043 or 958 BC – with Saul for 3 years; then David for 40 years. YHWH made His divine decision to stick with the status quo of kings "*officially*" with the death of Sampson and/or birth of Solomon in year 3060 or 941 BC. In recognizing their overlaps, this means, from the time Israel left Egypt, we can determine 450 of judges and 450 of kings.

8) The First Temple was completed in year 3100 or 901 BC.

9) Kings ended and the Babylonian exile began in the year 3510 or 491 BC.

10) The Babylonian exile ended in year 3580 or 421 BC.

11) The Second Temple was completed in year 3629 or 372 BC.

12) **The Messiah (*Yeshua*) was born in YHWH's Adamic year 4000 or 1 BCE (*Before the Common Era* or BC).**

13) Messiah was executed in the year 4049 or AD 49 (AMB - *After Messiah's Birth*).

With no deeper insights needed from YHWH and by not using other sources besides those of the Holy Scriptures themselves; we have walked together through biblical history and prophetic time from year one. We have walked I feel almost as accurately as possible. In that walk, we have arrived at YHWH's Adamic Hebrew fifth millennium. That is, if we trust the Holy Bible's numbers, my accounting of those years and objective minds feel my research does merit. Nevertheless, I am certain that due to the many vaunted *"Bible experts, theologians and historians,"* few may find this research and study has credibility. Nevertheless, from year 4049 or its Gregorian counterpart date, AD 49, if anyone insists; we can add on the *"two weeks"* from Daniel 9:26. Those are the fourteen years that I have contended are not to be allocated to the execution of our Messiah Yeshua. But, if dogmatism is to prevail; then comes unavoidably a much worse and an unlikely account of the year Messiah was cut off. From my humble perspective such a count would demand the Messiah's *"cut off"* year be AD 63. Considering nearly every Bible pundit I have heard speak to the subject regard AD 33, their about crucifixion date, one can see the obvious conflict in my contentious asserted date of AD 49. Let us not even go the route of the *"three score and two."* Surely that count is much more disastrous. For the meantime at least, let us maintain in your reading of this book, the compromise and more reasonable, even biblically solid and supported year AD 49. Now, let us continue forward and see if our Holy Bibles will solidify further, my claims and assertions concerning Messiah Yeshua's birth and his execution in other ways. Being honest, I do not think that is too much to ask of the Scriptures. And too, only speaking for myself; anytime someone asks of me concerning my beliefs, I would definitely consider such a request of my Biblical faith and truth, a reasonable spiritual challenge.

CHAPTER 12

WHEN THE WORD BECAME FLESH

"Who hath believed our report? and to whom is the arm of the Lord revealed? For he shall grow up before him as a tender plant, and as a root out of a dry ground: he hath no form nor comeliness; and when we shall see him, there is no beauty that we should desire him. He is despised and rejected of men; a man of sorrows, and acquainted with grief: and we hid as it were our faces from him; he was despised, and we esteemed him not. Surely he hath borne our griefs, and carried our sorrows: yet we did esteem him stricken, smitten of God, and afflicted. But he was wounded for our transgressions; he was bruised for our iniquities: the chastisement of our peace was upon him; and with his stripes we are healed. All we like sheep have gone astray; we have turned every one to his own way; and the Lord hath laid on him the iniquity of us all. He was oppressed, and he was afflicted, yet he opened not his mouth: he is brought as a lamb to the slaughter, and as a sheep before her shearers is dumb, so he openeth not his mouth. He was taken from prison and from judgment: and who shall declare his generation? for he was cut off out of the land of the living: for the transgression of my people was he stricken. And he made his grave with the wicked, and with the rich in his death; because he had done no violence, neither was any deceit in his mouth. Yet it pleased the Lord to bruise him; he hath put him to grief: when thou shalt make his soul an offering for sin, he shall see his seed, he shall prolong his days, and the pleasure of the Lord shall prosper in his hand. He shall see of the travail of his soul, and shall be satisfied: by his knowledge shall my righteous servant justify many; for he shall bear their iniquities. Therefore will I divide him a portion with the great, and he shall divide the spoil with the strong; because he hath poured out his soul unto death: and he was numbered with the transgressors: and he bare the sin of many, and made intercession for the transgressors" (Isaiah 53).

That was long, but worth every word to read. I am sitting here with tears in my eyes; as I attempted to try and understand, "...*what manner of love the Father hath bestowed upon us,*" (1st John 3:1) when **The LÕGÕS** (*pronounced* Log'-os; *translated*: **Word** - KJV) became flesh. I just do not get it. I think that is what John was conveying for himself and the entirety of the Messianic believers' movement of his time. I am prone to believe his sentiment still applies to all of us who profess Messiah Yeshua today. In this chapter, **"When the WORD became Flesh;"** I felt a need to put it in due to my claims on the life span and age of Yeshua. It is not right to ask readers to believe me; then offer them no compelling proofs of truth as to where I came from; or why I went there in the first place. Those declarations being the year Yeshua was born and year he was crucified, **according to the scriptures**; or as much of the scriptures that I believe are revealed to and understood by me. If people allow their objective minds to consider, I believe they will see my biblical logic.

IN MY OPINION, none-thorough logic says, "*Jesus*" died when he was 33½ in AD 33. Thoughtless logic suggests he was 63½ and died in AD 63. Why do **we** not all compromise and everybody agree with **me** on my determined age of 49 and also on my determined "*cut off*" date of AD 49? After all, 33½ plus 63½, when divide by two, "***in a compromise,***" is 48½. We would naturally round his age off to 49 - RIGHT? ☺ REALLY, I know a concession on this is not going to happen at all and it shouldn't. We all - each one of us and especially me - must "*prove all things*." Even though historians have their years varying oftentimes one from the other; we can use to a degree of effectiveness, the events that actually happened and take with a grain of salt the actual years that a certain historian might claim the events truly occurred. Then again, that is up to you. But, you already know my motto. "*Let God be true.*" Well, let us try to do another kind of compromise. Let us see if we can use in this case, both YHWH's **Holy Bible** and men's "*holy history*." Let us look to see if we can match up anything. Do not be fooled by me or anybody else - if at all possible. I caution. There will be those who will say, this chapter's words are so far off the rails they should literally be laughed at, being devoid of all sanity.

Some will say, even my argument that Yeshua was born in year 4000 or 1 BCE; should be determined as utter nonsense and as an absolutely ridiculous conclusion. See; so-called, *"historical fact"* declares that King Herod died in year 4 BC. With that date in hand, how could a dead King Herod have ordained the first real *"Christ* massacre" or *"Christ* mass" or *"Christ*mas;" as it has come to be known today, when *"Jesus Christ"* was a child of two? If he was not born until 1 BCE, as I do claim! Let us try and keep all of our claims, as basic for you as we can, Mr. Historian, Mr. Theologian or Mrs., Miss. or Ms.; however you choose to be addressed. Often, **recorded history** and our theories on an event are very different from the true realities of the event. Seriously, with all of the shenanigans going on in Washington, DC; is anyone not curious, what the far into our future history of this nation, *should it survive*; will say about our current president, Donald John Trump as of January, AD 2020. Who by the way, I believe is our **"Divine Hint"** from YHWH, to alert us to the lateness of our times. Consider the **messages** behind his names: **"Donald"** (Ruler of the world), **"John"** (Forerunner to Messiah Yeshua) and **"Trump"** (as in first and last) to be president as a Trump and quite possibly, the last to be inaugurated over the United States of America. Some may believe that is a bit of a *"stretch."* Maybe it is. But then again, maybe it is not. I am just saying. Notwithstanding, when we put all of the messages from all of his names all together; we can discern from them for the wicked, a terrifying premonition. However, to the righteous and the holy, it could be viewed as the prelude to **YHWH's Divine Coming Promise,** coming to fruition.

Bear in mind; the following, *which is by interpretation*, is nevertheless a

real meaning fact. President Donald John Trump's full name reveals who

he very well may be. What say you? Whom do you think or say this "son

of man" is? As for me, consider my findings.

1.   Donald (*Ruler of the world/earth*) = Who is **YHWH/Yeshua**

2.   John (**Forerunner to Messiah Yeshua)** – Malachi 4th Chapter:
     Highlighting verse 5 - as in the spirit of Elijah.

3.   Trump (Very likely ***the first*** and ***the last*** Trump to be president)
     = **The First Resurrection**

In Donald John Trump's name by discernment is found:

1.   True meaning and definition
2.   Divine prophetic symbolism
3.   Prophetic shadow picture fulfillment

Donald John Trump's name "by interpretation" is found in the following.

"YHWH's Forerunner to Messiah and the First Resurrection"

Take it or leave it, believe it or not. It is merely my statement of

sentiment after combining the three names. I do understand many people

find it hard to know, when the Holy Spirit is revealing. This is especially

true when it comes to a new bombshell revelation. And believe you me; I

did not want to include this perspective in this book. I felt it might be too

hard for people to receive; and thereby discourage them from reading the rest of this book. But, I was not given a choice on the matter. It is part of the core message behind this book. **It's Much Later Than You Think!**

A great number of the so-called history experts and even many of the Bible theologians do not believe the Holy Bible even in its original form, to be accurate without a doubt. That being no doubt the case, here is my challenge to all of the know-it-all Bible theologians and believe-none-of-its history experts. If you do not believe "*The Holy Scriptures*;" why do you or would you insinuate I am insane or some sort of history illiterate and unwise; because, I am not inclined and compelled to take you at your "peer-reviewed" word? Have **You** ever heard of, "The Fruit from the Poisonous Tree?" I have said it before and now I am saying it yet again. Whenever I am worried, whenever in doubt, I go with YHWH and "*Let Eloah be true.*" If I trust YHWH with my *Eternal Destiny*, why would I not believe **Him** and call every man a liar? I know we all must choose for ourselves. I get that. I choose Elohim and his Holy LÕGÕS (WORD) as The Truth. The way I see things, YHWH is my **only** hope in my quest to attain Eternal Life.

However and nevertheless, if the readers insist on a little bit of proof. Consider the revelations from Daniel 9:24-26. Many might consider the following perspectives to be preposterous and others may view them as highly debatable. I would encourage readers to study them in the light of what I have previously described as a type of "*dimensionalism*" in their fulfillments. While these are not the only fulfillment types concerning Daniel's seventy weeks, they are two of the easier ones to discern; if people from my perspective, have the wherewithal to consider them in sobriety. **Daniel's seventy weeks** has what I have coined as divine cases of **Root and Branch Fulfillment**. Meaning, they start from the same tree trunk in the ground or **year point in history**. **Root** (*extended*) fulfillment is chronological. They have no overlaps (*Each event occur one after the other in the fullness of time*). **Branch** fulfillments are individualized and all their events extend out individually from the same point in time. And also note they each end at their own respective times. There is no regard or connection to the other in terms of dependency. **Take note**: These are merely made-up theological terms, for loss of official ones. Based on my dimmed and limited understandings, there are prophetic fulfillments that indeed do overlap. Divine revelation of contexts, seems to be the key in discerning which is the case with a given prophecy. Do your own studies in Root and Branch fulfillment. See their concept in the seventy weeks of prophecy that Archangel Gabriel left behind to Daniel for the wise (*if you will*) of our end times to read, hear and discern from; with the invaluable assistance of YHWH's Holy Spirit. As I alluded to before, if one receives YHWH's inspiration, they **will** likely discover these following proofs are

by no means the only dimensions to Daniel's seventy weeks fulfillments.
Nevertheless, according to the primary premise of this book; we will just
apply what I have termed as their "**Root and Branch**" fulfillments in this
consideration of Daniel 9:24-26; as we seek out additional proofs for our
Messiah Yeshua's birth and death year, "*according to the Scriptures*" (1st
Corinthians 15:3-4).

Verse 24
"Seventy weeks are determined upon thy people and upon thy
holy city, to finish the transgression, and to make an end of sins,
and to make reconciliation for iniquity, and to bring in
everlasting righteousness, and to seal up the vision and
prophecy, and to anoint the Most Holy."

Verse 25
"Know therefore and understand [*Branch fulfillments*] that from
the going forth of the commandment to restore and to build
Jerusalem, unto the Messiah, the Prince, shall be seven weeks,
and threescore and two weeks"

Verse 26
"And after [*Root extensions fulfillments*] threescore and two
weeks shall Messiah be cut off, but not for himself: and the
people of the prince that shall come shall destroy the city and the
sanctuary; and the end thereof shall be with a flood, and unto the
end of the war desolations are determined."

Do you remember what I have claimed about the *threescore and two*
weeks? Recall, I said that only the *threescore weeks* were for Messiah
and the *two weeks* should have been assigned to the people of the prince.
Do you recall what year it was that Daniel received this prophecy? It was

in YHWH's Adamic year of 3580 or 421 BC. I made the claim to earlier concerning the point that most all prophecies are what I have termed as dimensional; meaning they have more than one meaning; and in their fulfillments, it is oftentimes duality or have multiple events until the final fulfillment. With that said, consider in particular – the 25th verse; "...*from the going forth of the commandment.*" **That is, from one specific point**. **Recognize** that **three events will unfold** from the same year in time; #1) To restore and to build Jerusalem, #2) To the Messiah and #3) To the Prince. Not only are events fulfilled separately from one point of origin; there is also a fulfillment in chronological order. As I have already said. **Prophecy is dimensional.** This is so that YHWH's hand can be seen at work in prophecy clearly; no matter which way a believer or nonbeliever is inclined to look and focus their theology or scorn on. That is one chief reason why the Bible declares we are, "*without excuse*" (Romans 1:20).

When we speak in terms of standard chronology, we understand Daniel's seventy weeks prophecy from its traditional fulfillment. In my experience, chronological order is that angle of understanding from every theologian and Holy Bible scholar I have ever heard speak on it, feel is its solitary understanding. However, I am declaring to every reader today that such understanding and interpretation is merely what we see in one dimension. There are at the least three (3) dimensions; from which I am able to view. Since this book's focus is time to the end and this section's topic is Yeshua's birth and death; I will only address two dimensions in this book.

Even though it is declared second. This leads me first, to the *root extensions* or **the chronological fulfillment** of Daniel's seventy weeks prophecy. Notice the language of Daniel 9:26 when compared to verse 25. While verses 25 and 26 in their writing, actually exploits the same number; which is "*threescore.*" Singular-directional verse 25 contends that it is to be identified with time leading up to the year and the birth of Messiah. Discern, if you will; it states, "***unto*** *the Messiah.*" On the other hand, without doubt verse 26 has the dogmatic intent on being identified with the death of the Messiah and the year when "*Messiah [shall] be cut off.*" Bible aficionados can see and say what they will and want. And, I am absolutely positive that most of them will. But from my vantage point and humble offerings for enlightenment, it is fairly obvious. One verse – "25" and its fulfillment addresses the birth of our Messiah. But our focus verse – "26," is fulfilled with Messiah's death. We will address *verse 25* shortly. But, first let us consider *verse 26*; which makes the switch from branch to root in its fulfillment. When we look to see YHWH's Adamic year 3580, we see theology's only accepted concept of chronology. Bear in mind from the commandment itself, up to the building and restoring of

Jerusalem and the temple was seven weeks (49 days/years). That takes us forward in time to the cumulative Adamic year of 3629 or 372 BC. Now comes verse 26 and notice that it states, "*And after...*" Generally when we say, "*This*" and then "*After this*" there is an extension or a combining (*addition*) of events. However, verse 26 is not speaking of a birth, but of a death. (*Root extended dimension*) Notice what it says in verse 26.

> **26.** "**And after** threescore and two weeks shall Messiah be cut off, but not for himself: and the people of the prince that shall come shall destroy the city and the sanctuary; and the end thereof shall be with a flood, and unto the end of the war desolations are determined."

We should see the chronological extension dimension - *if you will* - it references to the fact that the Messiah will be "*cut off*" threescore weeks **after** the seven weeks – believe it or not. In this set up or lay out, if one wants to see; with prayer and mercy they can see the hand of YHWH is at work; no matter whether one sees the individualized branch version or chronological root extension version. And please bear in mind, many of the "*terminologies*" I am using here are surely no theological gems. They are simple articulations, from a simple and hopefully humbled heart, that are meant to help make visible, a simple picture formation in the readers' mind that depicts these revelation perspectives. If we see the prophecy as having their "*dimensional fulfillments*," we should also discern how they work in cooperation with each other, without conflicting with each other.

Notice what is revealed, as we depart from YHWH's Adamic year of 3580; in what I have at present termed as the prophecy's chronological dimension. From 3580, we go forward in time forty-nine (49) years to year 3629. "*After*" we add the "*threescore weeks*" or 420 years. Then we arrive at Adamic year 4049 or AD 49. According to the prophetic event of <u>Daniel 9:26,</u> this is the year when Messiah is "*<u>cut off</u>.*" By now, we all know what I have claimed this revelation means for Yeshua's age.

Still, for this book to make its "*assertion*" for Yeshua's age to be at forty-nine (49) when he was crucified; there should be of necessity, some sort of confirmation to his birth year that supports such an outlandish and against our traditions assertion. This book claims such proof exist and is found in the 25th <u>verse of Daniel nine;</u> by way of its branch dimension fulfillments. Recall - <u>just like the branches of a tree</u> - each of the three prophecies from verse 25 reach forward individually into the future from the same "*tree trunk*" or date in history. In the case of <u>Daniel 9:25</u>, that date is YHWH's Adamic year of 3580 or 421 BC. Each prophecy in its verse, <u>branch</u> out from the same **Royal Proclamation by Cyrus**.

25. "Know therefore and understand, that **from the going forth of the commandment** to <u>restore and to build Jerusalem</u>, <u>unto the Messiah, the Prince</u>, shall be seven weeks, and <u>threescore</u> and <u>two weeks</u>."
   a. <u>Restore and to build Jerusalem and the temple</u> (*seven weeks – 49 years*)
   b. <u>Unto the Messiah</u> (*threescore weeks – 420 years*)

c. The Prince - his people (*two weeks – 14 years*)

> **Note:** All three prophecies in verse 25 branch out from the same trunk event - "*the going forth of the commandment.*" Recall that, "*the commandment*" went forth in Adamic year 3580 or 421 BC.

From this book's perspective and of course everybody already know I claim by the divine revelation of YHWH's Spirit; let us examine and judge the branch extension fulfillments, as they give support to my claim that the Bible reveals the birth year of Messiah Yeshua. From YHWH's Adamic year 3580, in seven weeks or forty-nine (49) days fulfilled in years, The Second Temple is completed. Making the count from 3580 would take us to the Adamic year of 3629 or 372 BC. **Most important**, taking note from the same dimension and from the same Adamic year of 3580, counting out threescore weeks or days of 420, fulfilled in years; *Gabriel reveals to Daniel and we who believe, the long-awaited Jewish Messiah would come*. (Verse 25) The text did not say, imply or assign any event akin to death. It clearly affirms "*...unto the Messiah.*" If we are able to accept it; we have biblical confirmation or at the least, support for the year Messiah *came to his temple*. (Malachi 3:1) Does it not make you wonder? Even if Y'hudah (Judah) still rejects **Yeshua** as Messiah today; how can they remain in denial that Messiah has come (*as the suffering servant*) and was "*...cut off*" "*...out of the land of the living*" "*...according to the Scriptures?*" (Daniel 9:25, Isaiah 53:8)

Now then, according to my claims of YHWH's revelations to me, in this book we now have both the birth year and the crucifixion year of the Messiah's time, in hand and "*according to the Holy Scriptures*." In turn, such an acknowledgment and confirmation offers – from my perspective – extraordinary support to my *"premise"* for the age of Yeshua at the time of his crucifixion. When we make the count up from year 3580, the 420 years account out precisely to YHWH's Adamic year of 4000; or 1 BCE. Then, as far as the two weeks in this same dimension from 3580 is concerned, it appears there is a leadership change from Cyrus; likely to Ahasuerus (*or Artaxerxes*) in the year of 3594 or 407 BC. Making way for that extended period (*30 years*) of social resistance and conspiracy against efforts of returning Jews of the captivity to rebuild Jerusalem and YHWH's second temple. Those three prophecies fulfill themselves as the extension branches from the prophetic tree trunk year of 3580. Each one individually reaching out from year 3580 to three independent, different and completed in their fulfillments of YHWH's once sealed (***BRANCH***) dimension of Daniel's seventy weeks. Nevertheless, its root fulfillments culminated with the complete annihilation and overthrow of **The Second Temple**. People will believe what they will. But, the evidence is there. That is, if one chooses to research it and perhaps believe it. That is also provided YHWH has mercy on them and reveals to such a one. As an added offering of supportive proof - *here is a bonus* - before we move on

with the time. View the following passages of biblical scripture. I believe

with additional study on the part of all interested parties, one may find a

discernible connection to my makeshift illustrations and narratives of the

branch. There is also a bit of evidence contained that man; i.e. the Jews,

will not be responsible for constructing the third temple of YHWH at the

Holy City at Jerusalem. So - *if you will* - judge the passages for yourself.

> *"Hear now, O Joshua the high priest, thou, and thy fellows that
> sit before thee: for they are men wondered at: for,* **behold**, I will
> bring forth my servant **the BRANCH**" (Zechariah 3:8).

> *"And the word of the Lord came unto me, saying, Take of them
> of the captivity, even of Heldai, of Tobijah, and of Jedaiah,
> which are come from Babylon, and come thou the same day, and
> go into the house of Josiah the son of Zephaniah; then take silver
> and gold, and make crowns, and set them upon the head of
> Joshua the son of Josedech, the high priest; and speak unto him,
> saying, Thus speaketh the Lord of hosts, saying,* Behold the man
> whose name is* **The BRANCH**; *and he shall grow up out of his
> place, and* **he shall build the temple of the Lord**: *even* ***he shall
> build the temple of the Lord***; *and he shall bear the glory, and
> [he] shall sit and rule upon his throne; and he shall be a priest
> upon his throne: and the* [**mighty**] *counsel* [**-or**] *of peace shall
> be between them both" (Zechariah 6:9-13).*

The reality of Messiah should be rather apparent. This ***prophecy*** was

not addressing "*Joshua* [Yahushua] *the son of Josedech* [Yahutzadak],

the high priest [cohen gadol]." He was merely the shadow picture of yet

future events in dimensions. The fulfillments of this prophecy would not

begin for roughly another 400 years. It would be with the birth of the true

BRANCH; Yahushua/Yehoshua (<u>Yeshua</u>), thought to be the son of Yosef (Joseph). The prophecy's "*final fulfillment*" is roughly 2000 years after that; with Yeshua constructing his true and as far as I understand it right now, his eternal temple of saints at the first resurrection; believe it or not.

Notwithstanding, let us suppose for a moment I am insane; and, the detracting pundits are right on Herod the Great dying in 2 BC and their traditional guesses regarding the birth of "*Jesus Christ.*" Should I not also concede to their condemnations of my arguments concerning the Roman Numeral concept; and its usage in the Mosaic writings, and in Prophecy? I mean, while I am on the backtracking and back-stepping trail, I might as well backtrack and renege on basically all of my major sticking points of dissention on this subject, as comparable with all of the standards of their so-called, "*theological expertise*" - Right? That means we will have to backtrack to the time of the Great Flood of Noah's day, disavow the Roman Number concept in scripture and do a recount from the year 1660 (2341 BC). Presuming that YHWH renewed the face of the earth in the Adamic year 4000 BC. When we recount, we gain significant years in the process. In seven generations following the flood, we gain forty (40) years. A forty-year discrepancy may not be very much in the eyes of the historians; but, consider what I wrote earlier and then go and add it up in the traditional route.

"Remember, in our walk we are in the year of 1660 or 2341 BCE with the birth of Arphaxad. Arphaxad lived, *"five and thirty years"* (25), and begat Salah. Salah lived, *"thirty years"* (30), and begat Eber. Eber lived, *"four and thirty years"* (26), and begat Peleg. Peleg lived, *"thirty years"* (30), and begat Reu. Reu lived, *"two and thirty years"* (28), and begat Serug. Serug lived, *"thirty years"* (30), and begat Nahor. Nahor lived, *"nine and twenty years"* (11), and begat Te'-rah" (pp. 155-156).

Let's do the count again. This time we will use the numbers of tradition!

1) Arphaxad, *__"five and thirty years"__* (25).
   That becomes thirty-five (35) .... **plus ten (10) years.**

2) Eber, *__"four and thirty years"__* (26).
   That becomes thirty-four (34)............................ **plus eight (8) years**.

3) Reu, *__"two and thirty years"__* (28).
   That becomes thirty-two (32)............................. **plus four (4) years**.

4) Nahor, *__"nine and twenty years"__* (11).
   That becomes twenty- nine (29) ....**plus eighteen (18) years**.

When we add ten (10), eight (8), four (4) and eighteen (18) we get a total of forty (40) additional years, as I said. We actually gained an entire generation. So as when we approach Te'-rah's seventy (70) years, instead of us being at year 1910 or 2091 BC, we arrive at and find ourselves at date 1950 or 2051 BC. From there it is fairly easy to count the years to Daniel's, "seventy weeks." Add the following numbers to year 1950.

1) Abraham to Isaac .... 100 years

2) Isaac to Jacob .... 60 years

3) Jacob to Egypt.. 130 years

4) Israel in Egypt .... 430 years

5) Israel in the wilderness .... 40 years

6) Israel enters the Promise Land under judges .... 410 years

7) Israel demands a king. Net overlap years after judges .... 450 years

8) The Babylonian captivity .... 70 years

Added together for a total that takes us to the year 3640 or 361 BC. Here is where things tend to get interesting again – if you ask me from my perspective. Supposedly now, we are at the year 3640 or 361 BC. Understand now, in the same manner, we are still coming up from the Babylonian captivity. However, we are - _traditionally wise_ - sixty (60) years ahead of where my research had landed us. So now, according to information given to Daniel by the Archangel Gabriel, there was to immediately follow the Babylonian captivity, some seventy (70) weeks of prophecy; where its days are fulfilled in years. We are to make our observations here in the chronological dimension. Let us now recount the numbers and reconsider their values.

1) Forty-nine (49) years or seven weeks to rebuild Jerusalem and the Second Temple.

2) 434 years until Messiah is cut off or crucified – if you take the "_threescore and two weeks_" (Daniel 9:25) without my/YHWH's perspective and insight; as a majority of religious experts would have you to view things. It would total out to be 62 weeks or 434 days fulfilled in years.

3) Then the last "*one week*;" the seven years with the shenanigans of the "Antichrist" in the midst of that last week; which the week is infamous for. (*Many think this week will occur the last seven years of the age before "Jesus" returns. It is not needed to prove my point*)

True enough, list item number three, the last week or the supposed seven-year period that includes that special covenant involving the Jews and the Antichrist, will be an important enough development to look for in the world's countdown to Messiah's return. But, that supposed future and historic covenant that lead to many Jews' doom, is not on *that list* of items – *the reasons for my theological dissent*. It is not vital to my claim and not needed to make my point that something is wrong concerning overall Christendom's interpretation and perception of and in Daniel's seventy weeks. The issue on point stands at list item number two. And, from my humble perspective, it is the careless blunder, the thoughtless mischaracterization of the largely unvetted and to this date the fairly unchallenged assumption through presumption about the "*threescore and two weeks*" of Daniel's ninth chapter. It is contained in verse 25. But – *at least for this exercise* – let it be as far from me, as the east is from the west, to challenge the historical and theological savvy of the "experts" on this matter. This is for ***instructional purposes*** only; with the possibility of enhancing reader insights. If we persist with historian's cites and we insist on sticking with the belief that, "*Jesus*" had to have been born no later than 4 BC (*pundits believe Herod the Great died 4-2 BC*); those base dates are wrong. However, if we back step and disavow the Roman Numeral concept revelation and return to using the experts' traditional concepts on mathematics. If we choose to have confidence of belief that using our established western-gentile thinking in **assuming addition,** in which case *order would not matter in adding and multiplication*; would accuracy with a culture much more ancient and distant from our own be even fairly acceptable in this case? I will limit my perspective in this one. The following is what we will actually end up with. Once again we start from the year we have newly established from the traditional approach of counting, year 3640 or 361 BC. Now, let us do the simple addition. Shall we? Add on seven weeks or forty-nine (49) years to 3640 or 361 BC for the temple. We have year 3689 or 312 BC. Now comes the "*insane*" part of the equation. Now add on the experts' "*threescore and two weeks*" or 434 days/years. **WOW!!!** I don't know about you concerning your phone calculator, but I come to the year 4123 or AD 123. That's right! Doing a basic add count, it being determined by the pundits; Herod the Great died between 4 and 2 BC. This would make "*Jesus Christ*" (*And, it is likely Jesus was **no less** than five (5) years old when Herod's death occurred*) very-very close to [**WOW!!! - Again**] **130 years old** at the time of his crucifixion! **That is what I call a total theological disaster**! Right now, from my perspective; my *asserted* forty-nine (49) years are not looking too extreme. Considering what we have so-called "**_expertly_**" come to, I think I prefer YHWH's revelation of discovery over human traditions.

It being a very good example - *notwithstanding* - in case my previous argument was not convincing enough for everybody in making my point; please be patient and allow me to put out one more example on my list of what I maintain, YHWH has allowed me to discern. I now consider them to be erroneous presentations from tradition. Please, don't be offended. If you consider what I am about to say without bias, you may see my points have little to do with preferential doctrines of belief. It is just the simple mathematics of addition. Everyone is okay with adding, right? So we are good? Let us continue. Now listen carefully to these next two questions.

These are not trick questions!

1. What does tradition say is the year "*Jesus Christ*" was crucified and died?

2. What does tradition say was the age of "*Jesus Christ*" when he was crucified and died?

3. When does much, if not most of history says is the year in which Herod the Great died?

Within the scope of the answers to these questions is revealed my final point before moving on.

- #1 - Most think "*Jesus*" was crucified between AD 30 and 36 (*AD 33 being the average*).

- #2 - Most every source I could cite feel *"Jesus"* was between 30-33½ years old at death. 33½ years old seems to be most popular.

- #3 - Historical sources cite Herod the Great died around 4 to 2 BC. (3 BC *is the average*)

Forget all those other discrepancies in the older numbers and years. Even if we were to ignore all of them and objectively, only consider what is right in front of our faces and right up under our noses. I would say we should all smell the stench of error and deception. There is good reason why in the book of Revelation the Holy Spirit reveals Satan, *"deceiveth the whole world"* (Revelation 12:9). People (*myself included*) have the tendency to push aside and ignore new ideas and concepts that push out against any of our long held traditions and beliefs. I know from firsthand experience. The challenge of spiritual logic against presumed and long-held, but thoughtless and unvetted tradition and belief is not comfortable. Do you really think I accepted the spiritual revelations I am declaring to you in this book, without a **BIG** spiritual fight with my fears and doubts? There are few things more powerful in the human psyche than our fears of being wrong and being deceived; then afterwards, having been called out and having to face critics, doubters, non-believers, enemies and yeah, sometimes friends and family with a sometimes thoroughly embarrassing error. Very few people like to be called out, when they are in the wrong.

It's Much Later Than You Think!

Think about this last example for a minute. <u>Note</u>: For a long time this was "MY" position regarding "*Jesus Christ's*" crucifixion and death. I actually believed that "*Jesus*" was 33½ years old when he was crucified. Because, I basically did not study enough in the right areas for to even think about any plausible objections that I might have discerned for such a basic belief and doctrine. Still, permit me to present the above numbers and bullet points; along with what I call, YHWH's thought-provoking Holy Spirit curiosities and my common sense <u>in-my-face</u> realities. What was I saying and establishing when I stated that I believed "*Jesus Christ*" was crucified in AD 33; he was 33½ when he died and Herod the Great died on the average, 3 BC? If we will objectively do the numbers; what the facts say is in the following. "*Jesus Christ*" was not 33½ years old when he was crucified. Instead, by our own numbers no less and then by our own admissions or omissions - *you can choose* - "*Jesus Christ*" had to have been around the age of forty (40) years old, at the time of his crucifixion. <u>Let us really think about this for a moment</u>. If we choose to accept that Herod the Great died in 2 BC (<u>*Choosing the lesser of three evils*</u>); then surely, specific issues should tend to become very apparent, perhaps even spiritually painful; but, absolutely biblically clear and bare to our common spiritual senses. "*Jesus*" was alleged to be two years old when Herod the Great ordered his attempt to snuff out the Messiah's life.

Personally and quite honestly, I have continuously asked myself the question, "Why Cuz?" If Herod really thought YHWH was truly at work. How did he (*Herod*), reason as a man, that he would be able to thwart Elohim's divine effort? I find Herod's attempt, absolutely extraordinarily ignorant. In any case, continuing. If "*Jesus*" was two; and by generous estimates, it took Yosef and Myriam (*Joseph and Mary's real names*) six (6) months to get into Egypt and again six (6) months on the return trip - with a practical two-year stay in Egypt; reasonably speaking; when AD 1 approached, "*Jesus*" would have surely been approaching seven (7) years of age. Basic human logic and just the plain exercise of literacy would dictate. When we add the AD 30 to 36 to the mixture; we eclipse age 33 and come nearer to age forty (40). Can you see my point of dissention in this last example with my own once and long-held traditions surrounding the crucifixion and death of our Messiah Yeshua? Is my reasoning sound in your own mind and to your own senses of objectivity? I should hope so. Come on people, guys and gals, critics or otherwise; even supposed brothers and sisters. Are my claims so outrageous, so out of sorts, so off of the rails to the point that I am seen as traditionally rebellious? Simply because I compare them - *in my perceived spiritual logic* - to unvetted or suspect customs. Whereas, many Christians and Christian organizations suspiciously overlook suspect beliefs in regards to their potential for falseness and paganism in the broader public of Christendom; I hope my breakdown of all this is not viewed as sounding superior or being mean-spirited. I don't mean to sound that way. I simply want to establish truth. Still, the Holy Scripture calls upon us all - *leaders and laymen alike* - to **study, watch** and **pray**; among other **spiritually enhancing actions**. We are all encouraged to do this so that we may all gain knowledge and understanding. Consider my critical analysis in contrast to the claims of this book about Yeshua's age at the time of his crucifixion. Decide in your own heart what seems likely the truth, what fits biblically and not robotically accept what history and one's denomination has traditionally claimed and taught. I trust you will be less confused with what I would deem, a proper implementation of my encouragement to contrast. As far as this book is concerned, and for your sanity, we will step away from the traditions and return yet again to the premise originally contained in and touted from this book of revelation and perspective. It was YHWH's Adamic Hebrew year of 4049 or AD 49; in our discerning of threescore weeks and not threescore and two weeks. Messiah Yeshua was forty-nine (49) years up in his age, when he was condemned to death and crucified. So then, continue to accompany me – *if you will* – in this walk through biblical and prophetic time. At worst, if nothing else; I pray readers are and will continue to engage; while I make every effort to challenge every objective spiritual mind and entertain the dogmatic denominational mind.

Believe me when I say, I am being honest when I say to you, I do understand the position that many historians are in. That being this; after nearly every event - *and this is true for the most of them at least* - their written history is god over anything the Holy Bible could ever record as true or exact. If the Holy Bible stand in opposition to anything their gods of history may claim, witness to and write; the Holy Bible has no seat of authority. Here is one of the few things I might suggest to you the reader. Do not be too hasty to side with these so-called witnesses for the vaunted historians. If there be any disagreements when comparing our witness in the Holy Scripture to the written history according to men, I would say to the seeker of the spiritual truth. Check to see first is the claims of history a dogmatic notation or simply a guess, estimate or theory. Then - *if you can* - see whether a good and proper translation of that Bible passage was employed. In other words, was the Holy Bible in reality, saying what it appeared to be saying? I'm not being dismissive of the Bible or anything close to that; but just the opposite. This is merely my exhortation to you and everyone else (*including my own holy aspirations*) to be biblically thorough as we can possibly be. After all, the Holy Bible does say this.

> "Study to show thyself approved unto God, a workman that needeth not to be ashamed, rightly dividing the word of truth. But shun profane *and* vain babblings: for they will increase unto more ungodliness. And their word will eat as doth a canker: of

whom is Hymeneus and Philetus; who concerning the truth have erred, saying that the resurrection is past already; and overthrow the faith of some. Nevertheless the foundation of God standeth sure, having this seal, The Lord knoweth them that are his."

(2nd Timothy 2:15-19)

If the Bible version you use acceptably matches those of the original writings in the Holy Scripture; you the reader, as the seeker of The Truth, when it comes to any dispute over questions to the trueness of the Holy Bible, is left with a choice of faithfulness. You therefore have to make a decision. Is the Holy Scripture witnessing to a truth or is man's so-called recorded history true? Prior to one deciding on the above dilemma; let me ask a qualifier to ascertain in your opinion, your ability to properly answer my qualifier question. It's a very simple inquiry. Which authority has made you that extraordinary and unique offer of eternal life? Was it YHWH (*The Holy Bible*) or men's rendition of history? I rest my case, for those who have hope in immortality through our Messiah Yeshua. As far as the Holy Bible skeptics and as far fools go, we know they do not believe the Bible. Understanding this as a fact; there is only one thing to say regarding their end – if they will not repent. As Paul Harvey use to say, "*And now, the rest of the story.*" As far as any Holy Bible detractors' scorn; who these people truly hate is YHWH Elohim through our Adonai Messiah Yeshua. So as far as I am concerned, "To hell with them all!"

"THAT'S RIGHT! I SAID IT!"

It is likely where they will all end up anyway and possibly a host of others. I am referring to those holy hypocrites; who hold back the truth of Yeshua our Adonai in unrighteousness. They don't believe; and they take great pleasure in discouraging the hearts of the unaware into choosing a "questionable" history book - over a thoroughly vetted translation in the pages of their Holy Bible from the Holy Scriptures. And, I understand no English translations of the Holy Scriptures are absolutely perfect. **I am just trying to be honest here guys.** In any case, 2nd Timothy 2:15-19 is generally the remedy to every intolerable entry or rendering of the Holy Bible - **STUDY!** That is my stand. What is yours? Again, with all of that said; let us continue on with our walk through YHWH's ordained time for Adam. But before we step forward in time; on the following page is my artistic attempt to help all my readers to obtain a mind visual through illustrations of the *Root and Branch fulfillments*. I feel it shows how both are able to exist together, work separately and in cooperation with each other to mark the Messiah's visitation in their exact fashion. Whether one believes their fulfillments or not, I believe they make the hand of YHWH in our history seeable – even by the carnal eye.

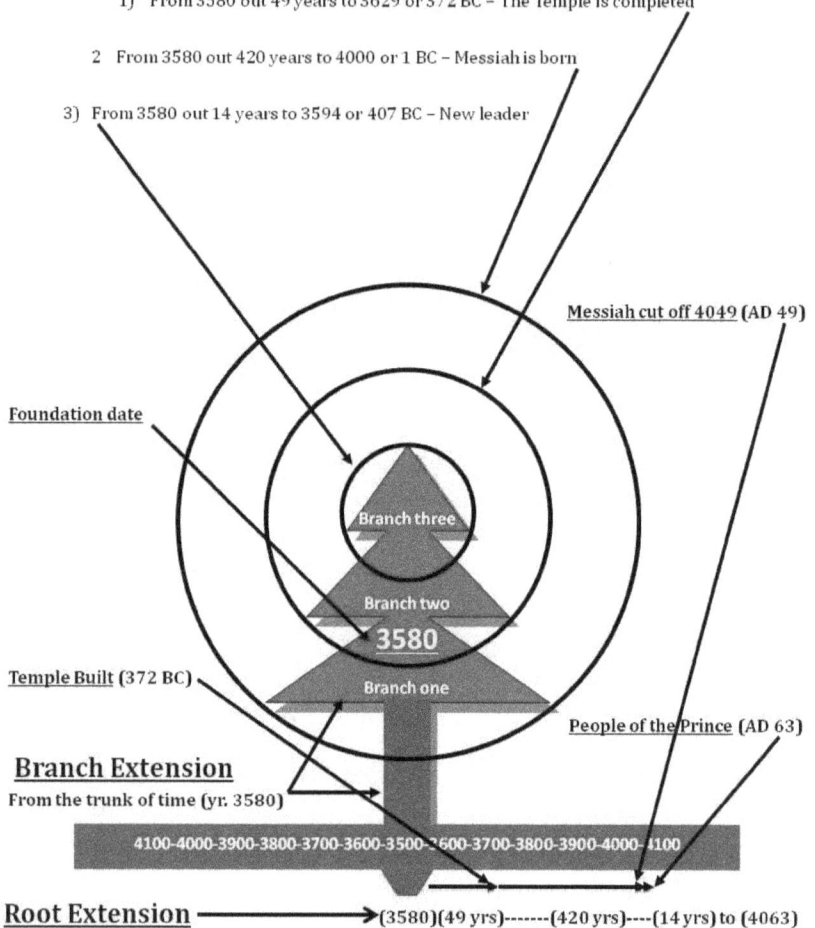

Visual - Branch and Root Fulfillment (Daniel 9:25 & 26)

1) From 3580 out 49 years to 3629 or 372 BC – The Temple is completed

2 From 3580 out 420 years to 4000 or 1 BC – Messiah is born

3) From 3580 out 14 years to 3594 or 407 BC – New leader

Messiah cut off 4049 (AD 49)

Foundation date

Branch three

Branch two

3580

Temple Built (372 BC)

Branch one

People of the Prince (AD 63)

Branch Extension
From the trunk of time (yr. 3580)

4100-4000-3900-3800-3700-3600-3500-3600-3700-3800-3900-4000-4100

Root Extension ———————➤(3580)(49 yrs)-------(420 yrs)----(14 yrs) to (4063)

CHAPTER 13

___THE FLAVOR OF FIRE___
(*Daniel's final three weeks*)

Within the "*two weeks*" and the "*one week*" which remain and mark

the conclusion of the "***root version***" fulfillments to the seventy weeks

prophecy of Daniel – from Daniel's day, we are given the future in

history's view to Rome's tyranny and overthrow of Jerusalem and

YHWH's second temple. At the societal level, Roman occupation and its

tyranny upon the Jewish people were the results of Judah's sin that

caused its desolation from Nebuchadnezzar's days. Because YHWH is

quoted as saying it was "*perpetual desolations*" (Jeremiah 25:9), not very

much relief, if any was going to be experienced by the Jewish people,

from Babylon up until the Roman occupation, and quite probably

beyond. In strategic terms the desolation of Jerusalem and the temple

was done in order to build up the exploits and boost the military resume of the then inexperience <u>Prince</u> (Titus). In prophetic terms and primarily, that great devastation was done to Jerusalem and her temple in order to fulfill the prophetic memos - *again because of Judah's great sin* - of what the Archangel Gabriel had given to Daniel (*9:26&27*); and also the prophecy of our Messiah Yeshua. (*Matthew 24:2*) The wicked spirit of corruption and sacrilege – *according to Daniel's seventy weeks prophecy* – would materialize in about the sixty-ninth (69) week and would rapidly disintegrate the Jewish people's resolve for the peaceful coexistence with the people of the prince (*The Roman Empire*).

If you will recall from the front side of my most recent *divine pillar of digression*; we were into the merits of why year 4049 (AD 49) was Yeshua's "*crucifixion year*." I hope my narratives support as well the tumultuous years I claim follow directly after his execution (<u>The believer should dub it as calculated murder</u>). I will try to describe in general what appears to be a slow but steady build-up of social and religious hostilities between the Jew and Hellenisation forces for Greco-Roman culture; until and beyond the destruction of the second temple by Rome. Of the fateful, but prophesied event, I would cite, it was quite literally all, " hell-on-a-nation" [*Roman retribution*] that broke out on the Jews at Jerusalem and their surroundings (Judea). Consider that we are told by historians, in 63 BCE, "The Romans invaded Greece and also conquered the Hellenistic

Seleucid Empire in the Middle East region. [The Seleucid Empire was a Persian/Iranian kingdom. And the vast majority of Iranians are Muslims - britannica.com.] Though the Jewish people were granted some measure of autonomy, inside of Jerusalem; Judea was in their reality, ruled from Rome" (History-of-israel.org). Even though Rome would occupy and govern Jerusalem for centuries to come, our focus will be that twenty-one (21) years time period following Messiah's murder/execution by the Jewish leadership - at the hands of the local Roman authorities; until the words of prophecies spoken by the prophet Daniel and by our Messiah Yeshua concerning the destruction of the second temple were fulfilled. So then, let us list those remaining perceptible segregates of the last twenty-one (21) years from Daniel's seventy weeks prophecy; which we failed to address during its run on page 205, where we cut them off from.

(Daniel's final three weeks)

3) The people of the prince will come after, "*two weeks*" to negotiate a seven-year covenant with supposedly some of its most likely, corrupt influential heads of the people and the corrupt High Priest of Judah.
   a. Two week is a total of fourteen days and is fulfilled in fourteen (14) years.
   b. After which, "...*he shall confirm the covenant with many for one week*" (Daniel 9:27)

4) The Covenant (part I) "*And in the midst of the week he shall cause the sacrifice and the oblation to cease*" (Verse 27).
   a. One-half week or three and a half days - equaling three and a half (3½) years into the enactment of the covenant agreement.

    b.   Major conflicts ensued and unprecedented war would break out.

5) The Covenant (part II) "…*the prince that shall come shall destroy the city and the sanctuary; and the end thereof shall be with a flood, and unto the end of the war desolations are determined*." (Verse 26)

    a.   One-half week or three and a half days; equaling three and a half (3½) years later the war took its toll on Jerusalem and its temple.

    b.   Of YHWH's second holy temple, there was not left one stone upon another that was not thrown down. (Matthew 24:2)

From Daniel's narrative, Yeshua's prophetic judgment and my perceived revelation from YHWH and history, that time span covers the years from AD 49 to 70. We will attempt to revisit that time period in hopefully a revealing narrative from my own study. After which, we will need to address an obligation of correction for insight; before we can walk on to the Millennial Sabbath Day of YHWH. That is in year 6001; as it has come to be known in many Messianic factions. Then from there, we will walk until the end of time as we understand it to be, up to the Last Great Day of YHWH. Many now recognize this period in time as the more apprehensive, **"JUDGMENT DAY."** It has come to be asked of us, on that great day of woe, "…*who shall be able to stand*?" (Revelation 6:17)

I would think no one needs to be reminded of this. After Messiah's execution, there was a major persecution focusing in on every Messianic believer in Yeshua as their Messiah. In that short period following the crucifixion, persecutions of Messianics only intensified. And believe it or not; from that period forward to date, said persecution has not decreased by any discernible degrees. The Holy Bible warns those professing the name of Yeshua/Yehoshua/Yahoshua/Yahushua/YHWH as the Messiah. **What!? You can't see it!?** You say potatoes, they say potahtoes; he says tomatoes, she says tomahtoes. I say, "**SEMANTICS!**" "*he that hath ears.*"

"And when the dragon saw that he was cast unto the earth, he persecuted the woman which brought forth the man child. And to the woman were given two wings of a great eagle; that she might fly into the wilderness, into her place, where she is nourished for a time, and times, and half a time, from the face of the serpent. And the serpent cast out of his mouth water as a flood after the woman, that he might cause her to be carried away of the flood. And the earth helped the woman; and the earth opened her mouth, and swallowed up the flood which the dragon cast out of his mouth. And the dragon was wroth with the woman, and went to make war with the remnant of her seed, which keep the commandments of God, and have the testimony of [*Yeshua the Messiah*]." (Revelation 12:13-17)

Is there anybody who is seriously thinking that at any time since that moment recorded in Revelation, that Satan the Devil has taken a day off and allowed the saints any accumulated relief? There is no doubt; Satan has not. Nevertheless, as far as the persecution of professing Christians are concerned, to hear the issue from modern media; or shall I say, to experience their deafening silence on their behalf, one might think "*that* old serpent" was vacationing someplace that makes him feel closer to his future home – like in the Mohave Desert in California. What would be even better, maybe he is not even on this planet! Perhaps he is cooling it out in our sun or preferably, someplace even further away – like the other side of the creation. That's wishful thinking - on Satan's part. Besides; he already tried that. It didn't turn out well. So I guess not and you're right. When we look around us, we can plainly see. <u>SATAN IS ON EARTH</u>!

Look; few people among the pundits today call things the way they are. Our masses have been made drunk by their wine of fornication. Because we ourselves are guilty, we have allowed ourselves to become at ease when we are describing those who commit their almost unspeakable atrocity, as being sick. Because, if we were to call things what they really were, which would be wickedness and sin; we would evoke the Spirit of YHWH. We would in the processes condemn ourselves. Not to mention, bring that same world of wickedness we have just condemned, down on our heads. To all of the righteous who are afraid, but not too afraid to speak out; I say, hear and understand this. Satan the Devil may have had a little problem finding you in this wilderness in the past. Possibly, you might have been keeping your head low in silence. Or maybe it was your go-along to get-along spirit, which convinced Satan the Devil to linger at bay. However, YHWH's Holy Spirit will speak to his own, oh professing

Christians and my Messianic brother. YHWH will tell you himself. Such an attitude, just plain and simple will not get you to the place ["Heaven?" for some - the kingdom of YHWH for others] where it is that you say you want to be. Self-condemnation or not, there are some who are not afraid and will call sin, wicked and twisted - openly and in public. If you want to have any chance of making it into where you want to be, you better be or become one of them. They speak out because they know Satan the devil is more than motivated. **He is an activist**! Satan is angry to the degree that many in silence do not comprehend. You only need to read history, to see some of that anger demonstrated against the early Messianic believers in Yeshua; and, the Jews seeking and looking for their Messiah to come. In my perspective, I assert that twenty years leading up to the year that the Romans destroyed The Second Temple, violence against Messianics and Jews was rampant. That violence and Jewish history could be and should be at this point, considered as being synonymous. The only discrepancy might be that the Messianic believers in Yeshua frequently received acts of violence from both ends of the spectrum, in the actions of the Roman authorities and Jews. Some cases on point would be Steven (*He was stoned by the Jews*), Apostle Shaul, (*Shaul was routinely mobbed and persecuted, to the point of an appeal to Caesar. The Holy Bible signifies Shaul may have likely been executed in*

Prison.) and most infamous, Messiah Yeshua himself was beaten beyond recognition (*by the Jews with the hands of Rome*) - almost to death. Then he was hanged on a stake (*crucified*) until he was **actually dead**. I would like to think we can all agree that Yeshua's sacrifice, although literally indescribable, speaks to his own for itself. It is obvious, after Yeshua's illegal trial; his scourging and crucifixion had to have been a horrible and gruesome sight to have to witness. As often as I speak to it, I do not truly comprehend the reality of such an evil act and event of envy and hatred.

> "Behold, my servant shall deal prudently, he shall be exalted and extolled, and be very high. As many were astonished at thee; his visage was so marred more than any man, and his form more than the sons of men:" (Isaiah 52:13-14).

If we match up history with YHWH's seventy weeks prophecy from Daniel's 9th chapter; after Messiah is "*cut off;*" for fourteen years tension among the factions (*The Jewish people were adversely manipulated by corrupted Jewish leaders and Roman authority*) would start to build to a violent head. Then after that frail seven-year pact for peace, things would make its shifts toward war. If we can believe Gabriel; the final upheaval would start after that, **69th week** (Daniel 9:25-27); which was in AD 63. I am not as meticulous and accurate in my narrations as is the Holy Bible, but there is a *reasonable* match up for the prophesied events of Daniel's 9th chapter in man's historical record. I am aware that some of the dates history gives us when compared to the Scriptural record, might be a little suspect. But, I believe for our witness, certain of the prophetic events are accurately depicted in men's history books to help confirm our faith in YHWH's authority to manipulate time and space. I have matched <u>Daniel 9:26-27</u> to specific events of which skeptics might view as coincidental resemblances in Roman/Jewish history. My study found key year binders to the ultimate destructions of Jerusalem and her second temple. Many of the causes relating to their ruin, were intensely entwined with the social, political and religious backdrops. In the form of "eye-witness" records of history left behind for to gather, classify and possibly judge over; the few that survived were too convoluted and controversial in nature for them to be satisfactorily presented in this small book. Although from time to time in this book I have and will make comments on certain moral or doctrinal issues; this book's main focus is on the passage of historical years, in contrast to the total allotment of years; which were ordained in YHWH's tender mercy for man's week of self-rule (six days/6000 yrs), Millennial Sabbath and Judgment Day. Judgment Day requires another 1000 years. In my book that is 8000 "discernible-chronological" years we must find.

This book started from year one using the biblical record. It has journeyed up from Adam to the time of the flood. It has scrutinized the generations after the flood leading to the patriarchs. With the Egyptian slavery, it was forced to forsake the Messianic bloodline for Israel's overall historical experiences. In laying out the passing of time, we have accounted for their wilderness wondering in Sin, Judges and Kings, the destruction of the first temple, the Babylonian Captivity, the construction of the second temple, the first coming of and sacrifice of Messiah and now we are at the destruction of the second temple. From here on out we will make our walk through history to what many feel will be the time of "***The Antichrist***," then on until the return of Messiah and then unto the judgment. But first it is vital we reflect on "that decisive match-up in history," as we compare it with the final week of Daniel's seventy weeks. That last week foretold in clear outline - *from my perspective* – the two crucial events between AD 63 and **AD 70**. It captures the spirit of the spiral that spun out of control into war violence. Through that war, we should well come to recognize **AD 70** as being that point where YHWH dropped his prophetic anchor in history. That anchor allows us the ability to steady the Biblical ship for a deeper prophetic discernment. **AD 70**, as it turns out to be in time reality; is, "***The Bridge to Prophecy***." **AD 70** in essence, helps us maintain proper perspectives and like a bridge, from its point in history; it links biblical history to future prophetic times. It stands as the foundational footing for the fulfillment of Yeshua's final two major prophecies, leading up to his return. In hope that you might find confidence in that anchor point, take time to reflect deeply on both Daniel and Yeshua's prophecies of destruction and desolation; as this section reflects on the antagonistic times leading up unto that infamous occasion that overflowed onto Jerusalem and her second temple.

> "And he shall confirm the covenant with many for one week: and in the midst of the week he shall cause the sacrifice and the oblation to cease..." "...and the people of the prince that shall come shall destroy the city and the sanctuary; and the end thereof *shall be* with a flood, and unto the end of the war desolations [*Plural*] are determined" (Daniel 9: 27; then 26).

> "And [Yeshua] went out, and departed from the temple: and his disciples came to *him* for to show him the buildings of the temple. And [Yeshua] said unto them, See ye not all these things? verily I say unto you, There shall not be left here one stone upon another, that shall not be thrown down."
>
> (Matthew 24:2)

Procurators and kings managed and ruled Judea and Jerusalem for many years from what history tells us was 63 BCE. As we stated before, corruption was as natural among the authorities over people's social lives as the Sabbath day was dominant in people's spiritual lives. The people lived daily with the burden of heavy taxation, also social and religious disrespect. Sometimes, there was outright blasphemy. While exercising their power over the Jews, the Roman authorities did many atrocities. The Jews would stage different protests in response to the way they were being treated and oppressed by Rome. Rarely did their protest render the desired results. Most occasions it was anxiety, pain and regret. These became the Jews' normal. Acts of violence, slaughter and murder was not viewed as off the rails and tyranny was a normal condition in Rome's occupation of Jerusalem. Nevertheless, it seldom escalated into anything much beyond their small local social skirmishes in and around the city. In frustration, the Jews were increasingly growing wearier of their dire condition. So that by the year AD 63 things were getting desperate, more so than the usual. The history books bear record. Many ambiguous things happened simultaneously in Rome and Jerusalem. Their perfect storm in friction caused that Jewish quake. This resulted in that spiritual tsunami; which Daniel preserved for us in his seventy weeks of prophecy. It was continuous acts of sexual indiscretions and debauchery from the highest authority in some of their Roman governors, to base troops in the Roman guard posted over the Jewish community. Stifling corruption continually pressed its weight of tyranny on the common citizen in both the social and spiritual arenas, to the point of no return. A vicious cycle of robbery, rape and murder were habitual. Sometimes they were done strategically for the devious purposes of provoking a response that required a ruthless retaliation. Once a protest was crushed, the cycle merely repeated itself. "Mother Rome" cared little for the troubles of the Jews at Jerusalem, or surrounding areas. Those Jews were a long way from her, and she cared only for the Jew's tribute money to keep coming. Rome's local kings and procurators were responsible for keeping that happening. Above all, they were to make sure the people understood - who was ultimately in charge.

Bible students have read about the brutality of Herod the Great and Pontius Pilate. Herod the Great ordered that evil assassination attempt on Yeshua, when he was two. Many children died in that prophesied event. (Jeremiah 31:15) Herod's son had "*John the Baptist*" beheaded (Matthew 14:10). Pilate, the governor in Yeshua's day, decreed that some Galileans be executed and their blood mingled with their temple sacrifices. (Luke 13:1) History states after Herod the Great died, Judea came under direct Roman rule. Rome exerted her direct authority over the Jews through the procurators. In the procurators' hand was life and death. Such judgments fulfilled themselves all too often among the Jews. Because of this type bloodshed, the High Priest made agreements and understandings with the Romans. In return, the priests would quell any anger with the purpose of keeping all the people in line. While all the time, they (*The High Priests*) gorged and profited from the financial misfortune of their people. On top of that, Roman Emperors tended to forget they were mere men. In their exalted minds they would enter into the plane of godhood. It was during these periods the faith of the Jewish people was tested to its fill. Emperor Caligula (*AD 37 - 41*) ordered during his reign that a statue of himself be put in the temple at Jerusalem. After an extraordinary protest that could have turned violent and into a Jewish massacre, the order was not carried out (biu.ac.il). However, it would appear that **"An Agreement"** or some sort of understanding to do sacrifice(s) **for - *which in disguise was really sacrifices to* -** the emperor, was in effect, still offered. Emperor Claudius (*AD 41 - 54*) did not take small tumults that sprung up from time to time in Jerusalem serious. The same held true with Nero (*AD 54 - 68*); at least not in the beginning, as new unrests started up around AD 63. That might be why the Romans had the minimum and untenable number of guards in their Jerusalem garrison. Too few were available and at the ready for that major uprising they might, ***but unlikely*** would encounter. Unfortunately, for all combatants involved, especially for its Jewish citizenry; social and religious unrests throughout Jerusalem and Judea, began to take the more perilous trail. Judea then caught the attention and the rage of the Roman authority. It caused Jerusalem and surrounding areas to become Rome's *class clown*; which needed to be taught a demoralizing lesson socially, politically and religious wise, by their *"true"* god and master, the Roman Empire. In this, Rome made the city of Jerusalem, Judea and the Jews an example their entire subjugated masses would take *"**grave**"* notes from.

Even if people have only read the New Testament, it would not take a lot of reading to understand the Jews detested living under Roman rule.

Amongst the many social and religious abuses by the Roman authority, the raising of taxes was a mounting burden on the people. At one point, certain of the Jewish leadership - *in an attempt to make Messiah Yeshua in his day, into some kind of poster man or savior catalyst for some type of revolutionary revolt against Rome* - asked Yeshua about the need to pay Rome's oppressive taxes. However, Yeshua responded with his now famous *angry* reply, "<u>*Render therefore unto Caesar the things which be Caesar's*</u>" (Luke 20:25). Also, from reading about that illegal mistrial of Yeshua from the Bible; even then one could sense an uneasy cooperation between - *who it is said to be* - Herod Antipas and Pontius Pilate (*who in the area of Judea was Rome*). Nonetheless, at one point during the illegal proceedings, in a desperate effort to murder Yeshua; the High Priest even used blackmail to try and pressure Pontius Pilate to authorize the Roman death penalty in a matter pertaining to then, Jewish law. (John 19:12-13) Most students of the Holy Bible are aware Judah, being under the Roman occupation, had no legal governmental authority to put any man to death. (John 18:31) That is why they needed the Roman law (*Pontius Pilate*) for their wicked treachery against Yeshua. **<u>In any case</u>** - in those final years leading up to Jerusalem and the second temple's desolations, nearly 126 years had passed since Rome first entered Judea; and life had only gotten worse. The harshness of the Romans' oppression would cause a growing number of hostiles among the Jews. They wanted nothing more than to

have the Great Roman Empire **"Foot,"** off of their Jewish necks.

> "Few would argue with the Jews for wanting to throw off Roman
> rule. Since the Romans had first occupied Israel in 63 B.C.E., the
> Jews social circumstances and religious condition only grew
> more desperate with time. From near the beginning of the
> Common Era, Judea was ruled by Roman procurators. The
> procurator chief responsibility was to collect and deliver an
> annual tax to the empire. Whatever the procurators collected
> beyond Rome's quota went to their profits. Second to taxes,
> procurators were also charged with maintaining peace in the
> areas they governed. Not surprisingly, they often imposed
> confiscatory taxes and any disruptions in the tax flow or any
> peace disturbances, was oftentimes met with lethal force.
> Equally infuriating to the Jews, Rome took over the appointment
> of the High Priest...As a result, the High Priests, who
> represented the Jews before God...came from corrupt Jewish
> priests [*who were likely to have more political leanings than
> spiritual faith and devotion to YHWH*] and for money and power,
> many of the Roman appointed High Priest collaborated whole-
> heartedly with Rome. [*With these happenings and other
> sufferings under the oppressive environment, all being aware of
> the wicked situation involving their High Priest appointments, it
> is no stretch of the historical imagination why the drums for
> revolt was sounded and the explosive kegs for war was lit.*]. As
> justified as the Judeans' actions might have been, "The...Great
> Revolt [*and War*] against Rome in 66 C.E. led to one of the
> greatest devastations perhaps in Jewish - *Common Era* - history.
> [*The event of the Jewish Holocaust inflicted by Nazi Germany
> during WWII is thought by most to be its superior or no less than
> its equal rivalry – <u>when one considers in the destruction of the
> Holy Temple of YHWH in the year of A.D. 70</u>*].'"
>
>   (jewishvirtuallibrary.org - "[*italics*]" author's comments)

Prior to that disaster/tragedy of "**<u>AD 70</u>;**" the Jews in year AD 63 knew tensions were on the rise again - *but this time* - while it was not unprecedented, the declaration for revolt was in all of the air. Rome had insulted and debased the people in almost every aspect of life; from appointing High Priests, determining the types and sometimes to whom (*The Emperor*) they sacrificed, even dictated some of the daily activities in the temple, by way of their corrupted High Priest comrades and their procurators - all appointed by Rome. After that year, in AD 64, back at Caesarea, over Judea and Jerusalem the next and the last procurator - *as historians claim* - Gessius Florus is appointed. Florus was purportedly in that office from AD 64 to 66. Gessius Florus has been judged by many historians as perhaps the "**very worst**" of all the previous procurators. According to noted historian Josephus, just prior to Florus there was the procurator Albinus. Albinus is said to have worked in conjunction with criminal enterprises for his own enrichment. That sort of activity further exasperated the already depleted tolerance of the Jewish people between AD 63-64 (Josephus: War 2.14.1 272). Among Gessius Florus' historical records of financial exploitation, his criminal actions and abuse of power as governor over Judea, is what historians cite was **The Act**; which cause Daniel's prophesied war. Some say the action was planned in advanced and meant to cause the violent response that it did; in order to conceal his own wrongdoings in Jerusalem and his high crimes against Rome. As planned, Florus' lawless deeds were indeed lost to the violence he was sure would ensue. They are now merely addendums in history.

> "In the spring of 66 C.E., he (*Gessius Florus*) robbed the Temple treasury of a great sum of money. The outraged populace mocked him by taking up a collection. Florus took revenge by allowing his troops to plunder part of the city of Jerusalem. Attempts at mediation by the priests failed, and when departing troops did not respond to friendly overtures of the Jewish crowds, the people began slinging insults at Florus. Slaughter ensued. But in a bloody street battle, the people eventually gained the upper hand, took possession of the Temple mount, and cut off the passage between the Temple and the Roman-held fortress of Antonia. Further attempts at mediation by Agrippa II, leading Pharisees, and the priestly aristocracy could not quell the revolt. Rebels retook the fortress of Masada, taken earlier by the Romans, and, at the direction of the son of the High Priest, Eleazar, the sacrifices ~~in behalf of~~ [*to*] the emperor were stopped. This was, in effect, a declaration of war" (*The Jewish World of Jesus*) (pages.uncc.edu/james-tabor).

Sources with more history on the events and conflicts of the first Jewish-Roman War were not especially bountiful or diversely insightful. But the book, ***The Great Roman-Jewish War*** by Flavius Josephus is available. And, from fairly credible to very credible sites with *dotcoms* or *dotorgs* are on the internet; i.e. a *Jewish Virtual Library* exists. The First Jewish–Roman War, which is often called the Great Revolt, is the first of three conflicts Jews waged against Romans. But, **AD 66 was cited in prophecy by Daniel**. It connects to the second temple's destruction. In real time the war commenced "*three and one-half years*" prior to AD 70, about the spring of AD 66 or in Daniel's term, in "*the midst of the* [final] *week*" (Daniel 9:27). Years prior to that time, around AD 62 and 63; then Emperor Nero (*AD 54 - 68*) had very little worry in reported disturbances about Jerusalem and Judea. A few lives lost here and there did not much matter. Besides, Jews were not Roman citizens or soldiers. Long as their tributes to Rome kept coming and in the temple Rome was still receiving her honor in the sacrifices; which showed priests' loyalties over any God they might claim they had allegiance to - Nero was satisfied, for the most part. He was aware of the irreverence involved with respect to sacrifices being made "*to him*" in the temple by the priests before YHWH. So far as the Roman Empire emperors were concerned, the sacrifices in **(to)** the Emperors' honor went a long way in letting know to the people who their priests felt was really in charge. With the High Priest indeed authorizing to perform such sacrifices; as far as the Emperor was concerned, it was not YHWH or any other would be "Jewish God." It was the Emperor. Despite the people and priests' claims of devotion to YHWH.

> "The First [*Roman-Jewish war*] was the [*end*] results of a long series of clashes in which small groups of Jews offered sporadic resistance to the Romans [authority]...In the fall of AD 66 the Jews...expelled the Romans [representatives] from Jerusalem and overwhelmed...their Roman punitive forces...A revolutionary government was then set up and [rebels] extended its influence throughout the whole country. Vespasian [*an accomplished military leader and trusted aide to Emperor Nero*] was dispatched by...Nero to crush the rebellion. He was joined by

Titus [*his son*] and together the Roman armies entered Galilee, ***where the historian Josephus headed the Jewish forces***. Josephus' army was confronted by that [*army*] of Vespasian and fled...Josephus gave himself up, and the Roman forces swept the country. On the 9th of the month of Av (August 29) in AD 70 Jerusalem fell; the Temple was burned...the Jewish state collapsed" (britannica.com). This event (*the end of the war*) was three and one-half (3½) years after ***Gessius Florus*** robbed the temple and war was prescribed.

It is **very well** worth noting that Vespasian was not the military leader who destroyed Jerusalem and the Holy Temple. But instead, it was Vespasian's son Titus who is credited with that great Roman victory over the Jews. "*Prophetically*," it was this same Titus who became "**The Prince**" of Daniel 9:25; when his father Vespasian returned to Rome in the summer of AD 69, after he had received word of the untimely suicide death of Emperor Nero; to eventually be named Emperor and to ascend to the throne over the Roman Empire. Vespasian left Titus in charge of tying up any loose ends and to decisively bring to a close The First Roman-Jewish War. As Daniel's seventy-week prophecy would dictate, it was in the spring of AD 70 that **Prince Titus** laid siege on Jerusalem. According to matching records, "history and the Bible;" in the fall of the year, he captured and destroyed Jerusalem and with it, the Second Temple.

Some historians and critics would argue over some of what I might have chalked off as minor details of the occurred events; but, in my oversimplification of their historical records, my overall narration stands as it is. The problem for me is, as far as I have been able to establish things; the only eye-witness on record to the destruction of Jerusalem and of the second temple was a, **"Jewish Turncoat;"** *if you will excuse my expression and my opinion.* That would be the ***vaunted*** historian, **Josephus**. He went from being the **"Captain of the Jewish forces"** that were to engage with General Vespasian in battle; to the **intimate**, **highly regarded** and **highly trusted confidant** of the **"Prince"** Titus. Nonetheless, since his are the only eyes we can use to scrutinize that tragic event in history; let us consider now a portion of his words as we seek to relive a bit of that infamy, to see if we can ourselves taste, ***The Flavor of Fire***.

"Roman legions surrounded Jerusalem in a siege. Once her outer walls were breached, murder and mayhem began. There was much death and despair between the outer walls to the approach of the temple. As the Romans approached the temple...a clash followed between the guards of the sanctuary and the troops who were putting out the fire inside the inner court; the latter routed the Jews and followed in hot pursuit right up to the Temple itself. Then one of the soldiers, without awaiting any orders and with

no dread of so momentous a deed, but urged on by some supernatural force, snatched a blazing piece of wood and, climbing on another soldier's back, hurled the flaming brand through a low golden window that gave access, on the north side, to the rooms that surrounded the sanctuary... the flames shot up...the Jews...flocked to the rescue...for the sacred structure that...was vanishing before their very eyes...No exhortation or threat could now restrain the impetuosity of the legions...overpowered by their rage, their detestation of the Jews, and an utterly uncontrolled lust for battle...Most of the slain were peaceful citizens, weak and unarmed, and they were butchered where they were caught. The heap of corpses mounted higher and higher about the altar; a stream of blood flowed down the Temple's steps, and the bodies of those slain at the top slipped to the bottom...While the Temple was ablaze, the attackers plundered it, and countless people who were caught by them were slaughtered. There was no pity for age and no regard was accorded rank; children and old men, laymen and priests, alike were butchered; every class was pursued and crushed in the grip of war, whether they cried out for mercy or offered resistance. Thousands of Jews were slaughtered. Thousands more were enslaved and sent to toil in the mines of Egypt; others were dispersed to arenas throughout the Empire to be butchered for the amusement of the Roman public" (Eye Witness to History).

In the retelling of the tragic events of AD 70, I intentionally left out, what I considered to be Josephus' theatrical expressions - as we go on to consider some of the key historical events of the

First Great Roman-Jewish War; alongside and in comparison to YHWH's Seventy Weeks prophecy delivered by Gabriel to Daniel in the 9th chapter. I am hoping almost everyone will be able to see the matchups. I do not connect all the prophetic dots. But I do feel enough of the dots are connected, to argue for some semblance of credibility on my part. For many of you - *even if you have not yet accepted my findings or believe my premises* - hopefully, I have given you a reason for additional studies. Consider the following prophetic matches. See if enough dots are connected for you to say with me, "***The seventy weeks prophecy in the book of Daniel, root and branch dimensions have been fulfilled.***" If you do not recall in our study of the Holy Scripture regarding the destruction of the first temple Solomon built; that tragic event marched us up in time to the year 3510 (491 BC). From that realization, we gained a different and all new perspective, relating to several important Scriptural events. Believe them or not, they are presented for your inspection and evaluations. On the subject and in context of the seventy weeks prophecy, we have entertained a bombshell that our Messiah was 49 years of age when he was hanged on a tree to die. From that perspective it would make Yeshua's "adult ministry" officially nineteen (19) years long. I would like for everybody to take note that I said, adult wise. Unofficially though, we know very little concerning Messiah Yeshua's youth years. We can witness to Messiah's own word from the Holy Bible when he spoke to Joseph and his mother Mary at the age of about twelve (12), "*How is it that ye sought me? wist ye not that I must be about my Father's business?*" (Luke 2:49) With the insights this book has presented, let us take a look to see as much of the prophetic fulfillments of the seventy weeks of Daniel as we can, in the time leading up until the Second Temple's destruction.

✓ From 491 BC, add the 70 years of captivity and 70 weeks (490 yrs) of Daniel, it brings us to AD 70; which is the year of the Second Temple's destruction. Any literate can do that math.

✓ Within the captivity and the seventy week prophecy there is this matching up of times in their relationship with years of the BC and AD assignments. Continue reading to see what I mean.

   a. From 491 BC we step forward through the time of the seventy years of the Babylonian captivity and we find ourselves marching up to, matching and coinciding with 421 BC.

   b. From 421 BC we step through the first seven weeks (49 years) of the total seventy weeks for Jerusalem's walls to be repaired and the Second Temple to be built and we match with 372 BC.

   c. From 372 BC we go forward threescore (60) weeks (420 years). We come to the date the Messiah is cut off by execution; hanged on a stake until dead. However, in a controversy, this date coincides with AD 49 and not the popular and traditional AD 33. I chose to keep with my professed revelation from YHWH. To believe the alternative is disaster. Readers are free to trust what they will. Recall too the Babylon exit (*3580 or 421 BC*) going ahead in *Branch fulfillment*, those same threescore (420) years; reveals Messiah's birth year as we come to year 4000 or 1 BCE.

d. From AD 49, we step forward in time according to Gabriel's revelation - two weeks. Over the next 14 years the political landscape, Jewish social conflicts with Hellenisation and an incessant intolerable religious hostility and blasphemy by Rome, polluted the environment and enflamed the people's hearts to the point of insurrection against the Roman authority. As unruly entities in the social backdrop heated up even more; and because of the simmering unrest with the common Jewish people, an allegedly unofficial/official agreement/covenant was tentatively established amongst the High Priest and its influential Jewish leaders with Roman authority, to bolster a weak week peace to keep the people from a revolt. Under the last two tyrannical and corrupted Roman procurators, Lucceius Albinus (AD 62 until 64) and Gessius Florus (AD 64 until 66), the Jew's resiliency and passiveness finally broke up. Sometime shortly after Florus robbed the Jew's temple treasury, the High Priest's son Eleazar, ordered sacrifice to the emperor to be stopped. Then, complete war broke out in AD 66 - it coincided with the three and one-half days/**years** and "***the midst of the week***" inside Daniel's 9:27 prophecy. Then three and one half day/**years** later in AD 70 "*the people* (The Roman war machine) *of the **Prince** (Titus);*" who in fact had just recently become prince by virtue of his father Vespasian ascending to the emperor's throne of Rome - after the unexpected suicide of Nero and a brief power struggle in AD 69; arrived and besieged Jerusalem. The following fall of AD 70, Jerusalem fell as it is described in prophecy, "...***with a*** [*Roman*] ***flood***" (Daniel 9:26). With that flood - we finish the seventy-week time span of Gabriel's words of prophecy to Daniel. However, there are yet insights to be gained for later retrospect and discernments. Take note: **Bible wise** - we have now stepped up through time from Adam and year one, to the destruction of not just one of YHWH's temples, but two of YHWH's temples. **THERE WILL BE NO THIRD TEMPLE OF YHWH**; due to divine reasoning and the Jews' incessant rebellions, "...for the overspreading of abominations he shall make *it* desolate, even until the **consummation**, and that determined shall be poured upon the desolate" (Verse 27).

I will be discussing the obscurity of the **"CONSUMMATION"** in a later chapter of this book. In the meantime, what is an amazing significance and needs to be cited is the fact that even though we stand *"accurately"* though *"unofficially"* at YHWH's Adamic year of 4070 or AD 70; we do have an issue. If you will recall – we accidentally failed to account for Isaac's sixty (60) years at the birth of Esau and Jacob. Instead, we recorded forty (40) years. That "officially" put us twenty years behind where we would have been; had we added the full amount of years. Had I followed my own understanding, instead of the YHWH's instructions, I would be situated in the Adamic year of 4090 or AD 90 for the temple's destruction. I desperately needed YHWH to help me understand. At that time though, I simply did not know how YHWH was going to accomplish this, *"intellectual"* feat.

CHAPTER 14

THE ABRAHAM - ISAAC CORRECTION

Whether you believe all, some, little or none of this book's research, you have to admit, it has been a thought-provoking walk thus far. There is more! We have only walked 4070 year and are only up to AD 70. By standard math, we still have theoretically and theologically 1931 years of time to go before we arrived at what is supposedly the millennial Sabbath reign and judgment. And of course, there is still the challenge to match up exact bible years with those 8000 years my study has determined is all we have in ordained time. Some may still believe this is a crazy quest. Nevertheless, I would greatly appreciate it; if others of you will at least entertain the idea that our *"crazy quest"* is at the least, possibly within reach. Hold on to that thought of what **Amos 3:7** is a promise of and believe it. That is not too much to ask for at this point, is it? Think about where we came from. It was **Biblical Year One**!! Think how we got here (4070/AD 70). We only used passages from Holy Bible text. "<u>Do you not find that amazing!?</u>" Why has not someone done this full count before? Seriously though, I am sure many have tried. So, would you like to know why no one to date, has succeeded. I will tell you why I think this is the case and I will give you at the least – two reasons. 1) "*<u>No man can serve two masters: for either he will hate the one, and love the other; or else he will hold to the one, and despise the other. Ye cannot serve God and mammon</u>*" (Matthew 6:24). What I am saying is many so-called Bible scholars hold man's history in the greater regard than they do for Holy Scripture authority. YHWH sealed the prophetic knowledge of time from most all of them, until these last few minutes of man's time before the end of the age. Personally, I have no confidence that anybody could arrive at any hidden spiritual truth; unless YHWH reveals it to them... for whatever the reason he might have for doing so. 2) Even if YHWH showed them, most will not receive it. Because, "...<u>when they knew God, they glorified him not as God...but became vain in their imaginations, and their foolish heart was darkened</u>" (Romans 1:21).

Consider this book's claim the Holy Scripture used Roman numerals. How could anyone have "<u>figured that out</u>" with all of the denominational static from the world, without YHWH revealing it? It is really impossible in my opinion. We just can't. I try not to give a lot of static in this book. On top of the nonsensical static, there is way too much of man's arrogant intellectual interferences. Claiming to know something he really does not know. He will use "theory" and say it is undeniable and factual; i.e. Our intellectual creation existing without an intellectual creator. Anyhow, I must digress. In getting to our here point on YHWH's Adamic date 4070 and to AD 70; we have used nothing more than established mathematical theory in practical applications of the numbers - with YHWH's guidance of course. And thus far, our Holy Bible history, prophetic dictations and declarations have determined; 3930 years remain on YHWH's calendar for humankind. Still, before we should continue; it is needful that we go backward in order to formally verify how the Holy Bible reveals the true and important year of Abram's birth.

That said, in case no one recalls, in *The Isaac Shift and the Te'-rah Error* section; I said an error was made that was not obvious to me, at the time of my initial study; and hence, also in my potential for accuracy in my addition of the years accounted for in the time of intellectual man. I did not realize it at the time and YHWH allowed me to continue with my count. In my reflecting back on the matter, I found it to be amazing in the fact that YHWH kept me on the right years - as far as the BC and AD sequences were concerned. I suspect he did this in order to allow me to keep a clear vantage of years and events, without major confusion. I was assured in my mind, but I was wrong in my actuality. YHWH gave me all the right numbers in years after Abram's birth so as to allow me on to reach the date of concrete certainty (*my words*); which was the Jewish recounting of the destruction of the second temple. Adamic year 4070 is parallel to AD 70. And, AD 70 is concrete. YHWH seared it onto Jewish hearts as "*__a date which will live in infamy__*" (Franklin D. Roosevelt, 1941). I suppose YHWH took me to that devastating time in history so I could afterwards; easily backtrack to Abram's time; to know confidently and understanding to the truest degree of clarity, the year when Abram was born. Settling my Abram birth issue along with the contingency of the twenty years deficiency in my count regarding Isaac's age when he begets Jacob, was fundamental to me maintaining my own standards of trueness required in Bible research and confidence of faith. Clarity was also needed – *in my opinion* – to perhaps be taken a bit more serious by the objective investigators, in their studies. If we're going to continue our walk through the time of intellectual man, those glaring discrepancies have to be addressed. Let us go back to verify, if we can; before we go to other seals that blind our eyes to knowing what time we stand in today. If you recall, the incident that endangered the credibility of my research and study of the times and my accounting of the years was caused when I read out of context and misunderstood <u>Genesis 25:20-21</u>. After I misread

my full tally reflected, "<u>Isaac was **forty (40) years old**, when he begat</u>

<u>Jacob</u>." I was tired. It was late at night or early in the morning. You have

probably heard all of the excuses, when error is involved. But, in the end,

YHWH set me straight. At least, I believe so. The following passage is

what I used to back up my claim. Read it for yourself; and afterwards we

will see if I can explain in an acceptable manner, why this misread had

the potential to knock my count off by significant years. I will also show

why a corrected date for Abram's birth is critical to my study proving

and maintaining what I am confident is Holy Spirit inspired truth in my

accounting of biblical history up to AD 70. It will also play well with the

Bible's yet future prophetic times. In its truth and with **the historical**

anchor date of AD 70 we were given (*The desolation of the Second*

Temple); we are now able to overlay them and see, as they relate to and

correspond to mankind's awareness of his apparent times and his utter

unawareness of YHWH's ordained real time overall. In other words,

Abram's correct birth year in the correct chronological order, is essential;

if we are to discern *what time we are really in and how much time we*

have left. That said; let us continue with my misread mistake concerning

how old Isaac was and when Rebekah gave birth to her twins in Esau and

Jacob. It is essentially Jacob, since the Messianic birth line continued on through him. After I reiterate to you my ~~excuse~~ <u>reasonable explanation</u> as

to why it happened, I will tell you how YHWH delivered me from error.

> "And <u>Isaac was forty years old when he took Rebekah to wife</u>,
> the daughter of Bethuel the Syrian of Padan-aram, the sister to
> Laban the Syrian. <u>And Isaac entreated the Lord for his wife,</u>
> <u>because she was barren: and the Lord was entreated of him, and</u>
> <u>Rebekah his wife conceived.</u>" (Genesis 25:20-21)

Like I said, it sounded good as I read it to myself. Isaac was forty –

right? He married his sweetheart Rebekah. Isaac asked YHWH to make

sure that Rebekah was fertile. YHWH showed Isaac that she was by

allowing her to become pregnant. The case is closed. Move over to the

next son in Messiah's ancestral line - right? Even though I did have my

concerns over <u>Abram's birth</u> - that is what I did by faith. I believed that if

something was off, in due time YHWH would inform me. That is, if he

blessed me to know and to understand the given matter. And, if YHWH

did not care for me to know, it is simple. The truth would have avoided

my discernment and I would not have known. Until such time perhaps,

that YHWH changed his mind and had mercy on my ignorance. In case I

forget to mention it later. The issue with the Isaac to Jacob years is when

I counted with forty (40) instead of sixty (60), it put my accounting

twenty (20) years behind in time than where I should have been. In short,

not considering the obscure dates in time and with all other numbers

remaining the same; had I done the correct count in adding the sixty (60) instead of forty (40) the destruction of the Second Temple would have counted out on AD 90. Needless to say that such a big discrepancy would have been total disaster for my premise of my so-called, "**<u>Anchor of YHWH</u>**" and "**<u>*date of concrete certainty*</u>** (AD 70)**." AD 90 would have crushed any semblance of credibility whatsoever on my behalf, in my accounting of Biblical time. Where the numbers stand right now is at the least, reasonably probable. At least, I believe so. Actually, I think they are spot-on. You should have been keeping count along with me. What do you truly think of the numbers - so far - <u>honestly!</u>?

Actually, in my original walk through time, I stepped all the way to the end of time as we understand it to be today. But, in all my many reviews, I found it easier and more effective during my presentation to others about time; to resolve my issues about Abram's birth from, "**<u>The Anchor Date</u>**" of <u>the destruction of the Second Temple</u>. When I got to the end, I thought I had everything wrapped up into a neat little box. Neat that is, until I went back to see if I could find more on the matter of Abram <u>not being</u> born part of triplets with Haran and Nahor. I still have not completely resolved my issues with the *triplet thing*. Not to worry though. I am not sure that the *triplet thing* is significant in the matter of our walk through the time of intellectual man. Besides, I am sure at some point the critics will enlighten me on my Abram question, one way or the other. Here is the important thing, from my perspective. In my reviews to double-check the irritating, (*to me*), matter of Abram's birth, I ran into an upsetting unexpected. And it threatened to neatly un-wrap what I thought was my "*neatly wrapped*" little box of chronological time. Come on!! I knew the whole time Isaac was sixty when Rebekah had Esau and Jacob. But, like I said before; for me, after a while, numbers just run together. Despite - when I reread the time accounts leading up to Israel's Egyptian captivity; I "*just happened*" to notice the following passage *in my total alertness*. In actuality, I am sure that YHWH simply opened my eyes and showed me. After which, I remember what I had recorded earlier and realized "**my own**" careless error. I suppose we all make them – Right?

> "...the Lord said unto her [*Rebekah*], two nations are in thy womb, and two manner of people shall be separated from thy bowels...And when her days to be delivered were fulfilled...the first came out red all over like a hairy garment, and they called his name Esau...after that came his brother out...and his name was called Jacob: and Isaac was threescore (60) years old when she bare them" (Genesis 25:22-26).

Isaac was sixty years old and not forty; as I had recorded. But I knew that! I just read the wrong verse - Really! A person who has not done the entire count might say in effect, "It is only a twenty year difference. Just add the twenty years on to your overall times and be done with it." However, for me, someone who had researched the counting, twenty years was a huge discrepancy. And, most notable was the fact that from my revelation and perspective, if I nonchalantly add on the twenty year discrepancy to my original work, it would make Messiah sixty-nine (69) years old instead of my already objectionable to most age of forty-nine (49), as my initial research concluded. I knew age sixty-nine (69) was not possible in light of the scriptural witness that reveals Messiah had not reached the fiftieth year of his life (*John 8:57*); when he was late into the process of preaching the final year of his human ministry. With such, he preached the acceptable year of YHWH (*Luke 4:19*). I felt in my heart I knew better. But I was not sure I would be able to reasonably prove on paper by way of a presentation, what my position was on that twenty years discrepancy; which weighed so heavily inside of my mind. I, I and more I. The truth of the matter is this. "I," was afraid of being found in a stupid error before a ruthless pack of critical theologians, historians and non-believing naysayers. My worry was unfounded! YHWH showed me a simple mathematical tool that addressed what would be certainly the legitimate concerns of any open-minded and rational spirit. The tool was subtraction! YHWH had me count backwards from the destruction of the Second Temple.

Counting backwards, starting with the seventy weeks of Daniel is biblical common sense and logical math. With Daniel's 490 years, the seventy-year Babylon captivity, the 450 net years of the kings, the 450 years of judges, the 430 years of their Egyptian slavery, Jacob/Israel's 130 years (*his age when he went down into Egypt*), "**THE SIXTY YEARS OF ISAAC!!**" (*his age when Rebekah gave birth to Esau and Jacob*) and then, those last 100 years of Abram/Abraham (*his age when Sarai/Sarah gave birth to Isaac*); I knew the strategy and found it to be, **full-proof**. That is, if one has enough faith to believe the seventy-week prophecy in <u>Daniel nine (9)</u>. More importantly, *that it has already been fulfilled*. The fact we have that virtually undeniable earmark date of **AD 70** in history, is absolutely paramount. I would not care to wager that every historian, and every theologian and every Bible student, with little doubt understands that even a slight referencing to that date is the solemn invitation to evoke that infamous event of when the Romans completely destroyed the second temple. <u>It is the one historical date fact that for me is "The Bridge" to knowing and understanding how to synchronize future prophetic times with discernible times and dates of yesterday and today.</u> **AD 70** is also the date in history that matches chronologically "***perfect***" - *according to my count* - with the final year of YHWH's Seventy <u>Weeks</u> of Prophecy that Gabriel gave to Daniel. Their matching is not an easy thing for the critics to ignore. Along with that, the Holy Bible records clearly and states numbers of years and simple revealed numbers. I will gladly choose them over what in my opinion are the more confusing and therefore the less dependable accounting methods of time employed by the vaunted historians and theologians. I am sorry guys, but most of you cannot agree on essential dates; whereas, if we used Bible verifications - where possible - it would be revealing. <u>That is exactly what I have done</u>! That is why I am totally confident with the years on record from the Holy Bible. Because I am, I only needed to count backward from the anchor - **AD 70**. Can you understand my math strategy? <u>If Daniel's seventy weeks are in their right chronological positions; and they are</u>. <u>If all of the other numbers are right and in their right chronological position; and they are</u>. <u>If we count back it will take us to the right year of Abram's birth</u>. How can we go wrong; if indeed we are using years the Holy Bible gives us? We are counting backward from the "***universally acknowledged***" date of the second temple's destruction in **AD 70**. Now, when I say "***universally acknowledged***;" I mean man and YHWH agree. Trust me. That is rare. <u>If we all feel we can trust the Bible, <u>and I do</u></u>. We will all *in this case* count back undeniably and with <u>very</u> <u>little</u> debate, to the true year of Abram's birth. So then, consider the following, counting backward from YHWH's Adamic Hebrew **year of 4070**; which in our present counting is - **AD 70**.

(Daniel's seventy weeks prophecy ends)
- AD 70 (4070) minus 490 goes back to.......................... <u>421 BC</u> (3580)

(Babylon captivity ends)
- 421 BC (3580) minus 70 years goes back to................ <u>491 BC</u> (3510)

(Kings end)
- 491 BC (3510) minus 450 years goes back to ....941 BC (3060)

(Judges end)
- 941 BC (3060) minus 450 years goes back to ....1391 BC (2610)

(Israel leaves Egypt)
- 1391 BC (2610) minus 430 year (Egypt) back to.......1821 BC (2180)

(Jacob's age when he went down into Egypt)
- 1821 BC (2180) minus 130 years goes back to ....1951 BC (2050)

(Isaac' age at Jacob's birth)
- 1951 BC (2050) minus 60 years goes back to ....2011 BC (1990)

(Abram/Abraham's age at Isaac's birth)
- 2011 BC (1990) minus 100 years back to..................2111 BC (1890)

(Abram/Abraham's birth)
- 2111 BC (1890) ....2111 BC (1890)

Counting back from **AD 70** has carried us to YHWH's Adamic year of 1890 or 2111 BC - Abraham's true birth. Now, starting from YHWH's base year one (1) - the year YHWH created Adam; retracing our original steps forward from that first year of Adam, back up until when Te'-rah (*Abram's father*) was seventy (70) years of age, we arrive at YHWH's Adamic year of 1910 or 2091 BC. In a bit more compact and simplified accounting of the years, we have thc following.

(Adam to the flood)
- 1 plus 1656 years goes up to year ....1657 (2344 BC)

(Arphaxad born)
- 1657 (2344 BC) plus 3 years goes up to year.............1660 (2341 BC)

(Arphaxad/Salah born)
- 1660 (2341 BC) plus 25 years goes up to year .... <u>1685</u> (2316 BC)

(Salah/Eber born)
- 1685 (2316 BC) plus 30 years goes up to year .... <u>1715</u> (2286 BC)

(Eber/Peleg born)
- 1715 (2286 BC) plus 26 years goes up to year .... <u>1741</u> (2260 BC)

(Peleg/Reu born)
- 1741 (2260 BC) plus 30 years goes up to year .... <u>1771</u> (2230 BC)

(Reu/Serug born)
- 1771 (2230 BC) plus 28 years goes up to year .... <u>1799</u> (2202 BC)

(Serug/Nahor born)
- 1799 (2202 BC) plus 30 years goes up to year .... <u>1829</u> (2172 BC)

(Nahor/Te'-rah born)
- 1829 (2172 BC) plus 11 years goes up to year .... <u>1840</u> (2161 BC)

(Te'-rah/Abram)
- 1840 (2161 BC) plus 70 years goes up to year .... <u>1910</u> (2091 BC)

The count from year one with confirmed and revealed ages and numbers brings us to Adamic year <u>1910</u> or <u>2091 BC</u>. Excuse my repetition, but to help ensure we all see it; I feel the need to list YHWH's Adamic dates once more. I will match them with BC/BCE–AD/CE up to year **AD 70**.

YHWH's millennial week, which adds on an eighth day for judgment and reward, has the first 6000 years set apart for YHWH-rejecting man to self rule. This is so he can prove to himself the gravest error was made by accepting fruit from the tree of the knowledge of good and evil. In truth it was a tree of death. (Genesis 2:17) We can know time left by subtracting the Bible record from YHWH's full time. If the years are right, whether from the beginning up or the end back, if we find all the years, it will be 8000. We are at 4070 (*AD 70*) and facing the enigma of more prophecy. But before we go there, it is vital we clear the air here concerning the birth year of Abram. Being the times are right, we can count both ways from and towards **AD 70** to align the years. If we do the counts, we can match up YHWH's Adamic count of those years on our Gregorian count of the years in exact fashion. However, when we did our recounts, regarding my miscount with reference to my dispute over the correctness of Te'-rah's age at Abram's birth; take notice coming back from the temple destruction in **AD 70** to Abram in one case. Then from Adam going forward to Te'-rah in the next. There is a glaring twenty year overlap. We can see it when we compare their four above end points with the time of 2111 BC; which corresponds to Adamic year 1890. Then the time of 2091 BC; which corresponds to Adamic year 1910. Compare – 2111 BC minus 2091 BC is equal to twenty (20) years. And when we subtract from Adamic year 1910 – when Te'-rah was seventy (70), after going forward from the year one (1); the year of 1890; after coming back through time from AD 70 – when the second temple was destroyed – to the birth of Abram; we get those same twenty (20) years. Year 1910 minus year 1890 equals twenty (20) years.

While Bible critics may object to those years coming forward after the flood, considering the Roman Numbers concept which was employed in determining the years; those years moving back from the Second Temple's desolation are for the most part, incontrovertible. Moreover from my study and research, all the years moving backward in time, strongly supports my declarations about my contentions concerning what I have called YHWH's accounting of time. Unless, one is willing to condemn the Holy Bible as unreliable; or worse yet, declare the Bible as a total fraud. **I am not** willing to make any such claim. What does this all mean, upon our closer examinations of the passages in question? Simply stating through my research, Te'-rah was not seventy (70) years old when Abram was born. He was merely fifty (50) years old. Years later when Abram reached the age of twenty (20); the reason for witnessing Te'-rah's age in Genesis, 11:26-30; was not for the birth of triplets, but for a double marriage when sons "*Abram and Nahor took them wives: the name of Abram's wife was Sarai...the name of Nahor's wife, Milcah*" (Verse 30). After YHWH made me to comprehend that truth, I felt I had that green light to continue with then my walk - now our walk - through YHWH's ordained time for humankind. Still, I knew more difficulty for conventional and non-conventional faiths (*Labeled to be so by the so-called mainstream*) was yet to come. But for then and now, I feel the

year of 4070 (**_AD 70_**) is well-established and with it the time of Abram's birth at YHWH's Adamic Hebrew year of 1890. Year 1890 is equivalent with the date of 2111 BC.

Why am I so confident in my findings? Consider the following with your best objectivity. Going backwards from **AD 70** (*The date in which it would appear is the universal consensus for the destruction of the second temple*) with all of the years witnessed from the Holy Bible, we end up at Adamic year 1890 or 2111 BC. Nevertheless coming forward from year one, if we used the traditional counts versus the Roman Numbers concept, we would gain 40 years. What that would translate to being is Te'-rah would have just turned ten (10) years of age versus being what I have asserted as fifty (50) years of age at the time of Abram's birth. While I must admit, after that last assertion concerning Te'-rah's father Nahor being eleven (11) years of age when he beget Te'-rah and my **kidshealth.org** site cite, which supports an even lower age saying that, "*Theoretically it could be as low as age nine* (9)." Though it was not likely, it was not out of the question, this might have possibly been the case with Te'-rah himself. I did not dismiss the possibility. But I was able to determine Te'-rah's age of ten (10) **was not** the case. When I took the count forward to the second temple's destruction. Using that count, it would take the temple destruction above AD 110. Since such a date was clearly error and therefore unacceptable; the concerns for Te'-rah's age was discounted. Also, if ten year separate the births, Te'-rah is always ten years older than Abram. No matter when we say Te'-rah is born, it is <u>not</u> Bible sound; if we <u>know</u> Abram was born in Adamic year 1890 (pp. 279-280). I return to the Roman Number concept. It makes more sense to me.

With YHWH's revelation of the Roman Numbers concept in tow, it allowed for harmony among all of the biblical numbers YHWH showed, disclosed and revealed to me. That is – *if you recall* – up until the year I had the misread with Isaac and the birth of sons Esau and Jacob. If you remember, with that correction, I had gained twenty (20) years, as I headed into the future of biblical time. If I had been allowed by YHWH to reach that historical anchor point; which was the destruction of the second temple, I certainly would have been all discombobulated. That is the chief reason why I believe YHWH established a **corrective plane** for Abram's true birth with me. That, *"corrective plane,"* even though I was essentially in an error, was very important to the overall count for my accounting of time. It is also how YHWH kept me on track as I went up through my accounting of the years. You see originally when I lost those twenty (20) years at Jacob's birth; YHWH in turn gave them right back to me with my misunderstanding concerning the birth of Abram. YHWH prepared my eyes before laying the foundation to reveal to me my *Isaac* *shift and my Te'-rah error*, later on in my walk. When he finally did, the two events would offset each other. I have to believe, that is how YHWH planned it all from the very beginning. I am pretty sure; I would have probably seen the Isaac thing. But – not in a million years would I have seen the situation with Abram's birth year; at least, not on my own. And to be honest with you all; it was completely amazing for me, how in my opinion, YHWH caused the years *to just happen* to offset each other and at the same time, kept me on the right number as far as my accounting of his ordained time (*The Millennial week*) was concerned. The twenty year subtraction off from Abram's birth completely absorb and neutralize the twenty year gain which I had to add, when I rediscovered that I had put the wrong date down for Isaac's sons birth. Since, they were born twenty years later than I originally recorded it. In other words, all is well in my accounting world. For a visual, I hope the following two charts will help you solidify the number discrepancy correction in your head some way.

The years coming back from AD 70 (*the destruction of the second temple*) to Abram's birth year.

	Isaac to Abraham	Jacob to Isaac	Egyptian Slavery to Jacob	Egyptian Freedom to Slavery	Kings to Egyptian Freedom	Babylon to Kings	Freedom to Babylon	Seventy Weeks
				BC/BCE to AD/CE				
4000 BC								AD 70
	100 years	60 years	130 years	430 years	450 years	450 years	70 years	490 years
Plus (1) 2111 BC	← to	←	←	←	←	←	←	← From

This chart shows the years going forward from Adam to Te'-rah's seventieth (*70*) year of life.

Adam to Arphaxad	Arphaxad to Te'-rah was 70							
				BC/BCE to AD/CE				
Year (1)								Year 4070
1660 years	250 years							
→ From 2091 BC	Minus (1)							

If you will see - there is the twenty year overlap from 2111 BC (*when Abram was born*) to 2091 BC (*when Te'-rah turned seventy [70]*). This clearly marks Abram's birth in the year that Te'-rah was fifty (50) years old, instead of the presumed seventy (70). These illustrations were done in a BC/AD chart for their computations of the years. That identical twenty year overlap is present in the chart which was computed from YHWH's Adamic year one (1) through 4070 (*Not printed in this book*). I pray these charts are useful to you and serve as the visual they were intended to be.

So, let us sum it all up one more time and put a lid on it. Abram was not born when Te'-rah was seventy (70). I contend that the only reason that Te'-rah's age was ever mentioned is to make known to us how old he was when Abram (*Abraham*) and Nahor **_took them wives_**. In fact Abram was twenty (20) at that time. Te'-rah *begat* Abram at the age of fifty (50). Do you not think YHWH has proven this unquestionably, in this section? YHWH also showed, despite my "Te'-rah Error" and "Isaac Shift" earlier in my walk - he kept me on track in time. Until I was ready to receive his insight and proof that was most critical. Abram was born when Te'-rah was age fifty (50) in YHWH's Adamic Hebrew year of 1890. That year corresponds to the Gregorian calendar date year of 2111 BC. To date and not so vital; it is only likely that Abram was not born as one of triplets.

CHAPTER 15

TIME FLIES WHEN YOU SLEEP

"Then shall the kingdom of heaven be likened unto ten virgins, which took their lamps, and went forth to meet the bridegroom. And five of them were wise, and five were foolish. They that were foolish took their lamps, and took no oil with them: but the wise took oil in their vessels with their lamps. While the bridegroom tarried, they all slumbered and slept" (Matthew 25:1-5).

Now, I need to create in my/our minds; the new route I need to take when trying to explain to you, how YHWH led me forward from Adamic year 4070 or AD 70. It was not easy, as I had hoped; because it involved the ability to articulately reveal one of YHWH's formerly hidden truths. The truth is, it takes a fair bit of faith to have confidence in an insight; it seems no one else in the world holds. That - *in and of itself* - is enough to frighten off a significant majority of *"believers."* My situation could be comparable to being the driver of someone else's car, driving in the dark;

while the owner is giving me the directions to a location that I have never been before. I was sort of like this child riding; only I was driving. I was gazing all about in "Bible Land." I was awestruck by YHWH's sparkling spiritual lights (*seeing them darkly*). Lights most have likely never been blessed to see. In truth, I had never discerned these insights before either. So, their revelations to me, became for me a heavy yoke – sad to say.

Actually, when I am driving for somebody else; and, I am going to a place I have never been before; I am in, "*La-La-land*." I am enjoying the, dark highway visages. The only thing I am attentively listening for, is the directional orders saying, "Turn left here" or "Turn right there." I cannot rightly speak for anybody else's "sense of direction." But, once I get to where it is I am supposed to be going, I am just there. But, if my life was dependent upon me directing someone else to that same location; I would be pushing up daisies. That is my crude example of the mindset I was in and I am now using to explain YHWH's counting path with. I hope my "*redirection*" skills will get readers close enough to how YHWH directed me, in my accounting of the years. Then again, readers would be wise to do their own studies. Readers might even come to the same conclusions; which I have come to. It is kind of like a scientific experiment. If your independent study, based on my premises, yields the same results; then there is an excellent chance that previous results (*my conclusions*) are valid. That is sort of the way, <u>Bible Study</u> really works.

Remember, we started out with 8000 years. And right off the bat, we sliced off 2000 years for the 1000-year millennial reign of Yeshua and another 1000 years for the Last Great Day. Recall, that is Judgment Day. I am aware some people out in reader land, do not hold to my premises. No worries - because those of you who do not believe what I am saying and will not entertain the possibility of what I am saying is true; I am not speaking to you Bible education wise. You are just reading this book for entertainment. And, I am okay with that. I like being entertaining. I also like giving people sensible Bible information to think about at the serious level too. That is the most important reason for this book's existence. It is for all readers who are ready to take on seriously, its considerations (*in debate - if needed*). Because, **It's much later than you think!** Do not forget. We had 6000 years we needed to account for. Starting at year one, we have already accounted for 4070 years. This leaves us 1931 years yet to account for; before we run out of time and start having to address all of the foolish naysayers of the Holy Bible clamoring and mocking.

"Where is the promise of his coming? Huh?"

Anyhow - *to my surprise* - YHWH showed me the next section of years in a much simpler way. Once I accepted Daniel's seventy weeks as "*dimensionally*" root and branch fulfilled; it was easy for me to see for subtraction, the next section of years in time. I think it was only fitting, the very same Daniel would later reveal to us; in regards to those next years that should be deducted from YHWH's prophetic week. Daniel records those years for the wise who are among us, to read and discern in these last few minutes, before the end of the age. "**It is a really simple insight from YHWH.**" It is recorded in Daniel's twelfth chapter.

> "And from the time ~~that~~ the daily ~~sacrifice~~ shall be taken away and the abomination that makes desolate set up, ~~there shall be~~ a thousand two hundred and ninety days." (Daniel 12:11)

Italics in the KJV are not in the original transcripts. YHWH revealed to Daniel through, "*one* like unto the Son of man," perhaps even Yeshua himself, before his incarnation (*Compare Daniel 10:4-11 to Revelation 1:12-18*); between the times of the Second Temple being destroyed and that wicked son of perdition (2nd Thessalonians 2:3), the abomination of desolation set up or consummated (*Daniel 9:27*) will be **1290** days/years. When we **add** the 1290 years to AD 70, we step to the year AD 1360. The year of AD 1360 corresponds to YHWH's Adamic year of 5360. When we subtracted those same 1290 years from the final 1931 years we have left on YHWH's Adamic count; which we have already accounted for by adding to the AD totals. We find ourselves down to 641 years. After the 641 years, we cross the fools' threshold and open up our faiths to obvious religious and secular ridicule. What do you think about that?

It does not get any simpler than that. Granted, in the particulars of events and fulfillments, I am sure there are revealing passages of scriptures that itemizes identifying markers in history. However, as I have said before, this book is more about the passage of time. Its primary focus is as the subtitle states. It is about "*What time we are really in and how much time we have left*." And as far as the passing amounts of days/years spoken of in Daniel 12:11 is concerned, it is all about a huge chunk of elapsing time being cut off. It is simple to surmise by making the following declaration. After the second temple is destroyed (*totally desolate*), and it was; at the minimum the temple will remain in perpetual desolations for the aforementioned time of 1290 years - believe it or not. But, you do not have to take my word for it! Take a gander over in Jerusalem at the site of the second temple in our now and if not "***perpetual desolations***," what is it do you see? I view **The Dome of the Rock**! More properly ascribed, it is "The dome over, "**The STONE**."" I will not elaborate deeper on what many Jews consider an Islamic "eye sore!" In many Jews' view the dome cannot stay. That is, if YHWH's third temple is to go under construction. **Why must that Dome be destroyed?** If you honestly do not know and desire to do a separate study; because this book of time must continue on. I will give you a great starting point. Do a biblical research that includes The Dome of the Rock and **The Holy of Holies**! I believe what you will find will be nothing short of amazing. You might even get some proof on how close Jews are coming to getting a third temple under construction. We will talk a little bit more on that, a little bit later. But for now, suffice it to say the 641 years left as far as my basis for total time is looking a bit thin. By Gregorian standards, adding the 1290 years to its calendar from AD 70 puts us at AD 1360. It is a date we passed over a half millennium ago and counting. Does the Bible have anything to say about the tight spot we are in? I mean really, it was like *"snap"* and over 1¼ millennia were simply chopped off of our remaining time – ***as if we were sleeping***. I suppose we were. But as I said, we still have 641 years left to go before my, *"hypothesis¿"* collapses and my theological chaos ensues.

Of course, on the one hand, it would appear we have already crossed over that threshold. You see, in our Gregorian reality; we already have a theological crisis of *"Overdueness."* Think about it. Even though I took a ***"brief intermission"*** at AD 70; that was not ***our*** time. If we acknowledge the fact of our reality, practically every living historian that I have heard speak on the issue of time, dates our present, *the time of this writing*, at the year AD 2020. And according to the doctrine of most Bible experts, *"Jesus Christ"* is nineteen years in the rears. I am not one to beat a *"dead horse;"* but I believe this unpleasant, ***"fact¿"*** has been mentioned before. Rather than we imply Messiah Yeshua is a liar; should not we all at this point simply be willing to admit, something has clearly not been counted right in our men's civil, social and religion accounting departments as for our chronological totaling of time? "I" had no other theological option at the time of my spirit's _unenlightenment_, but to judge our modern history and thus our accounting of time, as being in biblical error. If I did not use that option, then prominent historians of old were corrupt and lied about the years in time they lived. That is a distasteful option; but it is certainly not out of the question. Do an indebt study about what some of the critics are saying and writing about historian Josephus and his writings over his depictions of a heroic **Prince** Titus, in the Roman siege at Jerusalem. If there and with Josephus, then the questions must be asked; where else and with whom else? <u>I certainly do not believe it is YHWH Elohim who is lying</u>. **Do you?** When I looked back into history for the dates of events and occurrences, oftentimes there was this fair amount of uncertainty and confusion. In the end one has to determine in their own heart, what they choose to believe. Your situation and mine are not so much that different. Are we going to believe on those university trained and self-proclaimed pundits in every field of study, over the Holy Bible? Believing the Bible over humans' recollections of things and events was not a tuff pill for me to swallow. I can imagine it is for some, because of the scholarly crowd's effect on so many trusting souls. Scholars tend to carry a lot of so-called, *"credible academic weight¿"* when they oftentimes assert that the holy writings have not been preserved well enough for, us to be able to trust them wholly for their accuracy and truth. When scholars look at people with their self-assured and often snobbish eyes; it can be just a little bit unnerving. Add too, today we now have different languages and cultures. Another critical factor is we are thousands of years detached by the death of, "**every witness**." It can make events deep into our past, unknowable at worse; culturally dim at best. And far as being told the truth about things, where are these guys (Matthew 24:5&24) in the mix?

In fact, I am witnessing to you before YHWH today; he has made the genuine effort to get through to me; to help my spiritual deafness and my blindness. I was in truth, at an impasse. On the one hand, I was 640 years away from accounting for the entire 6000 years of the millennial week I had been researching. But, on the other hand, in theory of time at least, I was *supposedly* twenty (20) years past all scorners' thresholds of *"Jesus"* and the Messianic Yeshua's great and grand promises of their returns and redemptions. We will not mention the "Jewish Messiah" here. Since they are still at year 5780. In truth, Jews in Israel have no earthly idea of what year it really is. It seems they are in this similar confusion of time as we are. So, where do we all go from here? Any suggestion? Of course, those questions were rhetorical. I happen to know exactly where we are going.

CHAPTER 16

THE LITTLE SEASON

I was afraid I had come to the place I feared from the very beginning. I cannot remember clearly enough, so as to tell you exactly how things proceeded from this point; but I will retell it the best that I can. I do recall praying to the Holy Spirit of YHWH. I asked him why was I so blinded and without understanding? Why was I able to look directly at some written divine thing, with what I thought were two good spiritual eyes and still not be able to see that divine thing clearly enough to make out what it truly was? Then I said to YHWH, with all of the sincerity and humbleness that I could muster up from my heart, "I cannot see anything, unless you show me. If you do not reveal the way to me I will be lost." Those words are not the exact or according to my reality. Just know the event did happen. After which, YHWH's Holy Spirit resumed guiding my walk by asking me some questions of his own. Below are the recall

versions for some of those questions, along with my recall responses.

1) Why are you and everyone else who has thrown their hats into the prophetic arena trying to account for the 6000 years before Messiah Yeshua's return - _supposedly at year 6001_?
   a. I could not readily answer then.
   b. Here is my response now.
      i. I am sure, knowing the day and the hour wasn't what I really wanted to know in particular from YHWH. What I really wanted to know was if he was still really speaking to me. How could I know it was YHWH and not some familiar spirit? In these last days there are many false Christs, false prophets, there are false gospels and the spirit of antichrist in mentioning the top five. I wanted the real YHWH to stand up and show as much of himself to me as his will. In doing that, I asked him to reveal to me knowledge that could be known, **but few knew**. I asked him could <u>the last year</u>, <u>the last day</u> and <u>the last hour</u> be truly established among his true and trying believers. <u>My assertion is this book is part of what YHWH showed me</u>.

2) Did not I [_Yeshua_] say that I would shorten those days leading up to my return? You are one that believes me. But what does it say for the rest who insist without knowledge that it is year 6019? (_Translated to AD time, it is year AD 2020_)
   a. My answer was yes I do believe/know he would shorten the days.
   b. I had no good reply for those who felt Yeshua was not to return until year 6001 or AD 2001.

3) Is there any place in the Holy Scriptures that would reveal to you, or anybody who has faith to believe, by how many days of "_those days_" (Matthew 24:22), I will shorten them?
   a. At the time, I did not know?
   b. <u>But then</u> and <u>now are two different times</u> (_However, it is only by the Grace of Eloah_).

The Holy Spirit told me to assess the *Little Season*. That enigma had come up in my mind before when studying. I was amazed listening to the media, to devout Jews, Messianics and a few gentile ministers talk about Messiah returning in the year 6001. I would always say in my heart, "Did not Yeshua declare, "*For the elect's sake those days shall be shortened*" (Matthew 24:22)? I would then ask myself; why is it that I hear no one - *when they are **preaching** on our end times* - take Yeshua's statement into **serious** consideration? From my view, when those who make the claim, "Yeshua is to return in 6001" (*Whenever that is or was*); they are clearly calling him a liar. If Yeshua waited and came back in the year 6001, in truth he is a liar; because he failed to shorten "*those days*" for the "*elect's sake*" as he had biblically promised. If YHWH, "*is not slack concerning his promise, as some men count slackness*" (2nd Peter 3:9) what were or are those who say he will not return until year 6001 thinking about? We all say, teach and *trust*; it is impossible for YHWH to lie (Hebrews 6:18). If true, then Yeshua must; I repeat, he "**MUST**" return some time **before** year 6001. **This is true; even if we do not have our years right.** Here is an absolutely terrifying notion. **What if the Holy Bible is a Wholly Lie?** That is a profane question that no believer I know, would ever seriously consider. If the Bible is false, then our condition is just as Apostle Shaul stated, "*...your faith is vain; ye are yet in your sins. Then they also which* *are fallen asleep in Messiah are perished*" (1ˢᵗ Corinthians 15:17-18); a bit later, "*let us eat and drink; for tomorrow we die*" (Verse 32). Just as a side note – *before we move on* – I would like to ask the question, "Who would dispute our perception, Apostle Shaul or Paul knew absolutely and precisely what **physical death** - **really is**?" For those of you who were unsure before; Paul confirms the Bible's truth. I believe the term, "*fallen asleep...*" says it all. As I have said before, I say again. Let YHWH be truth and men liars; even if they are "*preachin men.*" Now with that said, we all must conclude at this point, there is something inaccurate with the year, AD 2020. We who profess to have **sober minds** – have no choice at this juncture. If we witness 2020 as accurate, **our** Messiah has spent these last 19 years being a liar. If we expect him in Messianic year 6001, we have again relegated him to the status of liar. Either way, from these two points of views, no matter how we try to spin it in the Bible; Messiah is still made a "**LIAR.**" Again, know this. Jews: Orthodox (*Traditional*), Reform (*Liberal/Progressive*), Conservatives (*Middle–ground*) and the Reconstructionist (*They are a different kind of progressive – Do not start me to lying*) know that the modern Jewish year of 5780 is significantly off. It is possibly off by hundreds of years - **in the rears**! Consider the following article that was written for the Jewish calendar year 5775.

> "A challenge regarding the Hebrew calendar is that the year 5775 may not be so precise. Seder Olam records that the time

between the destructions of the two Batei Mikdash lasted 490 years. However, secular history records that the Churban of the first Beit HaMikdash took place in 586 BCE, and that the Churban of the second Beit HaMikdash occurred in 70 CE; this leaves us with a period of 655 years. Thus, there is a discrepancy of 165 years between Seder Olam and secular history!"

(Reuven Herzog and Benjy Koslowe, 2015/5775)

Herzog and Koslowe imply Jewish time may be off 165 years, in the rear. YHWH's revelations to me show that number is likely higher. We will speak more to its probability a little later. For now, I would only ask for it to be considered as a biblically implicated option that chronological context as far as historical Bible years are concerned has been *misplaced*. Nonetheless, should we not consider it as his divine act of mercy that in these, our last desperate minutes of ordained time – *in those words from Daniel 12:10* – YHWH is bringing to the light (*now revealing*) from his believable testimony (*The Holy Bible*), the proof of our time table error. Notwithstanding, if people choose the option to agree with non-believing historians who insinuate that YHWH's Word is "inexact" (*a lie*), or those who were inspired by YHWH's Holy Spirit, actually wrote a lie, be my guest. But for my part and in my opinion; that I must say, is exactly what I would judge as, "*Faithless Insanity*." Somebody is wrong. Only it is not YHWH Elohim, his prophets, his Apostles or his Word. So then, let us go on to see if we can find every year of man's time from the Holy Bible. And, as far as YHWH and his Word being a liar, let that thought perish.

When YHWH had me to look at his little season, things did not dawn on me all at once. It took time before he let me know what it was that he wanted me to know. In my previous arguments, I felt that I already had the answer to YHWH's first question from his list. From my perspective, YHWH had to return in the authority of Messiah Yeshua, before the year 6001. Untimely for me, that meant Messiah Yeshua should have already returned <u>before AD 2001</u>! Having to admit this pretty much put me in the same boat with other Bible Sad Sacks. Would I also end up making face-saving excuses with designs to unnecessarily defend the credibility of the Holy Bible? This often happens to us, due to our lack of knowledge and contextual understanding. Even though I felt theoretically, it might have been a long shot; with 641 years still on my Bible time chart; I was still in the race and hoping for divine revelation. Yet, I had "<u>BIG</u>" theological and biblical problems. If you are the serious Bible student, you tell me! <u>Where do I find 641 chronological years from *AD 1360* (or year 5360) to 6001 in the New Testament</u>? They appear not to be in there. Now you are beginning to see that tight spot belonging to every <u>Holy Bible</u> theologian, historian, laymen, student, weekend warrior – now to me and you. We all face that enigmatic **<u>BEAST of lost time</u>**. To this point, none of us seem to be faring very well. We all can and most likely, we all have guessed. I am guilty. I admit it. I have said it. "It won't be too much longer and the

Lord will be back" or I have said something similar. I was merely stating what was obvious to any professing Christian. We have been making that guess ☺ *I am guessing!* ☺ for about 1990 years. We are bound to get it spot-on one day. "*Even a broken clock is right two times a day*" – Right?

I wanted to be more than a, "*broken clock.*" My big question related to the then unknown. If you are wrong to think it is AD 2020 without a hitch, and you are; if Christendom is off, and it is; if the Jews inhabit "*blindness in part*" (Romans 11:25), and they do; if I was wrong – even if I did not know how, and I was; then is there not one who is right? I am not intentionally trying to be insulting or anything. It is simple fact. That is, if "*Jesus Christ*" or Messiah Yeshua or the Jewish Messiah has not yet returned or come; and, to date he has not. I was definitely at a loss and did not have any clue. Most frightening was were there any who could be right? Some of you guys maybe thinking even stronger than before now; your understanding of the passage which seems to declare no man knows the day or hour (Matthew 24:36) is holding its own very well against my so-called **"Divine Revelations of Insight;"** insinuating that perhaps I do know, "*that day and hour.*" Some of you still insist, "*Impossible*" - right? When I was at that point (*5360 or AD 1360*); where I have all of you at this moment, I was pretty much thinking that same thing. Was this as far as YHWH going to take me in time? And, if it was; the next question of my mystery, "Was it YHWH's Spirit to begin with?" To be honest, that

was always and foremost, the question skulking at the back of my mind.

If this spirit would not, or maybe even perhaps could not, take me any

further; I would have to entertain the frightening probability that I had

listened to and I had been led by a familiar spirit from Satan the Devil.

The Bible says try the spirits. So that is what I did. I know a wicked spirit

will have no dealings with pure righteousness, holiness and godliness. So

I simply built up the good courage to say, "I will not communicate any

supposed divine knowledge designed to lift me up. I will not try and

make a lie or a suspicious dogma into an absolute truth. Anything that I

think might damage any person, I will discard. Most important, I will not

adopt, promote or in any way preach and teach anything that **I know** and

understand originated from paganism, idolatry or man's traditions that

will provoke YHWH to jealousy." In other words, no matter what this

spirit told me or showed me; I would, "*Abstain from all appearance of*

evil" (1st Thessalonians 5:22). **Now come on you guys.** We **all** have the

ability to classify religious doctrines and practices that did not originate

from the Holy Bible. That is child's play. None of us are that blind. **Are**

we? In short order, that is what I did. I would not accept any understood,

non-Bible things for spiritual truth or holy doctrine. Simple enough. With

that act went my prayer that YHWH might see my humbled spirit; and have mercy on my lack of knowledge, understanding and wisdom of time or whatever else his Spirit chose to share with my spirit. I believed since I was committing to the pursuit of human godliness, "***on those grounds***," no wicked spirit would promote or engage in such actions and behaviors of spirit. So, no wicked spirit would aid in such an endeavor – Capeesh?

From there it was go or no. So... into the darkness I went. I had no idea from Adamic year 5360 or AD 1360 where I was headed. I only had the light of that spirit to guide me through. The immediate unknown was, could that spirit or would YHWH reveal to me what I felt was the next step for discerning the years between AD 1360 and the end of the age. How much time is going to be cut off by Yeshua from Elohim's original time for man? I suppose that I had every reason to be excited about the prospects. Nevertheless, like most "humans;" I needed merely one reason to doubt. My doubt was contained in a truth that I could not deny. I was nowhere close to being worthy of such an understanding and Satan let me know it in no uncertain terms. However, the little faith in me spoke to me in reason. For whatever reason YHWH chose, he put questions in my mind and I expect him to give what insight he wanted me to have. Albeit, I worried about the responsibilities that would come along with possibly knowing something that not too many other people on earth may know or understand. "This **calling** worried me a lot." But, I chose to step forward anyway. Now I want you to step forward with me in faith. So I can show you, what YHWH showed to me. You judge, if there be spiritual merit in what I claim is his revelations. Like I said, it took me a little while. But, YHWH finally led me over into His book of Revelation. After I read the following passage, he asked me two thought-provoking questions. First, I invite you to read the passage itself. And then, consider it for yourself. What questions might you have asked in your wisdom and forethought?

> "And I saw an angel come down from heaven, having the key of the bottomless pit and a great chain in his hand. And he laid hold on the dragon, that old serpent, which is the Devil, and Satan, and bound him a thousand years, and cast him into the bottomless pit and shut him up; and set a seal upon him that he should deceive the nations no more, till the thousand years should be fulfilled: and after that he must be loosed a little season" (Revelation 20:1-3).

Now, ponder the questions YHWH's Holy Spirit asked of me after. How would you have answered them?

1) Why **"MUST"** the dragon, that old serpent, which is the Devil and Satan, be loosed for a little season? (*Why is Almighty YHWH* _obligated_ *to free the dragon? [MUST FREE - Satan]*)

2) How long is a little season?

The first question as to why the Devil **must** be loosed again, after he had been cast into the bottomless pit; I have always wondered about; but I had not thought much to evaluate. I was not quite sure how to respond to the Holy Spirit. He asked me to think on it a bit. He spoke in me and said, since I was an "**_off-shoot_**" from the tree of the knowledge of good and evil; fact is, I thought similar to that old serpent. And, I should have a very good idea as to why he **must** be loosed for a last time, after he had been cast in that bottomless pit for the 1000 years. That quiz by the Holy Spirit made me to see what was actually going on with Satan's situation. Think with me for a moment, my brother and sister "**_off-shoots_**." If **WE** were in Satan's predicament, _which is by divine proclamation;_ and we knew we were going to eventually and very soon be cast into the lake of fire, to be _tormented_ day in and night out "_for ever and ever_" (Revelation 20:10). Not one of us would be in any hurry to get there. Think about this too! If you were Satan and found out Yeshua re-ordained to be shortened the days of your freedom from the Lake of Fire, what state of mind might you be in? How might you **_react_** to that cut? (**_Oh really? No He didn't!_**) I think it is similar to finding oneself drowning in the middle of an ocean, with no aid in sight. You know in probability you are going to die - soon. Nonetheless, you fight! You fight with all of your strength and for every precious breath you have remaining. Unlike a lot of us Satan understands torment and death - absolutely. Believe me, Satan does not want to be tormented and he does not want to die. Remember Paul's descriptions, "_fallen asleep_" and "_perished._" Realize this; just like YHWH gave to us a specific amount of time; he also gave Lucifer and his angels a specific amount of time. If you have read about it and can recall the episode with its demonic witness from the fierce two who were possessed. They gave testimony to a *__known__* "time limit existing" for them. Read the following.

> "And when he [*Messiah Yeshua*] was come to the other side into the country of the Gergesenes, there met him two possessed with devils, coming out of the tombs, exceeding fierce, so that no man might pass by that way. And, behold, they cried out, saying, "What have we to do with thee, [*Yeshua*], thou Son of [*Elohim*]? Art thou come hither to torment us **before the time**?"" (Matthew 8:28-29) In the Hebraic-Roots Version of the Holy Scriptures it says it in a more direct and revealing way, "Why have you come here, to afflict us **before the set time**?"

The same argument those lower level demons made, Satan the Devil would concur with. They both exist in parallel states of being; and, have similar amounts of time remaining. If it be for any reason whatsoever that YHWH Elohim was to not keep his Word, heaven and earth would cease to exist. "*Heaven and earth shall pass away, but my word shall not pass away*" (Matthew 24:35). The Spirit then said to me that the reason he gave Satan that "*little season*" on the back side - **after** his Millennial Sabbath; was because Messiah Yeshua had first taken it from Satan on the front side - **before** his Millennial Sabbath. It was so clear. If YHWH does not take this abrupt action in cutting short the days, man would have destroyed himself from off the face of the earth, long before Messiah Yeshua would have returned in his Adamic year 6001. (Matthew 24:22) Some believe that passage entails when the last trump sounds, only the dead will be raised *"incorruptible"* and none alive will be *"changed."* Amazing... Such an **altered event** would make the Word of Yeshua null and void. Because Yeshua has sworn by his Holy Spirit of Truth (*which is inside of us*) and faithfulness towards us, "...*upon this* **Rock**" (Petra).

> 4073. Petra, *Pet'-ra;* fem. Of the same as 4074; a (mass of or [*massive*]) rock (lit. or fig.): - rock.

> 4074. Petros, Pet'-ros; appar. A primary word; a (piece of) *rock* (larger than 3037); as a name, *Petrus*, an apostle: - Peter, rock. Comp. 2786. Kephas, *kay-fas';* Of Chald. or. [comp. 3710]; *the Rock*; *Cephas* (i.e. *Kepha*), a surname of Peter: - Cephas.

> (The word Yeshua used in *"upon this rock"* is "Petra, *Pet'-ra;"* not Petros (*stone*) the word translated Peter (*who is Kephas or Cephas*).

> *"...I will build My church; and the gates of hell* [sh'ol/bodily death] *shall not prevail against it"* (Matthew 16:18). Just so some of you know, Yeshua was speaking of *himself;* **not Peter**. Compare: *Pet'-ra* (Yeshua - chief corner **stone**) to *Petros* (Peter). Have we not all read Ephesians 2:20? Anyway, to preserve us and his creation, Yeshua can't lie. Yeshua had to give Satan and his demons their allotted time; even if he did make an emergency revision to cut off a piece of time by a little season for the survival of man, truly his elect. He restores the little season at the end of his Millennial Sabbath Reign before the judgment. I am persuaded by the power and revelation of the Holy Spirit and the authority of biblical truth that is the way it went. That is also the way it still stands today.

"And when the thousand years are expired, Satan shall be loosed out of his prison [*for the little season* -verse 3], and shall go out to deceive the nations which are in the four quarters of the earth...to gather them together to battle...And they went up on the breadth of the earth, and compassed the camp of the saints about, and the beloved city: and fire came down from God out of heaven, and devoured them. And the devil...was cast into the lake of fire and brimstone...and shall be tormented day and night forever and ever. And I saw a great white throne, and him that sat on it, from whose face the earth and the heaven fled away; and there was found no place for them. And I saw the dead, small and great, stand before God; and the books were opened: and another book was opened, which is *the book* of life: and the dead were judged out of those things which were written in the books, according to their works. And the sea gave up the dead which were in it; and death and hell delivered up the dead which were in them: and they were judged every man according to their works" (Revelation 20:7-14).

After I heard, received and believed what YHWH revealed regarding Satan's time warp; he next decided to reveal how long a little season is. Satan's dilemma in my understanding is quite logical and makes credible sense. It appears, when I look back on that episode of revelation; YHWH had little issue afterwards, with revealing and explaining to me precisely how long the little season was. Now recall at present, we are in YHWH's Adamic year of 5360. Year 5360 corresponds to our Gregorian year, AD 1360. We have 640 years left on YHWH's Adamic week until we reach the threshold of mockery and ferocious discreditation. **And, we have not been allowed to move!** When some of you learn of the Little Season's simplicity. If you believe me. You might likely have said the same things I said to the Holy Spirit of YHWH. "Why could I not see this truth? How was I not able to figure it out, before now?" I mean truly. I may live to be sixty-one years old this year. I have been reading the Bible almost since I knew how to read. So, as soon as the Holy Spirit plainly revealed to me, I could see it. Still, I was afraid of being wrong about it. And, because of that fear, I was unable to fully receive what was then for me a real divine end time illumination, right there in front of my face. Fear kept me from receiving the *little season's* simple concept as a valid revelation of truth from YHWH. So, forgive me now for maybe about to sound like things were *simple* or like I was some kind of genius and was able to so-called, *"figure it out."* In reality, I was far from its simple concept, as far as my realization and understanding. In reality, it took me well over six months to receive the full insight for YHWH's *little season*. The biggest reason for my lack of faith – *to my shame* – was because of all that I had learned from many of the vaunted and most prominent theological Professors and Doctors of Divinity concerning end time prophecies. I can only imagine; many reading this book are just like I was. Because of what teachers you have every confidence in have taught; many find it difficult to receive a tremendous amount of the insights and perspectives I have written inside this book. I sadly had to come to that understanding; things are what they are. However, I am confident in this book and I believe you will receive whatever it is you are supposed to receive. I would have kicked myself in the tush for not seeing it before - if I could. I had all of the resources and the knowledge. I was simply not able to put everything together. YHWH instructed me with the knowledge that I already had; and with concepts I already understood. YHWH revealed to me, how to literally assimilate two completely unrelated concepts, as they related to the Little Season's revelation. Now check this out. Believe it, if you can. The hidden truth to discerning YHWH's "*little season*" was revealed when he instructed me to, "take the millennial day and assimilate it with the annual seasons!" Yes, it was just that simple. But on my life I could not see it beforehand.

Truly, I cannot help those who will not believe or even consider my discernments as truth. But, for those who do accept the concept of the millennial week; if you will, I want you to take it another step further and receive this additional discovery; which you know about; but an idea you probably never thought much over. Here is an additional insight from the Holy Spirit. If a millennial day is 1000 years - the Holy Spirit building my knowledge made me to understand - then a *little season* (Revelation 6:11 & 20:3), was either 250 or 500 years long. The question for me was which one? YHWH made me to discern that a general (*long*) season **in context**, was an entire year. Yet, a year is divided into two seasons. We know both those seasons and call them summer and winter. Likewise, we understand that those two seasons are also divided into halves as well. Those two halves are called spring and fall. The divisions of the year that make up the four little seasons are spring, summer, fall and winter. **Still,** I needed the Holy Spirit to give the biblical record - *a witness if he will -* to prove what he was telling me in my spirit. I needed the Holy Bible to divide up the years for me. So anybody could go to it and read it - **if they wanted to**. Then, they could choose whether they wanted to believe it or not. I would find just one passage in the entirety of the Holy Bible, which fulfilled that requirement. It reveals first, YHWH's seedtime and harvest in the spring and summer times. Then for all of ya'll winter gardeners out there; you understand that YHWH indeed has a seedtime and harvest in the fall and winter times. Read the passage for yourself. "*While the earth remaineth, seedtime and harvest, and cold and heat, and summer and winter, and day and night shall not cease*" (Genesis 8:22).

   i. Note that a year has four (4) little seasons in it, seedtime and harvest in the spring and summer; and also there is seedtime and harvest in the fall and winter (Genesis 8:22).

   ii. The insight and understanding of the little season is manifested when we are able to convert the two concepts in the 1000 years of the millennial day to the four divisions of the seedtime and harvest seasons in summer and winter.

After YHWH alerted me to incorporate the four subdivisions of the seasonal year into a millennial day, I divide YHWH's millennial day into little seasons and understood that the, "little season" was 250 years long. YHWH revealing the little season allowed for more time to be accounted for and that meant more time off of the millennial week. According to YHWH, the sixth millennial day was reshaped and redistributed, because of man's imminent self-annihilation. So you may visualize it in your own mind and understand what I am implying, YHWH cut 250 years off of the original 6000. That meant in truth, we only needed to account for 5750 years before Messiah should have been expected to return. By the revelation of YHWH, we have already walked through 5360 years; and correspondingly, that placed us at AD 1360. We were down to only 640 years that we needed to account for. But, when we subtract the 250 years of the "little season;" we are down to 390 years. That is not much time, when it is considered; we started with the overall number of 6000 years.

I guess this all should sound well and good. That is, if we do like some people do and just don't think about things. However, if we choose to use our minds just a bit. We would see that our current accounting as it is now standing, simply does not add up right. And we now have, at least from my perspective; some glaring problems in our spiritual accounting department. You have already been informed that the base year of 5360 corresponds to year AD 1360. That meant we could walk at the most just another 641 years, until we reached that threshold of critical mass error; invoking Christians' and atheists' scorn. That is, if we use our existing hypothesis of the millennial week or 6000-year total, before Messiah was to return. Now according to my self-professed witness of insistence that YHWH has been directing and instructing me; I am now ***cutting off 250 years*** from those remaining 640 of the original 6000 years of time. 6000 years is what I claimed was allotted for our self-rule. But, when it was told to me that I should do this. It clearly sounded counterproductive to me. Let us do the math together - *if you will* - and see some of the problematic issues we are faced with, in our walk towards the end of the age. There are several concerns that we must be aware of. We need to recognize them. We will cite a few to get a taste of what we might expect secular counters and some elements in Christian organizations would bite off, chew up and then spit out; without much of any pause or questions; along with whatever - *if any* - credibility we may have had - out with it.

1) Currently it is AD 2020. In our Adamic count, we stopped at year 5360; which is AD 1360. It meant we only had 640 years to go, before we came to what basically amounts to in theory at least, the theological end of the age. That is without cutting off 250 years for the *little season*. If AD 2020 is correct, that means we have already walked well past those 640 years. In simple mathematical terms, we are nineteen (19) years past that 640-year limit and look, no Messiah. When we consider all of the implications. **No way is it kosher at all!**

2) Since we are obviously still waiting. It would appear at least on the surface that Messiah did not shorten the days as he told us he would

in the Holy Bible. <u>Now that is a **REAL** bummer</u>! Because, heaven and earth is still **very much** here. That implication alone, whether misunderstood or even understood in many cases – *either way* – to some it can be a legitimate faith-breaker.

3) If we go ahead and proceed to cut off the 250 years for the *little season*, what would that all imply if we considered it? Would not it imply that instead of being nineteen (19) years in the rears, *"Jesus Christ"* and Messiah Yeshua and possibly even the Jewish Messiah are all 269 years in the rears of their supposed, *"Promises?"* I am just trying to think with a sober mind here. So please, do not get upset with me and treat my writings like some variety of atheistic theology for demonology. That assessment could not be further from the truths of the matter. You see - *right or wrong* - according to our apparent hypothesis of theology, with that cutting off of the *little season,* Messiah Yeshua should have returned in AD 1750. That is, based on the millennial week premise. Clearly, there is still confusion lurking around in many (*really all*) of the churches accounting departments.

4) My time accounting methods are improbable, not feasible and does not work. (*Hey! What about yours Mr., Mrs., Miss and Ms BC/AD?*)

5) No man knows the day and hour. (*That thought has been lurking in some of your minds for a while now.*)

The supposed current date of AD 2020; all but speaks for itself. We are over the threshold of the traditional, prophesied and the promised Messianic returns; and have no good reasons as of yet, in our knowledge and our understanding for explaining it or excusing it. Any would be and might be reasonable choices that we could consider approaching even some partial explanation of that ***did not happen event***, becomes woefully painful to the spirit, unpleasantly odorous to the, *"Christian"* smell test and equally distasteful to the *"Christians'"* pallet of witness. Basically with the current date AD 2020, or at the least, our understanding of the date, the Messiah's return date and indeed the Messiah himself is thrown overboard and is dead in the water. We only have so many choices at this point with our limited insights. Among them being is that our Messiah Yeshua is still dead in the grave, so that he cannot keep his promise. He has risen, but perhaps there has been some sort of interstellar or cosmic incident and he is having to take care of it. Messiah is just running a little bit late. Last, but not least; maybe, "Your Messiah" is just a damned liar. With the little season cut out from this side of the Millennial Reign, what we have left is the ordained time of 5750 years; which corresponds to the AD date of 1750 on its face value. Hey, wait a minute! My threshold date has been passed as well – and for well over 260 years. This is not a good thing for me either. That would imply that, "My Messiah" is a damned liar too? At this point in my understanding, "My Messiah" is dead in the water, right alongside of, "Your Messiah." Wow! My self-righteousness did not see that curve ball coming then. But actually, I do now. I just said it for the dramatic effects. But seriously though, what is the sane-minded *Christian* supposed to think? God can't lie! But all we can envision at this point is a bunch of hypothetical lies. Because, we lack understanding and we truly and in our pride do not want to admit it.

Where do we go from here? 🌝 **I know!!** 😋 **We should all become damned liars too.** Then, we can do like many of our biblical theologians and Christian pundits have been known to do at times. And that is, we make up excuses and falsehoods as to why our renditions of God has been made a damned liar - before all of mankind no less. **God forbid!** Believe it or not, thoughts like that did pass inside my head when I hit this brick wall. But, I have to give all the glory to my Eloah – who told me to just, 'keep walking in righteousness, while seeking the truth. And, do not be afraid to be wrong. Because for me; there were more unrealized insights yet to be revealed.' After that I did not feel absolutely stuck. Nonetheless, after cutting off the years for the *little season*, I only had 390 years to work with on YHWH's Adamic week. If I used the **Gregorian calendar**, I was already over my mark of 5750, by 270 years! That meant I had a host of issues needing to be dealt with. I also knew if truth was going to happen for me, as far as me gaining that understanding I needed in order to *know what time we are really in and how much time we have left,* the Holy Spirit would absolutely be needed to sort the issue out; because (*and you can quote me on this*) **I had absolutely not a clue.**

The next vital insight YHWH revealed to me; which we will need to discern the real time we are in and the start of the Millennial Reign close upon us; was a mystery not many even know exist, let along praying to

YHWH asking for divine insight on it. YHWH placed it in an obscure, so spiritually in a controversial rendering in the ninth chapter of Daniel. The obscure rendering I am referring to, is prophesied with Daniel's seventy weeks. But as far as actual fulfillment; it is incredibly joined indirectly in YHWH's total time allotment. The stage for this mystery is set well after the time of Daniel's seventy weeks. From the far future of a certain date, beyond that of the seventy weeks; the wisdom of this mystery extends up to our modern times and will not conclude until the return of our Messiah Yeshua. Let us read together this obscure passage as I am referring to it. Do not be upset with me or yourself if with your meticulous examination and scrutiny, you do not see what I see. And, I do not want you to think I am making this comment to insult you; or because I do not think you will be able to see what I see - to imply I am more insightful than you. I am saying what I said only because of how YHWH showed this crucial piece of the puzzle to me. And, not because there existed before me this divine mystery of prophecy (*though it was*); and with my tremendous spiritual expertise, I figured this mystery all out and all by my lonesome. My reality was far from that narcissistic fantasy. In my reality, I was at a loss when YHWH showed it to me; and the question that came forth from my mouth, only echoed my utter dismay. **"How could anyone know this?"** In the end, I realize that no one could truly, **"know this,"** unless YHWH revealed, **"this"** to them. And, for the most part, being disbelieved when I relay, **"this"** information to others; for me, is just par for the course. Be that as it may, in the pursuit of spiritual growth and our lively challenge to free ourselves from all wicked inhibitions, due to the effect of spiritual drunkenness (Revelation 17:1-2); if we can, let us receive from the Holy Spirit. We can do so, by allowing his scrutiny to reveal to us the serenely seductive secrets of the enigmatic passage that caused me to literally and spiritually throw up my hands in helplessness. I was profoundly in need of YHWH's divine guidance. It seemed for me then, every *saintly* step I was taking, was beforehand trackless and devoid of any previous human travelers. <u>Once again I was unsure</u>. You see; I had never heard **"<u>anyone</u>"** speak to the enigma that is Daniel's, **"CONSUMMATION."** Have you?

CHAPTER 17

THE CONSUMMATION

"And after ~~threescore and~~ two weeks ~~shall Messiah be cut off,
but not for himself; and~~ the people of the prince that shall come
shall destroy the city and the sanctuary; and the end thereof shall
be with a flood, and unto the end of the war desolations are
determined. And he shall confirm the covenant with many for
one week: and in the midst of the week he shall cause the
sacrifice and the oblation to cease, and for the overspreading of
abominations he shall make it desolate, even until the
consummation, and that determined shall be poured upon the
desolate" (Daniel 9:26-27).

With the event and aging of the consummation was perpetrated no
doubt the biggest hoax of the age; along with it, surely the great religious
deception of our time. Short of the Garden of Eden deception, within the
consummation is quite conceivably the greatest religious deception of all
times. It came upon us in a time of duress. I must as a result, confront it
with empathy and serpent subtlety - *if you will excuse the expression.*

The Bible warns us in such matters, "*Behold, I send you forth as sheep in the midst of wolves: be ye therefore wise as serpents, and harmless as doves*" (Matthew 10:16). Granted, for all of us the consummation was shrouded in a mystery of divine darkness. However, the consummation event itself was facilitated by the emissary (*The beast who spoke as a dragon* - Revelation 13:11) of the *dragon, that old serpent, which is the Devil and Satan*. After the emissary's deed that begat the offspring of the consummation; compensatory adoration and horror wonderfully destroys as that offspring's bow veils his cruelty. His pious wickedness is steadily accepted by its encountered foes, if they lived. It mattered not whether they were uninterested observers, nominal believers, or they became true believers in the faith of the emissary. And, this was easy for Satan to do; because their lives mean nothing to him. Billions are filled with his wine of spiritual fornication. And yes, YHWH is allowing it. Believe it or not, YHWH is even assisting Satan in this effort. Listen to the Bible witness. "*God shall send them strong delusion, that they should believe a lie*" (2nd Thessalonians 2:11). I should imagine that few will be able to receive the doctrine behind the consummation. But still, I must make every effort to illuminate it for judgment. But, because the consummation is so deeply imbedded in our society and indeed the whole world in general, it must be handled very delicately. For me, the consummation is not an easy event to explain. For you see, in my explanation I must hold certain truths back; that to many, would be too difficult to hear; "...*not willingly, but by reason of him who hath subjected the same in hope*" (Romans 8:20). And, I believe that hope is that you will be able to receive the revealing of all the numbers first. So you might recognize, **IT'S MUCH LATER THAN YOU THINK!** And, no matter how great or how bad my articulations of the narratives go, it is the numbers that do not lie. It is the numbers that I encourage you to hold on to and boldly consider.

People ask and rightfully so. "What is the consummation?" or, "Why is the consummation so hard for me, at the least, to explain?" I want to believe, at least for the most of us; we are all mostly mature here. Since, in fact and after all; you are reading this book. So, before I attempt to answer your inquiry, allow me to ask a question of my own. With the only prequalifying condition being that you are now or you have been married. At what *moment* was your marriage consummated? Most will say your wedding day. That is a twenty-four hour period. Can we narrow it down a bit? Then you might say on your wedding night. That is a bit closer. Still, it covers a non-determinate period of time. Okay you say; on our wedding night, in our wedding bed! But, you still do not know the very moment. Do you? And for goodness' sake - You Were There! As a matter of facts, you were one of only two witnesses at your marriage consummation - *I would hope*. Still, you find it difficult to describe. And, even if you could describe it; who would want to get any more clinical or vivid than what has already been spoken - right? And, for the "X-factor" concerning this book; we are definitely not going to go the way of being too clinically articulate here. So then, let it suffice us all to simply say the marriage consummation time is an incredibly intimate sexual interaction between **One Male and One Female!** There are no exceptions and no in-betweens. In addition, and it needs to be **said** - *in case you did not know* - sexual acts of male and female interactions, should not or do not cheapen, degrade and otherwise abuse YHWH's natural laws for marital participation. Participants know when they act in defiance of the obvious natural laws and spiritual laws governing the intimacy of the male and female sexual bonding. Pretend and deny as they do. We all know what is natural and spiritually intended. Whether we want to acknowledge the truth concerning our sexuality or not, is irrelevant. YHWH will judge us all appropriately. There will be no years of appeals. Yeshua is the lower courts, the higher courts, the thirteen circuit courts of appeals and The Supreme Court; all divinely wrapped up into one judgment. This is why YHWH warns us beforehand. So, when all of the time and the numbers in the years of our ordained existence have run its course; we will be without an excuse. (Romans 1:20)

"...sexual immorality and all uncleanness and covetousness also [*desiring what their fornication and uncleanness **appears** to deliver them*], indeed, should not be named among you, as is becoming to set-apart-ones, And neither obscenities, nor words of foolishness nor of reproach nor of nonsense, which are not necessary, but instead of these, thanksgiving. But this you should know, that every man who is sexually immoral or unclean or covetous, who is a servant of idols, has no inheritance in the Kingdom of the Messiah and of Eloah, less anyone should deceive you with empty words. For because of these, the wrath of Eloah [*comes*] upon the sons of disobedience."

(Ephesians 5:3-6, The Scriptures, Hebraic-Roots).

"But if any man think that he behaveth himself uncomely toward his virgin, if she [*not he*] pass the flower of her age [*blossomed or has become bodily mature*]...and need so require, let him do what he will, he sinneth not: let them marry [*naturally unite by becoming sexually one in the bond of matrimony*]" (1st Corinthians 7:36).

"Thou shalt not commit adultery" (Exodus 20:14); by taking another man's wife. **Words of Advice** - It is most wise and holy to marry and to have your own wife.

Those above, are basic instructions from YHWH Elohim; governing intimate sexual male and female interactions. Unmistakably so, male and male and female and female sexual interactions are clearly considered "**abominations**" by YHWII. "**Thou shalt not lie with mankind, as with womankind: it *is* abomination**" (Leviticus 18:22). I am absolutely sure, no interpretation whatsoever is needed for the above or for the following.

"For this cause God gave them up unto vile affections: for even their women did change the natural use into that which is against nature: and likewise also the men, leaving the natural use of the woman, burned in their lust one toward another; men with men working that which is unseemly...receiving in themselves [*their bodies*] that recompense (*cost*) of their error which was meet...as they did not like to retain God in *their* knowledge, God gave them over to a reprobate mind, to do the things which are not convenient...filled with all unrighteousness, fornication, wickedness, covetousness, maliciousness; full of envy, murder [*hatred*], debate, deceit, malignity; whisperers, backbiters, haters of God, despiteful, proud, boasters, inventors of evil things, disobedient to parents, without understanding, covenant-breakers [*divorce*], without natural affection, implacable, unmerciful: who, knowing the judgment of God, that they which commit such things are worthy of death, not only do the same, but have pleasure in them that do them" (Romans 1:26-32).

Now is your chance to discern in clearer context, the consummation contained in Daniel's seventy weeks. You might also gain insight how it fits into and effect ordained time on the larger scale. To do this, let us first consider the consummation's base word: *Consummate* by definition. "*Consummate*" is a transitive verb. Verbs are words of action. Being transitive in nature, *consummate* show the transference of a relationship of action between two or more entities or objects: i.e. if there is some relationship between, "a and b" and between, "b and c;" then, the relationship will also exists between, "a and c." (Paraphrased: Encarta Dictionary: English - North America)

What is the act of consummation?

1. Complete a marriage
a. To make a marriage legally complete and fully valid by having sexual intercourse.

2. Fulfill a relationship through sex
a. To bring a relationship to completion, or gratify a desire, especially by having sexual intercourse

3. Completion of a deal
a. The finalization of something such as a business deal

4. Perfect ending
a. The bringing of something to a satisfying conclusion, or the final satisfying completion or achievement of something

(All definitions are from: Encarta Dictionary; English - North America)

To have the abilities to describe the exact emotion and the memory to recall that exact time of your physical consummation on your wedding night is likely impossible. It is an arousing event in most cases, couples only fantasize about, let alone recount. However, if it is experienced; it is always a part of our spirits in the backs of our minds. In many cases, we retain the emotions for the duration of our lives, but not the moment. We often reminisce, in hopes we might relive the experience. But, the time of the moment eludes us. Because no one is watching the clock and few will take a picture for a, "Kodak Moment." An orgasmic event is vagarious in nature. Emotionally, it is an indescribable experience. As I said; even the couple who engaged in it, will find it mentally impossible to cite the very moment. This is why it is tricky for me to describe the consummation in the spirit of the seventy weeks. But I can tell you what the consummation is and when the consummation event occurred according to the Scripture.

In prophecy, the consummation event is that point in time where a religious organization will enter into an intimate relationship with the image of a man that is of the androgynous nature and physicality. He/She will be its poster person for its facilitation of spiritual imagery (*idolatry*) and widespread growth (*winning and to win - Revelation 6:2*). After the secretive and history making affair of the consummation first occurs; the copious images of that hermaphrodite He/She will grow so popular that it will dominate most of the world's social, business, political and religious landscape. The imagery of that man/woman will infatuate untold billions, generation after generation. So strong will that image be seared into the minds of the observers and into the hearts of his believers; he will still be popular almost beyond belief, prominent and divinely situated when our Messiah Yeshua returns to deals with him personally. We all understand consummate in the physical. Now understand it clearer in the spiritual. The consummation that Daniel's prophecy is about, completes a religious agreement of oneness with that spiritual hermaphrodite man. The initial intent of fulfillment or to consummate that marriage is by psychosomatic intercourse. The ones who consummately engages that hermaphrodite is joining his family, adopting his values, beliefs and practices; not caring where his social/religious fundamentals originated from. Those lovesick for a release without consequences are intoxicated in his underbelly with the sensual allure of decadence and excess. With no real rules to speak of, all is fair underneath and within the shadows of his "love and war" coven. Devoid of any genuine or true commitment, besides the continual offerings demonstrating subservience by his <u>lost converts</u>, the only quid pro quo is this. Every convert must praise without question, that <u>He/She</u> [<u>The Spiritual Hermaphrodite</u>] "…<u>above all that is called God, or that is worshipped; so that [He/She] as God sitteth in the temple of God, showing himself (Himself/Herself) that [He/She] is God.</u>" (Adapted: 2nd Thessalonians 2:4) It is the completion of his covenant and the perfect ending for the loss inhibitions of his drunken converts (*Those who have ears to hear*).

The Apostle Shaul's markings for identification, aptly list all of the main provisions of the consummation. This GREAT unholy apparition is prophesied to begin its anti-messianic fulfillments at a biblically specific year and time in these last days. Believe it or not, the action itself (*The Consummation*) was official and intimately fulfilled in all. All means all or everyone and everybody. Remember that all ten virgins were asleep.

Meaning, they (*the virgins*) were unaware of what was going on all around them the whole time; while and because, they were sleeping. (Matthew 25:5) So comprehensive was and is his subtle deception, it shrouds the carnal minded view of YHWH's true intent for the human potential in their eternal social, religious and government capacities. The consummation was done so deeply and so intimately secretive inside the belly of the beast, to this date I have been unable to identify any specific event in the historical record I could point to and show without question and major debate to say that this was truly Daniel's consummation event. However difficult that discernment of the consummation act itself has been for my research, the date of the consummation event and the act of that *poured upon* period are revealed in Daniel 9:26-27 and 12:11. The two as we have touched on prior and will for sure elaborate them further; both, "*the consummation*" and "*the poured upon period*" are illuminated inside 2nd Thessalonians 2:3-4 and Revelation 13:11-18 among others. Consider the following passage. After doing so, ask YHWH for some of his given understandings that can be known by his will and Holy Spirit.

> "I beheld another beast coming up out of the earth…he had two horns like a lamb, and he spake as a dragon…he exerciseth all the power of the first beast before him and causeth the earth and them which dwell therein to worship the first beast, whose deadly wound was healed. And he doeth great wonders, so that he maketh fire come down from heaven on the earth in the sight of men, and deceiveth them that dwell on the earth by…those

miracles which he had power to do in the sight of the beast; saying to them that dwell on the earth, that they should make an image to the beast [*This is that mark of the consummation event and the commencement of the poured upon period*]...And he had power to give life unto the image of the beast, that the image of the beast should both speak, and cause that as many as would not worship the image of the beast should be killed."

(Revelation 13:11-15)

I regret that I am unable to give out at this time, the defining event which marks Daniel's consummation event from the pages of history. Nevertheless, I can make known to your faith, the year this intimately secretive and highly miraculous illusory event occurred. It was AD 1360. But, this was not because I was so theologically clever; I discovered that date. Not by a long shot. YHWH in fact, through Daniel, freely gave us that time in history - straight forward and up front. Without the need for in-depth study or deep analysis and revelation. Will we believe Him? Let us read yet again, Daniel 9:26-27. Notice the stacking of time as YHWH, through Gabriel, through Daniel lays it out. I hope no one minds it. This time, I took the liberty of putting that passage in its chronological order. We follow time from the year of the crucifixion, twenty-one years before the destruction of the second temple. Then fourteen years later there is an arrival of the envoy that makes the "covenant" on behalf of the people of the Prince. Three and a half years later, they undermine and violate that agreement. The first great war between Jews and Rome was a resulted of the undermining. After another three and a half years the Jews are utterly

defeated by Rome. Last of all, the complete devastation of Jerusalem and

the total destruction of her second temple by the Roman armies under the

command of "the Prince." Then comes the 1290-year desolation until the

event happening of the consummation.

From there, we must return to the Holy Bible; to determine if there is

any revelation that takes us beyond from there. If there be any, hopefully

they will take us on into the time that so-called "modern-day prophets"

dream about. I am referring to that often preached time where millions of

"*Christians*" will be looking for that infamous "**Endtime Antichrist**" to

appear. That will be an intriguing time; though I am afraid the reality of

it, will be a shocker for many. This book also claims some extraordinary,

but unexpected things will and will not come to pass during that time; as

you have read. Now read the incredible events in chronological order that

will take us up to and past the great enigma of the consummation. Recall,

the narration is picking up right after the crucifixion of Yeshua in AD 49.

"After...two weeks [*fourteen (14) years*]...the people of the
prince...shall come...he [*they*] shall confirm the covenant with
many for one week: and in the midst of the week he [*they*] shall
cause the sacrifice and the oblation to cease...and unto the end
of the **war** desolations are determined...[*The people of the prince
under Prince Titus' commands*] shall destroy the city and the
sanctuary...and the end thereof shall be with a flood...and for the
overspreading of abominations he [*they*] shall make it [*All
Jerusalem and the Second Temple*] desolate...even [up] until the

consummation...and that [*the consummation*] determined shall be poured upon [*added in addition to*] the desolate [*the temple's time in ruin*]" (Daniel 9:26-27 – Chronologically listed).

I view only destruction [*which is what makes Jerusalem and the Second Temple desolate*] through to a continuous period of desolation, up until the event of the enigmatic consummation [***which begins the mark of YHWH's ordained sign that bands together the spiritual/political entity and elements facilitating the great falling away*** - 2ⁿᵈ Thessalonians 2:3].

THERE WILL BE NO THIRD TEMPLE!
"THAT'S RIGHT! I SAID IT!"

The falling away period, once it was determined by YHWH, is to be poured out on top of and in addition to the sustained desolate condition of the Second Temple. This event was allowed by YHWH - in order to frustrate that condition of desolation with which the Jews at Jerusalem and the Second Temple in AD 70, found themselves under. By YHWH's allowances that "***Wicked***" troubling of Jerusalem, was set. In Jerusalem and around the world, we see only increases in treachery against Jews. It is by that "***Wicked***," under a facade of pious humility, will intensified violence and deepening desolation; "*destroy wonderfully*" (Daniel 8:24). This worldwide conspiracy will persist and escalate until that abominable desolation reaches a full fever-pitch and worldwide hatred on the head of the Jews is satisfied with their national blood. It is worth noting from the

Jews' enemies that whoever supports the Jews is a candidate for the same level of violence and destruction. Jews' foes fret no more. Israel's USA sentry is in total moral and civil decay. <u>Like Esau</u>, **<u>we despise our own birthright</u>**. And in the name of false freedom and tolerance; and the false promise of **"<u>Free Freedom</u>,"** citizens view with little concern the social, religious, political and the constitutional attacks that tears at our national fabric. **<u>Is it not terrifying to witness our own demise</u>** or cannot we even see it? I have always known it was coming. But never in a million years, did I think I would live to see our fall, up close and personal. As I write, <u>the propaganda</u> of <u>self-loathing and cultural class warfare</u> is destroying this country from within. <u>Not merely the U.S.</u>, but **"<u>US</u>."** That means <u>me</u>, <u>you</u>... our **<u>children</u>**. I am saying this so you know it. *"<u>Pride goeth before destruction, and a haughty spirit before a fall</u>"* (Proverbs 16:18).

Honestly - and from your heart - how long from our present moment do you believe that our United States of America, will continue to exist? And not as a strait Democracy, *because that is not what we are*; we are a **<u>Representative Republic</u>**! Will this Representative Republic still exist, when those events of the consummation and the pouring out period of religious and political desolation come to their ends? How long will the pouring out period last, after YHWH determined the defining event of the consummation itself? How much longer will time itself continue, before Messiah's return, after that *"poured upon"* period following the consummation event is over? I will admit to it. If we seriously consider the challenges of this book, the above questions should all be accepted as *"legitimate inquiries."* Apostle Shaul is one who gives us critical insights to the mystery concerning that, *"poured upon"* period.

> "Now we beseech you, brethren, by the coming of our Lord Jesus Christ, and our gathering together unto him...be not [*easily*] shaken in mind...or...troubled...as [*if*] that the day of Christ [*was*] at hand. Let no man deceive you by any means: for... except there come a falling away first, and that man of sin be revealed, the son of perdition; who opposeth and exalteth himself above all that is called God, or that is worshipped; so that he as God sitteth in the temple of God, showing himself that he is God. Remember ye not, that, when I was yet with you, I told you these things?...ye know what withholdeth that he might be revealed in his time. For the mystery of iniquity doth already work: <u>only he who now letteth *will let,* [*This mystery is being allowed by YHWH and therefore shall remain*]...until he [*That* **"*Wicked*"** *one*] be taken out of the way. And then shall that **"*Wicked*"** [The Hermaphrodite He/She] be revealed, whom the Lord (*Yeshua*) shall consume with the spirit of his mouth, and shall destroy with the brightness of his coming...whose coming [Yeshua's]</u> is after the workings of Satan with all power (*abundant miracles*) and signs and lying wonders, and with all deceivableness of unrighteousness in them that perish; **because they received not the love of the truth...for this cause God shall send them a strong delusion, that they should believe a lie...**[*since they*] believed not the truth..."
>
> (2nd Thessalonians 2:1-12)

There are take-a-ways we may reflect on from this passage. Consider the following list as partial.

1. Shaul was under no delusions that "*the LORD*" could return at **any day and time.** Shaul understood and knew that was not the truth then; and I dare say, it is not the truth today.

2. Before the return of Messiah, first the mystery of iniquity (That **Wicked** one - son of perdition) had to be formally established or consummated with – **I dare say** – a professing **"Christian"** faith and religion. That is, this must be; in order for that great falling away to take place.

3. His **Wicked** word; which is "*...another gospel*" (Galatians 1:6), his dark dogma; which is the "*...doctrines of devils*" (1ˢᵗ Timothy 4:1) and his persona will preach against YHWH's Godly authority over man and of course himself as being inferior to his own preaching of counterfeit truth. He'll "*...speak great* words against the Most High...and think to change [YHWH's] times and laws:" (Daniel 7:25). He will claim in the name of progressiveness. He will say YHWH's laws and days are to be viewed as old and outdated. For the billions taken in or deceived by this "antichrist;" they will allow and submit to the exchanging of the "*lively oracles*" (Acts 7:38 - *Commandments of God*) to that **Wicked**'s own (*Actually it's Babylon's - Revelation 17:1-5*), made up (*Actually it's plagiarized*), modern (*Actually they're ancient*), non-YHWH sanctioned holy days and laws, for their "now gospel" and for his poisonous purposes of having the "all-inclusiveness" status for his abominable kin, into his gospel of lawlessness, with the rest of this, "whole evil world" (Revelation 12:9). His **Wicked** counterfeit spirit will reject all names (*not titles*) other than his own to be called on as Almighty God.

4. That **Wicked** spirit was already at work in Apostle Shaul's day. But his imagery and visage was not to be revealed as that "**Wicked**" to the world, until the end of his appointed time.

5. Once that **Wicked** was consummated and concealed; Eloah is allowing him to continue to conduct his spiritual business of deception, up until the day of the return of Messiah Yeshua.

6. To the ones who will not receive this truth, YHWH will send them "*strong delusion*" and they will believe The Great Lie; which is that **Wicked** and obey his gospel of lawlessness.

7. Upon Yeshua's return, it will be visibly apparent to the world they had been deceived by that subtle **Wicked** pretender. Then the world will hear Yeshua's True Gospel concerning The Kingdom of Eloah; until it is full of his knowledge for its opportunity for repentance.

The above list dissects Shaul's witness above it; which shed light on that obscure "*poured upon*" period that follows *that marked event* of the consummation in Daniel's seventy weeks prophecy. So then again, we could ask the question that remains. "How long is the combination of the determination that marks the consummation and the poured upon period? It is like I have stated before; I was unable to identify the mark in time; which was the determination of that consummation event, in the official record of man's history. But I do have the biblical record when it occurs. It is AD 1360. It is good enough for my faith. However, I can only speak for myself. Also as I have testified to before, the act of spiritual intimacy is deeper than physical intimacy. If one finds it difficult to express when the act of the physical consummation takes place; the same should truly appreciate the difficulty in trying to identify that defining event in time, when the spiritual consummation took place. I have to imagine such an effort is especially tough; when that *wicked* determination mark of the consummation involves the act of dark miraculous "<u>witchcraft</u>." And this mark event of consummation, surely has that dark stain of, **"<u>witchcraft</u>."** I suppose that is why YHWH made this next to final step for the answers to our time questions, more an exercise in faith and acknowledgement, than a victory for theological intellect.

As I have stated before, no matter what all of the wicked ones in our modern times would advocate, decree and have everybody to believe and accept; every consummation that occurs, involves one real man and one real woman. Everyone that truly understands what a marriage is, know it is "<u>**IMPOSSIBLE!**</u>" for two **REAL men** or two **REAL women** engaged in an ***abominable relationship***, <u>to consummate</u> a ***marriage relationship***. So the wicked ones and their supporters needed to change the definition of the <u>civil law</u> by claiming discrimination (They **can't** change the physical or spiritual law). The civil distortion gives out the aura of legitimacy and "*legal*" status to reject reality. Without courageous opposition from the sane, the righteous are supposed to accept their vile delusions. We are all suppose to secede from true reality; to concede no matter where one man sticks his penis, or tongue into or on another man's body; that area by demonic psychosis is now a consummation spot to host their repulsive non-sex act of nonunion twosomeness. The same goes (*tongue wise*) with two women. And, if any refuse to go <u>*schizo*</u> with them and say so; they are viciously attacked and are accused of being *"homophobic"* and/or making hate speech. No matter what some claim is progressive ideology. Their own **_"tolerance"_** seems to suffer in the face of any dissent. Eloah's fixed law for the marriage consummation is a lifelong _spiritual covenant and_ the *"**natural union**"* of **one male and female**. Hebrews 13:4 is clear.

Is there a male/female merger/union in the prophetic consummation? Can we find it in the Bible? In Revelation 1:11, Messiah Yeshua told Apostle Yochanan (*John*), to write what he saw in a book. Revelation 17:3 says Yochanan saw a woman sitting on a scarlet colored beast. Then, of course, at that particular time, The Great Whore was wearing her face covering – as did most Harlots. This ploy helped to disguise age and identity in the light. Whereas in the cover of darkness, such a tactic was not needed, nor did it matter a lot. In discernment and to our dismay, Apostle Shaul envisioned this same *"woman"* without her veil. How he describes her is quite different from the description that Yochanan gave. Shaul reveals, "Let no man deceive you by any means: for *that day shall not come,* except there come a falling away first, **and that man** of sin be revealed, **the son** of perdition;" (2nd Thessalonians 2:3). Understand it. **Shaul reveals a man** while Yochanan saw a woman! We should all be able to acknowledge that the word "He/She" is quite descriptive here and is indicative of our modern times of sexual and gender identities and confusion. I could also point out the synonymous attitude of this spiritual hermaphrodite. Shaul stated that he "opposeth and exalteth himself above all that is called God, or that is worshipped;" (Verse 4). He also states that this abomination of "spiritual nature," this **Wicked** son, will actually be sitting in the temple of Eloah, palming himself off as Eloah. Now compare the mannerisms of that **Wicked** man to that of the Great Harlot Woman of Babylon. (Revelation 18) Her witness to the world is self-glorification; proclaiming from her heart, "I sit a queen, and am no widow, and shall see no sorrow" (Verse 7). The **GREAT** take-away here is "**SHE HAS A HUSBAND!**" and *they twain shall be one* [spirit]. I would argue, though separately described; they are one. I would also assert of this singular entity, their spiritual union with the religious and political engines of church and state, officially through physical imagery, is the event of the consummation that begins the "*poured upon*" age that Daniel warns us about and Yochanan and Shaul gives us insight to. What is this "*poured upon*" age? How long will it last? **I am glad you asked!**

Section Update Now Available!

CHAPTER 18

AGE OF THE POURED UPON

Undoubtedly, you have noticed many times throughout this book, when making my scriptural claims; I have referenced the passage without quoting it directly. I have left it up to you, the reader; to go straight into the Bible itself for verification of my claims. Of course, I do understand my biblical "verification" may depend on your own interpretation of that particular passage. This is intended to promote a wide variety of things; from an emotional response, to self-study and proving. But most of all I suppose, I have employed this tactic for you to determine in your own heart how sincerely you want to know this "*truth¿*" I am professing to be called by YHWH to distribute. Here is yet another tactic I must employ; due to the somewhat "***limited scope***" (time) of this book. I am going to call it - *for loss of a better term* - the "*Write-to-me for the rest.*" It applies mainly to what I said in the last section and what I am about to cover in this section. If you have a question concerning an obvious and intentional omission. I hope to let the Holy Spirit reveal to you what exactly that, "*omission*" is and whether you should write to me for *the rest of the story*. If and when you write, I would hope that you take time to send a contribution of any amount to help offset the cost of operation to print and mail this additional information. But, if you will not, we will still make every effort to get that information to you nonetheless. We will for as long as it can be sustained. My present mailing address: PO Box 231, Richfield, North Carolina 28137. I apologize for the mysterious nature of this statement, but I find it necessary to write due to the realities and not to be insulting. Some of this book's readers may not be spiritually mature enough to receive the other end of this revelation and I do not want it to be a hindrance to anyone reading this book completely. This read is hard enough as it is. So by reason, I am making the omission of these sections a little more complicated to receive. So I guess the question is this. If the Holy Spirit reveals and inspires, "How bad in this instance and under the circumstances I have lain out, do you want to discern the rest of this truth story entitled, **"The Omissions of the "*poured upon*" age?""** With that question, I guess that is all that needs to be said about that, for now at least. There is also the update in the prior section. Do not forget it.

In an effort to lay the base for moving forward. I would like for us to reflect for a few minutes on the widely accepted, but a much debated and divisive belief. This is a reconsideration of that assumed belief. Naturally this reconsideration argues against this major element and foundational doctrine for nearly all Christendom. It is the near blasphemous proposal we, humans **are not** already <u>immortal</u>! Now I know many reading might disagree with me on this subject. That is okay. Everybody is at liberty to do that. First know; strangely enough, my "*at odds*" is not about being right or wrong. It is about our perspectives. Nonetheless and despite what many of our so-called religious pundits would have us all believe, let us state and challenge this old claim regardless. To begin with, I assert; if Elohim (*through our Messiah Yeshua*) does not allow for us to put on, "***Immortality***;" we will <u>remain</u> subject to **the power of death**. Because, "...<u>this mortal</u> (*that means us – you and I*), *must* **put on** immortality" (1st Corinthians 15:53). Bible text directly declares at present, we have yet to put on already, this almost universally presumed existence. I know none who would contend that our flesh and blood **can** inherit the kingdom of Eloah. We know truth is the opposite. (1st Corinthians 15:50) Because the creation is from everlasting to everlasting and "<u>WE</u>" are not. This truth is absolutely a condition of our now existence. Even Lucifer and his angels understand this truth. If YHWH does not have mercy on them and at this point I doubt very seriously if he will, at least on behalf of life. <u>Satan and his angels are going to die</u>! True, from our fragile lives' standpoint, they have yet unimaginable years remaining on their covenants as the hireling of YHWH. In any case however, that covenant will run out and with it, their lives. How can I proclaim seemingly such an outlandish statement? Since we know what the great majority of our popular Christian pundits and even most spiritual gurus in other religions contend with respects to their indoctrination platforms. Most of them have taught to the latter-day generations in some form, a propaganda encouraging them to believe in the immortality of their souls. I believe if we could think about this <u>with</u> our spiritually sober minds and without outside influences (*propaganda*); it is <u>not</u> an impossible concept to understand. "...**the soul that sinneth, it shall die**" (Ezekiel 18:4). I have to believe many out here, truly think our modern-day religious leaders (*pastors, preacher and whatnots*), <u>are</u> more insightful than a <u>Real Prophet</u>. Because of their confidence in these guys, they have come to believe, the second death is indeed, not a second death at all; but instead, it is in reality, **Eternal Life**, in <u>eternal fire</u>… ***Really?***

Come on y'all. *Minus on some occasions, the blinding influences of denominational indoctrination;* what do "**YOU**" **honestly** think it means when the Bible says that people will have their names, "*blotted out of the book of life?*" (Revelation 3:5) Hear this and understand. As the day is to the night and summer is to winter – **_so too_** – life is to death. Life is the

very antithesis of death. **When people are alive** we "_move, and have our_

being" (Acts 17:28). **When people are dead**, we do nothing and have no

awareness. Because in death, our capacity for movement and thought has

perished. (Ecclesiastes 9:5-6) As long as we are in the grave, we remain

in the **"deepest sleep"** humanly possible. (Daniel 12:1-2, Acts 7:60 & 1st

Corinthians 15:6) Because of the hard-core, dogmatic doctrines of many

groups, I felt compelled to use both Old and New Testament passages in

my references. And, as far as any bizarre notion that Satan the Devil has

some inferior form of immortality, recognize this as a biblical fact I feel

we have already established. And, let every theological implication sink

profoundly into your brain housing groups. We know only the True God,

our Eloah Elohim through Messiah Yeshua has eternal life. (1st Timothy

6:16) And less we forget - _as far as the state of the dead_ - there are many

passages that speak to their reality. I have shared only a few with you. If

I tried to give them all, the time in this book would be greatly extended.

That is not feasible in a book that is focused mainly on an accounting of

ordained time. Still I will cite one more human and angelic passage point

in order to put this subject to rest - at least in my mind. Messiah Yeshua

in St. John 11:11-14 **"clearly describes"** to us in no uncertain terms, the

human state of death. What was that we said before, "**_Let God be true_**"?

"…[*Yeshua*] saith unto them, <u>Our friend Lazarus **"sleepeth;"**</u> but <u>I go, that I may **awake him out of sleep**</u>. Then said his disciples, Lord, if he sleeps, he shall do well. <u>Howbeit [Yeshua] **spake of his death**</u>: but they thought that he had spoken of taking of rest in sleep. Then said [**Yeshua**] to them plainly, **Lazarus is dead**."

Now really; is there anybody out there; who honestly believe that our modern-day Bible and religious pundits, understand more about life and death than "*Jesus?*" <u>If</u> <u>there</u> <u>be</u> <u>one</u>, not trying to be ugly, but I must label him or her **insane**. As far as humans and immortality is concerned, it is simple. Our Messiah Yeshua, he is "*the blessed and only Potentate, the King of kings, and Lord of lords; **who only hath immortality**, dwelling in the light which no man can approach unto; whom no man hath seen, nor can see: to whom honor and power everlasting*" (1st Timothy 6:15-16). I for one think Yeshua's witness puts "soul-sleep" opponents to rest. Now, as for Satan the Devil and any wicked angels who did not, would not and will not repent - *as I have stated before* - their future prognostications are not very bright. So, consider Satan's spiritual, but **non-immortal** state of "**life**" he finds himself to be in from the Bible witness - *believe it or not.*

"Ye are of your father **the devil**, and the lusts of your father ye will do: **he was a murderer from the beginning**, and abode not in the truth, because there is no truth in him [*neither is there abiding in the devil - eternal life*]. When he speaketh a lie, he speaketh of his own: for he is a liar, and the father of it."

(John 8:44)

"Marvel not, my brethren, if the world hates you. We know that we have passed from death unto life, because we love the brethren. He that loveth not his brother abideth in death. Whosoever hateth his brother is a murderer: and **ye know that no murderer** [*which the devil was from the beginning*] **hath eternal life abiding in him**" (1st John 3:15).

Despite what many religions teach as their truth. I might hope these passages of scripture speak as clear to you, as they do to me. I will admit the topic continues to be hotly debated. Still, I do not think it is biblically unreasonable to combine the two passages above and say this regarding Satan the Devil. And you can quote me on this one; to those it applies to. "*Your father the devil, he was a murderer from the beginning and you know that **no murderer** hath **eternal life** abiding in him.*" No worries though. In this book, we do not have to agree on the state of the dead, in order to proceed. Our *focus* is the time and that balance of time available. I only brought up the issue of our limited time and mortality to stress my claims about time running out. It is vital to receive that concept as a key to discerning in a clearest way the "*poured upon*" age that is scheduled to commence at the **mark event** of the consummation. Read the truth of our limits in the following passages. Most important, note also in their *words* how a man's *days*, *years*, *life*, *age and events of his life* are seen and used numerically interchangeable throughout the entirety of the Holy Bible.

"Seeing his days are determined, **the number**s of his months (*life or years*) are with thee, thou hast appointed his bounds that he (*mortal life*) cannot pass;" (Job 14:5).

"The wicked man travaileth with pain all his <u>days</u>, and **the number** of <u>years</u> [*days*] is hidden to the oppressor" (Job 15:20).

"And ye shall serve the Lord your God, and he shall bless thy bread, and thy water; and I will take sickness away from the midst of thee...**the number** of thy <u>days</u> [*years*] <u>I will fulfill</u>."
(Exodus 23:25-26).

"Lord, <u>make me to know</u> mine end <u>and</u> the <u>measure</u> [*count or calculate*] of <u>my days</u> [*years*], what it is; that I may know how frail I am. Behold, thou hast made <u>my days</u> as a handbreadth; <u>and mine age</u> is as nothing before thee;" (Psalms 39:4-5).

"And the Lord said, My Spirit shall not always strive with man, for that he also *is* flesh: yet <u>his days</u> [***number***] <u>shall be</u> a hundred <u>and twenty years</u>" (Genesis 6:3).

"He weakened my strength...he shortened my <u>days</u> [***years/life***]. I said, O my God, take me not away in the midst of my <u>days</u> [***years/life***]..." (Psalms 102:23-24).

In the meaning of many passages "*<u>the number of a man</u>*" (Revelation 13:18) is the totality of one's age, or a year or date in future time from a "<u>marked</u>" event. The word "*<u>number</u>*" is used a lot. It is synonymous with years in age at the time of death. <u>With this knowledge and the context</u>, **the number** of something or someone will also signify or "mark" an end to some specific period or of an age after a special event or some specific moment in time. Such is the case as with an anniversary. **The number** in itself **marks** the time, length of life or time after, since some event. Read Jacob's witness before Pharaoh in <u>Genesis 47:9</u>.

*"The **days** of the **years** of my pilgrimage are **a hundred and thirty** years: few and evil have the **days** of the **years** of my life been, and I have not attained unto the **days** of the **years** of the lives of my fathers in the **days** (years) of their pilgrimage."*

Now compare Jacob's words with Yochanan's in the great prophetic enigma in Revelation 13:18.

*"Here is wisdom. Let him that hath understanding count [meaning to count and to calculate] **the number** of the beast: for it is **the number** of a man (The number identifies the son of perdition's visage and time – his days, his age in years or it is after some specific anniversary date from a specific mark in time) and his number is Six hundred threescore and six [Days are fulfilled in years – believe it or not]."*

The question could be asked. What is the number 666 representing? Is it some unknowable thing? Hardly. Revelation says wisdom knows how to "count and calculate" the number. Since we see it is the number of a man - *if we can believe* - we know it does at the least, one thing. It identifies his person, or his age, or a specific anniversary of his, or the coming of his death. Maybe the number identifies a combination of them or all. The matching relationship between any man's time/years/number, or special anniversary and this infamous enigmatic man's same should be reasonably obvious to most. The Bible will swap out time/years/number, and use them interchangeably in identifying the length of men's lives or some significant anniversary event; i.e. Shaul's third heaven experience. (2nd Corinthians 12:1-3) In this example, *"such a man's"* number was an anniversary in this case. It was "*above fourteen (14) years*." I just listed a few passages in hopes of establishing my point of assertion. I pray they also establish in your heart this truth and this insight YHWH has put into mine by his Spirit. "*Behold, God is great, and we know him not, neither can the number of his years be searched out*" (Job 36:26). Inconceivably, the reality is YHWH does not have a number as we humans certainly do. Our Eloah is immortal and he "...*inhabiteth eternity*" (Isaiah 57:15).

I would like to think now; it is a bit clearer where I am going with this path I am trying to blaze. Unsure? Read what most Christians think is **THE most infamous ENIGMATIC** passage of **ALL** passages in the Bible. Which in truth, **it was** once shielded by YHWH's divine darkness of prophetic mystery. Here however, I am claiming Eloah has revealed to me at least **"one layer"** of this, his multidimensional prophecy regarding **"THE IMAGE of the BEAST"** in Revelation 13:1-7. Let us read it again.

> "Here is wisdom. Let him that hath understanding count [and *calculate*] **the number** of the beast: for it is **the number** [*years*] of a man; and **his number** [*years, age and/or anniversary date*] is Six hundred threescore *and* six" (Verse 18).

Revelation 13:18, as with most all prophecy has no less than dual (2) meanings and fulfillments. Among other things, the count and calculate secret behind the number of 666 is a mark that stands ready to reveal the actual name of this enigma. It can therewith tell us who the image of the beast is (*Or as he has come to be known in modern times;* ***The Endtime Antichrist***). That revelation is by far the most common understanding for interpretation of the 666 number itself. In the addition of revealing by identification - <u>The Endtime Antichrist</u>; understand also that this number (*I contend*) will allow us to discern the number of years which will ensue after that dark magic event – ***yes indeed, it will be witchcraft*** – of the consummation. <u>Why is this "***event date***" and its "***poured upon***" period so important - from the standpoint of this book?</u> That is an insightfully good question. Going forward, there are *two things* you will want to consider. Read and understand me. Then hopefully, by the grace of Eloah's Holy Spirit "*every reader*" will be in agreement with me on those "*two things*" from the perspective of this book.

1. "Seeing <u>his days are determined</u> [*the consummation of the image of the beast - Daniel 9:27*], the numbers of his months [*days - years*] are with thee, <u>thou hast appointed his bounds that he cannot pass</u>;" (Job 14:5).

Forgive me. I took the liberty of somewhat taking <u>Job 14:5</u> out of context. If just to exasperate a point; which I felt was already established. **We all** have limited days/years/numbers. And none of us can go past any boundaries set by YHWH's divine authority; especially not Satan and his **Wicked** son of perdition. Here is a key to my insight and foundation to focus on in this book. I would like for us to take the time to compare the relationship with a few passages of scripture. I took the liberty to record them in this book, because of their vital importance to my assertions on the time gone by and the time we have left. Consider the following.

a) "~~And he shall confirm the covenant with many for one week: and in the midst of the week he shall cause the sacrifice and the oblation to cease,~~ and for the overspreading of abominations he shall make it desolate [3 ½ years later *the people of the Prince* utterly destroys the temple], even until the consummation, and that determined shall be poured upon the desolate" (Daniel 9:27).

b) "And from the time *that* the daily *sacrifice* shall be taken away [*the temple destroyed*] and the abomination that maketh desolate [*the son of perdition*] set up, *there shall be* a thousand two hundred and ninety days (**years**)" (Daniel 12:11).

c) "Now we beseech you, brethren, by the coming of our Lord Jesus Christ, and by our gathering together unto him, that ye be not soon shaken in mind, or be troubled, neither by spirit, nor by word, nor by letter as from us, as that the day of Christ is at hand. Let no man deceive you by any means: for that day shall not come, except there come a falling away first, and that man of sin be revealed, the son of perdition; who opposeth and exalteth himself above all that is called God, or that is worshipped; so that he as God sitteth in the temple of God [The Church is the temple - there will be no third brick and mortar temple - not even after Yeshua comes; consider Revelation 21:22] showing himself that he is God" (2nd Thessalonians 2:1-4).

d) "Here is wisdom. Let him that hath understanding count the number of the beast [*his age after the consummation event*]: for it is the number of a man [*the time/years, the age or* **anniversary** *of son of perdition – the image of the beast*]; and his number *is* Six hundred threescore *and* six [*in his 666th year anniversary*]" (Revelation 13:18).

e) "**And then** shall that **Wicked** [*son of perdition*] be revealed, whom the Lord shall consume with the spirit of his mouth, and shall destroy [**WHEN NOW!?**] with the brightness of his coming: even him [**Messiah Yeshua**], whose coming is **after** the working of Satan [*through his son of perdition - who exercises*] all power (*miraculous miracles*) and signs and lying wonders [*In man's sight*] and with all deceivableness of unrighteousness in them that perish" (2ⁿᵈ Thessalonians 2:8-10).

Because they [*carnal and religious men alike*] received not the love of the truth, that they might be saved, for this reason [YHWH] sent them this strong delusion, that they should believe arguably the greatest lie (2ⁿᵈ Thessalonians 2:10-12) perpetrated on humankind. This is so they all might be condemned; who rejected truth for convenience! These are they who teach "...*for doctrine, the commandments of men*" (Matthew 15:9). Just as important, understand these passages reference entities within the realm of Christianity. "*Then if any man shall say unto you, Lo, here is Christ, or there; believe it not. For there shall arise false Christs and false prophets* [**Not false Buddhas** and **false Mohammeds** or any other dissimilar religions. The falling away will be and is with those professing Christianity] *and* [many of the false Christ and false prophets] *shall show great signs and wonders; insomuch that if it were possible they shall deceive the very elect*" (Matthew 24:23-24). Understand what it is I am saying, in all soberness. YHWH has given that **Wicked** abomination who makes desolate, 666 years to pour upon those already desolate conditions of the Jews, the land of Israel, the city of Jerusalem and the temple. The whole world, including much if not all of Christianity, will be affected by this imagery. But he (*the son of perdition*), cannot go beyond those years ordained of him by YHWH. So while I admit to the truth. The passage of scripture from (Job 14:5) is not a direct link (*as is prophecy*) to the beast image of Revelation 13:18, nor the consummation event of Daniel 9:27. Nevertheless, it is an accurate depiction to the limitations and ordinations of the times concerning our human and (*I contend*) certain of the angelic entities conditions of existence. It is also a condition of existence for that, **Wicked**, "**son of perdition**;" who **billions** of professing Christians over the centuries to this day, look for to appear on the scene in the very near future, to **Mark** the end of the age. Most Christians expect a true-to-life man they called "Antichrist;" a human Satan with supernatural powers to boot. Many felt in Shaul's day this would occur; but, Shaul made it clear.

2.   "And now ye know what withholdeth [*YHWH's divine mystery shrouds the identity of the* **wicked son of perdition**] that **he** might be revealed in his time. For the mystery of iniquity doth already work: only he [*YHWH*] who now letteth *will let,* until he [*the son of perdition*] be taken out of the way. And then shall that wicked be revealed, whom the Lord shall consume with the spirit of his mouth, and shall destroy with the brightness of his coming:"

(2nd Thessalonians 2:6-8)

Regarding the Mark event of the consummation, I have stated prior; even though I have biblically; I have not as yet; been able to historically identify that very act (the consummation itself) which begins the "*poured upon*" period. I only know that it occurs in Adamic year 5360 (*AD 1360*); an event exactly 1290 years after the destruction of the Second Temple. Progressively worse in the "*poured upon*" period, **The Truth** will be evil spoken of. By various methods during this time, the *son of perdition* will deceive much of the world through elements within Christendom. Shaul says Yeshua will destroy Satan's *son of perdition* when he comes and not before. His destruction must come to fulfillment at the 666th anniversary of that Mark event which commences the consummation "*poured upon*" period. Hear me well and take heed.

There will be no 667th anniversary of perdition's consummation event.

"THAT'S RIGHT! I SAID IT!"

I understand this is shocking and unbelievable to everybody; but the end has to come at some point. **Do you not agree?** I can appreciate most, like myself, felt it was only an outside chance "*the end of the age*" would occur in our lifetimes. But, I did all of the numbers. **I** did not doubt them then. **I** do not doubt them today. The numbers researched are reasonably accurate. Nonetheless, in ways I did not understand; those same numbers were now invalidating the very credibility of my original argument for an "ordained" millennial work week for Adam. Do the math. I know it has been a minute or two since I last mentioned it. But remember. We only had room for <u>390 years</u> in our time vault. We just busted the bank by stuffing in <u>666 years</u>. In the back of my mind, I was always a little afraid something like this would happen. Now it did. I do not recall what I was thinking when YHWH brought me to this point. Of course now, unlike you at this point; me with my **20/20 spiritual hindsight**, I am completely confident. So then, please. "<u>Let us continue in **my confidence**</u>." I had all of the numbers. I checked them over a bunch of times. ***They were right!***

> "Man *that is* born of a woman *is* of few days...He cometh forth like the flowers, and is cut down: he fleeth also as a shadow, and continueth not...<u>**Seeing** *that* **his days** *are* **determined**</u>...<u>thou hast appointed his bounds</u>...<u>**he cannot pass**</u>;" (Job 14:5).

I'd discerned Adam's number prior to Messiah Yeshua's return was 5750 years. Yet, I had exceeded that number by a lot! <u>Did I mention already</u> - I rechecked the numbers a bunch of times? Based on my goals for writing this book, I felt all of the numbers were reasonably correct. Oh! I said that too – did I not? Come on guys. You know when we get intellectually lost, we tend to ramble a bit and repeat. <u>I was at a loss</u>! <u>I admit it</u>. While a few of the counts (*40 years worth*), will be dubious for the unbelieving; the big, major, really crazy controversy is the <u>*666*</u> count YHWH *<u>revealed</u>* to me. I concede that much. Yet, I feel if we can rally our faith; the truth in this book can be seen. If we can/will study it with open objective eyes.

Here are my conclusive thoughts; I offer as proofs of truth. The first item I am secure with thinking that everybody is in agreement on to be accurate is what I call YHWH's anchor. <u>The Second Temple was totally destroyed and leveled with not one stone being left upon another that was not thrown down</u>. (Matthew 24:2) The anchor being; that infamous event occurred in **AD 70**. And, believe me when I say this. I know how it must sound for many, when I claim that YHWH has revealed something to me that he may or may not have revealed to merely a few in the world. But, I am going to say it to you anyway. Along with the passage of <u>Daniel 9:27</u>, YHWH made known to me through a series of revelations that reference other passages - not limited to - but include the likes of <u>Daniel 12:11</u>.

> *"From the time that the daily sacrifice shall be taken away* [**AD 70**] *and the abomination that <u>maketh</u> desolate set up there shall be <u>a thousand two hundred and ninety days</u>* [in years] [**Until the Son of perdition consummation: AD 1360**]*"* (Daniel 12:11).

> *"Let him that hath understanding count* [and calculate] *the number of the beast...<u>his number</u>* [**anniversary**] *is <u>Six hundred threescore and six</u>* (666) - [<u>days in years</u>]*"* (Revelation 13:18).

<u>Six hundred threescore and six</u> (666) as it is claimed in this book, is a <u>count</u> and <u>calculate</u> number. Among end time revelations, it is fulfilled in the passing of years <u>after the Second Temple is destroyed</u>; in cooperation with the one other specific time period already mentioned. The 666 years commenced after 1290 years of sustained desolation and is to be poured, was poured, is still being poured out directly over top of it; with no relief

356

from desolation. I will mention two biblical promises that come together to dictate this path. 1) The *son of perdition's* consummation *poured upon* age cannot go beyond his 666th anniversary. 2) It is Yeshua's promise the days would be cut short. I stress they are cut short by the 250 years of the "*little season;*" which is to be later added back after the Millennial Reign of Yeshua. YHWH has made known to me these following things; which in my view, readers should take notice of and take to heart with their own sober, spiritually objective study and research.

1) The sixth day of the seven-day millennial week will be cut short by 250 years - which is the time period represented by the, "*little season*" spoken of in <u>Revelation 20:1-3</u>. It is added back after the Millennial Sabbath; or the thousand years Messiah will rule on the earth as it exist today, and just prior to the Last Great Day of Judgment. (Revelation 20:3&7-15).

2) The Second Temple remains desolate 1290 years until the consummation event. (Daniel 9:27 & 12:11)

3) The consummation "*poured upon*" period will be added to and on top of the time of the Second Temple's desolation and is an overlay with the physical times the spiritual. (Daniel 9:27)

4) The consummation "*poured upon*" period is 666 years in duration. (Revelation 13:18)

5) The consummation cannot exceed 666 years before Messiah returns. (Revelation 13:18)

6) Messiah must destroy that **Wicked** before he reaches 667 years of age, or <u>the number of a man - that man</u> (*that* **Wicked** *son of perdition*) would not be 666 years; but instead, it would be 667 years. That would make Messiah Yeshua a liar. **THAT IS NOT POSSIBLE**! Yeshua being Adon.

It's Much Later Than You Think!

What does all I have just listed really mean? The steps I made; which had caused me to arrived at the year I did in my walk through YHWH's ordained time - *now our walk through that aforementioned period* - again gave me pause to re-evaluate. You see - *when I added everything all up, the way my research and study had dictated* - I was not where I thought I would be - to say the least. However, I still remained firm in my faith, to whatever end I came to; it was YHWH's Spirit was guiding me. So then, I would be satisfied. Though from the place in time where I was standing then; my understanding of the overall picture of time was on really shaky ground. All the basic years, once counted up; still exceeded not only my 5750 years; but, also the 6001 years permissible by the Jewish tradition, most Messianic beliefs and also practically every *Christian* organization which believes in the so-called, *"Millennial Reign of Jesus Christ."* I was again at an impasse and right now, I got you in the same mess. You will see that on my following chart. Of course now in all fairness, the modern Jewish calendar year is at 5780. While it does exceed parameters in this book (*which includes a deduction for the little season*), those years have not exceeded their own allowances; which totals 6001 years before their Messiah is expected to come. If the Jews are close to accurate, we have a considerable sum of years left before the Jew's Messiah can be expected. That requires another 221 years to be exact. That means every one of us are absolutely going to die off from this life. Contrary to many Christian organizations, but according to Judah, the Messiah cannot come at any moment, unless he risks being well over 200 years earlier than he has purportedly revealed by prophets to their ancient fathers. It is contrary to Jews, but according to Christians. We are already twenty years past the 6001-year mark. They have in reality, the same count as many Messianic believers; who also claim we are nineteen years on the other side of the sixth day into the Millennial Sabbath of Yeshua. For Messianics, Yeshua and Christians "*Jesus*" seems to be running a tad late. I'm thinking sober. Notwithstanding, from where I am standing at this particular point in my study and research; I am not the one who should be judging at this time. My study in, **"IT'S MUCH LATER THAN YOU THINK!"** was faring no better than any other study. The chart below reads AD 2018. It is from my unfinished study in *Discovery and Perspective;* from years back. If one must be current, just add two years to reach AD 2020. It does not in reality matter. The Messiah is still "overdue" (**LATE!**). See for yourself.

							6001-7001		
Millennian Week							Millennial Sabbath to begin 6001	Messiah's Expected Return	Messiah's Great Judgment
Tradition	1st Day	2nd Day	3rd Day	4th Day	5th Day	6th Day	Actual year	7th Day	Currently	8th Day
Jewish	Some Messianic believers adhere to this date					(+)779 yrs	5779	(-) 222	Not yet	Yet future
Messianic	Some Messianic believers adhere to this date.					Beyond	6018	(+)18 yrs	Overdue	Yet future
Christian	Some Messianic believers adhere to this date.					Beyond	2018	(+)18 yrs	Overdue	Yet future
Discovery Perspective	Even with the, "little season" cut off - Discovery and Perspective - still stands at this date.					Beyond	6018	(+)18 yrs	Overdue	Yet future

Note: "Discovery and Perspective" should read "IT'S MUCH LATER THAN YOU THINK!"

1. The modern Jewish calendar is at 5780. That is 780 years into the 6th day with 221 years left.

2. Many Messianic Jews and believers sit at year 6019. That put Messiah 18 years in the rears.

3. The Gregorian calendar and therefore most all Christians sit at AD 2020. Basically, AD 2020 is equivalent to 6020. The Christian Christ *"Jesus"* is still, all the same, 19 years in the rears of his, *"promise¿"*

4. Taking from my unpublished study and research work of: <u>Discovery and Perspective</u>, **"IT'S MUCH LATER THAN YOU THINK!"** is also, almost at the of year 6020. At this point, my book is in the same predicament as most all Messianic Jews and professing Christians. Whether directly or indirectly, we are essentially all at this juncture, calling "Messiah Yeshua" and *"Jesus Christ"* liars. You see, from our present date line perspectives, they are both 19 years in the rears of their "<u>UNBREAKABLE</u>" promises. At this stage, only the Jewish Messiah is standing with potential for divine credibility. His remains to be seen. That is, if he can indeed keep his "<u>PROMISE</u>" to come.

The typical Jew still has 221 years to go until their Messiah becomes a liar. This is only true because the Jewish religion is not confronted and confounded with that head-scratching Bible pledge made by our Messiah Yeshua or *"Jesus Christ"* of shortening days. (Matthew 24:22) And, you can quote me on this, "For many Holy Bible theologians, understanding and explaining the *"shortened"* days <u>concept is "biblical," a theological mess!</u>" Actually it's a nightmare! I have even heard one prominent group preach (*teach*) that *"Jesus Christ"* was going to shorten *"those days"* by a "<u>**poultry one**</u> - <u>literally 365 days</u> - <u>**year**</u>!" Really!? I won't bother to ask the obvious questions of, "What for?" or "Why?" Don't do me no favors.

But seriously, what makes *"one year"* worth *"Jesus"* even mentioning it; as for as *"shortening"* the time span from the end of 6000 years or in the great scheme of things? I am sure they know some things I do not. In my eyes, it is still a mess for them to explain in the traditional. However, that can only be a mess in our eyes, if we are spiritually sober minded and being honest with ourselves. Many of us, most likely, are all too familiar with problems of honesty and coming clean in the face of biblical errors and theological embarrassments. That is just not kosher; right? YHWH knew, not only did I not; but likely all of the historians, theologians and chronologist put together, did not have the true adequate understandings needed of those ancient cultural times; nor do we now have the righteous foundation from our fathers, from those ancient times; to be able to fully grasp and recognize what divine talents were possessed and used in order to have spiritual discernment to know the many ancient mysteries veiled behind prophecy. Many are only today being revealed. I suppose in this case, I was ready to hear it straight. So, YHWH told me straight. He later proved it, when he instructed me to step down memory lane. Before then, it seemed that "**<u>EVERYBODY</u>**" was off in their count concerning the time of man. It had to be for one reason or another. It is like I said before. While the nation state of Israel (*The Jews*) was still under the 6000 years threshold – by 221 years; everybody else, for yet unknown reasons, had gone beyond their thresholds for a truthful and promise-keeping YHWH. The dilemma everyone except for all the believers in traditional Judaism find ourselves in, is the prideful inability to admit of truth, we have erred. Most all of professing Christianity say it is year AD 2020. Most Yeshua Messianics believe this year it will be 6020. <u>Even my own study at the time agreed with both groups</u>. So a new question emerged. One we have to seriously ask. Did "*Jesus*" and Yeshua lie? Wow, do I sound like a self-defeatist in saying that? Hey! **I knew everybody else was wrong!! And, I also knew why!!** None of the pundits I had read, took into serious consideration, the Holy Bible witness where Yeshua **promised**, "*For the elect's sake those days* **shall** *be shortened*" (Matthew 24:22). From my perspective, that is the fatal error for ever being able to even potentially understand the truth shrouding the time of "Jesus" or Messiah Yeshua's imminent return (*Christians and Messianic believers*); or the arrival of Messiah (*Judaism*). But, from my **HOLIER-THAN-THOU** outpost; and I was sure Holy Spirit was guiding me; *at least pretty sure*. So, if that was the case; **_why was I off and in error just like everybody else_**? It was only natural; I painfully began wondering if my ears were just too dull to hear and my eyes were just too dim to see. *I think both were true*. That is why I believe YHWH just came out and told me the last part of his accounting mystery. He wanted to see. Did I have enough faith to believe what was being told to my spirit by His Holy Spirit? **It is tougher than it sounds!** I cannot speak for anybody else. But in the back of my mind, most times, when I am studying new material that could lead me to new revelations, or insight; I wonder if it is YHWH that I hear or is it some familiar spirit. Remember, Messiah Yeshua warns us about deceiving spirits that will be rampant in the last days before his return. (Matthew 24:3-25) Like I have said; I do not want, **IT'S MUCH LATER THAN YOU THINK!** to be a stumbling block of lies and misinformation to anyone. Because, I do not want to stand before Yeshua or any of his set-apart ones in the judgment (*In the event I miss out on the first resurrection*), having to explain why I was in the religious trading and spreading of lies ministry. No Siree! I am totally sure. That is not the altar for me. And as controversial as this book might be; I do not want to ever steer anybody away from YHWH's truth. But, once I had gone over my ordained threshold; I was in spiritual drift mode. Still, I drifted forward by faith. I trusted where YHWH would lead me, in the end. This was true for me even though where I seemed to be at the time, and where I was unknowingly headed to (*which seemed to be nowhere*), and also whom it was that was in fact leading me, started to become somewhat unnerving and gave me a pause. I suppose that is the general processing of thoughts for our modern-thinking gentile mindsets. Besides all of this, YHWH expects us not to always be sure we are being led by HIS Holy Spirit. That is absolutely one of the central reasons He inspired Apostle Yochanan to record this passage. "*Beloved, believe not every spirit, but try the spirits whether they are of God: because many false prophets are gone out into the world*" (1st John 4:1). I have no intention whatsoever of being <u>one of them</u>. That is, be a false prophet. I encourage everybody who reads this book to try my spirit. Especially try my words in an honest search for **the spirit of righteous intent**. But, the most important try, is you must try my words by <u>The Word</u> (*Holy Bible*). Study my claims with righteous motivations. Let revealed wisdom from YHWH; which I say is the foundation of my revelations of truth; inspire you to new spiritual - *as in Holy Spirit* - heights. You have read all of my words about the "*poured upon*" period. If you have proved them possible or true; you are blessed and ready to see the last insight to our walk in time. But first I have a unique read for you sticking with me in this belief and denominationally challenging time walk. If you feel you have a firm enough understanding of the numbers, you may opt to skip the next two parts in the *Itemization of Time* and *BC/AD Corresponding Chart*. Then, you can read them later in condensed review. But, if you feel the press to take in all of the numbers attained so far better and deeper; I see no better time to read the *Itemization of Time* and *BC/AD Corresponding Chart*. I encourage everybody to go over them and take time to enjoy their read.

CHAPTER 19

THE ITEMIZATION OF TIME

In my spirit of desperation for truth, I asked YHWH, "Why can I not see this? I am looking right at it. And, I know I am looking right at it. But I just cannot see it. I know it is there. But I just cannot see it. I need for you to help me. Heal my eyes so that I might see! I will not see anything unless you have mercy on me and then show me." I said these words and much more. I said them in a bunch of different ways. But the bottom line was, if YHWH did not show me; I would not see and I would be 100%, without any doubt, deceived. Not very long after - in a matter of days I suppose - I heard from heaven. The Holy Spirit continued on with his directing of me. It asked me was I sure about all of the numbers? I said based on the instructions from the Holy Spirit I felt my heart was able to hear; my count should not be off one year - *maybe*. Look, I am just being real here people. Then YHWH instructed me to check and to recheck the numbers. Maybe you missed something. I did so. Then he had me to check and to recheck them again, and again, and again, so on and so on. I did so. It is like I said before. I was sure that everybody else's advanced counts were off. I simply did not know what the problem with my count was. When I tried counting the way the world would have had me to count - *and I admit I did take a stab at it, just in case* - my accounting discrepancy merely got worse. After that experience, I retreated to where YHWH had guided my research and studies from the very beginning. I suppose YHWH let me do all of my restarts and all of my redresses from my lack of understanding; to allow my mind to confirm that I had left no stones detected, unturned. So that I would be confident; the direction he was going to take me in and what he was about to show me, was the only logical biblical choice. YHWH asked me if I was content that all of the numbers accounting for the time of Adam were accurate. I said, "Yes." Next he asked me was I sure with the chronological order of the numbers that I used? I said yes. Not for YHWH and me, but in order to make sure you and I are on the same page; I am going to show you a rare treat. I am going to show you my itemized chronological listing of all biblical time!

Event/Years	**Dates**
1) Adam created by YHWH Elohim	(1)
2) Adam (130) to Seth	(131)
3) Seth (105) to Enos	(236)
4) Enos (90) to Cainan	(326)
5) Cainan (70) to Mahalaleel	(396)
6) Mahalaleel (65) to Jared	(461)
7) Jared (162) to Enoch	(623)
8) Enoch (65) to Methuselah	(688)
9) Methuselah (187) to Lamech	(875)
10) Lamech (182) to Noah	(1057)
11) Noah (500) to Shem	(1557)

100 years later: "The Great Flood" (1657)

Noah was 600 year old (*Genesis 7:6*)

The flood period lasted one (1) year (Genesis 7:11 & Genesis 8:13-14)

Arphaxad born 2 years after the flood (*Genesis 11:10*)

12) Shem (103) to Arphaxad	(1660)

This next section of the Messianic Bloodline was
"Sealed with Four Babel/Roman Numbers"
until the time of the end - then to be revealed.

13) Arphaxad (25) to Salah	(1685)
14) Salah (30) to Eber	(1715)

15) Eber (26) to Peleg ....(1741)

16) Peleg (30) to Reu ....(1771)

17) Reu (28) to Serug..(1799)

18) Serug (30) to Nahor ....(1829)

19) Nahor (11) to Terah ....(1840)

20) Terah (50) to Abram ....(1890)

21) Abram (100) to Isaac ....(1990)

22) Isaac (60) to Jacob ....(2050)

<u>"Jacob goes to Egypt and is enslaved."</u>

23) Jacob (130) to Egypt..(2180)

The Messianic Bloodline by count is concealed
from the Hebrew Scripture's historical records.
A renewed count must emerge by events of time.

24) Egypt slaves (430) to freedom ....(2610)

25) The wilds (40) to Promise Land..(2650)

"The Judges of Israel" **(In Bold)** and the
<u>Adversary</u> (*In double Underlined Italics*)

26) <u>*Chushan-rishathaim*</u> (8) to **Othniel** ....(2658)

27) Othniel (40) to <u>*Eglon*</u> ....(2698)

28) <u>*Eglon*</u> (18) to **Ehud**..(2716)

29) Ehud (80) to <u>*Jabin*</u> ....(2796)

30) <u>*Jabin*</u> (20) to **Deborah**..(2816)

31) Deborah (40) to <u>*Midianites*</u>..(2856)

32) *Midianites* (7) to **Gideon** ....(2863)

33) Gideon (40) to *Abimelech*...(2903)

34) *Abimelech* (3) to **Tola** ....(2906)

35) Tola (23) to **Jair** ....(2929)

36) Jair (22) to *Philistines* ....(2951)

37) *Philistines* (18) to **Jephthah** ....(2969)

38) Jephthah (6) to **Ibzan** ....(2975)

39) Ibzan (7) to **Elon** ....(2982)

40) Elon (10) to **Abdon** ....(2992)

41) Abdon (8) to *Philistines* ....(3000)

42) *Philistines* (40) to **Sampson** ....(3040)

43) Sampson (20) End of Judges...(3060)

"End of Judges"
Special Notes:

The prominent period of the Judges ended in the fourteenth year of King David's reign. Date wise, it would be in YHWH's Adamic year of 3060 or 941 BC. Of course that date's landmarks, would be in the death of Judge Sampson and arguably with the birth of Israel's future king in Solomon. We can discern this date since we can count back from the date that King Solomon "*began to build the house of the Lord*" – or the First Temple. That occurred 480 years after the Children of Israel left Egypt.

It's Much Later Than You Think!

(1st Kings 6:1) It is as well the fourth year in the reign of King Solomon. We note year 3060 or 941 BC in time, because it is in our accounting of time; what we call, the beginning of the *net years* of kings. With our use of the term *net years*, we want everyone to recognize. We are referencing in our count of all ordained time, the numbers of years as they relate to the more important chronological accounting of the years. So, when we cited Judges ended; we were referencing that chronological account as it relates to our count of time from the Holy Bible in this book. And we are not implying that Israel no longer had judges. Because, indeed Israel did. As a matter of fact, the Jews to this day retain that branch of governance within their civil government. Notwithstanding, with Israel's rejection of YHWH as their Adon and their establishment of the *"sovereign"* human kings, the role of the Judges would rapidly dissipate. Soon thereafter, the Judges' influence as the symbol and as being Israel's backbone of hope, strength and wisdom, the defender and hero of the people would come to its close as long as Israel and Judah would occupy their Promised Land. How we came to our solid date in history is a tad bit sneaky, but truly the mathematics is uncomplicated. We know the Judges ended in YHWH's Adamic year of 3060 (941 BC). We know that the Children of Israel left out from Egypt in the year of 2610. We add 480 to 2610 and we arrive at the year of 3090. That is the year when King Solomon *"began to build the house of the Lord*." If we subtract four (4) years from that date, we have 3086; which was the first year of King Solomon's reign. From there we merely count back forty (40) years and we get year 3046 (955 BC); the first year of King David's reign. If you will take notice, there is an overlap going forward to the end of Judges in year 3060 and stepping backwards from the start of the First Temple - forty-four (44) years: Solomon's four (4) and David's forty (40) years at year 3046. From there we basically count the first fourteen years of David's reign, "Shazam, Hocus Pocus and Voila!" We have come to the end of Judges and the beginning of the net years of king at 3060. But it is not any kind of magic my friends. It is simple mathematics. Like I said, the math is sneaky, but truly unremarkable.

"Transition Complete"

Though there would never be any peace in David's reign as king; due to his, *"wayfaring"* behavior against Uriah (*A weaker low-ranking soldier in David's army*); when David committed adultery with Uriah's wife Bathsheba; and later, even being totally complicit with the cruel and merciless murder of Uriah himself. (2nd Samuel 12:1-**10**) We can state, even with treason constantly lurking, – *with the maturing of David's son Absalom*, – the concluding thirty years of David's reign, would see Israel expand their territories and authority over their enemies still in their land.

David would eventually get a new heart and a right spirit. (Psalms 51:10) Such a tender act of mercy from YHWH would enable David to endear the hearts and minds of the people in his kingdom. That bond would be a valuable tool in the coming years with the fulfillment of the prophecy against him by YHWH (*Because of Uriah and Bathsheba*); when inside corruption and conspiracy would temporarily rip away the kingdom from David's hands. Even so, with the birth of Solomon, David received in essence, the confirmation of YHWH's forgiveness. Solomon was the heir of David, YHWH would come to love and honor as unified Israel's next and last king of the ages. Solomon's acceptance also solidified the events of eventual redemption from the hands of Absalom and his heartbreaking treachery he would mount against David. Absalom was that temporary, would-be-king; whom YHWH summarily rejected - but tolerated for a minute, for David's chastisement. Now, let us refocus back on time.

It is YHWH's Adamic year of 3060 (941 BC). From the transition overlap of Judges and Kings, we have the kings' net years commencing with David's final twenty-six (26) years. Even though the kingdom of Israel was later, "*rent*" (1st Kings 11:29-37 & 14:8) from David's hand in the reign of Rehoboam (*His grandson*); then 307 years later, one tribe Naphtali was taken away as captives by king Tiglath-pileser of Assyria in 3367 (634 BC) and yet again later, in 3383 (618 BC) the rest of Israel was "*escorted*" to Assyria by then king Shalmaneser. From that end we are unable to continue to follow Israel in the accounting of time. But, let us not forget about the tribe of Judah. YHWH, in His mercy for David and His Holy City Jerusalem, left Judah in the land and in the hands of David's heir (*Grandson Rehoboam*). Because we have Judah's record; we are able to account biblical time through history in the kings of Judah up until Nebuchadnezzar. From YHWH's Adamic year 3060, we count.

"Kings of United Israel"

44) David (26) to Solomon..(3086)

45) Solomon (40) to Rehoboam ....(3126)

"The Kingdom is separated?"

The kingdom is separated or is divided. This is often alleged to have described what happened to Israel after the reign of Solomon. However, the general theology behind that statement or notion is false at worse and misleading at best. The actuality is YHWH did not separate the Kingdom of Israel. My contentions are only valid if one can believe the very words of YHWH himself. "**Thus saith the Lord, the God of Israel, Behold, I will rend** [*slash, tear or rip*] **the kingdom** [*of Israel - the whole thing*] out of the hand of Solomon and will give ten tribes to thee (*Jeroboam*): (**but** [*Rehoboam*] **shall have one tribe for my servant David's sake, and for Jerusalem's sake...**)" (1st Kings 11:31-32). Recall now, Levi had no inheritance in the land. They were the priests of YHWH and he is their inheritance, "...*the Lord spake unto Aaron, Thou shalt have no inheritance in their land, neither shalt...have any part among them: I am thy part and thine inheritance among the children of Israel...I have given the children of Levi all the tenth in Israel for an inheritance, for their service which they serve, even the service of the tabernacle of the congregation.*" (Numbers 18:20-21) YHWH never divided the Kingdom of Israel. He merely left one tribe (*Y'hudah*) in Jerusalem for **David and Jerusalem**'s sake. Y'hudah (*Jews*) is not biblical Israel. They never have been and never will be. I do not say so disparagingly. I only say it for the purposes of **spiritual bearing** and *mainly my own*. I have to keep myself reminded that when I am speaking of the Jews, I am not referencing in any way: The Nation of Israel. It is not scriptural nor a divine possibility. Perhaps this discloser of biblical understanding will help others in their future studies on the heritages of the Jew and the real Kingdom of Israel.

"Kings of Judah"

I have said it before. Now I am saying it again. The records of the reigns of the kings of Israel and Judah were extremely meticulously and also extremely exhausting for me. When I read their records through the recorders and the Prophets, it was almost like I was reading them in three (3) dimensional writing and sometimes dual in dialects. Most of the time, when one king's reign ended in one kingdom, another was continuing in the other - listed by years. Far as recorders were concerned, it counted as a reigning year for each king involved. Sometimes a king's reign would overlap by years with his son. Father Kings would hand over partial reins to son King while his father helped him transition over as the sole leader at the death of his father and old king. While my descriptive skills may suffer. The numbers are tight. After all, I did read them in 3-D. If I sense the need, I might use an initial to describe an event: i.e. D - death, A - assassinated, ODK - overlap & dual kings and Ø - means other. So, let us get started again. Remember that we paused in the end of Solomon's reign at 3126 or (875 BC).

King's years	Reign dates	End date
46) Rehoboam (17)	*[3126-3143]*	(3143)
47) Abijam (3)	*[3144-3146]*	(3146)
48) Asa (41)	*[3146-3186]*	(3186)
49) Jehoshaphat (25-ODK)	*[3186-3210]*	(3210)

4 year overlap

50) Joram/Jehoram (8-ODK)	*[3207-3214]*	(3214)

2 year overlap

51) Ahaziah (1)	*[3213-3214]*	(3214)
52) Athaliah (6)	*[3214-3220]*	(3220)

*King **Ahaziah's** mother ruled Judah - **A woman**!*

King's years	Reign dates	End date
53) Jehoash (40-ODK)	*[3220-3259]*	(3259)

3 year overlap

54) Amaziah (29-A)	*[3257-3285]*	(3285)

His son Uzziah was only 4 years old at the time. Nevertheless, because he was the king's son, he was heir to the throne of Judah. He would likely be under tutors and whatever protection availed until such time he would ascend to the throne.

Azariah finally began his reign at the age of 16.

55) Uzziah Azariah (52)	*[3297-3348]*	(3348)
56) Jotham (16)	*[3349-3364]*	(3364)
57) Ahaz (16)	*[3364-3379]*	(3379)

3 year overlap

58) Hezekiah (29)	*[3377-3405]*	(3405)
59) Manasseh (55)	*[3405-3459]*	(3459)
60) Amon (2)	*[3459-3460]*	(3460)
61) Josiah (31)	*[3460-3490]*	(3490)
62) Jehoahaz (3 months!)	*[3490-3490]*	(3490)
63) Jehoiakim (11)	*[3490-3500]*	(3500)
64) Jehoiachin (3 months!)	*[3500-3500]*	(3500)
65) Zedekiah (11)	*[3500-3510]*	(3510)

"The End of Kings"

Timothy B. Merriman

"The Babylonian Captivity"

Mattaniah–Zedekiah was the final "King of Judah," **and not Israel**, to sit on the throne of "Judah," before their captivity. The "Kingdom of Israel" had been carried away into what was then the kingdom of Assyria by king Shalmaneser; after he laid his siege on Samaria 130 years earlier. **A note:** Shalmaneser's siege, lasted around three years. The period of the Babylonian Captivity was seventy years. The Prophet Jeremiah giving us witness "**nineteen (19) years**" earlier; saying to the peoples and to their wickedness, "*this whole land shall be a desolation, and an astonishment; and these nations shall serve the king of Babylon for seventy years*" (Jeremiah 25:1-11). Daniel would later confirm that Jeremiah wrote the prophecy (Daniel 9:2); as Daniel himself would experience its precursory warnings in years 3500-3501 (*501-500 BC*) when Eliakim (Jehoiakim) was taken to Babylon. Daniel was intimately familiar with the ultimate fulfillment of Jeremiah's nineteen-year old prophecy of the desolation on Jerusalem. Daniel in fact would endure the full interval in the prophecy's primary captivity. We have the years, seventy (*70*). With little debate, we can chronologically advance. From year 3510 (*491 BC*), we can continue to walk and to do the work of accounting for the biblical years to discern,

"What Time We Are Really In And How Much Time We Have Left."

66) Babylon Captivity (70)........... [3510-3580]...............................(3580)

"The Seventy-week Prophecy"

Not without issue and debate, the seventy weeks of Daniel covers a time period of 490 years. Each day within Daniel's prophecy, represents one literal year in the counting of time off man's calendar. Of course, the main controversy and complaint from the so-called experts of history and practically all the theologians concerning this book's claim, is the break-up and the major conclusion that were drawn, because of those divisions. All matters of which, are discussed in reasonable details, inside the book, **IT'S MUCH LATER THAN YOU THINK!** Consider those divisions in Daniel's seventy weeks from the perspective of the book, at the end of the Jews' Babylonian captivity in YHWH's Adamic year 3580 (*421 BC*).

"The Seventy Weeks Divisions"

Seven (7) Weeks
(Total 7 weeks)
After forty-nine (49) days/years
"*Restore and to build Jerusalem;*" and the temple.

The event and years	Start and End of the Event	YHWH's Adamic Year
67) Temple rebuilt (49) .... [3580-3629] .... (3629)		

Threescore (60) Weeks
(Total 67 weeks)
After 420 days/years
"*After threescore…weeks shall Messiah be cut off.*"

The event and years	Start and End of the Event	YHWH's Adamic Year
68) The Crucifixion (420)	[3629-4049]	(4049)

Two (2) Weeks

(Total 69 weeks)

After fourteen (14) days/years (*Prince's people*)

"He confirms the covenant with many for one week"

The one week being seven (7) days is seven years.

The event and years	Start and End of the Event	YHWH's Adamic Year
69) 7-year peace treaty (14)	[4049-4063]	(4063)

One-half Week

(Total 69 ½ weeks)

After ½ week (3½) days/years (the security/covenant is breached) *"In the midst of the week he shall cause the sacrifice...to cease"* (Daniel 9:27).

The event and years	Start and End of the Event	YHWH's Adamic Year
70) Jew/Rome War! (3½)	[4063-4066.5]	(4066.5)

One-half Week

(Total 70 weeks)

After ½ week (3½) days/years (Jerusalem in Ruin)

"...and the end thereof...with a flood" (Daniel 9:26)

The event and years	Start and End of the Event	YHWH's Adamic Year
71) Jews defeated (3½)	[4066.5-4070]	(4070)

It's Much Later Than You Think!

For those who may not know it as of yet, YHWH's Adamic year of 4070 is indirectly equivalent to Gregorian's AD 70. To translate into an AD number from one of YHWH's Adamic Hebrew years, just subtract 4000 off any number presented above 4000. If the number is 4000 and below 4000, just subtract 4001. This is due to the fact there is no zero year. This will leave you with a negative number. From there, discard the negative sign before the number and after the number add BC, BCE or my personal favorite BMB (*Before Messiah Birth*).

Let us now refocus and understand where we are at in time. It is year AD 70. Jerusalem and the second temple are in desolation physically and spiritually. Sadly, this is not the end of the desolation, nor its low point. Listen closely to YHWH, as he describes what he was and is doing to the Jews (Judah and **HIS** Holy City – Jerusalem).

> *"Thus saith the Lord...Because ye have not heard my words...I will send...Nebuchadrezzar the king of Babylon, my servant, and will bring* [him] *against this land, and against the inhabitants thereof, and against all these nations round about, and* [he] *will utterly destroy them and make them an astonishment and a hissing and perpetual desolations"* (Jeremiah 25:9).

YHWH's witness states that the Jews and Jerusalem would become, "*an astonishment and a hissing and perpetual desolations*." While all three curses are serious in nature, I want to focus at this time on the term, "perpetual desolations." If we believe YHWH then we should understand that perpetual means the desolation will be continuous or forever or until the end of a specific time or the end of the age. In the fact that the word desolation is not used; but, **desolations** – with an "**s**;" we must conclude, there will be more than one. Daniel is among other places that confirms the premise of Jerusalem's desolation being of the plural in divine nature. Topic of biblical fact, Daniel confirms three herald desolations that will continue as this detailed document contends - until the end of the age and the return of Messiah Yeshua. It would be difficult to speak to the Jews on that one. However, know this is truth for sure. The initial destruction of the Second Temple was merely the first of **three** enduring desolations.

After the Second Temple was to be destroyed, which it was; Gabriel informs Daniel it will remain in that state for another 1290 years (*Second Desolation*) until the coming of the third desolation (The Consummation Event). Upon its arrival, the first two desolations would not end; but to the contrary they persist. And the third desolation (the Consummation's "*poured upon*" period) will be poured out on the first two desolations. Read carefully to what happens after the Second Temple is destroyed.

> "...for the overspreading of abominations (Judah's continuous and escalating sins), he shall make *it* desolate [Jerusalem and the temple in particular], even until [over some undisclosed interlude of time] the consummation [up until this unknown event], and that determined [the event and its time] shall be poured upon the desolate" (Daniel 9:27).

Daniel is not informed here by Gabriel; but, is later made to know how long the interlude period would be. This is disclosed in Daniel 12:11.

> "...And from the time that the daily sacrifices shall be taken away [*The Second Temple destroyed*], and the abomination that maketh desolate set up [*Satan's enigmatic consummation*], there shall be a thousand two hundred and ninety days [**years**]."

So we add on - *from the time of the destruction of the Second Temple* - the time ordained by YHWH, revealed by Gabriel and then recorded by Daniel; which is **1290** days/years -- **PLUS** -- "*added to*" 4070 (*AD 70*).

The event and years	Start and End of the Event	YHWH's Adamic Year
72) The Hissing (1290)	[4070-5360]	(5360)

"The Consummation" (The Final Desolation)

YHWH's next to "*final mystery unveiled*" if we can call it that; was YHWH's revelation concerning the truth of the consummation. They are offered up for your study and explained with biblical logic in the book;

"IT'S MUCH LATER THAN YOU THINK!"

If you do not have your copy, I encourage you to get an edition as soon as you can. If you are reading this section as part of the book, then you already know a lot in relation to the consummation. Conversely, there were some matters about the consummation that I could not write in the book. If you think you would like to know, I encourage you to write to me now for that information. I am ashamed to say that we need your help when you write to help with our cost of getting the word to the world. If you will, send $15 or more with your request for the *article of omission*. If you cannot, we will do what we can for as long as we can. The book will hopefully be available very soon at Amazon, Barnes and Nobles or wherever fine books are sold. If not there already, keep watching. I will make the *article* available as long as possible. The beast is here to silence free speech; especially The Gospel of the Kingdom of God. Well, I think that is enough begging for one booklet; back to the consummation.

The Consummation Event, according to the revelations of Daniel, is to commence **1290 years** after the Second Temple has been destroyed. The Consummation Event is a **666 years** period for increasing appalling atrocities and abominations. It will also see an unprecedented up tick of ***Anti-Semitic*** sentiment around this world. And the term, "***Anti-Semitic***" is putting things a bit on the mild side; if I should say so myself. Right now, with the information available to you in this pamphlet and if you have it, from the book; the most important thing you need to remember about the 666 year period is that nothing super divine can happen at 665 and the year number of 666 *cannot* go on to 667 without the super divine happening." If you know what I mean. If you do not. Here is a little hint.

> *"The mystery of iniquity doth already work: only he who now letteth will let, until he be taken out of the way. And then shall that **Wicked** be revealed, whom the Lord shall consume with the spirit of his mouth, and shall destroy with the brightness of his*

coming" (2nd Thessalonians 2:7-8).

With that said, the last number the Holy Bible offers as part of the biblical history and prophetic future, before the coming and return of the Messiah (*Yeshua*) is 666; **as in 666 years**. It is the infamous number of the beast **man** - believe it or not. Even if you do not believe it, try and humor me a bit more and hear me out. Let us adjoin that number as the final account of years before my book's expected date for "the second coming of Messiah (*Yeshua*)" to the recent sum to see the end of the age¿

> *"Here is wisdom. Let him that hath understanding count the number of the beast: for it is the number of a man; and his number is Six hundred threescore and six"* (Revelation 13:18).

Once YHWH had determined those numbers of years, then that final desolation was ordained to be poured upon *those current Jerusalem and second temple conditions of the first two old perpetual desolations.* The consummation's "*poured up*" time period is 666 years.

The event and years	Start and End of the Event	YHWH's Adamic Year
73) Final Desolation (666)	[5360-6026].............................	(6026)

> ***"Why, seeing times are not hidden from the Almighty,***
> ***do they that know him not see his days?"***(Job 24:1)

For those who do not recognize YHWH's Holy Week Calendar year of 6026; you can convert it into the AD standard by subtracting 4000 from YHWH's Adamic Hebrew year of 6026 and you will get AD 2026.

Timothy B. Merriman

"The Final Dilemma of Impasse"

The great premise of the book, **"IT'S MUCH LATER THAN YOU THINK!"** and this booklet you are now reading, **"The Itemization of Time"** is based on two biblically sound doctrines. The first doctrine is YHWH has a set ordained time for man's self-rule. Our studies have led us to think, determine and conclude this ordained time is seen in shadow picture throughout the entirety of the Holy Bible. A focus point of study would be in an annual Holy Bible feast of YHWH (Leviticus 23:33-34). This time is mainly recognized in our western hemisphere as the Jewish Feast of Tabernacles. As with all holy days, it is cited as a gathering for worship. Tabernacles is the thanksgiving feast for YHWH's grace given phenomenon, our dwelling here on this earth in our temporary flesh. In Tabernacles, Jews honor YHWH for our opportunity at everlasting life. Without a drawn-out study here, F.O.T. is a seven day observance; it also signifies in its shadow, YHWH's millennial week for man's self-rule after he rejected YHWH's authority in the Garden of Eden. The period is 6000 years - plus the Sabbath Millennial Reign of Messiah. The second doctrine is Yeshua said he would shorten the days or we would destroy ourselves. (Matthew 24:22) The impasse is that at year 6019 or AD 2020, we have passed 6001 and 666 ends in 6026/AD 2026 - no shortened day. Why is Yeshua not here? It is because there is a final revelation to time!

CHAPTER 20

BC/AD CORRESPONDING CHART

The list items below correspond to the list items above in their numerical

sequencing in order to see the BC/BCE and AD/CE determinations from

YHWH's Adamic times referenced. Discern YHWH's times in BC/AD

terms now and later learn why his promise of return has not yet occurred.

Name	Age	Lived/Died
1) Adam created	(*)	(4000 BC)
2) **Adam**	**(930)**	*(4000-3070 BC)*
3) Seth	**(912)**	*(3870-2958 BC)*
4) Enos	**(905)**	*(3765-2860 BC)*
5) Cainan	**(910)**	*(3675-2765 BC)*
6) Mahalaleel	**(895)**	*(3605-2710 BC)*
7) Jared	**(962)**	*(3540-2578 BC)*

8) **Enoch** (*Translated*) ....(365) .... (*3378-3013 BC*)

9) **Methuselah**................................(969) .... (*3313-2344 BC*)

10) Lamech......................................(777) .... (*3126-2349 BC*)

11) **Noah** ....(950) .... (*2944-1994 BC*)

12) Shem ....(603) .... (*2444-1843 BC*)

13) Arphaxad..................................(428) .... (*2341-1913 BC*)

14) Salah..(433) .... (*2316-1883 BC*)

15) Eber...(456) .... (*2286-1830 BC*)

16) Peleg..(239) .... (*2260-2021 BC*)

17) Reu..(235) .... (*2230-1995 BC*)

18) Serug ....(230) .... (*2202-1972 BC*)

19) Nahor.......................................(130) .... (*2172-2042 BC*)

20) Terah ....(205) .... (*2161-1956 BC*)

21) Abram/**Abraham**......................(175) .... (*2111-1936 BC*)

22) **Isaac**.......................................(180) .... (2011-1831 BC)

23) Jacob/**Israel**..............................(130) ....(*To* **Egypt**-*1821 BC*)

24) Israel left Egypt..........................(430) .... (*1821-1391 BC*)

25) Wilderness of Sin........................(40) .... (*1391-1351 BC*)

26) king Chushan ....(8) .... (*1350-1343 BC*)

27) **Judge Othniel** ....(40) .... (*1342-1303 BC*)

28) king Eglon.................................(18) .... (*1302-1285 BC*)

29) **Judge Ehud**...............................(80).....................(*1284-1205 BC*)

30) king Jabin...................................(20).....................(*1204-1185 BC*)

31) **Judge Deborah**.........................(40).....................(*1184-1145 BC*)

32) Midianites..................................(7).....................(*1144-1138 BC*)

33) **Judge Gideon**...........................(40).....................(*1137-1098 BC*)

34) Abimelech..................................(3).....................(*1097-1095 BC*)

35) **Judge Tola**...............................(23).....................(*1094-1072 BC*)

36) **Judge Jair**................................(22).....................(*1071-1050 BC*)

37) Philistines..................................(18).....................(*1049-1032 BC*)

38) **Judge Jephthah**.........................(6).....................(*1031-1026 BC*)

39) **Judge Ibzan**..............................(7).....................(*1025-1019 BC*)

40) **Judge Elon**...............................(10).....................(*1018-1009 BC*)

41) **Judge Abdon**.............................(8).....................(*1008-1001 BC*)

42) Philistines..................................(40).....................(*1000-961 BC*)

43) Judge **Sampson**.........................(20).....................(*960-941 BC*)

44) King David (*Net yrs*)...................(26).....................(*940-915 BC*)

45) King Solomon.............................(40).....................(*914-875 BC*)

46) Rehoboam..................................(17).....................(*874-858 BC*)

47) Abijam......................................(3).....................(*857-855 BC*)

48) Asa...(41).....................(*855-815 BC*)

49) Jehoshaphat................................(25).....................(*815-791 BC*)

50) Jehoram .... **(8)** .... (*794-787 BC*)

51) Ahaziah .... **(1)** .... (*788-788 BC*)

52) Athaliah (*woman*) .... **(7)** .... (*789-781 BC*)

53) Joash/Jehoash .... **(40)** .... (*781-742 BC*)

54) Amaziah .... **(29)** .... (*744-716 BC*)

55) Uzziah/Azariah .... **(52)** .... (*704-653 BC*)

56) Jotham .... **(16)** .... (*652-637 BC*)

57) Ahaz .... **(16)** .... (*637-622 BC*)

58) Hezekiah .... **(29)** .... (*624-596 BC*)

59) Manasseh .... **(55)** .... (*596-542 BC*)

60) Amon .... **(2)** .... (*542-541 BC*)

61) Josiah .... **(31)** .... (*541-511 BC*)

62) Jehoahaz .... **(3 months)** .... (*511-511 BC*)

63) Eliakim/Jehoiakim .... **(11)** .... (*511-501 BC*)

64) Jehoiachin .... **(3 months)** .... (*501-501 BC*)

65) Mattaniah/Zedekiah .... **(11)** .... (*501-491 BC*)

66) Babylon Captivity .... **(70)** .... (*491-421 BC*)

67) Second Temple(*7W*) .... **(49)** .... (*421-372 BC*)

68) Messiah cut off(*60W*) .... **(420)** .... (*372 BC-AD 49*)

69) Covenant (*2W*) .... **(14)** .... (*AD 49 - AD 63*)

70) **War!** (*1/2W*) .... **(3 ½)** .... (*AD 63 - AD 66 ½*)

71) Jews defeated(*1/2W*) .... (**3 ½**) .... (*AD 66 ½ - AD 70*)

72) Perpetual desolation .... (**1290**) .... (*AD 70 - AD 1360*)

73) The Consummation .... (**666**) .... (*AD 1360 - AD 2026*)

After the Consummation is set up (*consummated*) - that abomination

of desolation cannot exceed YHWH's "*determined*" time of 666

years (Daniel 9:27 & Revelation 13:18).

CHAPTER 21

THE FINAL REVELATION OF TIME

According to the presentation and contentions inside this book, "IT'S MUCH LATER THAN YOU THINK!" the "*poured upon*" period of the consummation is to be the final desolation, prior to the coming or returns of Messiah, Yeshua and "*Jesus Christ.*" Of course now, that depends on which Messiah any one particular faith accepts. Regardless to which Messiah any religious group or one may accept as biblically the real deal **or dare I say right now**, "**DEPENDABLE¿**" it makes no difference to me. At this moment and for the time being, I am face to face with the more pressing problem. After I added on the years of the "*poured upon*" period of the consummation, YHWH's Adamic Calendar is sitting at 6026. With little opposition, I say its corresponding Gregorian date is AD 2026. This *problem*, has newly forced me to take notice of **my**, "*theological glitch¿*"

It's Much Later Than You Think!

Conversely, in theory at least; I have made this your problem too. Just to make sure we are all clear on my angle. Since you are reading along with me in this book; you are also walking with me through biblical history and prophetic time. Based on the arguments of my lecture in this book of research and study, my revelation to you of the consummation prophecy puts "us" twenty-five (25) years past the general ideas and consensus of a great many people who believed or felt "*Jesus Christ*" might-would have come in the year AD 2000; or may have proposed the 6001 year mark for the return of our Messiah Yeshua. It is without a doubt that many of our atheist *friends* are smirking. That's not the half of it! Recall; after I added on the 1290 years of *continuous desolation*, after the second temple was destroyed (Daniel 12:11) and subtracted the 250 years of the *little season* (Revelation 20:3) 390 years are left. I don't recall saying; but if everyone was paying close attention. They would realize that adding 1290 years to AD 70, only takes us out to AD 1360. Even if I had found the 390 years later in my walk - *exactly to my satisfaction* - it would have only taken us to year AD 1750. **We are in the year of AD 2020!** We passed AD 1750 exactly 270 years ago and we are still counting. When one thinks about it, the United States of America was not even a nation in AD 1750.

Those being awkward add-ons to literally and spiritually, an already contemptuous biblical stand, *as far as many Christians are concerned*;

my declared revelations of the 666 years, in regards to the consummation prophecy, puts me well passed my own revelatory mark; which is 5750 accountable years for man's self-rule or sadly, AD 1750. Again, we have already passed that mark by 270 years. There is no denying our current reality of the issue as far as all of our concepts of calendar are concerned. Error is afoot. It would appear no matter how one slices the pie, year AD 2026 is well passed my so-called, "*revelatory*" mark! Truth be told, AD 2020 is decades past everybody's mark - *except for Judaism* - of course. But, even the modern Jewish calendar has gone passed my mark. As you already know; it stands at year 5780. In translating my AD 1750 to their years, we get year 5750. Are you confused and concerned? Yeah, I was at the least, concerned! Other than that, I was still confident YHWH was the spirit guiding me.

I am very glad to say, I did not panic! I held on to what bit of faith (*if one could call it that*) I had until YHWH gave me what modern Christian thought would call, "**A Breakthrough**!" But for that time being, YHWH let me remain in what I can only describe as Holy Spirit stasis; due to my error, misunderstanding or whatever it was of time. I could not figure out what was off with what I will call right now, "My hypothesis." It was not really a hypothesis. YHWH illuminated my mind to see. Look, I am not expecting anybody at all to envision that I am some kind of divine genius of the Holy Bible. **For me at least**, the Bible has many secrets I have not begun to sort out for understanding. Questions like, "Why is not "*Sodom and Gomorrah and the cities about them*" still burning?" I mean they were all burning with eternal fire - right? (Jude 7) I am confident I know the answer. But, for those who have not a clue; I could not resist bringing that question up. How about this. Now, I understand no one can see him. Nevertheless, if a clueless soul were to say accidentally walk through the path that leads to the Garden of Eden and the Tree of Life, would they be mortally struck down or wounded by Cherubim with his flaming sword? Then there are those questions that I think about, but I do not ask about. Because, I understand that no one can answer them in serious mode. For an example - how long do you think it took Elohim to count and name all of the stars? (Psalms 147:4) Then there are those *useless questions* (*Or so we presume*), where the Holy Bible provide answers; but, no one sees the need to ask about them in questions. There may be many reasons why we do not know a thing or do not ask YHWH a question of ignorance. But our lack of curiosity **should not** be one of them. But, it may be the worst of all. It may be the big reason why we do not know a thing we could or should know. "*O taste and see*" (Psalms 34:8). The Bible dares us!

> "If any of you lack wisdom, let him ask of God, that giveth to all
> men liberally, and upbraideth not; and it shall be given him. But
> let him ask in faith, nothing wavering...For let not that man
> think that he shall receive any thing of the Lord. A double-

minded man is unstable in all his ways" (James 1:5-8).

"...ye have not, because ye ask not. Ye ask, and receive not, because ye ask amiss..." (James 4:2-3).

Like I said before. I did asked. I believe I received. But, sometimes our spiritual self-worth, is not as high as it might be (***which is not always a very bad thing***); and our spiritual roots are so shallow, we do not know truthfully what we should be asking. Even worse; at times, we feel like those grounds **The Seed** has been thrown on; ***every kind of ground but good – that is.*** Then there are times, even if we are good ground; we can feel overwhelmed by enemies on every side, or because in our eyes, our seed is so small. (Matthew 13:1-32) Yet Yeshua knows our struggles. He is "...*not a high priest which cannot be touched with the feeling of our infirmities; but was in all points tempted like as we are, yet without sin* " (Hebrews 4:15). This section here, for accounting time, was in a similar situation. I was able to ask questions, just not the type of questions that would allow me to attain their deeper discernments. So, along with his teaching, YHWH through the Holy Spirit asked me questions. He asked me what I see today as sound and basic questions; but then they made my mind work overtime in thought-provoking supernatural fashion.

YHWH grilled me on all the numbers I had studied for well over a year. And from where I stood, besides a debated concession (*through somebody's lack of faith that YHWH revealed this truth to me*) for the revelation of the consummation's 666 years, the years I '*listed in order*,' were the only years the Holy Bible and Spirit, released to my spirit, for distribution to any reader, who is seeking out Biblical "*illumination*" low in major controversy. With YHWH's instructions for me to go back over my accounting of man's ordained time; the numbers I listed out for you in this book, in itemized and exhausting details (pp. 365-390), were the only numbers I had to offer YHWH, in response to his instruction for me to review. He asked again, if I was satisfied to their accuracy in my accounting. Again, I said yes I am. The Holy Spirit asked my yet again; how many years did I need to account for? I said based on the knowledge and understanding that your sixth millennial is cut short by a little season and a little season is 250 years; I subtracted 250 years from the totality of the 6000-year time period that covered all of Adam's (*mankind*) self-rule before the Sabbath millennial reign of Yeshua and I had the remainder of 5750 years in total to account for. Those of you who followed along with me and did the count too, should ask the obvious question, "If I only had 5750 years to account for, why am I standing at the abominable number of 6026 years?" That is a real good question. At the time, I was at a real loss for a real good answer. YHWH would later instruct me to do a count down from the end of time point (*5750 years*) in its reverse chronological order with all of my accounted for times and verify my end results to be

absolutely sure going forward and backwards. So, I did that. Here is how

it went counting back from 5750.

1) 5750 - 666 = 5084 (From end of the *poured upon period*, *to the* *"consummation event"* of *"that determined,"* - consummation)
   a. **Daniel 9:27, Revelation 13:18 & 2nd Thessalonians 2:8**

2) 5084 – 1290 = 3794 (Time between the consummation and 2nd temple being destroyed)
   a. **Daniel 12:11**

3) 3794 – 3.5 = 3790.5 (From destruction of the 2nd Temple to the beginning of the war)
   a. **Daniel 9:26** - *"...unto the end of the war desolations are determined."*

4) 3790.5 – 3.5 = 3787 (From the breach of the covenant [*War!*] back to the "unofficial" covenant's confirmation agreement)
   a. **Daniel 9:27-27**

5) 3787 – 14 = 3773 (From the people of the Prince (*Titus*) arriving to confirm the covenant to Yeshua's crucifixion)
   a. **Daniel 9:26**

6) 3773 – 420 = 3353 (From Yeshua's crucifixion at the of age 49 [After threescore ~~and two~~ weeks Messiah cut off – *already explained*] to the completion of the Second Temple.)
   a. **Daniel 9:26**

7) 3353 – 49 = 3304 (From the completion of the Second Temple, back to when it is started at the end of the Babylonian captivity)
   a. **Daniel 9:25**

8) 3304 – 70 = 3234 (From the beginning of the second Temple construction and the end of the Babylonian captivity to the start of the Babylonian captivity)
    a. **Jeremiah 25:11 & Daniel 9:2**

9) 3234 – 450 = 2784 (From the start of the Babylonian captivity to the net overlap or gain from the transitional beginning time of the kings of Judah; which is 450 years)
    a. Kids, "**DO NOT TRY THIS AT HOME!**" Unless you feel that you have to for personal verification. That count was exhausting; but, I put it in my book for you!

10) 2784 – 410 = 2374 (From its net overlap transitional beginning time of the kings of Judah to the beginning of Judges, with 40 years in the wilderness that totaled 450 years)

11) 2374 – 40 = 2334 (You can also do a count here too - *if you like* - it's not as bad as kings)
    a. **Acts 13:17-20**
    b. Note: The 40 years cited in Acts 13:21 meant David, not Saul (1st Kings 2:11).
    c. The Holy Bible only records three years regarding Saul's reign (1st Samuel 13:1).

12) 2334 – 430 =1904 (From Judges and the wilderness to Israel's Egyptian slavery - albeit during the first 30 years Israel time was pleasant and their thrived)
    a. **Exodus 1:7** (*Then consider verses 8-22*)
    b. **Genesis 15:13 & Exodus 12:40-41**

13) 1904 – 130 = 1774 (From the Egyptian slavery to the year of Jacob/Israel's birth)
    a. **Genesis 47:7-9**

14) 1774 – 60 = 1714 (From Jacob/Israel's birth to Isaac's birth)
    a. **Genesis 25:26**

15) 1714 – 100 = 1614 (The age of Abram/Abraham when Isaac was born)

    a. Genesis 21:5

And finally, to make a longer story shorter…

16) 1614 – 1889 (From Abraham/Abram all the way back to Adam) = *Negative¿* (**-275 years**)

    a. Again, you can do the recount yourself – *if you think you need to*. Do not forget to use the Roman number rule for the second Messianic bloodline. If you want to get close to the same number as my count.

    b. From Abram back to the flood is 233 years (*Roman numbers' rule*)

    c. From the flood back to Adam's creation on the sixth day of year one - 1656 years.

With all of that back counting, we ended up with negative 275 years.

Am I serious!? Yes I am! And, **Really** I am! How could I end up with negative years? Not only that - but all of my event dates were now in this "time warp" of confusion. For example; or most notable to the average Bible novice, Item #3: The destruction of the Second Temple was no longer aligned with the date AD 70, but 206 BC. Furthermore, Messiah's crucifixion date was now insisting that Yeshua was put to death in 227 BC - Really!? Based on the Holy Bible's verified numbers; which I had determined to be extremely accurate, from my perspective. There were unacceptable surplus years. It did not matter which way I went. This next thing is important. I need everybody to follow with me closely. All of the years in biblical history and prophetic times starting from year one, come to a maximum of 6026 years.

    a. If we presume Yeshua is a liar and did not shorten the days as he promised; going forward from year one, I still transgress the 6001 maximum years mark by a considerable twenty-five (25) years. **Unacceptable.**

    b. If we presume Yeshua is a liar; even if he did shortened the days by my asserted 250 years in the little season, going forward from year one, he would still be overdue at the end of the 6026 years by 275 years. I find this scenario also - **Unacceptable.**

    c. If we presume the spirit I say revealed to me concerning the 666 years was not the Holy Spirit, but a deceiving familiar spirit; in reality, we are still apparently in year AD 2020. Obvious the years were not shortened. And, neither did the Messiah keep his promise to reign in the Millennial Sabbath. This is also - **Unacceptable.**

    d. If we presume yet again, Yeshua is a liar as he was in scenario (a) and we count the years back from the maximum 6001 years (according to the concept of the Millennial week) we wind up at the negative twenty-five (-25) years mark. Surely, I do not need to tell anyone. That is ludicrous and **Unacceptable.**

Clearly, there is way too much going wrong; when we go the route of, "Yeshua being a liar." We could be here for a long time, sorting all of the scenarios out. **How about we consider this?** Let us presume that Yeshua "**IS NOT**" a liar. Let us see if that will allow us to fair any better.

    e. Let us presume Yeshua **is not** a liar and he did shorten the days. Then let us also presume in shortening the days, it was by the revealed 250 years in the little season. Counting back from that year (5750), we still come to what most would consider the untenable number of negative 275 years. As I comprehend; it is still **Unacceptable**. For me however, it is truly much better I am called the liar; than to insinuate, imply or indirectly call Yeshua the liar – **Capeesh?**

While I acknowledge all of the things I "*presumed,*" all involve the correctness of the 666 years concept or as I like to call it - revelation; there is nothing else on the horizon in sight that makes any semblance of common spiritual sense as far as history, prophecy and our current reality is concerned. If there is and somebody reading this book knows about it, I would sure love for them to use my contact information to write and enlighten me about it. Because I for one - am sick and tired of so-called Bible Scholars, calling Yeshua a liar. Maybe the worse thing about it all; is sadly they have quite a few elements in professed "*Christianity*" doing the same thing. And, I "*presume*" that most of their converts, do not even realize they are doing it. Even though I was somewhat at a loss, with my years predicament; the Holy Spirit inspired me into which path I should pursue my effort. It was scenario (e.). Scenario (e.) was the only scenario listed; which did not insinuate, imply or indirectly call Yeshua the liar. It was what I called, the process of elimination. (e.) was the more tolerable and lesser of all the listed evils of error. (e.) only insinuates, implies or indirectly calls me the liar. I can admit on those very rare occasions when I am wrong; unless I am "*discussing things*" with my wife. Then, I am always wrong. (*I know, no other married men out here has a clue of what*

I am talking about.) Anyway, let us get on with the more serious note.

As far as I was concerned, there was still no spiritual logic in play. In dismissing (a.) through (d.), I was still in the negative (275) concerning Adam's creation and my entire base of dates, such as the destruction date of the Second Temple were off. That is, after I had totaled the back step verification of my walk through those years of intellectual man. I asked YHWH a series of questions that ranged from, "How do I go forward from here?" to "What does this negative and positive (depending on which way we count it out) excess of numbers mean to the big picture of counting the time?" YHWH, in his response to all of my confusion; gave illumination to alleviate my time darkness – by asking me two questions of his own. Within the compass of their answers - *at least for me* - new discoveries and a fresh perspective brought to crystal clarity, the insight as to why prophecy and so many historical dates are cited in doubt with debate. Consider YHWH's questions below and how you would reply.

1) **How long was Adam in the Garden of Eden?**

2) **When did prophecy begin?**

I did not have to consider long. YHWH revealed to me by his Holy Spirit. Adam was in the Garden of Eden for the duration of the 275 years before he sinned; when I was supposedly in the impossible negative of history, when I had stepped backwards from the end to the beginning of

Adam's time. The truth of this situation and what YHWH revealed to me was this. I was attempting to negotiate "***two different***" *spiritual weeks* as one - in my quest to appreciate what time and date we are living in. Truth is we have Elohim's original foundation clock or millennial week; which included an eighth day for the purpose of presenting Eternal rewards to Adam and elected descendants. Also, as I claim; **here and now**, there is **ADAM'S WEEK!** *Adam's week* is an overlay of that original plan Elohim sketched out for man's ordained and eventual everlasting takeover of all the earth. (Genesis 1:26) Doubters may ask, if my insight is true; why is there not a Bible witness? ***There is!*** The trail is still here. ***We just walked it!*** Did not we just follow it back to its origin? We already know with our 20/20 biblical hindsight – Adam failed to qualify in order to take over his everlasting post. With Adam's failure to fulfill Elohim's week, YHWH ordained that Adam to be given his own full Millennial work week (*6000 years*); to prove for and to himself, what YHWH knew from the very beginning. There is only **one way** which leads to joy, peace, happiness and of course, Eternal Life. Also, that our quest to gain Eternal Life; is not infused with the outright lies and deceptions of the Serpent. With the beginning of Adam's "***auxiliary***" millennial work week - for "***self-rule***;" divine "***prophecy***" from YHWH to manage Adam's "**deferred destiny**," simultaneously commenced with his expulsion from the Garden of Eden.

(Genesis 3:14-19) This contextual insight is central to our understanding; in order to discern biblically, why it appears we are at year 6019 and AD 2020. In truth of total years, we are in year 6019 and AD 2020. However, those year counts **are not** in their proper and therefore their discernible context of Adam's **auxiliary/second** week. Years 6019 or AD 2020 is in the context of YHWH Elohim's **original intent week** - believe it or not.

> **"Mr. Merriman, we believe <u>YHWH's original time for man is the only time and started on the first day of the first week of the first year</u>. We do not believe there is any such thing as this <u>auxiliary week</u> in the background, overlay or wherever."**
> ☹ **(Signed: All My Detractors)** ☹

Fair enough. I have no issues with your primary claim. Actually, it is not just a claim and Bible wise it is generally simple to prove. You can easily support your claim by having me turn to Genesis in the Holy Bible and read it as the faith fact that it is. I can acknowledge that much. My only question to you Mr./Mrs./Miss or Ms. Detractor, regarding the immediate matter of this, is this. "<u>Why cannot we both be right on this one</u>?" Let me try to explain it the best I can; my claim of the two weeks over this next sections. Please stick with me. But first, let us read - **your** Bible proof.

> "And God said, Let us make man in our image, after our likeness: and let them have dominion over the fish of the sea, and over the fowl of the air, and over the cattle, and over all the earth, and over every creeping thing that creepeth upon the earth. So God created man in his *own* image, in the image of God created he him; male and female created he them. And God

blessed them, and God said unto them, Be fruitful, and multiply, and replenish the earth, and subdue it: and have dominion over the fish of the sea, and over the fowl of the air, and over every living thing that moveth upon the earth. And God said, Behold, I have given you every herb bearing seed, which *is* upon the face of all the earth, and every tree, in the which *is* the fruit of a tree yielding seed ; to you it shall be for meat. And to every beast of the earth, and to every fowl of the air, and to every thing that creepeth upon the earth, wherein *there is* life, *I have given* every green herb for meat: and it was so. And God saw every thing that he had made, and, behold, *it was* very good. And the evening and the morning were the sixth day" (Genesis 1:26-31).

Year one, sixth day, man made; I got it. My claim is not in dispute of Biblical fact. My contention is "**prophecy**" for Adam did not begin until he chose to take the serpent at his word through Eve. After which, since Adam decided he *did not* want to *carry on* with Elohim's week. YHWH made a divine executive decision to ordained a reset. YHWH gave Adam his own complete week to "painstakingly" explore his new/Old path (*We understand spiritually - Satan had previously run that course - to his own eternal demise*). In that new/Old path "**prophecy**" commenced. With the promise of Adam's Messiah in those early years (Genesis 3:15) Elohim's original plan for YHWH's "divine visitation" for "fellowship;" became a divine rescue mission for his salvation (*my words*). Adam's sin required a Messiah. The visitation, which was planned before the renewing and our world began; was not contingent on Adam's week. However Messiah Yeshua's sacrifice, his resurrection after his sacrificed, his going away to receive for himself the Kingdom as <u>KING of Kings and LORD of Lords</u>, then his return in "***power and great glory***;" (Matthew 24:30) would logically and divinely be intimate with Adam's week.

YHWH knew Adam's week would not run its completed course. Our "<u>acquired satanic nature</u>" for evil wanton violence made self-annihilation inevitable. Those chickens truly and visibly came home to roost after that fallen angel took the key that he had been given charge over (Revelation 9:1-11) and used it to open up, "<u>the bottomless pit</u>;" as Daniel prophesied pertaining to 2356 years earlier. Daniel confirms our "*knowledge shall be increased*" (<u>To the points of our intellectual limits, but without YHWH's direction</u>) (Daniel 12:4). Why do you think we have atomic, nuclear and other weapons formed for mass destruction? It is evident for our survival, we would need Eloah's divine interventions. It is why YHWH shortened **Adam's sixth day**. Still, it appears <u>YHWH's week</u> continued on - base on the fact that his promised and prophesied *visitation* (Genesis 3:15 & Psalms 8:4), still occurred on Elohim's base calendar, "*in the midst of the week*" (***1 BCE - AD 49***). YHWH simply overlaid his week - **at the 275 year mark** - with <u>Adam's week</u>. Do a review of this book and its claims, along with back up reading in the Bible. I do pray if there are any doubts; they will be alleviated. I cannot imagine it will get any more complicated than what I have explained from this book. **<u>The Numbers tell the Story</u>!**

CHAPTER 22

SERIOUS?

To this point, some are still in a daze. What am I saying? What did this book just claim?" They ask themselves, "Is this guy actually saying, what it is I think he is saying?" "**I**" don't exactly know. What exactly is it do you think "**I**" am saying? Are **you** asking **me** if this book is predicting that the return of Messiah Yeshua will be at the head of YHWH's true Adamic Hebrew and Holy Bible year 6026? **And,** are **you** asking **me**; if this book is claiming the year 6026, matches up with the Gregorian year AD 2026? Truly **"this book"** is not necessarily saying anything of the sort. In **"this book"** is written merely those numbers the **"Holy Bible"** clearly records and the Holy Spirit has revealed to me. So now then, if **you** are asking **me** if this book is proclaiming that the Holy Bible reveals that our Messiah Yeshua will return, based on the Holy Bible's recorded numbers, when combined with prophecy as revealed by the Holy Spirit at YHWH's Adamic year 6026; "**I**" must reply to **you** with an enthusiastic, "**Yes!**" And, if **you** are asking **me,** if year 6026 corresponds within a 207 days period with the Gregorian calendar year AD 2026; then as far as my Bible perspectives are concerned, my answer to you must be <u>Absolutely,</u> <u>Undoubtedly</u> and <u>Unequivocally,</u> <u>Enthusiastically</u> and <u>Unapologetically,</u> "**<u>YES!</u>**"

"THAT'S RIGHT! I SAID IT!"

<u>What do you mean, "I can't be serious</u>?" Then I must seriously guess you are seriously unconvinced with my many serious biblical arguments. Some readers might ask, "<u>How can I state so strongly, a definite day and</u> <u>hour Messiah Yeshua is "**truly**" due for his return? When the Holy Bible</u> <u>says so plainly, not even "*Jesus Christ*" himself, knows the day and the</u> <u>hour.</u>" If they then remembered where for to look, they would find that alleged discrediting text, and have me read it; or read it out loud to me, verbatim. So, yet **again** we will read, "...*of that day and hour knoweth no* *man...*" (Matthew 24:36). "There!" They will say. *Actually*, to this point I have just claimed to know the year. Ultimately, proving one knows, "*that* *day and hour*" would create an entirely different challenge with the many Christian mindsets out here. This is especially true with all of the pagan influence in culture today. I recently recall trying to explain the insight of

"***possibly***" *being revealed to by YHWH and* **knowing** to an acquaintance of mine. After generally all had been said; the only words that they could come up with for their rebuttal, as if there had to be one; was the text we already cited. Then in a moment of spiritual epiphany; I understood our impasse. It was not about establishing the truth. It was more about them not letting me overturn their apple cart of traditional denominationalism.

I want the reader to know it is not about me being right or you being wrong; or vice-versa. It is about not being afraid to challenge the Bible. It is about not being afraid to declare what it is you believe that you have found inside of the Holy Bible to the world for its scrutiny. It is about developing the spiritual attitude to trust YHWH's spirit; no matter where he leads you and no matter what condemnations you might receive from the wickedness in this world's population; even if that populace includes prominent members from the dissimilar religions communities. Yeah - I recognize the way the Bible is translated and we are told to understand it; it seems to imply "…*of that day and hour*," only **The Father** in heaven knows them for sure. But with a closer "sober-minded" scrutiny; I would argue that there is more to the passage than the average denominationally challenged and shackled mind, might be able to see. No offense intended.

See, since the most ancient of its tradition surrounding and within the Israelite Tribe of Judah, **Yom Teruw'ah** or **The Feast of Trumpets** has come to be known as, **"The Day That No Man Knows!"** It is also in reference to - *according to the knowledge and understanding of a great number in the theological studies on the Holy Scripture* - that day in shadow when, *"The Jewish Messiah,"* more properly cited, *"The Eloah of Yisra'el"* is to return and restore **the kingdom to Yisra'el**. Most people I know; stand in agreement with the understanding of Matthew 24:36. It is a day no man knows or can know. I ask, "Are they sure." They say, "Yes, not even the angels know!" Then, on some of the faces you can see, **The People's Eyebrow**. Those familiar with actor Dwayne **"the Rock"** Johnson, know what I am talking about, *if you smell what the Rock is cooking*. Then they go in for the kill! To slam the door on my insane notion some have said in all confidence, "The Bible says not even *"Jesus Christ"* know!" [Check] I say, "Really? But I thought *"Jesus"* was GOD!" And now, with an incredulous look of sully disdain on many of their faces, they state their declaration. **"HE IS!!"** Then without shame, and nearly a total absence of humility, unwilling to resist that urge inside of my *"human"* psyche to feel the sensation of **"Gotcha!"** With an equal look of incredulousness on my face I say, **"But I thought GOD knew everything!"** From that point few reply with anything sounding remotely close to intellectual sanity. If you heard many of their replies, you would know what I meant and would know what I was thinking. [**Checkmate!!**]

Look, in all truth; most of the time my, **"Gotcha!"** moments with these people - for me at least - has more to do with keeping our powers of thought and reasoning on line, versus being more right about a given situation minus the input of my fellow debater or conversationalist. I am not a <u>spiritually devout Jewish traditionalist</u> at all or in any sense of those words. I do not even have an "indirect" inherited connection to the race of Jewish people; which I am aware of at least. Moreover, any branches that conceivably, I might have had connecting me at all, to any of the lost tribes of Israel; would have been a long time ago snapped-off, dried-up and severely withered away under pagan influences, as the living oracles of YHWH dissipated from my heritage down through the many former generations to me; by me not being connected to the True Vine of family, which is in Yeshua (John 15:1). Any claim I might be tempted to make today; would have to be from YHWH's extending his merciful grace in granting his knowledge, understanding and wisdom. With that said, I do claim something of a connection to the Judah of Israel, through Israel – somewhat. But nevertheless, I am not dogmatic with the possibility about having any physical heritage with Israel. Though the spiritual heritage no doubt is definitely alive and growing. Whether it will be ample to get me into the wedding feast of Messiah Yeshua as part of the five wise virgins, remains to be seen. Time will tell. This witness is to how I count myself.

"Not as though I had already attained, either were already perfect: but I follow after, if that I may apprehend that for which also I am apprehended of [Messiah Yeshua]. Brethren, I count not myself to have apprehended: but *this* one thing *I do*, forgetting those things which are behind, and reaching forth unto those things which are before. I press toward the mark for the prize of the high calling of God in [Messiah Yeshua]."

(Philippians 3:12-14)

YHWH called me to preach the simplicity of his gospel. Not as some dogmatic convincer of you or else, in order to conquer the world; but as a witness to the truth before those who may encounter me in the world. My availability is to those who may scrutinize me concerning the hope of salvation I have in me. We all live by faith. Faith is that lively hope by which we seek to establish YHWH's truth in our spirit. I know many will still insist on the one hand just be ready; for no man knows the day or the hour (Matthew 24:36). Yet on the other hand, knowing what I believe I know about Yeshua, **"There will be a man!"** My same affirmation in questions: "Could there be some man **"today"** who knows the day and hour?" "If Yeshua is **GOD** manifested in flesh, **how could he not know**; being who we discern as **GOD** and all?" If Yeshua knows, why would he hold back from his own; who have come to see the end of our final age?" Of us Yeshua has said, "*Unto you it is given to know the mystery of the kingdom of God*" (Mark 4:11)." **Do not misunderstand me now**. I truly understand that his disciples did not know everything. Yeshua did not tell them "*everything*" while he was with them on the earth. (John 16:12) But he did say to them that many end time things would be revealed to them at some later date, by the Holy Spirit. (Verses 13-15) The possibility and the probability that someone now, does know **that day and hour**; is that matter this section will concern itself with.

Are there any men alive now who does, will, or even can know *that day and hour*? Would it be profane for any to make such an outlandish assertion? I am absolutely confident that few biblical theologians would go on record and out on the proverbial limb, to risk their reputations to deny Messiah made that statement. It is easy to find it in the Holy Bible in black and white; or "Red!" Anyone can read John 16:12-15. It is pretty clear to me through its reading. Yeshua states he will reveal "everything" the father tells him to his own. Now everybody with any kind of common spiritual sense, understands that it is a given for – eventually. Still, allow me to interject at this point in time; to cite what from my viewpoint is an interesting question for debate. "Who in their right mind, does not think Messiah Yeshua at least knows by now, that day and hour? I would love to open up the floor for rhetorical challenges, debate and rebukes to that spiritual notion.   **'You got five minutes!"**

Seriously. Simply because the statement made by Yeshua appears to say that no man or angel knew the day and the hour was completely, unambiguously and unquestionably true at the time when Yeshua made it; does that mean that his statement still has to be true, even today? If Yeshua is to continue to be in our eyes the Messiah, we have to believe in some rational capacity he at least knows now, what it is we presumed he did not know when he spoke those words to his disciples. I would also have you keep in mind, addition to the words of his statement, Messiah Yeshua gave us a well-known Bible event; to help clarify to us the actual point behind his words, "that day and hour knoweth no *man*." Our age is to be viewed in like fashion as far as spiritual similarities go, but from the reality of our own end age today. I can admit it. Yeshua's words were true, when he made them. I also know Yeshua followed up that statement with the following revealing words!

> "But as the days of Noah *were,* so shall also the coming of the Son of man be. For as in the days that were before the flood they were eating and drinking, marrying and giving in marriage, until the day that Noah entered into the ark, and knew not until the flood came, and took them all away; so shall also the coming of the Son of man be" (Matthew 24:37-39)

From my perspective, there is no getting around Yeshua's testimony. Yeshua's terrifying words bring us right into our now; and on until when he returns. So then what is my beef? First as an aside so you can perceive its reality. Children, infants and pregnant women were part of that world Noah and family were able to escape from, because of YHWH's mercy. That is for those who claim YHWH, *"Never harms innocent children."*

They say every time something like that happens, it is the enemy Satan. However, unlike Satan, I know YHWH is able to and will raise up those *innocents* up along with their parents, in that Last Great Day of YHWH and judge them in righteousness and mercy. And that is all I want to say about that - in this book.

Next up, is that obvious question Yeshua allows us to ask by his challenge that we should compare the two eras. **Was there a man who knew it was going to rain?** Well of course there was! **Noah knew!** And, unless Noah built the entire ark by his lonesome; everybody who helped Noah in building the ark, also knew it was going to rain. And I have to believe Shem, Ham and Japheth all knew. Since Noah, Shem, Ham and Japheth were all married; I am reasonably sure all four of the wives knew too. It is also a fairly reasonable assumption that the oldest man to have ever live in, Methuselah (*969 years*) likely knew. As a matter of record, Methuselah died the year of and very likely before the flood; not, in the flood. Was it coincidence? I would like to imagine not. I liken the man Methuselah, to the man Moses. Even though we are not given privy to any indiscretions on the part of Methuselah; it is likely YHWH Elohim determined Methuselah would not go to the other side of the flood. As it was with Moses, who was himself denied entry into, The Promised Land. Of course, without biblical proof, my determination is all conjecture and only for interesting and "*entertaining¿*" biblical discussions.

Discovery: Not only did the people I have mentioned likely knew it was going to rain - *I got one more **bombshell** for ya* - Everyone under the sound of Noah's voice knew it was going to rain! However, it has to be rather obvious none of them actually believed "*that ole fool*." **You** had to know they felt Noah was insane. He was preaching to people about some future event that had never occurred in history. Granted, for the next 100 years after YHWH's announcement, no one knew "when" it was going to rain. **Noah did not know until "Seven Days" before the rain started**. (Genesis 7:4) I tell you, Noah's notice from YHWH is a shadow picture in days then, for our years today. "*He that hath ears to hear*" (Mark 4:9).

How many of us would have believed Noah? Be honest. What might we have said to Noah? Think it may have sounded anything close to this?

> "Gimme a second to get my head around this okay? Cause I rilly wanna git dis story rite. Makin sure I understan now. You talkin bout water comin down from the sky rite? Okie-dokie. You mind if we take a break here Noah? Smoke-em if ya got-em! Come on man. Rain from the sky... really?" (Timothy B. Merriman, 2020)

Be true. We tend to make fun of the people of Noah's day. But, we know had we been there; it would be no humor. Sadly, I am quite sure I would have been one who at the first drop - *in a moment of mortal clarity* - that moment YHWH's truth was being fulfilled in my formerly *non-believing* eyes, wishing I had fish gills to breathe with and fish fins to swim with.

Anyway, let us get back to being real seriousness here and know this for sure. Yeshua's idiom was "never" meant to imply there would be no man who would know "*that day and hour*" of, and at the end of our age. That is precisely why Yeshua gave the Noah comparison. It was for those who could believe to understand. He would show us or to whom he chooses to reveal to, "*that day and hour*." The fig tree parable (Mark 13:28-30) with the idiom was not meant to show "*that day and hour*" would be hidden. In their revelation, it shows the very opposite. Yeshua was telling us he would let someone know. And while I reserve the right to be wrong, I am about to tell you what I feel was my shocking discovery. I give all glory and praise for any and every revelation to YHWH, for his tender mercies. Truth is, I do not know but for mercy and grace; any other reasons he would tell me, what I am about to tell you.

Mind you, it will be a bit difficult for me to articulate the path that Messiah instructed his angel to take me through. But, I will do my best to make that path known to you. It started when I was taught how to count biblically with age and prophecy. But before I go further, I would like to inform you briefly concerning the idiom Messiah spoke in relation to the day and the hour. An idiom, in accordance to Merriam-Webster, is "*a group of words established by usage as having a meaning not deducible from those of the individual words.*" Based on only the need for a limited study, an idiom, while it may make sense in one culture or language, may be viewed as assumed insanity, if taken literally in another culture or language. "It's raining cats and dogs" in English is an easily understood reference to heavy rain downpours. All the same, a different culture not abreast with ours might think of it as very crazy, or incomprehensible. Messiah was speaking a Hebrew idiom when he reference what most people within the Christian faith view as utter or complete ignorance in heaven (*Messiah himself and the holy angels*) and in the earth (*Mankind and all demons*) when it comes to knowing when Messiah was to return as **KING of Kings and LORD of Lords**. Christians are very quick to reference that defining passage, "*But of that day and hour knoweth no man, no, not the angels of heaven, but my Father only*" (Matthew 24:36). But, if we are able to look closer; we might see additional insights. The following is a reasonable enough explanation. I am sure there are deeper insights to Messiah Yeshua's words. As I have said. The truth of YHWH is dimensional. And, the following gives some credibility to our premise that, "*no man knows*" had no direct reference to the mainstreams of Christianity's widely held belief no one can know. Just like Noah knew, somebody will in this time also know. Take notice in absence of, or in lieu of your own additional studies on the subject. Because, if we can establish even a possibility that some people will know; it assists my efforts to put forth insights and perspectives on when I claim Messiah is

returning, just slightly a bit easier. I have insight on the day and the hour.

Be patient and do not shut me out. Not just yet.

"The Feast of Trumpets was known by those in ancient
Jerusalem as "The Day That No Man Knows." And why was this
feast nick-named by this Hebrew Idiom? It is because [*Yom
Teruah or Yom Teruw'ah - Feast of Trumpets or The Day of
Blowing*] is the only feast [*or holy day*] that is determined by the
sighting of the new moon [*very first sliver*], therefore, "no man"
can calculate the exact day nor the hour of when it begins."
(Double Portion Inheritance Ministries, 2008).

While I am not exactly positive concerning the current accuracy of

their statement, especially now in our modern times of technology; I can

vigilantly agree with their general premise of their statement. From my

perception, Yeshua's idiom had less to do with people not knowing the

day or the hour, especially the wise in the end times (Daniel 12:9-10);

and more to do with us **actually being able to identify** the day in which

His return or His coming would take place to His end-time believers. The

Festival of Trumpets is a direct reference to, and the shadow picture of a

final fulfillment in the trumpets of Revelation. The Feast of Trumpets is

especially identifying; when it comes to what the seventh trumpet in the

book of Revelation embodies. That is, the return or coming of Messiah

and first resurrection. The Seventh Trump is the last trumpet of prophecy

in man's self rule and it witnesses the fulfillment of the very foundation for all of our hopes and faiths; no matter what you may and may not believe regarding the Bible or this book. We all hope for divine life after this life, and the shadow picture in the Feast of Trumpets offers us that hope of salvation, through Messiah Yeshua's promises and in his return.

> "Let not your heart be troubled: ye believe in God, believe also in me. In my Father's house are many [*abode/rooms to stay in*]: if *it were* not *so,* I would have told you. I go to prepare a place for you. And if I go and prepare a place for you, I will come again, and receive you unto myself; that where I am, *there* ye may be also" (John 14:1-3).

> "...I show you a mystery; we shall not all <u>sleep</u> (*there's that word again*), but we shall all be changed, in a moment, in the twinkling of an eye, <u>at the last trump</u>...the trumpet shall sound, and the dead shall be raised incorruptible."
> (1st Corinthians 15:51-55)

The Feast of Trumpets (*Yom Teruah, Yom Teruw'ah or the Day of Blowing*), takes place in the fall of the year. It is the beginning of the Jewish civil year in Israel and the fall Holy Days; of which most Christian believers, primarily view as Jewish festivals. I will reserve to comment on our Christian attitudes in regards to the only holy days recorded inside of the Jewish Holy Scriptures; and also incidentally, inside every full Christian Holy Bible. Besides, that is not what this book is alerting you to. This book is mainly focused on the times; time used up and time left. Identifying if we can and as accurately as we can; when we can expect Messiah to come or Yeshua to return. From my perspective, in the research and study of this book, we have the year. It is Adamic year 6026. That year corresponds to the Gregorian of AD 2026. I am also persuaded that we have **The Day**. It is the Feast of Trumpets; "*The Day That No Man Knows*." But, I am afraid that is as close as I can get. And before anyone starts again with the dismissals, take note that Yeshua said precisely, according to the **KJV** translation, "But of that day **and** hour knoweth no *man,* no, not the angels of heaven, but my Father only" (Matthew 24:36).

Also recognize, when it comes to the KJV, *italics* words were added by the translators in their efforts to make reading more comprehensible to average laypersons. Sometimes, I believe their effort had the opposite effect. Nevertheless, based on rules governing our English language, the word '*and,*' show we have a compound sentence. That means in order for the compound statement to be true, all claims of the report has to be true: i.e. "I went to the grocery store *and* bought some food." If I went to the grocery store, but I got motor oil my statement is false. Even though I did go to the store and I did make a purchase; motor oil is not considered a food item. So in truth, I did not perform what my statement claimed. In retrospect and from my perspective, if anybody made the claim Yeshua's statement is false today, they would have to prove that they; or someone knew "the day *and* the hour." I cannot readily claim both. So then, upon further study, from my new perspective; I can no longer imply Yeshua's statement he made in <u>Matthew 24:6</u> may no longer be true. "*<u>Oh taste and see</u> [to] <u>prove all things</u>*" (Psalms 34:8 & 1st Thessalonians 5:21). Nevertheless, here is the real kicker. In making his statement, Yeshua never said or claimed that no person would know that day **<u>or</u>** the hour; but, that no person would know that day **<u>and</u>** hour – *and there is a* **<u>marked</u>** *difference* – if we can trust the translation of the KJV. Some may accuse me of mincing words. Maybe that is true; but I do not think so. At times, when guarding against going overboard, I believe it is important to be precise. Then at times, it just does not matter. Based on my research, I have to believe in this case the "**<u>and</u>**," could be of some significance.

I would have those who do not know and understand, The Feast of Trumpets is observed in the Jewish month of Tishri. Tishri is the first month of the year on the Jewish civil calendar. But, it is the seventh month of their religious year. Since most theologians would concur that the number seven represents completeness - ***then theological wise*** - the seventh month of Tishri is a type of first and a type of last. In its shadow picture Tishri can signify with its first feast day (*Feast of Trumpets*), the first and the last trumpet, the first through the last trumpet or in their final fulfillment, the completed blasts of all seven trumpets. I said all of that to give readers the full array when in the future they may consider the beginning of the month of Tishri with its declaration of *Yom Teruah, Yom Teruw'ah, the Day of Blowing and the Feast of Trumpets;* which in the Hebrew idiom is, <u>The Day That No Man Knows</u>. The Hebrew/Jewish month of Tishri generally happens during our September-October on the Gregorian calendar. If one follows the "new moon sightings" to the start of the <u>Jewish civil year</u>, one could know when to expect their seventh religious month. They are generally one in the same, but with provisos!

There you have it. Based on all of my research you have the year, the month and the day - but not, <u>The Hour</u>. You see, days overlap. While one day is ending, the other is beginning. Who can tell when there are equal amounts of daylight as there is darkness? <u>I can't</u>. But if one can prove for themselves the insights and revelations this book has cited, then gain this book's outlook; I dare say one is close enough. <u>Trust me</u>. <u>The hour will not matter</u>. I don't know when <u>the hour</u> comes "<u>absolutely</u>" starting "<u>that day</u>" or any day; but if this book is true and one who has read it believes it, they will know. Spiritually and biblically I believe it. If I am still alive at "**<u>that year and day</u>**" (***6026 which is AD 2026 – Feast of Trumpets***); I will know "<u>absolutely</u>" within a few seconds, when "**<u>that hour</u>**" is gone.

On that note, I challenge you to get to work. Repeat this Bible study. See if you get the same results. If you do, then unlike the carnal world - *on the one hand* - which will not read this book and the ones who have read it, but do not and will not consider to the slightest degree that its research and ideologies might be true; you who have believed - *on the other hand* - now know this tremendous truth as your new reality. "Now is [your] salvation nearer than when [you] believed" (Romans 13:11). In believing its recorded numbers that from the beginning of the Holy Bible until its end and from the start of this book until its end; which I have contended do not lie; minus an occasional religious pause for thought-provoking biblical references and inferences for to change, if one has doctrinal fortitude and can perhaps put a pin in their debate issues; to consider this book's insights only as it relates to time; I do not hesitate to say you have the world's rarest view. You now have the view that every Bible truth seekers has continually wondered about as to when – for their entire lives. You have in your hands this book; which gives you the real ability - *if you attain with it YHWH's divine blessing to discern its truth -* to literally "*see, the [unknowable] day approaching*" (Hebrews 10:25).

CHAPTER 23

WHY SHOULD ANYONE BELIEVE ME?

To this point and after all that has been said, "<u>Why should people believe me?</u>" is a fitting question for survey (<u>**See p. 467**</u>). This book is clearly religious in nature. By being so; is there an advantage for me; if people should believe any of the controversial claims I have made? I am just saying. One generally does not make a lot of money off of unpopular controversy. Unpopular religious things are what they call a, "hard-sell" and real tuff to do. It's not like I'm asking for monthly gifts (*$$$*) or half your life savings as a love/seed gift. I guess curiosity could translate into a few book sales. Or if people actually liked it or believed me, they might buy additional copies for their friends to read. Then again, one could just as easy loan them their copy. There is always the opportunity, if enough people seriously believe its Bible numbers to be <u>fairly accurate,</u> a second excursion into book writing may occur for me. I guess that is motivation enough for many. My goal however, as stated before is simply to get the word of this book into the broader public and *"Christian domain."* I have no other motivations I can speak of at present. So again, why should one believe me? In your position it is likely the question I would ask myself. It is a fair question. ***Why should you believe?*** That is, believe how I have accounted for all of the numbers in man's current and total existence? On the one hand, many Bible tweaks and spiritual lectures I made inside this book; which may appear to be doctrinal in nature, could be argued based on, beliefs. On the other hand, numbers have a uniqueness. Numbers can be real precise and are much easier to interpret. If the same mathematical process is employed, minus error, the same result will always occur. The understanding of numbers gives one the tenor of confidence, because fact checkers can backtrack to verify accuracy in one's efforts; when they are listed in simplicity. Because unchanging mathematical concepts have put numbers together, even "obstinate minds" find them difficult to view and then refute; if they are detailed. One does not have to concede their final interpretation to conclude numbers are reasonably presented, if offered in an established mathematical format; i.e. The Roman Numbers. A format I assert and present in the book's subtitled chapter, *"**From Shem to Te'-rah.**"* I have listed **"Every Number"** the **"Holy Bible"** has for offer; that is focused on *what time we are really in and how much time we have left*. After time fulfills the last digit in the mark of the beast (666), the next likely and biblically sound event is <u>Yeshua's return</u>! (2nd Thessalonians 2:1-8) It is crucial for one accepting the numbers in this book - *from the Holy Bible* - as being chronologically accurate, <u>as far as time gone by</u>. As far as how much time we believe we perceive we have left; it will depend if whether a person believes the millennial week declared from this book and many other biblical sources, is that maximum time given by YHWH; <u>for self-rule</u> (*6000 years*), <u>Yeshua's 1000-year reign</u> and <u>"the eighth day"</u> <u>for judgment</u> is **<u>"Holy Bible"</u>** sound. All Judaism recognizes in its yearly observance that millennial week (*life and judgment*) in shadow picture, at <u>Sukkot</u> (*Feast of Tabernacles*) and <u>Shemini Atzeret</u> (*Last Great Day*).

This will come as no shock. I would love for everyone to believe the things I write in this book. But if they opt not, I get it. This is fact. People fear religion is filled full with lies. While they may be right; the **<u>real</u>** fear is truth seekers are having **<u>real</u>** trouble, identifying and accepting what a **<u>real</u>** lie is, how and why they hide. Who is to say, I am not lying now and unethically using sensationalism to try and sale this book? I do not doubt by saying it, I have given detractors an epiphany to say, "<u>You are right!</u>" Still, rightly they ask, "How do you know your interpretation of passages you cited are right?" In my own words, they are "*biblically sound.*" They fit into Bible place. As far as I am concerned, they are not interpretations. In a confident affirmation, I will say things revealed to the reader in this book is full of truth. I will say the Spirit of YHWH instructed me in all of these things. The tender mercies and grace of Yeshua revealed to me. He has caused me to discern what truths he wanted me to. Then, commanded me to present them in open public, through this book. To be honest, I am not sure what kind of **"proof"** I could provide; which would be sufficient enough to please skeptics or those who might be dogmatic over contrasts they now accept and judge is truth. Wait a minute! I may be able to ask a litmus question to assist possible stalemates with the more controversial accounted years. It is a yes or no question: "Does the dogmatic believer, believe Moses and the Prophets?" (Luke 16:31) Now analyze your reply.

General question: How did Yeshua's disciples know that they were hearing the truth; after he clarified one of his parables he taught them by, concerning the Kingdom of Eloah? **Answer:** After Yeshua explained and clarified his parables to them, they made common, righteous, holy and godly sense. His disciples **DECIDED** they believed Yeshua. I **DECIDED** to do the same. I will stick with that belief unless someone shows me I have encountered, heard or believed some familiar spirit of deception. If that happens, I will rebuild my faith; with that new perspective of truth I have received from my *loving* brother or sister who helped me to see. I believe the readers of this book, should seriously consider doing that same thing concerning the numbers contained inside of this book. However, before one makes such an important decision, here are some vital questions I think every reader should want to or consider asking themselves, when it comes to if they can believe the things written in this book. It is a series of thought not limited to, but might very well include allied questions to the following; as conditions to their deliberation and acceptance of my conclusions' truthfulness and accuracy.

1) Is the conclusion biblically concrete (**<u>ROCK</u>** hard - *if you will*) or <u>at the least</u> **<u>reasonable</u>**?

2) Can the conclusion withstand an honest and independent biblical scrutiny?

3) Is there precedent found for methods and patterns used for the conclusion?

4) Must the conclusion's view be right and its opposing view wrong, or can they coexist?

5) Does the conclusion's claim make spiritual common sense and flow/fit with scripture?

6) If a conclusion is believed, how will it affect the spirit life in and around those believing?

7) If a conclusion is wrong and is believed, what might the resulting harm be?

8) How is the Holy Spirit leading "you" regarding this book's claims and views?

9) Can harmful or wicked ulterior motives be found behind why the author wrote this book?

10) Considering all variables: could losing one's salvation be an issue if received or rejected?

Reflect on the following: If I gave you in chronological order, the two numbers of six (6) and two (2); then told you, I had put them in a mathematical equation, with the choice of answers being: **a)** *4*, **b)** *12*, **c)** *8*, **d)** *3* and **e)** *All of the above*; but you only know how to add – what would be your choice for the answer? There is of little doubt that your choice would be **c)** *8*. You know in addition, $6 + 2 = \underline{\textbf{8}}$. But if you knew subtraction, multiplication and division; you would say **e)** *All of the above*. It is the only choice. Your answer choices vary, depending on the scope of your math skills; which in turn, would determine what types of mathematical processes are used. Take a look.

---

a) $6 - 2 = \underline{\textbf{4}}$ (*Subtraction*)

b) $6 * 2 = \underline{\textbf{12}}$ (*Multiplication*)

c) $6 + 2 = \underline{\textbf{8}}$ (*Addition*)

d) $6 / 2 = \underline{\textbf{3}}$ (*Division*)

e) All of the above

All the answers are possible, when one has a wider range of math ability; which have to include subtraction, multiplication and division. In somewhat similar manner, <u>time is like the math</u>. If we are to see time with a clearer view, we must have a broader contextual perception of its circumstances. See, time will often overlap, interlock and go end on end. There are occasions when two or more events of time occur over the same periods in time. However (*as our math example asserts*), because I am only able to add and you can only multiply; we forever stand at odds with each other. I insist the answer is: **c**) *8*; while you know absolutely the answer is **b**) *12*; not recognizing we are both right and there are other outcomes equally right. True; sometimes I am right and you are wrong or vice versa. More often than we might like to admit it, we are both wrong about a spiritual matter and are just too spiritually immature to admit our mistake or even recognize our error. It happens. In such cases, non-belief becomes relative ignorance in manifestation. We all work spiritually with what we have. We should pray to our Eloah Elohim that he might have mercy on us and give us more of his knowledge, understanding, wisdom and grace through YHWH our Adon and Messiah Yeshua (*who is one*).

Because I understand that while I may see one event occurring in a specific stage of time, someone else (*a reader*) might perceive another event happening too; but not see a reconciliation of our two events by understanding that they could be occurring simultaneously, at the same time or overlapping. ***Why should one believe the things written in this book?*** Other than what I have already stated at the beginning of this chapter, I cannot say why anybody should believe me. But, I can say they should study! Perhaps, they should do their own research and studies on the things that I have written. I mean seriously, when we believe without doing as the Bereans did with Apostle Shaul; we tend to end up believing the wrong things most of the time; especially in our times and last few minutes before Yeshua returns. Think about it. Had Eve checked with Adam first, before she partook of the tree of the knowledge of good and evil (***The Tree of Death***); perhaps we would not be standing where we are today. **I mean seriously**, look at us; after over 6000 years! We still believe the **very same lie** that old serpent told Eve. "*Ye shall not surely die*" (Genesis 3:4). In other words, **you have an immortal soul and you cannot die**. Yes, I am afraid. "**That's a LIE**!" But, due to the likes of **not** Prophets, but rather ***philosophers*** like Socrates, Plato and Aristotle (469-322 BCE), then later with the founders of Catholicism and Protestantism; over the past 2½ millennia, **WE** have ***dressed up*** that **LIE** a bit. We teach new and naive converts in essence, "Yes, Satan was telling you the truth after all and God; well he was ***stretching*** the truth just a tad." We preach, "True, like the serpent said; we have immortality. But if we do not accept Jesus Christ as our personal Lord and savior; tragically we will spend our immortality burning in hell for eternity. Still, if anybody thinks my claim about **not being** already immortal is true; a legitimate question to ask me

would be, **"Why have not the masses caught on to the serpent's lie?"**
It is really quite simple, once we all get past all of the complexities in the
psychology of thought. <u>In our hearts</u> I think we know the real truth of our
mortality. But due to our "<u>vain and imagined self-importance;</u>" it is much
easier to imagine ourselves tormented while burning in the unimaginable
heat of *__hell fire__*, than to conceptualize the truly incomprehensible. How
will one **experience** the **Second Death**, if the *second death* is in reality
True Death; as to no longer exist in non-existence? Meaning; there will
be no hope for a future resurrection <u>for</u> **eternity**; because there no longer
exists of **US**, any things to be resurrected; no body, no soul and no spirit.
Finally, understand this. Not one living entity will recall, at the height
of all our glory or in <u>any</u> <u>former reality</u> that our human life <u>ever existed</u>.

    WE are, and **WE** will eternally remain, as though **WE** never were.
Meditate on that with your own non-existence in a time of deep spiritual
thought. The second death, should you experience it, is "*__YOU__*" no longer
existing and no one alive remembering you ever did. Attempting to place
oneself imaginatively in that state of <u>eternal</u> <u>non-existence</u>; is just too
unattainably terrifying for anyone living to imagine. And therefore, they
cannot grasp hold of, for its pre-experiencing, that state of death through
their psychological processing. That is why when it comes to eternity, in
the comprehension of our human thoughts, man chose sensation over the

nothingness of **True Death**. We would rather imagine ourselves burning in hell for all eternity (*Actually, it is others – and not ourselves*), than to discern our existing lives ending in such final fashion and non-resolution. It having then, zero value and no recourse for judicial appeal to a higher authority. Consider again, the rich man in the parable of Luke 16:19-31. Understand. If he is indeed cast into the lake of fire, as many presume he will. In that moment he will cease to exist for all of eternity; **no body**, **no soul**, **no spirit**, **No Life**! That is the end of his story; **PERIOD**. Believe it.

> "For the day of the Lord is near upon all the heathen: as thou
> hast done, it shall be done unto thee: thy reward shall return
> upon thine own head. For as ye have drunk upon my holy
> mountain, so shall all the heathen drink continually; yea, they
> shall drink, and they shall swallow down, and they shall be as
> though they had not been" (Obadiah 1:15-16 – Let God be true!).

To those remaining unmoved and incredulous to *my "assertions;"* if they insist on remaining at the second to the likes of Socrates, his students and their surrogates; have at it. Divinely, eternally, merciless - if that is what people think of our Eloah, ***whose mercy endures for ever*** (Psalms 136:1) and have the spiritual audacity to imply YHWH was misleading - **really lying** to Adam and Eve when he said the following; we are in bad shape.

> "*Of every tree of the garden thou mayest freely eat: but of the
> tree of the knowledge of good and evil, thou shalt not eat of it:
> for in the day that thou eatest thereof thou shalt surely die.*"
> (Genesis 2:16-17)

Why... that is the exact opposite of what that old serpent told Eve! Now again, who do "**they**" teach is telling us the truth? The way I see things, either we are going to **surely die** (Genesis 2:17); according to YHWH's words; or we are **not** going to **surely die** (Genesis 3:4); according to the serpent's words. If people do not believe YHWH over Satan, who am I?

Before I leave the last of the "*immortal or not immortal*" argument to all of the debaters, I need to remind everybody concerning this **one-time essential fact**, "...*the Scripture cannot be broken*" (John 10:35). When it comes to believing or not believing, consider this to be a suggestion to us all. Stop using difficult passages when trying to understand, when we are trying to establish our point and indirectly undermine clear scripture and simple instruction. Do not be afraid to step out to the unknown of biblical understanding - then examine the assertions of others. This is especially true and advantageous when one recognizes salvation is not on the line. People might be surprised with the perspectives they gain. I do not want people to judge me. I want them to read carefully, consider seriously and possibly believe the words I claim are of our Eloah recorded in this book. "...*believe not every spirit, but try the spirits whether they are of God: because many false prophets are gone out into the world*" (1st John 4:1).

Now then – where were we? Oh Yeah! That's right! In our great picture that is ordained time; I claim two separate, but somehow adjoined millennial weeks are at work with Adam's time. As a matter of fact other special weeks and times are not uncommon in the biblical readings and accountabilities. If you read the Bible often, you know Patriarch Jacob had to fulfill two weeks for his two wives Leah and Rachel, a week each. In Jacob's reality it was seven (7) days/<u>years</u> each, for a total of fourteen (14) days/<u>years</u> before his "father-in-law" Laban would allow Jacob to consummate his marriage to his wife Rachel. One could think of the two consummations as types or shadow pictures of Messiah Yeshua's binder to all Israel and marriage to his church. YHWH/Yeshua is fulfilling his millennial weeks in preparation to honor his marriage proposal; while his betroth, The Bride, The Church makes herself ready to be received for consummation, at their **Divine Marriage**. Just as a side note - if you will recall; <u>there were ten virgins</u> who were originally preparing themselves to meet the bridegroom. As holy godliness would dictate, <u>only five made it into the wedding feast</u>. One final aside, before we take our final steps forward in the time of intellectual man. "*Know ye not that they which run in a race run all, but one receiveth the prize?*" (1ˢᵗ Corinthians 9:24) While the two primary weeks I have cited aren't the only calendar clocks involving the unfolding of biblical time and prophecy; if a believer truly understands the two weeks and how they work in union with each other, they could become an invaluable tool and insight for positioning oneself with the possibility of going into <u>the great wedding feast</u> - **as the Bride!**

Remember, we spoke a while back about having, "**An absolute love of the truth?**" Consider that goal now, as we put together and take our final steps through revealed and ordained time for intellectual man. Consider next, YHWH's foundation week and Adam's week side by side to see and believe - *if one can* - how they exist and work in union with each other. And, why for as long as I have been able to study and research in my attempts to understand the Holy Bible or other religious documents; we have never recognized the existences of the two weeks. Neither have we understood the interlocking reality of the two nor how we have erred in our understanding of their "*contextual time*" as a result of it. First view YHWH's original plan for humankind through YHWH original week.

YHWH's Adam/Man Plan

	YHWH's Week						The Great Translation to YHWH Day	YHWH's Great Reward Day
Adam's Creation	Years 1000	Years 1000	Years 1000	Years 1000	Years 1000	Years 1000	Years 1000	Years 1000
Qualifying Day	<------Six (6) Millennial days------>						7th Day	8th Day

I would like to point out a few things that spoke to the advantage of not sinning.

1) No expulsion from the Garden of Eden.

2) No need to shorten days due to man's imminent self-destruction.

3) No need for a little season. (*Satan likely would have been confined in fire after day one.*)

4) There is no need for judgment (*Only rewards after the Sabbath millennial of celebration*).

Adam's Week started the year he sinned - 275 years after YHWH's week began.

	Adam's Week						Day of YHWH Millennial Reign Intervention	Adam's Week Officially Ends	
The 1st Man Adam is of the earth: Earthy *Natural*	Prophecy begins and Adam is given his week to explore his new path taken - with Satan at his helm to prove to himself the Serpent told him a lie and not the truth in that YHWH lied and will it lead him to the life he seeks.					6th Day is shortened by a little season due to man's imminent act of self-annihilation	The 2nd Man Yeshua from heaven: Spiritual	Satan must be Loosed for a little Season	The Last Great Day Millennial Judgment
Years	Years	Years	Years	Years	Years	Years	Years	Years	Years
275	1000	1000	1000	1000	1000	750	1000	250	1000
Adam lived 275 yrs before he sinned	<--------Six (6) Millennial days-------->						7th Day	Last quarter of the 6th day	8th Day

The commission of sin did not negate YHWH's foundational week. YHWH, only because of his love for Adam, mercifully made allowances for repentance and special divine opportunities. However, because Satan the devil through the old serpent, was now at the helm of man's direction (*Adam had rejected YHWH's authority over him by virtue of his freewill sinning*); it became of a necessity for YHWH to intervene; or deviate and make divine allowances from his original intent. Nevertheless, it became clear to YHWH early on Adam would not survive long enough to see the end of his tender mercies, contained in that ordained auxiliary/secondary week. We can see that, 100 years prior to the great flood of Noah's day.

> "The earth also was corrupt before God; and the earth was filled with violence. And God looked upon the earth, and, behold, it was corrupt; for all flesh had corrupted his way upon the earth. And God said unto Noah, The end of all flesh is come before me; for the earth is filled with violence through them; and, behold, I will destroy them with the earth" (Genesis 6:11-13).

Then in only three generations after the flood; we can see that man's wickedness began to exert itself yet again, at the Tower of Babel. When Nimrod's **_Great Tower_** first began to go under construction, YHWH bore witness of the people saying, "_Behold, the people is one, and they have all one language; and this they begin to do: and now nothing will be restrained from them, which they have imagined to do_" (Genesis 11:6). YHWH already knew man's self-annihilation was only a matter of time. That is why **Adam's week** has needed divine interventions throughout its history; i.e. **The founding of the United States of America**. That was by Divine Providence; **Our victory in WWII** - _you guessed it_ - Divine Intervention. Discernment reveals that the first fulfills prophecy and the latter to avert our premature self-destruct before Messiah's return for his Church and Sabbath Millennial Reign. Even with those, Yeshua still will cut the sixth day short. Arguably, there were three **primary** interventions that YHWH determined were necessary, to accomplish what was needed and prevent mankind from baseline premature self-annihilations.

- YHWH ordains that Adam gets a full six millennial days after his sin, to do his works and to determine if he wants to repent. Just like the Great Red Dragon, which is the Devil and Satan – along with some of his angels; will received their full allotment of days they have on their divine covenant of life, even after the judgment and interment to the lake of fire. YHWH has promised by his unbreakable word to give to all of those rebellious ones their number of days, long before they sinned, will be judged and/or cast into the Lake of fire.

- YHWH ordained a shortening of the sixth day for the elects' sake; which had to be added back after the 1000 year reign of Messiah to quell sure complaints by Satan the Devil that YHWH was a liar - just like he first implied to Adam through Eve back in the garden.

- YHWH's intervention in WWII to help the Allies gain the upper hand and eventually win the "**Greatest Tribulation**" this world has ever known. Come on you guys. Read some of the history surrounding WWII, such as the Manhattan Project and you will see. There was no way the Allies were "*supposed*" to come out on top. What if Einstein had been an Adolph Hitler loyalist and never wrote his persuasive letter to then President Franklin Roosevelt? Then, what if those many anti-Hitler scientists who contributed to the Manhattan Project, had not been anti-Hitler? What if Adolph Hitler had possessed the Atomic Bomb – instead of the United States? **What if both America and Germany had possessed the Atomic Bomb?** We often hear of various pseudo-historians semi-brag about how the United States had rebounded after Japan's vicious attack on Pearl Harbor effectively crippled our navy fleet; and therewith, America's military effectiveness in the Pacific Ocean. One underreported truth concerning the attack on Pearl Harbor is the Japanese squadron did not complete their mission - **as they were supposed to**. Had the Japanese returned with their originally planned **third wave of bombers** (*which for some reason or other it never came -* **Divine Providence?** *- I'd like to think so.*), the term, "crippled" would have been a major understatement. The term, "Dead in the water" would not have been some tasteless pun when describing the aftermath at Pearl Harbor as it might be taken today. But of our military's ability to respond in a meaningful way and in a meaningful time, it would have been very much closer to their reality and our truth, during that chaotic time in our nation's history.

If one is able to critic without prejudice, the concept of Adam's week and prophecy beginning 275 years after Adam was created, as sort of a divine reset, or discriminately described as YHWH's divine interlaying of times; explaining to oneself and others why two of the three respective Messiahs did not returned in their prescribed times (*The Millennial Week*) might be more flavorable and kind to our spiritual pallets and doctrinal stomachs. The acceptance of the start of Adam's personal 6000 years life-quest, in YHWH's year 275, is most essential if anyone is to have a reasonable understanding of *what time we are really in and how much time we have left*. Within their framed concepts, every number of chronological time in the Bible come together with precision to make sense; including one of the revelations hidden behind the enigmatic 666. You have read the book. What else can, how else will and how well has any book prior to this one, explained in clear detail, with Holy Spirit logic or any logic as far as it goes, why Yeshua has not returned? The truth, which I claim YHWH has revealed; Messiah Yeshua is not "***running late***" with his promised return. Based on this book's research, Yeshua has not broken his promise to his faithful believers. I will not presently speak for Judaism's Messiah.

Once again, take into consideration. Man's *self-rule in his millennial work week*, commenced in YHWH's Adamic year 275. What it means is YHWH interlaid his original week, with Adam's 6000 years work week, at that point. Messiah Yeshua would come to us later and reveal **Adam's sixth day** will be shortened by a "*little season*" (**250 years**). Certainly do not let us discount YHWH's **"Anchor in History,"** the destruction of the **Second Temple in AD 70**. Using all three understandings, we can know **why** Messiah Yeshua has not returned... yet. Using those three references for biblical time and bearing, to the point of exactness; again I say to the reader, every biblical number given as far as time goes (*the amount gone by and the amount left in Adam's millennial work week*) all fall neatly in place - **with biblical precision**. In reality, at least from my perspective; if **believers** would take a sober look at the overall years, they would find that Yeshua's Sabbath Millennial Reign is only delayed by the slimmest of *twenty-five (25) years*. But that is plenty of time for every haughty and wicked human soul to mock with those words cited from earlier. "*Where is the promise of his coming? for since the fathers fell asleep, all things continue as they were from the beginning of the creation*" (2nd Peter 3:4).

Look at the two weeks; YHWH's base week and Adam's prophetic week. Pledge to study them, not as being two wholly separated weeks, but being intertwined, in conjunction with and in cooperation with one another. I believe the better words to use would be that these two weeks are "*Interlaid and overlapped.*" YHWH's week is so, at the 275 years date mark (*the year that Adam sinned*); with Adam's week (*another 6000 years*). And again, <u>that is when prophecy began</u>. With YHWH's week remaining as what could verily be called the **Foundation Week** for the fulfillment of ***The Visitation*** (*Messiah's first coming*); the interlaying of Adam's week reveal YHWH's precise time limit of mercy for all of man to repent, "*...not willing that any should perish*" (2nd Peter 3:9) and avoid the believed ill-fate of "*...a certain rich man*" (Luke 16:19-31), the devil, who is to be cast into the lake of fire (Revelation 20:10) and the angels which kept not their first estate. (Jude 1:6)

YHWH's Adam/Man Plan

YHWH's Week

							The Great Translation to YHWH Day	YHWH's Great Reward Day
Adam's Creation	Years	Years	Years	Years	Years	Years	Years	Years
	1000	1000	1000	1000	1000	1000	1000	1000
Qualifying Day	<------ Six (6) Millennial days ------>						7th Day	8th Day

Adam's Week

					Day of YHWH Millennial Reign Intervention	Adam's Week Officially Ends
The 1st Man Adam is of the earth: Earthy *Natural*	Prophecy begins and Adam is given his week to explore his new path taken - with Satan at his helm to prove to himself the Serpent told him a lie and not the truth in that YHWH lied and will it lead him to the life he seeks.	6th Day is shortened by a little season due to man's imminent act of self-annihilation	The 2nd Man Yeshua from heaven: Spiritual	Satan must be Loosed for a little Season	The Last Great Day Millennial Judgment
Years	Years	Years	Years	Years	Years	Years	Years	Years	Years
275	1000	1000	1000	1000	1000	750	1000	250	1000
Adam lived 275 yrs before he sinned	<--------- Six (6) Millennial days --------->					7th Day	Last quarter of the 6th day	8th Day

Many things can be learned from study on the subject of the "<u>dual weeks</u>" of YHWH and Adam. A core idea for this book is to show where and why YHWH and Adam's week merge and how it has distorted our view of time as it relates to Messiah's promise of return. This book has shown in proper context how much time has really elapsed. If we have been given the occasion to know this, we must know how much time we had from the beginning. Then again, we must have a credible record of how much time has elapsed in order to deduct it from the total time we have determined that we had from the beginning. From the discussions in this book, readers have been inundated with the premise that YHWH's foundation week is seven days or 7000 years in total time; with a 1000 years period for rewards to his most deserving servants. Then because of Adam's sin, YHWH has overlapped his week after the 275 year mark (*the year Adam sinned*) with a second work week to give mankind **FULL** opportunity to spiritually evolve through carnal experiences, repentance and salvation. If one can entertain and believe those perceptions written and explained in the pages of this book, it would be really easy to use established mathematical methods to add up all of the time in overlap of the two weeks and determine that the entire time allowed for mankind by YHWH is 8275 years. Again, when we take all of the numbers that we have determined to be accurate, we can count them forward or backward and they give us the same certainty in calculations. <u>We can see them and we can count them</u>. And, according to the extent of our faith; **<u>we can believe them</u>**. We have divine insight to an incredible, biblically sound time, as to how much of it YHWH has ordained for man; and we have a reasonable date as to what year that ordained time for man is scheduled to run out. Let us see the biblical numbers one more time; reviewing the condensed version in an effort to save time.

1) From year one - Adam to Abram (To flood: 1656 & Flood to Abram: 233 = **1890 years**)

2) Abram/Abraham to Isaac (**100 years**)

3) Isaac to Jacob/Israel (**60 years**)

4) Jacob/Israel to Egypt and slavery (**130 years**)

5) From Egyptian slavery to the children of Israel's freedom from Egypt (**430 years**)

6) Wondering in the wilderness – (*The beginning of Judges*) (**40 years**)

7) After the wilderness until the end of judges (**410 years**) [Total years of Judges 450 years]

8) Net years: Kings of Israel and Judah until Jerusalem and the First Temple was destroyed (**450 years**)
   a. The total time period covered by the Kings of Israel and the Kings of Judah was 467 years
   b. Recall: **Net** is used in the chronological totaling of biblical and prophetic years.

9) Babylonian Captivity (**70 years**)

10) Seventy Weeks in the book of Daniel [Total of 490 years]
    a. Jerusalem's walls were rebuilt and the Second Temple constructed. (**49 years**)

b. Messiah cut off (**420 years**)

c. The people of the prince came to establish an agreement or covenant. (**14 years**)

d. The Sacrifices to the Emperor were halted and war begins (**3.5 years**)

e. Jerusalem and the Second Temple is destroyed (**3.5 years**)

f. Linking the Second Temple destruction and the Abomination of the Desolator is a specific amount of time (**1290 years**)

g. After the Consummation of the abomination of Desolation is done and set up, the "*poured upon*" period starts (**666 years**)

h. After the consummation's "*poured upon*" period; which is 666 years and before the image of the beast can turn 667 years of age, "**Our Adon Messiah Yeshua must return!**"

i. In truth, historic and prophetic biblical years take us up to 6026 (AD 2026). Based on knowing YHWH's Adamic year and also biblical holy day dates, we can look ahead and up for **Messiah Yeshua's** return at the "Jewish¿" *Festival of Trumpets* beginning 6026.

"THAT'S RIGHT! I SAID IT!"

The basic numbers above are all of the years this book - *through its research of the Holy Scriptures* - has been able to discern counting up from year one and day six (*with YHWH's creation of Adam*); until the supposed coming of the Hebrew/Israelite/Jewish Messiah, or the eminent return of the Jewish/Gentile/Messianic/Christian Messiah Yeshua and for **billions,** "*Jesus.*" Besides this book's declaration that prophecy did not begin until after Adam sinned, which was in year 275 after his creation; the Babel/Babylonian/Roman numeral concept revealed in the genealogy after Noah's Great Flood, unsealing their significant numbers for proper biblical and spiritual bearing and the counting of time, and Oh Yeah, that *"unbelievable"* claim Yeshua was forty-nine (*49*) years old at the time of his horrible crucifixion in AD 49; the two most revealing understandings from insights of all the determining numbers in this book's accounting of Adam's ordained times, are in the following acknowledgments.

1) After the Second Temple was to be destroyed (*desolated and in ruin*) in AD 70 - **and it was**; there would be an additional 1290 years of desolation time - **and it was**; between that time and that moment of the ***Enigmatic Consummation*** with the Abomination of Desolation was to be done and set up - **and it was, and is not, and yet is**. (Above item **f**: referenced in Daniel 12:11).

2) Once "**the Abomination that maketh desolate**" *through divine proclamation* has been set up (*which is after the 1290 years*), its anniversary date in age **CANNOT** - and I repeat - "**CANNOT**" extend beyond 666 years. Moreover, if we add-up all of the numbers established in this book for that determination of time listed from number 1) to 10e); the years will bring us up to the destruction of the Second Temple in AD 70. From AD 70 the final count is easy math. We add items **f**: 1290 years and **g**: 666 years to AD 70. From that vantage point we can see, **The Year!**

After those last two determinations of years, we run out of all the years opened to us to consider from YHWH's Holy Scriptures, before the time of the supposed return or Sabbath Millennial. I offer those numbers up to you for your own review, study and conclusions. As for our walk of the ages, we have come to its finish. We have accounted for all ordained years with those from the biblical record. And, the end of the 250-year shortened sixth day, is in year 6026 or AD 2026. The Bible has no more numbers to review; save the years that are to come after we have made the count from listing 1) to 10h) above. After all those time periods have expired; then next comes the thousand years of <u>The Millennial Reign of Messiah Yeshua.</u> Because the sixth millennial day is cut short by a "<u>little season</u>" or 250 years. After the thousand years have expired, that "<u>little season</u>" will be tacked back on at the end of it. That is just before **The Last Great Day of Judgment**. It is also one thousand years in duration. I have now lain out for everybody's scrutiny, all of the years in sequence; as far as my studies in the Holy Scriptures have been able to determine, discover, establish and conclude. <u>**EVERY LAST ONE**</u> of the chronological <u>years to be received by humankind from YHWH</u>; which would allow any book other than this book, to give people a reasonable summation of the times, <u>**is recorded and witnessed in this book**</u>. If anybody can believe them, this book offers plausible explanations as to why there is so much doubt and confusion as to *what time we are really in and how much time we have left*. I am prayerful the words offered in this book in some way helps you, with your biblical picture. So you may gain additional insights to run **The Race**; and to finish <u>your course</u>. All in all; and to what end is this book written? In all truth, it is for **our** spiritual aid. So all who have the capacity to believe and have an absolute love of **The Truth**, "*may know* [**Yeshua**] *and the power of his resurrection*" (Philippians 3:10).

"...knowing the time, that now *it is* high time to awake out of sleep: for now *is* our salvation nearer than when we believed. The night is far spent, the day is at hand: let us therefore cast off the works of darkness, and let us put on the armor of light."

(Romans 13:11-12)

Why should you believe me? I don't know. Maybe you should; and maybe you shouldn't. Every Bible teacher, Christian writer, you name it; would be foolish to claim no inspiration by the Holy Spirit. So my claims are relative. Not to be ugly, but honest; I really do not have time to worry over those who are dogmatic over denominational doctrines, to their own detriment. I have a race to run, a fight to fight and a course to finish. In a loving reminder to all of my brother and sister readers, so do you. I have claimed in this book, YHWH sent me to inform everybody I could. From reading this book, you know it was for a number of reasons. But, I know millions have asked YHWH in faith, as to **"*that day and hour.*"** I am one of you. I believe this book, is YHWH; delivering to our faith, his answer and witness. This is so we can know exactly how close we are, to his real finish line. "*And he saith unto me, Seal not the sayings of the prophecy of this book: for the time is at hand*" (Revelation 22:10). I have not. "*Who then is a faithful and wise servant, whom his lord hath made ruler over his household, to give them meat in due season?*" (Matthew 24:45) This is my meat for you. Let every soul eat. I encourage you to buy copies for your friends. It is much later than they think too!

449

CHAPTER 24

MY APOLOGY

Several people, who know my *"holier than thou"* side, also know of my criticisms against diverse believers' groups. There is one man and ministry in particular to whom this apology goes out to from this book. It is because of the primary subject matter of this book, (*Time*), as it related to a specific claim by this man, was why this final section of retraction needed to be written. This matter for me was especially unnerving when it came to the time when Yeshua returns. So before I ended this book, I wanted to make an acknowledgement and a sincere apology. It might seem a bit odd when I say this is to a person which I admire in numerous ways. My apology is extended because before I feel I was *"enlightened,"* I had determined that he was off in his years as far as counting off the years until our Messiah Yeshua returns. Yeshua's return, in this man's calculations, was supposed to have occurred in his Hebrew year 6001. In his reckoning of time, 6001 matches to AD 2001. As soon as he spoke from his mouth to imply year 6001/AD 2001, as the possible date for Messiah Yeshua's return - *in my infinite wisdom* - I knew he was infinitely wrong. I spread the word of his supposed error to as many people as I had the occasion to speak to on the subject and date of Yeshua's return. Even though I doubt if he or anybody with his direct chain of ministry to which my apology is directed, will likely read this or any significant portions of this book; unless directed to by a random but well connected reader (*hint-hint*) my retraction still must be made public.

First, I would like to introduce the man himself. The reason for this is because I think he can help many get a good start as far as their discernment of the more excellent way to YHWH. Of course now if one already feels that they are in the way of YHWH; I still believe this man can help them along their way to attaining a higher level of truth and understanding. I have gone to listen to him on a few occasions. While I am comfortable with saying I do not agree with "EVERYTHING" he says, that's not saying very much. Because many times I don't agree with "EVERYTHING" that I say. Just as I am comfortable with saying that I do not agree with everything this man preaches; I am just as comfortable with saying that this man has understanding, that if a person is willing to objectively consider **what** he says, rather than **how** he says it; that person can learn an invaluable amount of truth through a tremendous amount of knowledge and hopefully come to a greater understanding of truth. And, even though I think I am right about a couple of things, he might think I am wrong on or vice-versa; it does not prevent me from acknowledging his truth and my error. That is, when I can see myself on the short side of knowledge and understanding. I think this instance is such an occasion for such an acknowledgement.

I think I have said this prior. But as far as any notoriety in my book writing, I am a literature nobody. **"IT'S MUCH LATER THAN YOU THINK!"** was supposed to be my second book. But, it is instead my first published work. I believed because of the urgency of the information and the insights that it holds; additionally, it being **"Time Sensitive"** and all; it was necessary for me to get this word out into the public eyes of the "believer" as quickly as was possible. As I am sure I stated before, **"IT'S MUCH LATER THAN YOU THINK!"** was taken out of a chapter in one of my older, but unpublished manuscripts. However, I am afraid with the wayward paths that our free speech has taken and how it is being shut down today in the USA - *unless one subscribes to a certain social or political correctness* - oftentimes, in an effort to shut down freedom of religion and the truth of YHWH, words spoken are often being falsely described as "hate speech;" because of the current atmosphere. And it is only getting worse as far as I can see. This book could very well be my first and last. On the other hand, the man to whom my apology goes out to; he is an accomplished author and lecturer. So, in neither case will my condemnations or my endorsements make him or break him. I am pretty certain what I have spoken against him and what I am about to say for him now, this man will have no anxiety, regardless of. Neither should he. He is in his own lane to eternal life. I am in mine. He has his own course to navigate – as do I. Besides, I have no doubts that he has no shortages of enemies and detractors. Through this book with my apology, I want to publicly take my name off of the list. I do not want to sound self-serving; but the apology is really for my good conscience. He has no awareness of my criticism of him. Only those people who I have criticized portions of his research in front of know. Although, if he reads over these next few pages; he will learn of my arrogant and "*rude*" detraction. Which it was later shown to me by YHWH, I was the one in error… sort of. ☺ In candor, I pray the following is received as my public apology to him.

My apology goes out to one, Michael John Rood. For those of you who may not know of him, despite what some of his detractors might be saying about him; I would like you to have the opportunity to meet Michael Rood by way of self-introduction on his own terms in this book;

before I move ahead into the clarification as to why I owe this man my apology and my witness on a certain position. Now, allow me to allow Michael Rood to briefly introduce himself by way of his own website.

> "Michael Rood is an author, historian, teacher, broadcaster, and life-long student of the Bible - a most unique "Biblical Chronologist." His dig site is the Bible, and his tools are research skills gained from decades of Biblical study...Rood's live teachings and video presentations showcase some of the most intriguing and controversial discoveries about the Bible in modern history, all with one purpose in mind: to reveal the TRUE Gospel of the Kingdom."
>
> **(https://aroodawakening.tv/meet-michael-rood)**

Did mention already I went to hear Mr. Rood sometime around the year 2000? At the time Mr. Rood was in the process of introducing/promoting his new and *controversial* to say the least about it:

"Astronomically and Agriculturally

Corrected Biblical Hebrew Calendar."©

Mr. Rood was also purporting the "*real possibility*," according to him - *if his calculations were correct* - that Messiah Yeshua might return in the year 6001 of his *Corrected Biblical Hebrew Calendar*. Mr. Rood's 6001 date just happened to match up to the Gregorian calendar year of AD 2001. At the time of his lecture, I'm thinking it was year 2000. If that was the case and I believe it was; then Mr. Rood's *Corrected Biblical Hebrew Calendar* year would have been set at the year 6000. Have I already cited as of this writing AD 2020, Rood's year is 6019? I have already made my arguments to do with historical and prophetic time in this book - believe them or not. So, I do not need to go over them again. Obviously, everybody is encouraged to review the subject matter or the entire book as far as all of its *"insights"* and *"subjects addressed"* - at your own leisure.

It has been nineteen years since that lecture. That also means, according to his *Corrected Biblical Hebrew Calendar,* Yeshua is passed his threshold by eighteen years and counting. And still, Yeshua has not returned. Clearly there was and still is an issue. One of the first terms that come to our minds - for a lot of people is that shameful and debasing, "False Prophet" – right? Resist the urge! At least until you are familiar with the bigger story behind why the date was cited. Do not be like some critics, fastened on to what obviously appears to be an error by Rood and use it as a reason to slam everything he says. I challenge you even with the apparent error; get one of his lecture DVDs. In particular the four-set DVD entitled, *"Prophecies in the Spring Feasts."* I believe if people better understood the biblical feast and appointed times; then, recognize Mr. Rood felt he had correctly restored the *incorrect* modern Jewish calendar back to its original and accurate Hebrew date; then the rest from there on out to the end, as far as spiritually logical conclusions in the culmination of prophecy are concerned, is elementary. If year 6000 was calculated, and Messiah Yeshua had not shortened the days to the extent we expected - *it would seem spiritually logical and obvious* - Yeshua could not go past the year 6001. Because, according to his understanding of YHWH's witness of Scripture, and not just his, but many Christians, Messianics and traditional religious groups in Judaism, the year of 6001 begins the millennial reign of Messiah Yeshua or "Jesus" or the Sabbath millennial of YHWH (*Jews*).

Besides, Mr. Rood's supposedly bad prediction in his date setting was not the reason for my apology. In all fairness, Mr. Rood is witnessed as saying, during his teaching engagements, that if, <u>his calculations were correct</u>, this and that might happen. And, Mr. Rood has himself, cautions against <u>date setting</u> and <u>predicting</u>. Even though I appreciated all of his teachings, I had my own unease with his date of 6001; as far as when he thought it would occur and his overall perception of time in general. Like the most of us who would speak in the name of YHWH, we do not want to speak an error in his name. I do not feel anyone in their right mind wants to be that stumbling block for anyone seeking to find YHWH's truth. As I have testified before, I **<u>do not</u>** want to have to stand before YHWH; having to explain why I promoted some bald-face lies. I want to be right about everything I speak on. However, I recognize that I do not have the spiritual root system I need from YHWH, to be in that category.

It is hard for me to say that, but it is the truth. However, just because I said that; do not presume that this book you just read no longer has validity or anything to offer your spiritual wellbeing. <u>It absolutely does!</u> I tell you in these last few minutes before the return of Messiah; his Holy Spirit has hidden portions of his truth in the hearts of separate groups and individuals for safety. So that his devoted Messianic believers can search them out in relative obscurity for protection purposes. It is up to that good and faithful Messianic servant to get that word out to the Messiah's true believers for gathering up the truth of YHWH in their spread out increments. "*Who then is a faithful and wise servant, whom his lord hath made ruler over his household, to give them [**YHWH's household**] meat in due season*?" (Matthew 24:45) Then those believers, with the wisdom of Holy Spirit, can put together that set-apart jigsaw puzzle of YHWH's Divine Gospel. Then develop a working plan of steadfast obedience at their highest level that they might obtain. And pray that it is enough that they/we can make it into the wedding feast of the Lamb as the one true bride of The Lamb - ***Messiah Yeshua**.*

Though I would definitely tell people that I am somewhat confident; I tremble and I walk in fear before YHWH. Believing that I now know my own condition; I am learning not to be so quick when it comes to condemning or demeaning people simply because **I think** I know some specific thing that **I think** they do not. I try to share my knowledge with them and I hope they share their knowledge with me. And together we might help each other to develop our own spiritual pictures that will inspire us to run the race for immortality. I feel I have learned what was for me, a valuable lesson in my spiritual interactions with Mr. Rood on a claim of specific knowledge that I had - *to say the least* - some skeptical concerns over. In a moment of recall, I was entirely sure Mr. Rood was wrong about his claim of supposedly an irrefutable knowledge. But the truth was, in its proper context, I was the one in error for my dogmatic accusation against the apparent error of Mr. Rood. Let me explain.

It is really quite simple. But it is also important that I set the record straight the best that I can. Here is basically how it all went down. Of course this was all before YHWH showed me the time and dates that he revealed to me. It was either, when I went to hear Mr. Rood or when I was listening to him on recorded media. I do not rightly recall which. But Mr. Rood said back in year 2000, based on his calculations at the time; we were in the, "***Astronomically and Agriculturally Corrected Biblical Hebrew Calendar***"© year of 6000. He then went on to say that **if he was right**, the next year would begin the Sabbath Millennial of YHWH. Of course, upon hearing this, I was totally incredulous to his claim. Then he set out to prove his declaration. As he did so, he doubled down on his stance and said something **firm**. While it surely did not remove me from my cynical stance, it did perk up my ears. Still, if you must know. I knew to the highest degree; it was **impossible** for Mr. Rood to have been **right**. Remember, Yeshua said that he would shorten *those days* for the elect's sake (Matthew 24:22). So, unless the translators completely botched that rendering – Mr. Rood's calculations of the year AD 2001, corresponding with the year 6001 of his "***Astronomically and Agriculturally Corrected Biblical Hebrew Calendar***" ©, as far as I understood was, "*entirely and unquestionably*" Mr. Rood's own biblical fabrication. I knew as a matter of basic mathematics; 6001 is absolutely **not** a shortening of, *those days*. And I was definitely not prepared to call Messiah Yeshua the liar. As far as I was concerned, it was Mr. Rood in the deception. It was Mr. Rood who was the liar-liar pants on fire! That was the only way I could resolve the shortening of the days issue in my mind. So you can imagine the look on my face, when Mr. Rood stated that he had friends at, "**NASA**" (The National Aeronautics and Space Administration) who assisted him with the date restoration of his, "*Astronomically and Agriculturally Corrected Biblical Hebrew Calendar*" ©!

Now you want to talk about skepticism! **Really! NASA? REALLY!?** You must know about then, I was thinking **NASA** must have some really big dummies employed. But what can you expect from a bunch of rocket scientists - right? But then I started thinking seriously. How could **NASA** be wrong about the dates, with all of their mathematical expertise and all of their computer technologies they have available - *right there* - at their fingertips? I could not for the life of me come to terms with the question, *"**How could NASA be wrong?**"* Maybe it was a computer malfunction or something. Maybe **NASA** just lied to Mr. Rood. Now, there was a real possibility! Some scientists lie about so much. Many scientists are deeply involved with their scientific and political activism among other things. Do not even get me started on their claims and interpretations concerning creation and their - **"Big Bang Theory."** Hey! I will admit it. The Holy Bible acknowledges the existence of science. Why would it not? YHWH is the **Master Scientist**. Elohim is the Ultimate Master of it. He created it in this physical universe. Nevertheless, Elohim goes beyond the physical laws in science. Elohim is the divine spirit being. Elohim is not limited in or by the physical. HE dwells in the light with YHWH. And, even though the scripture uses the term, "science;" conversely on the heel of its usage was the Holy Spirit's condemnation of the expression's abuse. Exposing the real potential in those who would use the sciences' limited abilities to reveal ultimate truths, as a tool for deception - saying of such practices in science as, *"falsely so called"* (1st Timothy 6:20).

But, Mr. Rood said of his time-restoration assisters – *those people who aided him* – they were his friends. His friends would not lie to him. So they must have made some sort of mistake. Yes. That is what it was, a big mistake! It had to be! I have a thought and strategy, when it comes to how I deal with differences. While it is not foolproof, it is a start position that has worked well for me on the surface in debates. Here it is. When people have differences, either one is right and the other is wrong; or the other is right and the one is wrong; or both are wrong and there is yet a right way yet undiscovered by the one or the other. That makes sense - right? But wait. There is another thought. I never really thought about it at first; because like most, I figured my first three alternatives covered most everything. Usually, I do not use this consideration during a debate, because of our mindsets we oftentimes adopt. However, possibly the last attitude in debate, when dealing with differences is this. The one and the other are appositionally right. Appositional could perhaps be described as, looking at the same three-dimensional object, from a different one-dimensional angle of view. At the time, I did not know how applicable my last differences tool was. My perspective at the time would not allow it. That is why I could not figure out what the problem was; and, I had no discernible place to go intellectually. I gave to myself the option of being wrong about my dates – but based on the biblical record, on prophecy and what I believe was/is YHWH's inspiration, **I was solid!!** But, **I was**

absolutely positive Mr. Rood was in error. Because, there had to be a shortening of the days! (Matthew 24:22) So why was **NASA** telling Mr. Rood - **WRONG?** I was absolutely stuck. And, there was absolutely no way that I was going to figure it out – **PERIOD!!** ☹

But, I am not telling you anything you are not already aware of. You have read this book! I knew about Yeshua shortening the days during my criticisms of Mr. Rood's 6001 date, back in year 2000. However, at that time, I did not know how long the prophetic little season was. I now know it to be 250 years. I did not know, and it had never occurred to me, how long Adam was in the Garden of Eden; or that it even had any kind of bearing on prophetic time. I knew the first of prophecies in the Holy Scriptures were recorded right after Adam sinned. (Genesis 3:14-15) But, I had no clue a secondary reset, a full 6000-year millennial work week was "interlaid and overlapped" at the 275-year mark of YHWH Elohim's original divine week; and, it began along with Adam and Eve's expulsion from the Garden of Eden. But, we all possibly could have known; and perhaps even should have known. The understanding has been sealed - it appears - in the Ten Commandments for 3411 years. YHWH clearly tells us, 'Remember and do not forget it this time! You got six days!' (Exodus 20:8-10) How blind are we? These are keys to understanding and insight. Which if unknown; it absolutely obscures our biblical view of time. Once

YHWH revealed these keys from the Holy Scriptures to me I understood. **NASA was right!** And thus, **Mr. Rood was right!** **NASA** and Mr. Rood were spot-on with their declaration of the millennial times. I do not know how they calculated it out and with what devices they used; but, they were right on target as far as my study and research were able to discover and discern. **NASA** used wholly science. I used Holy Bible. With divine inspiration, my source is clearly immeasurably better, effective and true.

True, when YHWH showed his secrets to me, I did not understand all of the things I was being shown. But, I surely understood YHWH was showing me truths he had hidden from mankind as a whole, certainly for as long as I had been living. I believed what YHWH was telling me. And after, YHWH opened my eyes to discern *some of* their significances and impacts. Believe me, by no means am I bragging on myself; when I say that I have heard no one else speak to the matters with which YHWH has revealed - *in mercy* - to me. The situation is simply what I perceive of it.

I have to imagine Mr. Rood is a little bothered, by the fact that at this moment in time, his numbers seem to be nineteen years off - even though he **"was"** totally confident in NASA's projections and calculations. I can imagine nineteen years after the fact, he might be starting to wonder.

"Mr. Rood, there is nothing wrong with your base date of year 6019. And, I sincerely apologize for spreading falsehoods about you being in error to all that I came in contact with and discussed the matter."
(Timothy B. Merriman, 2020)

For my "scientific digs," it gave me some sense of satisfaction to demean "**NASA**." Even though I did know in the process, I was also putting down Mr. Rood with unfair criticisms. Again, I say to Mr. Rood and before everyone who reads these pages in this book; I was wrong concerning my criticisms of your *Astronomically and Agriculturally Corrected Hebrew Calendar* © year of 6001; when I did it in AD 2000. I now know that since your year of 6000 was correct, your present year of 6019 is also absolutely correct - from my perspective. *I was contextually wrong.* ☺ Notwithstanding, here is my challenge to Mr. Rood. Without going back over to the study of this book - you now know that your date is correct, but out of context. Today, the corrected Hebrew year is 6019. Indeed 6019, corresponds to AD 2020. But, to discern why, "**Messiah Yeshua**" has not yet returned or the, "**Jewish Messiah**" has not yet come (*In reality, they are one in the same*), no one needs to think the Holy Scripture is false or Yeshua broke his promise. Both are impossible. If you will dare to trust the base claim of this book, take **276 years** (***Date*** *of Adam's eviction from the Garden – when his new personal week and all prophecy began*), add to Adam's eviction, his ordained reset millennial work week or his 6000 years, then deduct 250 years (*for the little season - the shortening of those days*). You have your answer as far as when I expect Messiah to return. After that, you can add the 1000 years for

Messiah's Millennial Reign, after that, tack back on the 250 years for the little season Satan *"**must be loosed**."* And finally, the last 1000 years for The Last Great Day of Judgment can be added on. Now you have every year in time in short, proven from your Holy Bible. That is, if you feel the numbers are **"biblically believable."** If not, what more can I say? My witness is now public. In simplicity consider the following once more.

$$1 + 275 + 6000 - 250 = 6026 \text{ (\underline{AD 2026})} + 1000 + 250 + 1000 = 8276$$

I think and calculate on Mr. Michael John Rood's, *Astronomically and Agriculturally Corrected Hebrew Calendar* ©, the date which this book's research has determine would begin the Millennial Sabbath of Yeshua our Messiah, corresponds to Mr. Rood's year 6026. Based on the revelations of YHWH's holy feast and appointed times within that year, from my understanding and perspective, the date within that year would be, "Yom Teruw'ah" or the Feast of Trumpets! *"Then shall they see the Son of man coming in a cloud with power and great glory"* (Luke 21:27).

> *"He that is unjust, let him be unjust still: and he which is filthy, let him be filthy still: and he that is righteous, let him be righteous still: and he that is holy, let him be holy still."*
> (Revelation 22:11)

My apology to Mr. Rood, though sincere; it was not meant to be a whole-hearted, blanket endorsement over all Mr. Rood's teachings and doctrines. Neither is my lack of a complete endorsement meant to show any degree of animosity, reproach or accusation of error of any kind. As with any and all doctrines or teachings from anyone, including myself concerning YHWH's truths; I would encourage everybody to *prove all things*. As best as you can, do as the Bereans did, "*they received the word with all readiness of mind, and searched the Scriptures daily, whether those things were so*" (Acts 17:11). Thank you Mr. Rood for all you do to get the word out concerning the coming Kingdom of Elohim and YHWH (*His Messiah Yeshua*). Certainly before I started to write this book, I knew it was late on the prophetic clock. Even when I was but a child of fifteen, YHWH revealed to me that I might live to see the return of Yeshua. I thought he meant if I lived to be **ninety–something**. After YHWH walked me through his biblical history and prophetic times, I realized in one of my many moments of clarity, "**It was much later than most all of us thought!**"

> "...it is written, Eye hath not seen, nor ear heard, neither have entered into the heart of man, the things which God hath prepared for them that love him. But God hath revealed them unto us by his Spirit: for the Spirit searcheth all things, yea, the deep things of God...the things of God knoweth no man, but the Spirit of God...we have received...the Spirit...of God; that we might know the things that are freely given to us of God. Which things also we speak, not in the words which man's wisdom teacheth, but which the Holy [*Spirit*] teacheth; comparing spiritual things with spiritual...the natural man receiveth not the things of the Spirit of God: for they are foolishness unto him: neither can he know, because they are spiritually discerned."
>
> (1st Corinthians 2:9-14)
>
> ...Amen.

The Survey
(Why Should Anybody Believe Me?)

Focusing on the numbers (*Added comments can be added on the back or on separate sheets.*) I will do my best to read them and reply as necessary or by request. Keep in mind; I do not have a lot of help. Please be patient for replies. Keep in mind also – everything cost. Help us if you can.

(1) Will you judge the numbers in this book, apart from its doctrinal debate issues?

☐ Yes   ☐ No   ☐ I'm not sure   ☐ Require more study

(2) Did you believe God has limited man to an ordained Millennial Week (7000 yrs.)?

☐ Yes   ☐ No   ☐ I'm not sure   ☐ Require more study

(3) Do you believe there will be a millennial reign when Satan will be forced to rest?

☐ Yes   ☐ No   ☐ I'm not sure   ☐ Require more study

(4) Did you ever think or know a 1000 years "Judgment Day" is scriptural?

☐ Yes   ☐ No   ☐ I'm not sure   ☐ Require more study

(5) Do you think it now?

☐ Yes   ☐ No   ☐ I'm not sure   ☐ Require more study

(6) Do you feel the Babel/Roman number claim for the Bible was sensibly presented in this book?

☐ Yes   ☐ No   ☐ I'm not sure   ☐ Require more study

(7) Do you feel the numbers fit well in general within the scope of this book as it relates to and its claims go for biblical history and prophetic times from the Bible alone?

☐ Yes   ☐ No   ☐ I'm not sure   ☐ Require more study

(8) If not, which numbers do you find objectionable - why? (*Use extra paper if needed*)

_____

_____

(9) Based on your view of the overall numbers, do you think this book is "***reasonably***" accurate with its conclusions? Particular dissention can be put on a separate page.

☐ Yes   ☐ No   ☐ I'm not sure   ☐ Require more study

With any biblical *interpretation*, I recommend checking passages cited. Read adjoining scripture to the passage cited. Make as sure as possible that nothing has been taken "*unreasonably*" out of context. You already know Satan *deceiveth the whole world*. Do not let anyone fool you; present company included. We are alive in the ***last minutes*** of ordained time. Still, sadly for most, but no longer you; "**IT'S SO MUCH LATER THAN THEY THINK!**" **Please - Pass this WORD on.**

Timothy B. Merriman

Please send your survey to: **IMLTYT * PO Box 231 * Richfield, NC 28137**

References

Afary, Janet, and Peter William Avery. "Iran." Encyclopædia Britannica, Encyclopædia Britannica, Inc., 29 May 2019, www.britannica.com/place/Iran/Religion.

"Ancient Jewish History: The Great Revolt." The Great Revolt (66 - 70 CE). www.jewishvirtuallibrary.org/the-great-revolt-66-70-ce.

Chin, Felicia. "11-Year-Old Boy Fathers a Child." *The Asian parent*, The Asian parent, 19 June 2013, sg.theasianparent.com/male-sexual-abuse-boy-11-fathers-a-child/.

Double Portion Inheritance Ministries, (2008); "Yom Teruw'ah: 'The Day That No Man Knows!'" 1 Jan. 1970. doubleportioninheritance.blogspot.com/2011/05/yom-teruah-day-that-no-man-knows_3315.html.

"The First Roman-Jewish War." Encyclopedia Britannica, Encyclopedia Britannica, Inc., www.britannica.com/.

Frost, Robert. (1923). "Stopping by Woods on a Snowy Evening by Robert Frost." *Poetry Foundation*, Poetry Foundation. www.poetryfoundation.org/poems/42891/stopping-by-woods-on-a-snowy-evening.

Gadd, D., (2013). "11-Year-Old Auckland Boy Fathers Child." *Stuff*, 2013, www.stuff.co.nz/national/crime/8800704/11-year-old-

Auckland-boy-fathers-child.

"The History of Israel - A Chronological Presentation." *The History of Israel - A Chronological Presentation*, history-of-israel.org/ 2018.

Holy Bible: *KJV Super Giant Print Reference Bible w/Giant Print Concordance. Containing the Old and New Testaments: Authorized King James Version.* Holman Bible Publishers: 1996 and 1998.

Hom, Elaine J., 2013. "Roman Numerals: Conversion, Meaning & Origins." LiveScience, Purch, 15 May 2013, https://www.livescience.com/32052-roman-numerals.html.

"INDNJC." Our Daily Bread, 23 Aug. 1999, odb.org/1999/08/23/indnjc/.

The Jewish Revolt, Biu.ac.il. *www.biu.ac.il/.*"אילן-בר אוניברסיטת" אילן-בר, הקהילה למען, www1.biu.ac.il/ 2018.

"The Jewish World of Jesus: An Overview." The Jewish Roman World of Jesus, 11 Apr. 2013, pages.uncc.edu/james-tabor/the-jewish-world-of-jesus-an-overview/.

Josephus, Flavius, and William Whiston. The Works of Josephus. A.C. Armstrong and Son, 1902.

Kidshealth.org, 2018. "The Web's Most Visited Site about Children's Health." *KidsHealth*, The Nemours Foundation,.

Lauterborn, David. "Letter from Military History - January 2013."

HistoryNet, HistoryNet, 11 Feb. 2016,

www.historynet.com/letter-from-military-history-january-

2013.htm.

"Meet Michael Rood." *A Rood Awakening*, aroodawakening.tv/meet-

michael-rood. 6 August 2018.

Melton, James L. (2010). "God's 7000 Year Plan". *Bible Baptist

Publications*, Bible Baptist Publications, 2010,

www.biblebaptistpublications.org/gods7000yearplan.html.

Pope, Alexander. *An Essay on Man*. Alexander Pope, 1733. Written to

Henry St. John, Lord Bolingbroke

Reuven Herzog and Benjy Koslowe, 2015/5775. Articles, Kol Torah.

"The Hebrew Calendar and its Missing Years - Part One." Kol

Torah, 8 Aug. 2018, www.koltorah.org/halachah/the-hebrew-

calendar-and-its-missing-years-part-one-by-reuven-herzog-and-

benjy-koslowe.

Rich, Tracey R. "Shemini Atzeret." *Judaism 101: Shemini Atzeret and

Simchat Torah*, Judaism 101, Online Encyclopedia of Judaism,

5771 (AD 2011), www.jewfaq.org/holiday6.htm.

Robbins, Michael W. "Whose History?" *Historynet.com/Letters from

Military History, 2013*, World History Group, 2 Nov. 2012,

www.historynet.com/letter-from-military-history-january-
2013.htm.

"The Romans Destroy the Temple at Jerusalem, 70 AD." Eye-Witness to
History; www.eyewitnesstohistory.com (2005).

Rood, Michael J., (1999). *Prophecies in the Spring Feasts*. The Prophecy
Club, 1999.

Roosevelt, F.D., 1941. Speech by Franklin D. Roosevelt, New York
(Transcript). "A Declaration of War (WWII - Japan)." *The
Library of Congress*.
https://www.loc.gov/resource/afc1986022.afc1986022_ms2201/
?st=text.

The Scriptures, *Hebraic-Roots Version*. Institute for Scripture Research,
2009

Strauss, Valerie. "Hiding in Plain Sight: The Adult Literacy Crisis." *The
Washington Post*, WP Company, 1 Nov. 2016,
www.washingtonpost.com/news/answer-
sheet/wp/2016/11/01/hiding-in-plain-sight-the-adult-literacy-
crisis/?noredirect=on&utm_term=.0b677df0f1f1.

Webster Dictionary, (1913). "Online Dictionary and Translations."
Online Dictionary and Translations, www.webster-
dictionary.org/.

It's Much Later Than You Think!

Notes

Timothy B. Merriman

Notes

It's Much Later Than You Think!

Notes

Timothy B. Merriman

www.ingramcontent.com/pod-product-compliance
Lightning Source LLC
Chambersburg PA
CBHW021132090426
42740CB00008B/747